International Political Economy Series

Series editor

Timothy M. Shaw
Visiting Professor
University of Massachusetts Boston, USA

Emeritus Professor
University of London, UK

The global political economy is in flux as a series of cumulative crises impacts its organization and governance. The IPE series has tracked its development in both analysis and structure over the last three decades. It has always had a concentration on the global South. Now the South increasingly challenges the North as the centre of development, also reflected in a growing number of submissions and publications on indebted Eurozone economies in Southern Europe. An indispensable resource for scholars and researchers, the series examines a variety of capitalisms and connections by focusing on emerging economies, companies and sectors, debates and policies. It informs diverse policy communities as the established trans-Atlantic North declines and 'the rest', especially the BRICS, rise.

More information about this series at
http://www.palgrave.com/series/13996

Xiaoke Zhang • Tianbiao Zhu
Editors

Business, Government and Economic Institutions in China

palgrave
macmillan

Editors
Xiaoke Zhang
Alliance Manchester Business School
University of Manchester
Manchester, UK

Tianbiao Zhu
Institute for Advanced Study in
Humanities and Social Sciences
Zhejiang University
Hangzhou, Zhejiang, China

International Political Economy Series
ISBN 978-3-319-64485-1 ISBN 978-3-319-64486-8 (eBook)
DOI 10.1007/978-3-319-64486-8

Library of Congress Control Number: 2017959575

Printed on acid-free paper

This Palgrave Macmillan imprint is published by Springer Nature
The registered company is Springer International Publishing AG
The registered company address is: Gewerbestrasse 11, 6330 Cham, Switzerland

Acknowledgements

As editors, we wish to thank all the authors for their willingness to respond to our editorial suggestions and their valuable contribution to the book. We also extend our appreciation to Wyn Grant, Gregory Noble, Richard Whitley, Yongping Wu and the anonymous reviewer for their comments, criticisms and support. While organizing the international symposium in August 2014 and the publication workshop in January 2016 from which this book was born, we received and gratefully acknowledge financial support from China's National Social Science Fund (project number: 13BJL027) and the Zhejiang University Research Fund (project number: 188020-193810401/054). Finally, we are grateful to Timothy Shaw, the series editor, and Christina Brian, editorial director for politics and international studies at Palgrave Macmillan, for encouraging the project.

Xiaoke Zhang
Tianbiao Zhu

Contents

Notes on Contributors

Richard W. Carney is Fellow at the College of Asia and the Pacific, Australian National University.

Gregory Chin is Associate Professor at the Department of Political Science, York University, Canada.

Juanfeng Liu is Assistant Professor at the School of International Relations, University of International Business and Economics, China.

Tak-Wing Ngo is Professor at the Department of Government and Public Administration, University of Macau.

Yiping Wu is Associate Professor at the School of Public Economics and Administration, Shanghai University of Finance and Economics.

Yukyung Yeo is Associate Professor at the College of International Studies, Kyung Hee University, South Korea.

Changdong Zhang is Associate Professor at the School of Government, Peking University.

Jianjun Zhang is Professor at the Guanghua School of Management, Peking University.

Jin Zhang is Senior Research Fellow at the Cambridge China Development Trust and university lecturer at Judge Business School, University of Cambridge.

Xiaoke Zhang is Professor at Alliance Manchester Business School, University of Manchester.

Jiangnan Zhu is Associate Professor at the Department of Politics and Public Administration, University of Hong Kong.

Tianbiao Zhu is Executive Dean and Professor at the Institute for Advanced Study in Humanities and Social Sciences, Zhejiang University.

List of Figures

List of Tables

PART I

Introduction

CHAPTER 1

Understanding Business–Government Relations in China: Changes, Causes and Consequences

Xiaoke Zhang and Tianbiao Zhu

Introduction

This book brings together conceptual and empirical analyses of the causes and consequences of changing business–government relations in China since the 1990s, against the backdrop of the country's increased integration with the global political economy. More specifically, it provides an interdisciplinary account of how the dominant pattern of interactions between state actors, firms and business organizations has changed differently across regions and industries and how the changing varieties of these interactions have causally interacted with the evolution of key economic

X. Zhang (✉)
Alliance Manchester Business School, University of Manchester, Manchester, UK

T. Zhu
Institute for Advanced Study in Humanities and Social Sciences, Zhejiang University, Hangzhou, China

X. Zhang, T. Zhu (eds.), *Business, Government and Economic Institutions in China*, International Political Economy Series,
DOI 10.1007/978-3-319-64486-8_1

institutions in China. The basic theoretical premise of the book is that business–government relations comprise a key linchpin that defines the Chinese political economy and calibrates the character of its constitutive institutional arrangements.

In line with this analytical focus, the book has three different yet interrelated objectives. In the first place, building on the recent comparative political economy literature (Crouch et al. 2009; Hancke et al. 2007; Zhang and Whitley 2013), it develops a typological framework for identifying key dimensions to be included in cross-regional and cross-sectoral comparisons and for establishing the guiding principles for elucidating the diversity of business–government relations in China. Furthermore, the book advances novel theoretical propositions concerning the primary causes of changes and variations in the organization of state and business actors and in the configuration of power relations and interactions between them. Finally, it explores the causal pathways through which business–government relations, as a key set of sociopolitical structures and processes, have shaped emergent systems of economic control and coordination across the regional and sectoral levels of analysis.

This introductory chapter sets the general backdrop against which the central analytical objectives of the book are defined and its major contributions to theoretical and policy debates specified. It introduces a typology of business–government relations, advances the main causal propositions of changes and variations in business–state interactions, and explores the impact of such interactions on the emergence of new market institutions. It does so by drawing on, but not confining itself to, empirical evidence presented in individual contributions to the book. The chapter concludes by discussing the organization of the volume.

Key Contributions

By focusing on the above-mentioned three analytical objectives, the book is intended to make a number of contributions to current theoretical and policy debates on the changing nature of business–government relations and its impact on newly emerging economic institutions in China.

To begin with, existing studies of business–government relations in China have tended to be narrow in theoretical focus and fragmented in analytical perspectives. Some have shown political actors in the state domain as the causal agents of changes in business–government interactions and portrayed business actors and their organizations largely as passive and subordinate objects of control and co-optation through state corporatist mechanisms (Alpermann 2006; Dickson 2003, 2008; Foster 2008; Ong 2012; Unger 2008a; Walder 1995, 2003). Others have granted analytical primacy to the growing role of economic actors and firms in structuring relations with the state and emphasized horizontal interactions mediated through market institutions, business associations and social networks as an important defining feature of state–firm relations (Nee 1992; Nee and Opper 2012; Peng 2004; Sun, Wright and Mellahi 2010; Tjosvold et al. 2008; Xin and Pearce 1996). Still others have sought to advance a micro-theory of business and politics that explains the motivation of individual firms to develop connections with various party and governmental entities, the choices they make on tactics and strategies, and the impact of political ties on their performance (Du and Girma 2010; Guo et al. 2014; Li et al. 2006; Park and Luo 2001; Peng and Luo 2000).

While these approaches shed important light on the manifestations and consequences of changing business–government relations in China, they do not exhaust the categories of potential patterns of such relations. They have mainly concentrated on one set of analytical dimensions, largely to the exclusion of others that are constitutive of interactions between the state and businesses. As a result, they have precluded the theoretical possibility of more than one pattern of state–business ties existing in the Chinese political economy. The typological framework to be developed in this book, which focuses on both the authoritative governance of the economy and the market coordination of socioeconomic activities, provides a more encompassing analytical tool for developing a holistic understanding of changing and divergent forms of state–business relations, as will be shown below. This is particularly relevant, given that the ultimate objective of the book is to illustrate how the interrelationship between state agencies, firms and business organizations has varied across different regions and industries and explain how these regional and sectoral variations have shaped the pattern and trajectory of economic institutional changes in China.

Furthermore, the emphasis of many extant studies has tended to be more on understanding how business–government relations in China have been changing over time, particularly against the backdrop of the country's increased integration with the global economy and continuous market reforms, than on examining how and why such relations have changed differently at the regional or sectoral levels of analysis. To the extent that some studies have explored cross-regional or cross-sectoral variations in state–business interactions (see Ernst and Naughton 2008; Huchet and Richet 2002; McNally 2011; Segal 2003; Thun 2006), they have failed to provide a systematic explanation of the sources of these variations (the few exceptions include Kennedy 2005 and Tsai 2007). There has yet to be any satisfying account of why economic agents have been more powerful in shaping socioeconomic relations, business associations more autonomous, or state–firm relations more cooperative and development-oriented in some regions or industries than in others.

As indicated above, the typological framework that focuses on how authoritative governance and market coordination interact to generate different forms and patterns of state–business relations facilitates a comparative analysis of why such relations vary across divergent regional or sectoral sociopolitical environments. In advancing their respective causal propositions, individual contributions to the book explore how the impact of global and market forces on changes in the structure and practice of business–government ties have been mediated through the region-specific or sector-specific characteristics of ideological orientations, state institutions and market structures. By examining the causes and consequences of changing business–government relations within a cross-regional and cross-sectoral framework, this book introduces a more dynamic perspective into the study of the Chinese political economy and thus fills an important analytical lacuna in the literature.

Finally, the literatures on business–government relations in China and on economic institutions and institutional change have, until recently, developed largely in isolation from each other. While there have been scholarly efforts to integrate the analysis of state–firm interactions and industrial transformations (Breznitz and Murphee 2011; Kennedy 2005; McNally 2008; Segal 2003; Thun 2006), empirical studies on the impact of changing interactions between state and business actors on the emergence of new market institutions have been rare; cross-regional or cross-sectoral analyses of the causal linkage between different forms of business–government ties and divergent patterns of economic institutional reforms have been even rarer. This book aims to bring together both the temporal and spatial comparisons of how the structure of business–government relations has varied and of how these variations have exerted shaping influence on the process of institutional changes in China.

A Typology of Business–Government Relations

This section delineates the defining features of key analytical dimensions that underpin business–government relations, develops some guiding principles for categorizing and comparing the organization of these dimensions that generates the varied contours of interactions between state and business actors, and describes the different configurations of such interactions across regions and industries in China.

Key Analytical Dimensions

Developing a typology of business–government relations, in such a vast and diverse country as China, that is both conceptually parsimonious and empirically encompassing is difficult. The difficulty mainly rests with the lack of commonly accepted conceptual criteria for identifying key analytical dimensions that characterize business–government relations and for ascertaining the number of distinct types of state–firm interactions, although the regional and sectoral diversity of such interactions is widely recognized (Breslin 2012; Kennedy 2005; Ngo this volume; Unger 2008b). However, there appears to be general agreement in the emerging literature on the constitutive institutions of Chinese capitalism that the authoritative governance of the economy and the market coordination of socioeconomic activities are crucial components of interrelationships between state actors, firms and business organizations (Fligstein and Zhang 2010; Redding and Witt 2007; Zhang and Peck 2016).

The authoritative governance of the economy concerns the extent to which the state structures its relationships with the business sector through industrial targeting and intervention, market regulations and controls over associational arrangements among various economic agents. Despite the continuous process of market-oriented reforms, both central and local governments in China have remained involved in steering and organizing economic activities and outcomes, though the nature and levels of such involvement have varied significantly across regions and industries (Huang 2008; McNally 2008; Naughton and Tsai 2015). On the other hand, socioeconomic producer groups, particularly business, are also crucial agents that coordinate economic action and structure market transactions (Nee and Opper 2012; Redding and Witt 2007). Thus, to understand the organizational diversity of business–government relations in China, the authoritative governance of the economy needs to be viewed in close interaction with the market coordination of socioeconomic activities that pertains to the ability of business actors to organize themselves for collective action purposes. Such an ability is embodied in the degree of interfirm collaborations, the development of business associations and the density of interlinkages between firms and such third-party entities as financial and research institutions.

In the first place, the state structures its relationship with business actors through its efforts to protect or promote specific firms, sectors or industries. These efforts affect the development of new technologies, the restructuring of ailing industrial sectors and the performance and fortunes of various enterprises. Here, we are concerned with how the state management of industrial development shapes state–firm relations. In the less state-led form of intervention, the state facilitates industrial development and adjustment by organizing its strategies around public–private partnerships and even private initiatives and providing policy and institutional support; it often does not target specific sectors or firms for special promotion and discriminate against private domestic or foreign firms. In the more dirigiste form, the state deploys a wide array of elaborate policy instruments to manage resource allocation, production activities and investment flows directly, with the view to aligning the behaviour and incentives of market players with its industrial policy goals and socioeconomic development imperatives.

The extent to which state actors are actively involved in governing the economy through industrial targeting and intervention both derives from and influences their approaches towards managing and regulating the development of product, labour or financial markets. Such approaches vary, for instance, between the more market-oriented modes of regulation and the more state-controlled pattern of market development. These differences that have prevailed across regions and industrial sectors in China exert differential shaping influence over both state–firm relations and interactions among various socioeconomic actors. They are particularly manifest in the extent to which: state actors orchestrate the distribution of financial resources between economic agents through ownership means and administrative decrees; bureaucratic procedures favour some firms over others by restraining entry and reducing competition; and regulations influence relations between business and labour and their respective ties with state actors.

A final attribute of authoritative governance concerns the extent to which the state sets the rules and conventions that structure interlinkages between various economic agents and shape associational arrangements among them. Business–government relations are likely to be developed in a hierarchical, top-down and often narrow manner, where the state plays a dominant role in defining the nature of linkage relationships between market players and is reluctant to encourage the growth of business associations. By contrast, state actors are likely to be connected to business actors and organizations through broad, multiple and horizontally oriented mechanisms, where the state gives private players considerable latitude in developing their collaborative interactions, provides them with incentives to organize themselves and enlists the support of business associations in the formulation of strategies for strengthening networks of market governance.

The configuration of business–government relations is also contingent on how business actors coordinate within and between industries to resolve collective action problems (Evans 1995; Maxfield and Schneider 1997). As suggested above, the ability of business actors to organize themselves to interact with state actors is constitutive of interfirm collaborations and alliances. Firms that develop and maintain dense and durable inter-corporate networks and share managerial, informational and technological resources across an array of activities are more capable of deploying organizational and associational mechanisms to shape their relations with political actors. Strong interfirm collaborations enable business actors to effectively coordinate their decisions and actions and render them well organized and cohesive in a robust negotiating relationship with the state. By contrast, where firms share resources across a narrow range of activities and for limited purposes and interfirm relationships are conducted on an arm's-length, ad hoc and low-commitment basis, the private sector is likely to be fragmented and weakly organized. This not only undermines collective business efforts to interact with government officials but also makes it difficult for state agencies to elicit cooperation from the private sector and stimulate business participation in policy-making processes.

Not only do firms coordinate their decisions and actions through interfirm linkages, they may also develop collaborative ties with such third-party entities as financial institutions, research organizations or legal and consultancy services. Extensive and long-term networks with these entities, which can help firms build, integrate and reconfigure their internal and external competences, are likely to enable them to respond to rapidly changing business environments and tackle market and technological challenges in the process of organizing economic and innovation activities. Equally important, these networks may also broaden business actors' access to extramural resources, sharpen their mobilizational skills to pursue shared goals, and enable them to take independent action to initiate or strengthen public–private partnerships. It can be argued that business actors immersed in dense firm–third party linkages are well equipped to coordinate socioeconomic activities through network arrangements rather than seeking aid and guidance directly from the state.

Finally, interfirm coordination and firm–third party linkages also reflect the organizational structure and strength of business associations. Apart from their crucial roles in strengthening the functioning of markets by supporting the provision of such public goods as property rights and public administration, business associations also act as an interfirm forum to pursue collective interests and as a key network governance arrangement that links state actors to the business sector (Bell and Hindmore 2009; Doner and Schneider 2000). While the roles of business associations are crucial, the ways in which they organize themselves internally and externally to fulfil these roles differ considerably across industries and regions in China (Kennedy 2005; Unger 2008b). They are likely to be strong and effective, if they can aggregate and articulate interests coherently, discipline the behaviour of members, and develop institutionalized and stable linkages to state agencies. How regions or industrial sectors differ in these dimensions is an empirical issue and will be illustrated in the following analysis of the changing variety of state–firm interactions in China.

Four Ideal Types of Business–Government Relations

While these two constitutive dimensions of business–government relations are conceptually distinct, they are correlated because shifts in the authoritative governance of the economy may reflect the changing ability of business actors to coordinate economic action and develop collaborative links with other sociopolitical groups. The two dimensions can thus interact to generate different configurations of connections between state actors, firms and business organizations. Conceptualized more broadly than extant approaches that tend to focus relatively narrowly on state structures or policy networks as the fulcrum of business–government relations in emerging markets (Cali and Sen 2011; Cammett 2007; Weiss 1994), this framework is better able to capture the multiplicity and heterogeneity of interactions between the state and businesses in China.

Table 1.1 characterizes heuristically the different ways in which authoritative governance and market coordination interact with each other and

Table 1.1 Four ideal types of business–government relations

		Authoritative governance of the economy	
		Strong	*Weak*
Market coordination of socioeconomic activities	*Extensive*	I Interdependent	II Networked
	Limited	III Statist	IV Atomistic

the resultant configuration of business–government relations. When strong authoritative governance exists alongside robust market coordination (cell I), the state is connected to business actors through mutually dependent or interdependent relations. State agencies may possess rich and elaborate policy and administrative resources to shape and nurture the growth of new industries and promote technology development. They often do so by extracting vital information from firms, stimulating business participation in key policy areas and eliciting cooperation from a well-organized business sector. By the same token, firms rely on the state for developing governance structures that restrain the play of particularistic interests, coordinate competing claims and organize collective action among various socioeconomic interests. On the other hand, the ability of state actors to mobilize industry collaboration in advancing industrialization strategies and enhance the effectiveness of their economic policies is contingent on the contribution of firms and associations to policy development and implementation. This reflects, among other things, the relatively robust ownership integration of production chains or different markets, extensive inter-corporate collaborations or strong firm–third party linkages. In an interdependent mode of business–government relations, while the state establishes and monitors a broad set of sociopolitical objectives, these are often pursued through negotiations and cooperative relationships with business actors.

Where authoritative governance is relatively modest or limited but the role of key socioeconomic producer groups in coordinating market activities is crucial (cell II), the state is likely to develop close, cross-cutting and highly structured ties with the business community. While state actors may have considerable policy-making capabilities, they organize industrialization processes not so much through direct and dirigiste resource allocations and market regulations as through multifaceted, broadly based and sometimes horizontally oriented networks with various market players. The economic governance roles of both state and business actors derive from such networks that are shaped as much by informal norms of negotiating relationships as by institutionalized practices of public–private partnerships. Both as a cause and a consequence of this networked mode of firm–state interactions, business actors generally develop more collaborative relations through extensive intra- or inter-sector alliances and through the comparatively strong coordinating roles of collective interest-representing organizations. Among these organizations, business associations not only play a key role in organizing collective action among firms but also provide a strong basis for long-term and multi-level exchange relationships between state agencies, firms and sectors.

State–firm relations are likely to be organized in a top-down and vertically structured manner, in the case of strong authoritative governance coexisting with limited market coordination of socioeconomic activities (cell III). In this statist mode of business–government interactions, the development of policy-making rules, market institutions and innovation strategies is structured around state interests and actions, with firms and associations connected hierarchically to each other through the subornation of economic governance to state authorities. While state actors may solicit cooperation from the private sector and encourage business participation in policy processes, socioeconomic producer groups are more an instrument of development strategies than an equal and negotiating partner. This derives from the predominant role of a powerful and interventionist state in directing industrial development, allocating financial resources, orchestrating market regulations and controlling intermediary organizations. Equally important, state dominance weakens the development of independent and robust business associations and stifle private initiatives to promote collective action through close and long-term inter-firm or inter-sector networks. Large firms that operate in oligopolistic sectors or business groups, both state-controlled and family-owned, that coordinate economic activities between firms within groups may have direct entrée to the state and employ various means of securing influence. However, the business community as a whole that has limited associational resources to draw on to develop horizontal linkages and collaborations is likely to be too weakly organized and fragmented to shape relations with the state in line with its policy interests.

Finally, where the authoritative governance of the economy is weak and the ability of socioeconomic groups to coordinate market activities is limited (cell IV), the organization of state–firm relations tends to be atomistic. While state agencies may be directly involved in investment and production activities, their ability to promote industrial development, regulate product and labour markets and organize technological innovation processes is likely to be poorly developed. Likewise, business actors are unlikely to play an effective role in the coordination of economic and innovation activities in an institutional setting in which industrial structures are decentralized, interfirm relations fluid, firm-third party linkages ad hoc and difficult to sustain or business associations incohesive. Atomistic business–government relations often arise in regional political economies or industrial sectors where state officials demonstrate limited ideological and organizational coherence and have few stable and broadly based links to the business sector. To the extent that they are connected to major economic interests, these connections tend to be narrow and particularistic and are unlikely to centre on impersonal and institutionalized procedures. This makes it difficult for state actors to draw business into cooperative relationships and mobilize broad industry participation in formulating and pursing regional or sectoral development objectives.

Regional and Sectoral Variations in Business–Government Interactions

Contributors to the book apply and interrogate this typological framework in view of variations and changes in business–state interactions and the institutional consequences of such interactions in China. The objective is to develop an analytical approach that can distinguish different and changing forms of authoritative governance and market coordination in a clear and accurate manner. While the four ideal types of business–government relations delineated in the foregoing subsection may not be found pristine in the real sociopolitical world, they help establish a theoretically appropriate point of departure for understanding the varied patterns of interrelationships between political actors and economic agents in China. A key question being considered here is not so much whether state–business ties have changed over the past decades as how these changes have varied across regions and industries.

These four ideal types are empirically illustrated in the comparative analysis of regional and sectoral changes and variations in business–government relations in this volume and elsewhere. In the first place, state–firm interactions in the oil industry have shared many characteristics of the interdependent type. In her chapter, Jin Zhang argues that while the strong guiding hand of the planning agency, the National Development and Reform Commission (NDRC), tight party controls over the careers of corporate elites and extensive state ownership have underpinned the state steering of the oil industry, state planners have depended on lead petroleum firms for organizing technological and market developments, not only because of the latter's substantial financial and human resources but also because of their strong inter-corporate collaborations, increasing transnational networks and symbiotic ties with key line economic ministries. By the same token, ties between the central and local governments and leading multinational automakers have represented an interdependent variety of state–business interactions, as made clear in Gregory Chin's chapter. Such ties that were mainly structured around negotiations over market access, ownership levels and investment treatment in early years of the reform era have shifted towards a mutually dependent relationship that has hinged on the coordinating capability of state officials, MNCs' financial and technological contributions, and personal and institutionalized linkages between them. Likewise, other empirical studies (Luo 2001; Sun, Mellahi and Thun 2010) have also highlighted an increasingly interdependent relationship between government agencies and multinationals across various industries in China.

The interdependent genre of business–government relations also manifests itself in the regional pattern of industrial transformation. In Shenzhen, for instance, the municipal government has displayed a robust authoritative capacity to mobilize financial resources, foster collaborations between high-tech firms and academic institutions, and strengthen public–private policy linkages in its effort to direct the high-tech industrialization process. The effective state direction has co-exited with the strong business coordination of economic and innovation activities that has organizationally correlated with the governing role of large firms, dense interfirm networks and well-structured business associations. Shenzhen has thus cultivated a co-governed regime of technology development in which state and business actors have coordinated efforts to promote the growth of high-tech industries (Breznitz and Murphee 2011; Xiaoke Zhang this volume). In Beijing, Guangzhou, and Kunshan, state–firm interactions have also featured an interdependent structure that has combined authoritative governance with extensive business coordination to shape the transformation of the ICT and other sectors (Keng 2010; So 2004).

Business–government relations take on networked properties when the state organization of the economy is limited relative to the business coordination of socioeconomic activities. Nowhere are these properties more salient than perhaps in the evolution of interlinkages between local government officials and private market plyers in Wenzhou, Zhejiang Province. In their comparative analysis of associational underpinnings for business–government ties in this volume, Juanfeng Liu and Jianjun Zhang suggest that the limited ability of sub-state actors to steer local socioeconomic development in Wenzhou has been more than compensated for by their close, cross-cutting and multifaceted connections with a well-organized local business community. Such connections have both derived from and reinforced the roles of dense interfirm networks and business associations in coordinating local industrialization processes, shaping corporate financing patterns and promoting foreign trade activities. Similarly, Richard Carney's study in this volume also portrays state–firm interactions in the automobile industry of Guangdong as displaying many characteristics of this networked type. Local industrial planners have promoted public–private partnerships, inter-corporate linkages and major business associations as important institutional vehicles for reforming corporate governance practices and organizing the upgrading of production technologies in the industry.

It should be noted that the networked type of business–government relations has been a prevalent sociopolitical characteristic, particularly in the Pearl River and Yangzi River delta regions. While networked ties may vary in the density of public–private policy linkages, the tenacity of interfirm collaborations and the cohesion of business associations, they have converged on the combination of the facilitating role of sub-state agencies and actors with the dominant role of private market players in coordinating local industrial development. As meticulously documented in many region-specific studies (see Nee and Opper 2012; Wei et al. 2007; Yang 2014; Zeng 2010; Zhang and Liu 2013), private entrepreneurs, motivated by a perennial search for new business opportunities in decentralized economic systems and emboldened by local government efforts to foster associational arrangements among various socioeconomic actors, have developed both formal institutions and informal practices of commitments and collaborations along the same production value chains and across industrial boundaries. These institutions and practices have enabled private firms to share information about each other's business plans, mitigate opportunist behaviours, reduce uncertainties surrounding investment activities and develop competitive advantages in government-facilitated and self-organized industrial clusters.

The flipside of networked ties is the statist type of business–government nexuses. Such state-centred nexuses have manifested themselves in the dominance of state actors over giant telecommunications companies in policy and regulatory processes, as made clear by Yukyung Yeo in her contribution to the volume. The other sectors of strategic importance, including defence industries, finance and energy, have also had a top-down governance structure in which large firms organize and coordinate economic activities through their subordination to centralized regulatory and planning authorities (Hsueh 2016; Naughton and Tsai 2015), with the partial exception of the oil industry that features more interdependent state–firm relations, as noted above. This structure has weakened the ability of large firms in these sectors to shape their relations with state and other sociopolitical actors in line with their commercial and strategic interests, despite their increased lobbying power and operational autonomy from government agencies and despite the reliance of economic officials on them for information collection, policy implementation or technology development (Brodsgaard 2012; Deng and Kennedy 2010).

The regional variety of statist business–government relations is particularly salient in Shanghai. Contributions to this book (Carney; Xiaoke Zhang) and other key empirical analyses (see Chen 2009; Huang 2008; Thun 2006; Zhang 2015; Zhang 2016) have emphasized strong state direction and weak business coordination as the dominant sociopolitical structure of industrial governance across an array of high-tech and medium-tech sectors. The heavy dirigisme of industrial governance has been derivative from and concomitant with significant government controls over financial and product markets and elaborate and systemic policy interventions to target and promote specific sectors and firms. In stark contrast to the forceful state steering of industrial development processes, the business organization of economic activities through collaborative and associational arrangements has been weak in Shanghai. This weakness has been reflected in the segmentation of firms of various ownership types into mutually isolated groupings, organizationally incohesive and politically subordinate industrial associations, and fragmented linkages between business, financial and research entities. Business–government relations in other places, such as Chongqing, Jiangsu, Liaoning and Shandong, that have exhibited statist tendencies at various administrative levels have borne discernible resemblance to the sociopolitical attributes of state and business organization in Shanghai (Liu 2008; Liu and Zhang this volume; Mulvad 2015).

Business–government relations may become atomistic and individualized, when state actors have a limited authoritative capacity to direct the economy and weakly organized socioeconomic groups play an ineffective role in market processes. Recent studies on the changing roles of local governments in socioeconomic transformation (Chen 2016; Ong 2012; Zhou 2010) have contended that the ability of sub-state actors to align business interests with collective policy objectives has been significantly weakened against the backdrop of continuous market liberalization. This has generated an increasingly particularistic state–firm relationship and made it difficult for local governments to mobilize broad private-sector collaboration in advancing development strategies. These studies, while shedding light on the dynamics of business–government relations at the local level, have focused on the causal importance of sub-state institutions and actions, largely to the exclusion of that of business organization. In his comparative analysis of changing state–business ties across seven counties in Chongqing, Hunan, Shanxi and Zhejiang, Changdong Zhang (this volume) argues that collusive interactions between officials and businessmen have prevailed in many of these counties, not only because the governance capacity of local governments has been weak or weakened but also because the business sector has remained organizationally fragmented, and, equally important, public–private linkages have been narrowly based, exclusive and unstable. Due to the lack of steering and coordinating capabilities on the part of both state agencies and socioeconomic groups, political and economic elites have colluded to control the commanding heights of the local economy, giving rise to the personalized character of business–government relations.

There have been heated debates on the changing nature of personalized or guanxi connections in the process of China's transition towards a market economy. While some observers have contended that the significance of particularistic ties between officials and businessmen has declined, against the backdrop of continuously strengthened formal institutions (Guthrie 1999; 2002), others have emphasized the prevalence of such ties, despite institutional changes and improvements (Wank 1999, 2002; Yang 2002). Scholarly efforts to reconcile these opposing views have focused on the exploration of the process through which personalized ties have gradually taken on organizational properties (Wank 2002) or the co-evolution between guanxi practices and the peculiar socioeconomic institutions of

Chinese capitalism (McNally 2011). It is argued here that personalized connections between business and government have not only changed over time but also varied across regions and industrial sectors, reflecting, among other things, the different interests and strategies of private market players operating in divergent sociopolitical environments.

The interest of firms in interacting with government officials derives primarily from their desire to secure various resources that allow them to compete for survival and profits. However, firms may adopt different strategies to pursue the interest. At the risk of oversimplification, business efforts to develop and maintain state–firm relations can be differentiated between particularized and coordinated strategies. The particularized strategy rests with individual businessmen cultivating and sustaining personal ties with government officials, often at the expense of collective efforts to influence policy and regulatory processes through inter-corporate and associational linkages and broad-based interactions with officialdom. The coordinated strategy does not forsake relational ties with particularistic officials but places more emphasis on the organization of collective action to formulate and pursue shared interests by developing horizontal collaborations among firms, mobilizing associational resources and building inclusive and multifaceted public–private networks.

This variation in business strategies represents the responses of firms to their divergent sociopolitical institutional environments. While private property rights are enshrined in the Chinese constitution, their enforcement has been highly uneven across the country. In places where rules and laws for property rights protection are weakly enforced and the predatory practice of state agencies, such as informal taxes and fees, is rampant, firms are strongly motivated to maintain personalized and collusive relations with government and party officials in order to obtain protective privileges and regulatory favours (Li et al. 2006; Ngo this volume; Changdong Zhang this volume; Zhou 2010). Furthermore, the particularized approach to interacting with state actors is more prevalent in those regions or sectors in which the redistributive power of the state remains extensive. State controls over the allocation of scarce resources and services effectively obliges individual firms to offer government officials gifts, payoffs and personal rewards in exchange for discretionary privileges rather than to pursue collective solutions through inter-corporate arrangements and producer organizations (Nee and Opper 2010; Wank 1999, 2002; Zhu and Wu this volume).

While the particularized strategy may help politically well-connected firms cope with institutional uncertainties and predatory government behaviour, there are significant costs associated with personalistic networking with state and party officials. These come in the forms of excessive time and monetary investments, non-commercial commitments and obligations, and erratic and unreasonable requests for funds from state agencies (Li et al. 2006; Ngo this volume). Private firms may also face unpredictable political risks, as when officials with whom they are associated get demoted or purged in elite power struggles or implicated in corruption scandals. Equally important, there is no guarantee that firms seeking particularistic alliances with party–state officials and obtaining policy favours will necessarily be competitive and successful in the marketplace. Indeed, there is little evidence to suggest that guanxi connections generate any significant positive impact on the long-term performance of those firms that have attempted to cultivate such connections in the face of real and potential costs and risks (Nee et al. 2007; Park and Luo 2001).

Significant disincentives against particularistic efforts to interact with government officials have inclined firms to move towards or adopt the coordinated strategy. This is particularly true in those regional political economies and industrial sectors where government agencies have played a key role in facilitating the growth of the private sector, encouraging private entrepreneurs to foster new forms of business association and institutionalizing relatively symmetrical and even transparent patterns of business–government relations and where private firms have developed mobilizational and associational capabilities to nurture collaborative interactions both among themselves and between them and state actors (Liu and Zhang this volume; Zeng 2010; Zhang and Peck 2016; Xiaoke Zhang this volume). In the Pearl River and Yangzi River delta regions, the success of private enterprises that has depended more on their efforts to build social networks within close-knit business communities than on guanxi connections has generated a widespread demonstration effect, encouraging many others to decouple from the particularized strategy (*Economist* 2017; Nee and Opper 2012).

As noted above, the coordinated strategy does not preclude personal ties between firms and government officials; nor does it necessarily restrain rent-seeking on the part of both state and business actors. However, in those regions and industries where a well-organized private sector is connected with government agencies through regular and extensive consultation and coordination, business efforts at developing broad and collaborative interactions with state actors are stronger and more successful. As long as rent-seeking associated with particularistic practices is circumscribed by these interactions, interpersonal ties are likely to complement rather than compromise the coordinated strategy.

It should perhaps be emphasized here that each of the above-mentioned four types of business–government relations only rarely becomes established in its entirety in any regional political economy or industrial sector. Since few regions or industries have developed all the necessary features for any single coherent way of organizing interactions between state and business actors to be fully institutionalized, it follows that there are few empirical examples of these types with all their distinctive characteristics. More often than not, business–government relations, as a set of sociopolitical structures and processes, display hybrid and multifaceted features as in, for instance, the oil industry that combines a largely interdependent state–firm linkage with an elaborate system of state controls over key resources, corporate elites and finance or industrial clusters in the Pearl River delta region where predominantly networked ties between local government officials and private entrepreneurs are tempered with personalistic and particularistic tendencies.

Explaining Changes and Variations in Business–Government Relations

The second key question that this book addresses focuses on understanding and explaining the patterns and trajectories of changes and variations in business–government relations in China. The causes of these changes and variations can be theorized and categorized in different ways. Distinctions are commonly made between endogenous and exogenous causes; between economic, social and political causes; and between material and ideational causes (Haggard and Huang 2008; Hsueh 2016; Kennedy 2005; Nee and Opper 2012; Ong 2012; Unger 2008b). All of these distinctions are artificial and involve oversimplifications of some kind. In this book, the approaches to developing explanatory propositions represent a collective effort to break through these often artificial distinctions, illuminating the aggregated effects of various causal factors on the changing varieties of interactions between state agencies, economic actors and business organizations in China.

This does not suggest that contributors attempt to provide a unified approach to accounting for changes and variations in the configuration of business–government relations. Indeed, the empirical facts and causal processes remain too contested for analytical unity of this kind to be achieved in the book. However, individual contributions take the key structural features of power relations between the state and businesses in China around the early 1990s as their respective point of departure and set their empirical analyses against the typology of business–government interactions. More importantly, while individual contributions encompass a range of different cases, specific issues and diverse methodologies, they are all structured around the exploration of changing business–state ties at the interface between global forces, market pressures and sociopolitical changes. They examine how external and economic influences have altered the ways in which state actors are linked to businesses and how ideas, political institutions and market structures have intermediated systemic pressures to generate the varied patterns of these linkages across regions and industries in China.

The major causal variables that are empirically shown to have shaped business–government relations in contributions to this book and elsewhere are drawn from three levels of analysis: global market and normative pressures, national sociopolitical transformations, and regional and sectoral configurations of state institutions and market structures. The central argument to be developed here is that while global pressures and national transformations have been the most powerful stimuli for changes in the general pattern of state–firm interactions, regional or sectoral configurations are the primary sources of variations in the behaviour of similarly situated state and business actors.

Global Market and Normative Pressures

Political and economic rivalries among nation-state have been a major driving force behind industrialization across developing countries, including China (Zhu this volume). While these rivalries have both legitimized and strengthened the role of the Chinese state in managing the national development process, the open door policy instituted in the late 1970s has gradually, yet steadily, integrated China into the global economy. The resultant trade and capital flows and associated competition from foreign exporters have encouraged domestic firms to look for, and introduce, market-oriented managerial approaches and business strategies that have been at variance with the policy and institutional legacies of central planning and challenged the dominant role of the state in the process of market development and governance (Child 1994; Keister and Zhang 2009). Equally important, the internationalization of the Chinese economy has created tremendous opportunities for business actors to expand the scope of their operations, foster transnational linkages and upscale their organizational and technological capabilities. This has not only enhanced their preferences for more open, equal and independent relations with state actors but also endowed them with political and organizational resources with which to pursue such preferences (Story 2010; Yueh 2011).

Furthermore, through the constant expansion of their investment activities in China, multinational companies have become a major agent to push for changes in the characteristics of the host country's sociopolitical institutions, including government–business relations, in which they invest and operate. The role of MNCs in influencing the pattern of state–business interactions in general and of government–MNC ties in particular has tended to be politically significant, particularly when they and local firms have common positions on market regulations and form transnational alliances to lobby the relevant government authorities and shape public policies in their shared favour (Kennedy 2007). The growing influence of MNCs has not only reflected their ability to agitate for policy and institutional reforms by dint of their presence or even dominance in the key sectors of the Chinese economy but also stemmed from the eagerness of economic officials to attract foreign capital, acquire new technologies and maintain access to overseas markets. This goes a long way towards explaining why state planners, at both central and local levels, have been willing to accommodate more interdependent and cooperative relations with MNCs, as noted above.

The impact of economic globalization on the transformation of business–government relations in China has worked not only through market mechanisms and constraints but also through the more subjective pressures of transnational norms. China's integration into the global economy coincided with the growing dominance of neoliberalism in international policy circles during the 1980s and 1990s. Key international economic institutions, such as the IMF, the World Bank and the WTO, and major western powers and the United States in particular all espoused the virtues of a minimalist government and free markets. As China became actively involved in the decision-making process of these institutions and developed increasingly close commercial ties with leading industrialized nations, it was under heavy pressure to accept, and reorient state–market relations with, the neoliberal mantras (Kornberg and Faust 2005; Yang 2004). While the global financial crisis of the late 2000s appears to have debunked many of the neoliberal credos and vindicated the state-led model of development in China, the continued sway of liberal economic ideas among intellectuals and reformers within Chinese academic, state and party organizations has provided endogenous support for a more market-oriented, rule-based and institutionalized relationship between state actors and market players (Ferchen 2013; Hsu et al. 2011).

National Sociopolitical Transformations

While global market and normative pressures are remarkable and revealing in themselves, the impact of these pressures on changes in the ways in which business and government have interacted in China is less linear and more limited than one may expect. Two points are important here. First, the expectation that economic openness would be accompanied by a unidirectional movement towards more societal corporatist or pluralist frameworks in business–government relations has clearly been misplaced. If anything, the vagaries of the international market have necessitated the enhanced role of the state in promoting national competitiveness and legitimized the dominance of state agencies over socioeconomic actors and groups, particularly in the key sectors of the Chinese economy (Gabriele 2010; Zhu this volume). Second, the internationally centred accounts that have privileged the causal importance of global forces suffer from an endogeneity problem: the increased integration of the Chinese economy with the global market system has resulted primarily from the strategic decisions of national political leaders to launch and sustain market-oriented reforms (Naughton 1995; Shirk 1993). Such reforms have not only opened China up to the outside world but also triggered fundamental changes in state–society nexuses (Goldman and MacFarquhar 1999; McNally 2008; Oi et al. 2010).

Global forces thus need to be viewed in close interaction with national sociopolitical transformations in order to better understand state–firm relations in China. Two of such transformations that have had systemic implications for the changing nature of interactions between government and business are marketization and decentralization. While the process of nearly 40 years of economic reforms has been meandering, often piecemeal and sometimes punctuated with reversals, it has firmly put China in the transition towards a market economy in which price mechanisms have prevailed to allocate the majority of goods and services, central planning has ceased to exist, and, most important of all, a vibrant private sector has emerged. The private sector, which has now produced a lion's share of China's industrial output, has constantly encroached on the business reverses of SOEs, moved into new industrial and commercial activities and become the most dynamic sector across many regions and industries, although the influence of the state in the financial system and producer goods sectors has remained strong. As private firms have grown in economic importance, their regulatory environment has improved and their ability to circumscribe the absolute authority of officialdom, particularly at the local level, has been on the rise. While the continued existence of an authoritarian regime has made it difficult for business actors to politically challenge the state, the growing marketization of the economy has created more socioeconomic space for them to develop their interests and organizations. In those regional political economies and industrial sectors that are dominated by private firms, business actors have been better positioned to reshape their relations with state agencies as much as government officials have employed direct or indirect levers to reorient the interests and behaviours of the private sector with their policy objectives (Breznitz and Murphee 2011; Garnaut and Song 2004; Nee and Opper 2012; Tjosvold et al. 2008; Xiaoke Zhang this volume).

Concomitant with economic reforms has been the process of decentralization that has devolved decision-making powers from the central government to local officials and produced political and administrative cleavages between the centre and localities. Recent recentralization efforts do not appear to have fully reversed these developments (Huang 2008; Heilmann and Melton 2013). Decentralization, which has had far-reaching and long-term implications for China's socioeconomic development (Brandt and Rawski 2008; Montinola et al. 1995; Naughton and Yang 2004; Xu 2011), has generated two different but interrelated effects on the evolution of business–government relations, particularly at the local level. Together with the nomenklatura system of the Chinese Communist Party (CCP) that has emphasized economic development as a principal yardstick to evaluate the performance of local officials, decentralization has incentivized them to implement market-oriented reforms and promote local economic growth. However, the same process has also led to variations in the extent to which sub-state actors have nourished private firms as key agents for industrialization and incorporated them into local development coalitions. These variations have influenced the political status of private firms within regional political economies or industrial sectors, delimited their access to decision-making processes and defined the nature of their relations with sub-state actors (Breznitz and Murphee 2011; Mulvad 2015; Remick 2002; Segal 2003). On the other hand, administrative decontrols have given local government agencies considerable latitude in adapting centrally formulated reform programmes to local socioeconomic conditions and developing locally specific approaches to pursing economic growth and governing market activities. These approaches have exerted divergent shaping influence over state–society nexuses and especially business–government interactions in the same way as varied sub-state structures and practices have affected their effectiveness differently (Carney this volume; Heilmann et al. 2013; Rithmire 2014; Tsai 2006, 2007; Wang et al. 2014, Xiaoke Zhang this volume).

Regional and Sectoral Configurations of State Institutions and Market Structures

Market-oriented reforms, coupled with economic openness, have created a policy, social and institutional environment propitious to the rise of business power but have not fundamentally influenced the ways in which the balance of power between state and business actors has changed differently across regions and industrial sectors in China. Similarly, the process of decentralization has constituted a necessary but an insufficient condition for the emergence of regional and sectoral variations in the intersection between the authoritative governance of the economy and market coordination of socioeconomic activities, as identified in the previous section. Extant studies have offered explanations of why business–government relations have varied across regions (Breznitz and Murphee 2011; Segal 2003) or sectors (Hsueh 2016; Kennedy 2005) but have fallen short of developing an integrated framework for explicating variations both across regions and sectors. To develop such a framework, this subsection first assesses propositions about the sources of variations in business–government relations that focus on state ideologies and institutions and market structures and characteristics. It then summarizes and attempts to weigh the influence of these variables, reaching for a holistic understanding of variations in the four types of state–business interactions delineated in the preceding analysis.

State Ideologies and Institutions

While economic reforms and decentralized administrative systems have encouraged local officials to develop different preferences for supporting the growth of private firms and incorporating them into public policy-making processes, they do not answer the nagging questions of where these preferences come from and how they differ. As these situational factors cannot determine unambiguously the choice of state strategies to engage with business actors, ideologies may loom large as an explanation. Two antithetic ideologies—interventionism and liberalism—that reflect pre-existing development models, long-standing policy norms or international linkages generate differential effects on the strategic preferences of sub-state actors. Business–government relations are likely to be more state-oriented, where centralized industrialization processes that have historically been organized around large SOEs and planning rationalities that have been internalized as basic policy-making rules have institutionally entrench the dirigiste approach to controlling private economic actors and governing market activities (Huang 2008; Yeo this volume; Xiaoke Zhang this volume). By contrast, in those regions or sectors where industrial production has traditionally been led by small and medium-sized enterprises (SMEs) and linkages with international public and business entities are strong, local or sectoral officials are more receptive to liberal ideas, more heavily influenced by the hands-off ideology about the modest role of the state and more interested in engaging business actors in policy processes (Mulvad 2015; Remick 2002; Segal 2003).

Variations in the configuration of state–business relations are also a key function of divergent state institutions at the regional and sectoral levels. Two such institutional variables are the internal organizational structure of local governments and relations between the centre and regions or industrial sectors. The ways in which sub-states organize bureaucratic agencies and the availability of various resources at their disposal influence the degree of local government intervention in the economy and the nature of state–business relations. Local officials are more capable of asserting a dirigiste form of control over socioeconomic activities and shaping their interactions with private economic actors in line with their policy interests, if sub-state bureaucracies are not only centrally and cohesively structured but also command a wide array of organizational, informational and production resources (Carney this volume; Thun 2006). On the other hand, the state direction of local industrial development is likely to be limited, where sub-state agencies lack organizational coherence and are poorly equipped with policy instruments to control the behaviour of market players. As an important way to compensate for their limited governing capacity, local officials may encourage private firms to organize themselves through associational mechanisms and mobilize business participation in implementing development strategies. This is likely to be true in regions where state actors have a pro-business approach to market governance and transnational linkages are strong (Carney this volume; Liu and Zhang this volume).

The impact of centre–local/sector relations on the characteristics of state–business linkages varies mainly with the role of specific regions or sectors in contributing to the state coffers, strengthening national competitiveness and enhancing the geostrategic interests of top political leaderships (Ernst and Naughton 2008; Hsueh 2016; Leng 2010; Remick 2002; Thun 2006). Regions or sectors that are more valued in their contribution to the achievement of the centre's fiscal, technology and security policies operate more tightly under the yoke of the central government. This invariably leads to the extensive state direction of regional or sectoral development processes, encourages the centralized mode of economic management and institutionalizes vertical political connections between state and business actors. In those regions or sectors whose strategic contribution is less significant and whose relations with the centre is thus more distant, direct state involvement in production and investment activities is likely to be modest, the economic success of firms becomes increasingly independent of government interventions, and market governance tends to be structured around decentralized and horizontal ties between state agencies and socioeconomic groups. This both incentivizes and enables regional or sectoral officials to craft more interdependent or networked relations with private economic actors.

Market Structures and Characteristics

While state ideologies and institutions are important, they generate varied state–firm relations in conjunction with locally or sectorally specific market structures and characteristics, as will be shown below. Taking their cues from the extant literature (Kennedy 2005; Maxfield and Schneider 1997; Nee and Opper 2010; Park and Luo 2001), contributors to the volume have underlined the causal significance of three key market variables—the size of firms, regional and sectoral shares of state ownership and transnational linkages of specific regions and industries.

In the first place, firm size is an important attribute that not only shapes the behaviours and decisions of enterprises but also the disposition of state actors to structure their relations with market players through interactive and associational mechanisms. Generally speaking, SMEs tend to have stronger incentives to cooperate with other firms and cultivate policy networks with state agencies, primarily because they lack resources with which to overcome institutional disadvantages but are flexible and entrepreneurial enough to develop joint mobilizational skills (Liu and Zhang this volume; Park and Luo 2001; Xin and Pearce 1996; White et al. 1996; Xiaoke Zhang this volume). This is particularly the case if government officials encourage SMEs to organize through business associations and delegate policy and regulatory functions to these associations, as an important way to help them mitigate or resolve the collective action problem. Large firms, on the other hand, are likely to interact with party–state officials and influence policy processes through particularistic links rather than through interfirm collaborations and associational arrangements. This is partly because managers in large firms are eager to maintain their independent organizational identity and partly because many large firms are descendants of the central planning system and have inherently close connections with party–state agencies and officials and more favourable access to various resources (Carney this volume; Yeo this volume; Xiaoke Zhang this volume).

Furthermore, firm size often correlates with the regional or sectoral share of state ownership in their combined impact on the pattern of business–government relations. The statist genre of such relations is more likely to be prevalent in regions or sectors more dominated by large SOEs. With extensive state ownership come the strong redistributive controls of government agencies over scarce resources and the tight state regulation of interorganizational relations and associational activities. This enables party–state officials to pre-empt private-sector interests or thwart business attempts at collective action and renders industry associations subordinate and even irrelevant. By contrast, interdependent or networked state–firm relations may be more dominant in regions or sectors in which the presence of SOEs is relatively limited and the role of the private sector more robust in industrialization processes. Where state involvement in production and investment activities is weak, private players are likely to have more sociopolitical room for fostering their own networks and associations of interfirm interactions. Business organizations that are more fully developed and enjoy greater operational autonomy help small private firms build more institutionalized links with state agencies and get access to, and influence, local or sectoral policy-making processes (Carney this volume; Kennedy 2005; Liu and Zhang this volume; Nee and Opper 2012; Xiaoke Zhang this volume).

Finally, the impact of firm size and ownership forms on the configuration of business–government relations is intermediated by the extent to which regional political economies or industrial sectors are commercially and socially linked to transnational actors and entities. In regions or sectors where the presence of foreign companies is heavy, exposures to international market forces through trade and capital flows are significant, firms are extensively embedded in global production networks, interfirm competition is strong, state controls over market activities are limited, and government officials are more supportive of private economic interests and organizations (Caney this volume; Park and Luo 2001; Yang 2014; Xiaoke Zhang this volume; Zhu and Wu this volume). Business actors who are able to upgrade their organizational and technological capabilities through both localized and globalized networks of firms become increasingly independent of state apparatuses and more assertive in their interactions with party–state officials. This appears to be true even in those industrial sectors in which state ownership is prevalent (Jin Zhang this volume). Where regions or sectors have few transnational linkages, market competition is likely to be weak, government influences over the allocation of resources tend to be strong, and the growth of private sector interests and associations is subdued. Firms may have little choice but to depend on particularistic connections with party and state officials for obtaining policy and regulatory favours and overcoming institutional constraints.

An Integrated Explanation of Varied Business–Government Relations

Based on the causal propositions described and analysed above, this subsection explores the combined impact of ideological, institutional and market variables and presents an integrated explanation of regional and sectoral variations in the four types of business–government relations, as summarized in Table 1.2.

The regional variety of interdependent state–business relations is well illustrated in the strong authoritative organization of high-tech industrialization and the robust market coordination of production and innovation activities in Shenzhen. The ability of the municipal government to guide local economic development has had an organizational and

Table 1.2 State and market influences on the four varieties of business–government relations

Types of business–government relations	*State ideologies and institutions*			*Market structures and characteristics*		
	Ideological orientation	*Organizational cohesion and resources*	*Relations between the centre and regions/sectors*	*Firm size*	*Regional/sectoral share of state ownership*	*Transnational linkages*
Interdependent	Mixture of interventionism and liberalism	Relatively cohesive and resourceful	Varied	Balanced between large firms and SMEs	Some to considerable	Relatively strong
Networked	Largely liberal	Limited resources but relatively incohesive	Relatively weak and distant	Generally small; lead firms embedded among small producers	Generally limited	Generally strong and extensive
Statist	Strongly interventionist	Cohesive and resourceful	Close and strong	Predominantly large	Considerable to high	Varied
Atomistic	Little clear ideological orientation	Organizationally fragmented and incohesive	Generally weak	Small to medium-sized	Varied	Generally weak

ideological correlate in a largely cohesive and resourceful bureaucracy and in the growing influence of a statist industrialization strategy, particularly within the planning agency. However, this has been balanced out by the strong role of private sector interests and organizations that has derived from limited state ownership, extensive linkages with overseas markets and an industrial structure in which large firms have found themselves immersed in collaborations with SMEs. As a result, local state officials who are weakly tied to the central government have been keen to develop a mutually dependent relationship with private players in their effort to promote the growth of high-tech industries (Breznitz and Murphee 2011; Fu 2015; Xiaoke Zhang this volume). The state–market balance in interdependent business–government relations may not necessarily be even. In the sectoral example of such relations, the oil industry, dirigiste policy-making rules, close ties to and extensive controls by the centre, and an oligopolistic market structure have all weighed in favour of authoritative governance. But the broad thrust of state–firm interactions has remained more interdependent than statist, partly because lead oil companies have developed extensive collaborative interactions with MNCs and partly because line economic ministries have adopted a relatively liberal approach to organizing their relations with major market players and have been supportive of their efforts at collective action in the industry (Jin Zhang this volume).

The regional genre of networked state–business relations is particularly salient in Wenzhou and Guangzhou, as demonstrated in contributions to this volume (Carney; Liu and Zhang) and elsewhere (Mulvad 2015; Zeng 2010). These two places have both been characterized by a local government that has relatively limited organizational cohesion and resources but by a private-sector-dominated business system that is embedded in dense and deep interfirm alliances of mainly SMEs and transnational linkages through various commercial activities. Local government officials who have weak ties with the central government and have a pro-business policy orientation have seen their governing roles as implanted in, and supported by, broad-based, cross-cutting and horizontally structured networks with private-sector actors and organizations. There are few sectoral instances of networked state–business relations in individual contributions to this volume, but other empirical studies have depicted many sectors of high and low technology, ranging from electronics to textiles, that often conglomerate around industrial clusters across the Pearl River and Yangzi River deltas as having displayed many defining features of such relations (*Economist* 2017; Nee and Opper 2012; Zeng 2010). Underpinning the growth of these clustered industries have been the willingness of local government officials to engage with market players through public–private partnerships and, more importantly, a well-organized yet open business community built through collaborative linkages among small private firms and interwoven with global production and innovation networks.

The statist mode of business–government relations tends to be particularly prevalent in industries of strategic importance (Naughton and Tsai 2015; Yeo this volume) and centrally administered municipalities (Carney this volume; Leng 2010; Mulvad 2015; Xiaoke Zhang this volume). In these industries and municipalities, the various forms of dirigiste thinking have provided an elaborate and durable rationale for interventionist policies and the dominance of either large, central government-controlled firms or local SOEs. Extensive state ownership and concentrated industrial structures have strengthened the ability of cohesively organized and resourceful economic bureaucracies to steer sectoral or regional development but stifled business initiatives and efforts to coordinate socioeconomic activities through collaborative and associational mechanisms. In Shanghai and the telecommunications sector that have maintained transnational linkages, many of which are orchestrated by industrial planners, the role of these linkages in stimulating market competition, curbing government controls and fostering private sector organization has been more than countervailed by entrenched statist ideologies, institutions and practices.

The atomistic type of state–firm interactions correlates with local state bureaucracies that are incoherent in ideological orientations and fragmented in organizational structures. Sub-state actors have little incentive and capacity to encourage SMEs to organize themselves collectively through interfirm linkages and business associations; nor are they able to mobilize broad business participation in local development processes and isolate redistributive and regulatory policies from special interest groups. Weak ties with the central government make it difficult for national planning and regulatory authorities to monitor the behaviour of local government officials and amplify the influence of particularistic interests. Furthermore, atomistic business–government relations also tend to be prevalent in regional political economies that have limited transnational linkages and weak market competition. Firms that are under little pressure to acquire new knowledge and upgrade their research competences and thus remain technologically and organizationally impotent are eager to seek easy and quick profits through personalized ties with local state actors.

Equally important, where links to overseas actors and institutions are sporadic, global market and normative forces that may help enforce private property rights and restrain predatory government behaviours more effectively are subdued. Finally, where local bureaucracies are incohesive, ties to the centre weak and transnational linkages limited, personalistic tendencies in business–government relations tend to be particularly acute in regions with extensive state controls over production and investment activities. Such controls that reinforce the discretionary power of sub-state agencies to regulate market entry, favour some firms over others, and distribute rents incentivize business actors to seek particularistic privileges through collusive ties with government and party officials.

Institutional Consequences of Changing Business–Government Relations

The third and final issue to be addressed in the book relates to the ways in which business–government relations have impinged on the development and transformation of economic institutions in China. It focuses on corporate governance practices, market regulation, multinational corporate behaviour and technology development regimes. These have featured prominently in the reform of economic institutions in which state agencies are dependent on business organizations for change implementation and firms are incentivized to engage with government in order to shape the change process. While institutional dysfunction and performance crises associated with global competitive pressures have prompted reforms in these institutional arenas (Potter 2003; Rowen et al. 2008; Story 2010; Tenev and Zhang 2002), they are crucially intermediated by the structure and process of state–business interactions. Contributors to the third part of the book pay close attention to three key points in their efforts to examine the causal pathways through which changing business–government relations interact with economic institutional change.

In the first place, the analysis of this interactive process focuses on how dominant patterns of business–government ties, as a key set of sociopolitical structures, influence the ways in which political and economic actors formulate and implement institutional reform proposals. These structures not only shape the disposition of actors to favour certain institutional choices over others but also constrain their ability to pursue preferred institutional changes. A central argument of this book is that a more dynamic perspective into the nature and properties of institutional change needs to be based on a proper understanding of how the structural dimensions of business–government relations—the authoritative governance of the economy and the market coordination of socioeconomic action—impinge on the constitutive features of emergent market institutions. It is these dimensions that constitute one of the most critical and enduring endogenous sources of changes and variations in the contour of market organizations and practices in China.

Furthermore, while emphasizing the structural constraints of business–government interactions, contributors to the book also eschew the deterministic view of institutional change prevalent in much of the recent institutionalist literature (Mahoney 2000; North 1990; Pierson 2000). They devote explicit attention to the role of agency in determining how state actors, corporate executives and business leaders interpret and respond to pressures for institutional reforms. Prevalent patterns of state–business relations not merely impose constraints on the behaviour of individual actors but also empower them to challenge and redesign socioeconomic norms and practices. This suggests that state and business actors have the agential power to shape the character of economic institutions and institutional change. While individual contributions focus on diverse cases and deploy different theoretical approaches, they converge on the proposition that sociopolitical actors serve as change entrepreneurs supporting the reform or creation of market institutions that they deem to be aligned with their ideational orientations or self-interested purposes.

Finally, one of the central analytical objectives of the book is to explore how business–government relations differ across regions and industries in China and how cross-regional and cross-sectoral variations lead to divergent forms and outcomes of institutional change. While an emphasis on the causal importance of endogenous sociopolitical structures is crucial, the explanation of changing economic institutions would be seriously incomplete without a careful examination of exogenous causes. As will be demonstrated in the third part of the book, contributors examine how various forms of internationalization—global market integration, transnational norms and internalization of external pressures—interact to shape state–firm interactions and force changes in regional or sectoral systems of economic coordination and market organization. While international forces may be a key contributor to economic institutional change, they constitute a necessary but not an essential cause. External market and normative pressures, however powerful, manifest themselves through the infiltration of regional and sectoral configurations of business–government relations in China. They shape the ways in which state and business actors respond to external economic and political forces, intermediate the impact of exogenous factors differently and generate divergent processes and outcomes of institutional change across regions and industrial sectors.

In his chapter, Richard Carney emphasizes local state–business relations as a crucial intervening variable that has shaped the pattern of corporate governance reforms in the automobile industry of Guangdong and Shanghai. While corporate governance reforms were prompted by international market pressures—the desire to secure foreign capital through international listing in Guangdong and the need to obtain advanced technologies through joint ventures with automobile MNCs in Shanghai, the prevalent pattern of reforms has diverged between the two locales. In Guangdong, emerging corporate governance practices have more closely resembled those of the West in that they have offered stronger protections to minority shareholders due to leading car manufacturers being bonded to higher governance standards. By contrast, the municipal government in Shanghai has continued to retain significant influence over the dominant firms in the industry, both because of its extensive ownership stakes and due to less stringent information disclosure requirements and weaker minority shareholder protection. The divergent paths that corporate governance reforms have taken derive, argues Carney, from regional variations in key state–business dimensions. In Guangdong, weaker ties to the central government, a less cohesive bureaucracy and a better-organized private sector with more extensive localized networks and stronger associations have enabled international market pressures to exert greater shaping influence over local corporate governance structures and practices in the automobile industry. On the other hand, closer ties to Beijing and a more centralized and dirigiste state apparatus that connects relatively poorly organized private business actors via vertical sociopolitical structures have allowed industrial officials to continue favouring a few state-owned car producers and dampened the call for more forceful corporate governance reforms by minority investors and automobile MNCs.

Carney's contribution reinforces but goes beyond extant studies on the sociopolitical dynamics of corporate governance reforms in China. Many of these studies have tended to focus on state institutions and the policy preferences of state actors as the major determinants of changing corporate governance policies, structures and practices (Fan et al. 2012;

Nee et al. 2007; Oi 2010). While shedding important light on the political process through which state actors have pursued institutional and legal changes in the governance of firms, they have largely failed to consider these changes in tandem with business–government relations. Equally significant, extant studies have tended to pay inadequate attention to how and why political underpinnings for corporate governance reforms have varied across regions and industrial sectors. To the extent that they have explored regional or sectoral variations in reform patterns and trajectories, they have remained thin in the political explanation of these variations. Carney's chapter that advances such an explanation provides a new point of theoretical departure for thinking about the sources of economic institutional change across regional political economies in China.

This proposition is supported in the contribution by Xiaoke Zhang, which suggests that business–state relations bear strongly on technology development regimes by shaping the ways in which industrial policies and corporate strategies interact to manage innovation challenges. He develops this argument through a comparative analysis of technology development processes and innovation outcomes in the ICT industry of Shanghai and Shenzhen. In the dirigiste technology development regime of Shanghai, while the strong state organization of industrialization processes has underpinned forceful policies to help ICT firms deal with innovation challenges, the efficacy of such policies in improving R&D skills and competences, particularly among small firms, has been compromised by the inability of business actors to organize innovation activities across firms and sectors. By contrast, Shenzhen has cultivated a co-governed technology development regime in which strong state direction and robust business organization have generated the coordinated efforts of policymakers and market players to promote technology development in the ICT industry and appears to have achieved better innovation outcomes.

The major empirical findings of Xiaoke Zhang's chapter call into question the central propositions of prominent studies (Wan et al. 2015; Williamson and Yin 2014) that have taken a grossly aggregated approach to examining innovation processes across regions and industries in China. While more nuanced analyses (Chen 2014; Nahm and Steinfeld 2014) have demonstrated crucial regional or sectoral differences in technology development patterns and trajectories, they have tended to privilege empirical elaboration over causal explanation and have been less geared towards exploring the fundamental sources of these differences. Zhang's contribution has taken as its starting point the central idea that technology development regimes are not cut from the same institutional cloth but vary significantly with regional or sectoral structures of industrial governance. These structures that hinge on the interface between state organization and business coordination shape the process through which innovation challenges are managed. To better understand regional or sectoral variations in technological change and industrial competitiveness, we need to bring to the fore the divergent configurations of business–state interactions.

The political logic of varied business–state relations also asserts itself in the development of China's market regulation systems and the organizational behaviour of Chinese multinational corporations. In her analysis of a recent anti-monopoly investigation against state-owned telecommunications giants in China, Yukyung Yeo clearly demonstrates the institutional consequences of changing state–firm relations. Oligopolistic players in the telecommunications industry have recently acquired significant economic clout, partly because of their expanding scope of operations and partly because of China's integration with the global economy. Headed by powerful corporate elites who have ministerial or vice-ministerial statuses, these companies have enjoyed growing managerial autonomy from state economic agencies. However, despite this realignment of power relations between the state and business in China, large telecommunications companies have been unable to shape the formulation of regulatory rules and the process of market regulation in line with their commercial and strategic interests. This is mainly attributable, argues Yeo, to the ability of the Chinese Communist Party (CCP) to influence the career development of senior managers in these companies, the strengthened hands of the more intervention-minded state agencies, more specifically the NDRC, in regulating market activities and the continued resilience of state corporatist mechanisms.

In the oil industry, which is as strategically important as the telecommunications sector and also features an oligopolistic market structure, the more interdependent mode of business–government relations has generated different institutional and organizational outcomes. In her contribution, Jin Zhang shows that Chinese oil multinationals have been able to take more independent initiatives to improve their corporate governance practices, formulate overseas investment strategies and develop transnational alliances. In her explanation of the organizational behaviour of these companies, she emphasizes the sector-specific characteristics of state–firm interactions as a key determinant. While state structures remain similar across the strategically important sectors in that the NDRC has occupied an increasingly powerful position in the state apparatus and the career development of corporate elites is subject to CCP controls, the oil industry has been characterized by a different pattern of market coordination and government–firm links. It is stronger interfirm collaborations, more extensive transnational networks and more symbiotic and horizontally structured ties with key economic ministries in the oil industry that primarily account for a more important role of market players in shaping organizational changes and developments. These sector-specific state–firm dimensions have set the behaviour of state-owned giants in the oil industry apart from that of their counterparts in the telecommunications and other strategically important sectors.

Organization of the Book

This book addresses the above-mentioned issues through division into three parts. The first part presents a panoramic view of how business–government relations have changed differently across regional political economies and industrial sectors in China over the past two decades or so and forms the basis for analysing the sociopolitical causes and institutional consequences of varied state–firm interactions. This introductory chapter has discussed the typological framework for categorizing business–government ties, advanced theoretical propositions concerning the sources of changes and variations in the regional and sectoral patterns of interactions between state and business actors, and specified the causal linkage between such interactions and economic institutional change. The next chapter in the first part takes a further look at the key theoretical and empirical issues mentioned in the introductory chapter by focusing on the uneven relationships between the polymorphous state and hybrid businesses and identifying the factors contributing to such relationships.

The second part of the book examines how the regional and sectoral patterns and trajectories of changing business–government relations can be understood and explained. Representing a collective effort to interrogate and critically apply the theoretical arguments about the fundamental sources of the changing variety of state–business interactions developed in the first part, the chapters in this part assess the explanatory value of region- and sector-specific economic ideologies, state institutions and market structures against that of global forces and national sociopolitical transformations. The third and final part brings together chapters that explore the impact of varied business–government relations on the evolution and transformation of corporate governance practices, market regulation systems, multinational corporate behaviours and technology development regimes across the regional and sectoral levels of analysis.

References

Alpermann, B. (2006). "Wrapped up in cotton wool": Political integration of private entrepreneurs in rural China. *China Journal, 56*, 33–61.

Bell, S., & Hindmore, A. (2009). *Rethinking governance: The centralist of the state in modern society*. Cambridge: Cambridge University Press.

Brandt, L., & Rawski, T. G. (Eds.). (2008). *China's great economic transformation*. Cambridge: Cambridge University Press.

Breslin, S. (2012). Government-industry relations in China: A review of the art of the state. In A. Walter & X. K. Zhang (Eds.), *East Asian capitalism: Diversity, continuity and change* (pp. 29–44). Oxford: Oxford University Press.

Breznitz, D., & Murphee, M. (2011). *Run of the red queen: Government, innovation, globalization, and economic growth in China*. New Haven: Yale University Press.

Brodsgaard, K. E. (2012). Politics and business group formation in China: The party in control? *China Quarterly, 211*, 624–648.

Cali, M., & Sen, K. (2011). Do effective state business relations matter for economic growth? *World Development, 39*, 1542–1557.

Cammett, M. C. (2007). *Globalization and business politics in Arab North Africa*. New York: Cambridge University Press.

Chen, X. M. (Ed.). (2009). *Shanghai rising: State power and local transformations in a global megacity*. Minneapolis: University of Minnesota Press.

Chen, L. (2014). Varieties of global capital and the paradox of local upgrading in China. *Politics and Society, 42*, 223–252.

Chen, K. (2016). Two China models and local government entrepreneurship. *China: An International Journal, 14*, 16–28.

Child, J. (1994). *Management in China during the age of reform*. Cambridge: Cambridge University Press.

Crouch, C., Schroder, M., & Voelzkow, H. (2009). Regional and sectoral varieties of capitalism. *Economy and Society, 38*, 654–678.

Deng, G., & Kennedy, S. (2010). Big business and industry association lobbying in China. *China Quarterly, 63*, 101–125.

Dickson, B. J. (2003). *Red capitalists in China*. New York: Cambridge University Press.

Dickson, B. J. (2008). *Wealth into power: The Communist Party's embrace of China's private sector*. New York: Cambridge University Press.

Doner, R. F., & Schneider, B. R. (2000). Business associations and economic development. *Business and Politics, 2*, 261–288.

Du, J., & Girma, S. (2010). Red capitalists: Political connections and firm performance in China. *Kyklos, 63*, 530–545.

Economist. 2017. *The Pearl River delta: Jewel in the crown*. 8–14 April.

Ernst, P., & Naughton, B. (2008). China's emerging industrial economy: Insights from the IT industry. In C. A. McNally (Ed.), *China's emergent political economy* (pp. 39–59). London: Routledge.

Evans, P. (1995). *Embedded autonomy: States and industrial transformation*. Princeton: Princeton University Press.

Fan, J. P. H., Wong, T. J., & Zhang, T. (2012). Institutions and organizational structure: The case of state-owned corporate pyramids. *Journal of Law, Economics and Organization, 29*, 1217–1252.

Ferchen, M. (2013). Whose China model is it anyway? The contentious search for consensus. *Review of International Political Economy, 20*, 390–420.

Fligstein, N., & Zhang, J. (2010). A new agenda for research on the trajectory of Chinese capitalism. *Management and Organization Review, 7*, 39–62.

Foster, K. W. (2008). Embedded within state agencies: Business association in Yantai. In J. Unger (Ed.), *Associations and the Chinese state* (pp. 86–116). Armonk: M.E. Sharpe.

Fu, W. (2015). *Towards a dynamic regional innovation system: Investigation into the electronics industry in the Pearl River delta, China*. Heidelberg: Springer.

Gabriele, A. (2010). The role of the state in China's industrial development: A reassessment. *Comparative Economic Studies, 52*, 325–350.

Garnaut, R., & Song, L. (Eds.). (2004). *China's third economic transformation: The rise of the private economy*. Abingdon: RoutledgeCurzon.

Goldman, M., & MacFarquhar, R. (Eds.). (1999). *The paradox of China's post-Mao reforms*. Cambridge, MA: Harvard University Press.

Guo, D., Jiang, K., Kim, B.-Y., & Xu, C. (2014). Political economy of private firms in China. *Journal of Comparative Economics, 42*, 286–303.

Guthrie, D. (1999). *Dragon in a three-piece suit: The emergence of capitalism in China*. Princeton: Princeton University Press.

Guthrie, D. (2002). Information asymmetries and the problem of perception: The significance of structural position in assessing the importance of guanxi in China. In T. Gold, D. Guthrie, & D. Wank (Eds.), *Social connections in China* (pp. 37–56). Cambridge: Cambridge University Press.

Haggard, S., & Huang, Y. (2008). The political economy of private sector development in China. In L. Brandt & T. G. Rawski (Eds.), *China's great economic transformation* (pp. 337–374). Cambridge: Cambridge University Press.

Hancke, B., Rhodes, M., & Thatcher, M. (Eds.). (2007). *Beyond varieties of capitalism: Conflict, contradictions, and complementarities in the European economy*. Oxford: Oxford University Press.

Heilmann, S., & Melton, O. (2013). The reinvention of development planning in China, 1993–2012. *Modern China, 39*, 580–628.

Heilmann, S., Shih, L., & Hofem, A. (2013). National planning and local technology zones: Experimental governance in China's torch programme. *China Quarterly, 216*, 896–919.

Hsu, S. P., Wu, Y.-S., & Zhao, S. (Eds.). (2011). *In search of China's development model: Beyond the Beijing consensus*. London: Routledge.

Hsueh, R. (2016). State capitalism, Chinese-style: Strategic value of sectors, sectoral characteristics, and globalization. *Governance: An International Journal of Policy, Administration, and Institutions, 29*, 85–102.

Huang, Y. (2008). *Capitalism with Chinese characteristics: Entrepreneurship and the state*. New York: Cambridge University Press.

Huchet, J.-F., & Richet, X. (2002). Between bureaucracy and market: Chinese industrial groups in search of new forms of corporate governance. *Post-Communist Economies, 14*, 169–201.

Keister, L. A., & Zhang, Y. (2009). Organizations and management in China. *Academy of Management Annals, 3*, 377–420.

Keng, S. (2010). Developing into a developmental state: Explaining changing government-business relations behind the Kunshan miracle. In T.-K. Leng & Y.-H. Chu (Eds.), *Dynamics of local governance in China during the reform era* (pp. 225–271). Lanham: Lexington Books.

Kennedy, S. (2005). *The business of lobbying in China*. Cambridge, MA: Harvard University Press.

Kennedy, S. (2007). Transnational political alliances: An exploration with evidence from China. *Business and Society, 46*, 174–200.

Kornberg, J. F., & Faust, J. R. (2005). *China in world politics: Policies, processes, prospects*. Boulder: Lynne Rienner.

Leng, T.-K. (2010). Centrally administered municipalities: Locomotives of national development. In J. H. Chung & T.-C. Lam (Eds.), *China's local administration* (pp. 39–60). London: Routledge.

Li, H., Meng, L., & Zhang, J. (2006). Why do entrepreneurs enter politics? *Economic Inquiry, 44*, 559–578.

Liu, L. (2008). Local government and big business in the People's republic of China – Case study evidence from Shandong province. *Asia Pacific Business Review, 14*, 473–489.

Luo, Y. (2001). Towards a cooperative view of MNC-host government relations: Building blocks and performance implications. *Journal of International Business Studies, 32*, 401–419.

Mahoney, J. (2000). Path dependence in historical sociology. *Theory and Society, 29*, 507–548.

Maxfield, S., & Schneider, B. R. (Eds.). (1997). *Business and the state in developing countries*. Ithaca: Cornell University Press.

McNally, C. A. (Ed.). (2008). *China's emergent political economy: Capitalism in the dragon's lair*. London: Routledge.
McNally, C. A. (2011). China's changing guanxi capitalism: Private entrepreneurs between Leninist control and relentless accumulation. *Business and Politics, 13*, Article 5.
Montinola, G., Qian, Y., & Weingast, B. (1995). Federalism, Chinese style: The political basis for economic success in China. *World Politics, 48*, 50–81.
Mulvad, A. (2015). Competing hegemonic projects within China's variegated capitalism: 'Liberal' Guangdong vs. 'Statist' Chongqing. *New Political Economy, 20*, 199–227.
Nahm, J., & Steinfeld, E. S. (2014). Scale-up nation. *World Development, 54*, 288–300.
Naughton, B. (1995). *Growing out of the plan: Chinese economic reform 1978–1993*. Cambridge: Cambridge University Press.
Naughton, B., & Tsai, K. S. (Eds.). (2015). *State capitalism, institutional adaptation, and the Chinese miracle*. New York: Cambridge University Press.
Naughton, B., & Yang, D. L. (Eds.). (2004). *Holding China together: Diversity and national integration in the post-Deng era*. Cambridge: Cambridge University Press.
Nee, V. (1992). Organizational dynamics of market transition. *Administrative Science Quarterly, 37*, 1–27.
Nee, V., & Opper, S. (2010). Political capital in a market economy. *Social Forces, 88*, 2105–2132.
Nee, V., & Opper, S. (2012). *Capitalism from below: Markets and institutional change in China*. Cambridge, MA: Harvard University Press.
Nee, V., Opper, S., & Wong, S. (2007). The developmental state and corporate governance in China. *Management and Organization Review, 3*, 19–53.
North, D. C. (1990). *Institutions, institutional change, and economic performance*. Cambridge: Cambridge University Press.
Oi, J. C. (2010). Political crosscurrents in China's corporate restructuring. In J. C. Oi, S. Rozelle, & X. Zhou (Eds.), *Growing pains: Tensions and opportunity in China's transformation* (pp. 5–26). Stanford: The Walter H. Shorenstein Asia-Pacific Research Centre, Stanford University.
Oi, J. C., Rozelle, S., & Zhou, X. (Eds.). (2010). *Growing pains: Tensions and opportunity in China's transformation*. Stanford: The Walter H. Shorenstein Asia-Pacific Research Centre, Stanford University.
Ong, L. H. (2012). Between developmental and clientelist states: Local state-business relationships in China. *Comparative Politics, 44*, 127–150.
Park, S. H., & Luo, Y. (2001). Guanxi and organizational dynamics. *Strategic Management Journal, 22*, 455–477.
Peng, Y. (2004). Kinship networks and entrepreneurs in China's transitional economy. *American Journal of Sociology, 109*, 1045–1074.

Peng, M. W., & Luo, Y. (2000). Managerial ties and firm performance in a transition economy. *Academy of Management Journal, 43*, 486–501.

Pierson, P. (2000). Increasing return, path dependence, and the study of politics. *American Political Science Review, 94*, 251–267.

Potter, P. B. (2003). Globalization and economic regulation in China. *Washington University Global Studies Law Review, 2*, 119–150.

Redding, G., & Witt, M. A. (2007). *The future of Chinese capitalism*. Oxford: Oxford University Press.

Remick, E. J. (2002). The significance of variation in local states: The case of twentieth century China. *Comparative Politics, 34*, 399–418.

Rithmire, M. E. (2014). China's "new regionalism": Subnational analysis in Chinese political economy. *World Politics, 66*, 165–194.

Rowen, H. S., Hancock, M. G., & Miller, W. F. (Eds.). (2008). *Greater China's quest for innovation*. Stanford: The Walter H. Shorenstein Asia-Pacific Research Centre, Stanford University.

Segal, A. (2003). *Digital dragon: High-technology enterprises in China*. Ithaca: Cornell University Press.

Shirk, S. L. (1993). *The political logic of economic reform in China*. Berkeley: University of California Press.

So, B. W.-Y. (2004). State-business interaction in the IT sector. In R. Garnaut & L. Song (Eds.), *China's third economic transformation: The rise of the private economy* (pp. 209–224). Abingdon: RoutledgeCurzon.

Story, J. (2010). China and the multinational experience. In D. Coen, W. Grant, & G. Wilson (Eds.), *Oxford handbook of business and government* (pp. 346–380). Oxford: Oxford University Press.

Sun, P., Mellahi, K., & Thun, E. (2010). The dynamic value of MNC political embeddedness: The case of the Chinese automobile industry. *Journal of International Business Studies, 41*, 1161–1182.

Tenev, S., & Zhang, C. (2002). *Corporate governance and enterprise reform in China*. Washington, DC: World Bank and International Finance Corporation.

Thun, E. (2006). *Changing the lanes in China: Foreign direct investment, local governments, and auto sector development*. New York: Cambridge University Press.

Tjosvold, D., Peng, A. C., Chen, Y. F., & Su, F. (2008). Business and government interdependence in China. *Asia-Pacific Journal of Management, 25*, 225–249.

Tsai, K. S. (2006). Adaptive informal institutions and endogenous institutional change in China. *World Politics, 59*, 116–141.

Tsai, K. S. (2007). *Capitalism without democracy: The private sector in contemporary China*. Ithaca: Cornell University Press.

Unger, J. (2008a). The strange marriage between the state and private business in Beijing. In J. Unger (Ed.), *Associations and the Chinese state* (pp. 117–148). Armonk: M.E. Sharpe.

Unger, J. (Ed.). (2008b). *Associations and the Chinese state*. Armonk: M.E. Sharpe.

Walder, A. G. (1995). Local governments as industrial firms: An organizational analysis of China's transitional economy. *American Journal of Sociology, 101*, 263–301.

Walder, A. G. (2003). Elite opportunity in transitional economies. *American Sociological Review, 68*, 899–916.

Wan, F., Williamson, P. J., & Yin, E. (2015). Antecedents and implications of disruptive innovation. *Technovation, 39-40*, 94–104.

Wang, C. Y., Ye, J. Z., & Franco, J. C. (2014). Local state corporatism or neo-guanxilism? Observations from the county level of government in China. *Journal of Contemporary China, 23*, 498–515.

Wank, D. (1999). *Commodifying communism: Business, trust, and politics in a Chinese city*. Cambridge: Cambridge University Press.

Wank, D. (2002). Business-state clientelism in China. In T. Gold, D. Guthrie, & D. Wank (Eds.), *Social connections in China* (pp. 97–115). Cambridge: Cambridge University Press.

Wei, Y. D., Li, W., & Wang, C. (2007). Restructuring industrial districts, scaling up regional development: A study of the Wenzhou model, China. *Economic Geography, 83*, 421–444.

Weiss, L. (1994). Business-government relations in East Asia. *Asian Perspective, 18*, 85–118.

White, G., Howell, J., & Shang, X. (1996). *In search of civil society: Market reform and social change in China*. Oxford: Clarendon Press.

Williamson, P. J., & Yin, E. (2014). Accelerated innovation. *MIT Sloan Management Review, Summer*, 26–34.

Xin, K. R., & Pearce, J. L. (1996). Guanxi: Connections as substitutes for formal institutional support. *Academy of Management Journal, 39*, 1641–1658.

Xu, C. (2011). The fundamental institutions of China's reforms and development. *Journal of Economic Literature, 49*, 1076–1151.

Yang, M. M.-H. (2002). The resilience of guanxi and its new deployments. *China Quarterly, 170*, 459–476.

Yang, D. L. (2004). *Remaking the Chinese leviathan: Market transition and the politics of governance in China*. Stanford: Stanford University Press.

Yang, C. (2014). Market rebalancing of global production networks in the post-Washington consensus globalizing era: Transformation of export-oriented development in China. *Review of International Political Economy, 21*, 130–156.

Yueh, L. (2011). *Enterprising China: Business, economic and legal developments since 1979*. Oxford: Oxford University Press.

Zeng, D. Z. (Ed.). (2010). *Building engines for growth and competitiveness in China*. Washington, DC: World Bank.

Zhang, F. (2015). Building biotech in shanghai: Perspective of regional innovation system. *European Planning Studies, 23*, 2062–2078.

Zhang, Q., & Liu, M. (2013). The political economy of private sector development in communist China: Evidence from Zhejiang Province. *Studies in Comparative International Development, 48*, 196–216.

Zhang, J., & Peck, J. (2016). Variegated capitalism, Chinese style: Regional models, multi-scalar constructions. *Regional Studies, 50*, 52–78.

Zhang, X. (2016). Socio-political structures and market organization in regional industrial system. In R. Whitley & X. Zhang (Eds.), *Changing Asian business systems: Globalization, socio-political change, and economic organization* (pp. 229–256). Oxford: Oxford University Press.

Zhang, X., & Whitley, R. (2013). Changing macro-structural varieties of East Asian capitalism. *Socio-Economic Review, 11*, 301–336.

Zhou, X. (2010). The institutional logic of collusion among local governments in China. *Modern China, 36*, 47–78.

CHAPTER 2

State–Business Relations in China's Changing Economic Order

Tak-Wing Ngo

Introduction

In a capitalist market economy, businesses are recognized social actors engaged in legitimate economic activity for the pursuit of profit. These profit-making establishments are generally private enterprises with a well-defined ownership structure. The existing literature on government–business relations in advanced capitalist economies focuses largely on how the government facilitates or restrains business activities, regulates market exchanges to create a level playing field, and adjudicates conflicts between rival business interests. In contrast, comparative studies of developing countries have underlined the conditions under which government–business relations become collaborative or collusive. Some explore the capacity of the state for manipulating business investments for the sake of long-term development goals. Others examine the factors contributing to state-capture by business or the emergence of crony capitalism.

T.-W. Ngo (✉)
University of Macau, Macao, China

X. Zhang, T. Zhu (eds.), *Business, Government and Economic Institutions in China*, International Political Economy Series,
DOI 10.1007/978-3-319-64486-8_2

In contemporary China, government–business relations do not fit neatly within any of these strands of inquiry. Capitalists were once considered the number one enemy of the communist regime in China. Private business was thus completely eliminated during the Maoist era. When business enterprises emerged again following market reforms, profit making was not considered one of the main constitutive functions of business. At the same time, the ownership structures of business undertakings remained highly convoluted. There now exists a diversity of organizational forms and a plurality of ill-defined property rights with overlapping public and private ownership. These blurred boundaries affect the interests and behaviours of the state as well as business since the state is not only a policy maker and regulator but also an investor and active market player. While intense competition exists between business establishments, the market is anything but a level playing field. These contradictions and paradoxes defy the conventional characterizations proposed by existing theories and models of government–business relations.

This chapter seeks to characterize state–business relations in China by examining the polymorphous nature of the Chinese state and the rise of business as a hybrid actor. It begins with an assessment of existing concepts and approaches to the Chinese situation and argues that the forms of contention and the terms of exchange between state and business in China deviate from the existing categories of analysis. From the outset, state polymorphism and business hybridity point to the multiplicity and heterogeneity of interactions between the state and businesses, as Zhang and Zhu discuss in the introductory chapter. Seeing state–business relations in China as uniform or dominated by a specific form of interaction is a gross oversimplification. State–business relations are heterogeneous and not only vary across regions and sectors but state–business relations are also "uneven" across different kinds of business actors within the same sector in a region. To further complicate the issue, such interactions have changed over time, again in an uneven manner.

While the present volume, as a whole, seeks to develop a framework for categorizing and comparing state–business relations in China and to account for the patterns and trajectories of changes and variations, this chapter aims to contribute a micro building block to this endeavour by focusing on the uneven interactions between substates and hybrid businesses. We will not deal with regional and sectoral variations here; these are analysed in other chapters. However, such variations are to a large extent predicated upon the specific mixture of substates and hybrid businesses. By focusing on their interactions, this chapter seeks to identify the factors contributing to the unevenness. This may help generate informed hypotheses for empirical comparisons across regions and sectors.

In Research of New Theorization

To begin with, we prefer to speak of state–business relations rather than government–business relations because the latter is too narrow for our analysis, limiting such relationships to those between the executive arm of public authorities and business. In China, as we are well aware, a large variety of state actors, including not only the government bureaucracy but also the party, the military, state-sponsored people's organizations, and so on, have established close relations with business. Even public bodies such as universities, news agencies and hospitals have business ties. It is therefore more appropriate to adopt the broader view of state–business relations.

The challenge of characterizing state–business relations in China stems from both the ambiguous boundaries between the state and business and the multiple polarities of their interactions. Such ambiguity and multipolarity account for the limitations of existing theories in describing state–business relations in China. Kennedy (2005) reviews the Chinese case in terms of levels of firm autonomy, patterns of organization, cooperative versus competitive exchanges, and policy process transparency with reference to the theoretical models of pluralism, societal corporatism, state corporatism, clientelism, and monism and concludes that, to varying degrees, China fits into each of the frameworks, except monism (see Table 2.1). We can briefly repeat the exercise here without going into details by adapting Kennedy's framework to a different set of comparative criteria. Our reference points are not firm autonomy or policy transparency since they do not reflect our core concerns. Instead we underline the centrality of power and interests by comparing under different conceptual models the alleged institutional structures of the state and business, their respective interests, forms of interaction, terms of exchange, and the nature of relationships (see Table 2.2).

In contrast to Kennedy's conclusion, our comparison shows that China does not conform to any of the models in question. China obviously deviates from the pluralist model, which sees numerous sectoral interests as competing freely to influence state policies under an open political system. In China, not only is political accessibility restrictive, but more importantly,

Table 2.1 Expectations of government–business relations under different frameworks

	Pluralism	*Societal corporatism*	*State corporatism*	*Clientelism*	*Monism*
Level of firm autonomy	Firm has operational, financial autonomy	Firm has operational, financial autonomy	Formal autonomy undercut by pressures to adhere to state policies	Official patrons may influence firm operations, finance	Firm has no autonomy over personnel or operations
Avenues of interaction					
Indirect	Mediated via non-hierarchical, voluntary associations and other intermediaries (e.g., law firms)	Mediated via hierarchical, involuntary associations acting as arena for state-industry negotiations	Mediated via hierarchical, involuntary associations acting as transmission belts of state policy	Formal associations significant only as conduit for patron–client ties	Very limited role for associations and other intermediaries
From firm's perspective	Firm lobbies via associations and other intermediaries, promoting interests of firm and industry	Firm defers to association to represent their interests in negotiations	Firm follows orders of and reports to an association	Firm manipulates associations to benefit interests of itself and patron at expense of industry and state institutions	Firm does not participate in associations or rely on other intermediaries
Direct	Extensive direct state-firm interaction not part of clientelist relationship	Limited direct interaction	Limited direct interaction	Extensive direct interaction that is part of patron–client relationship	Extensive direct interaction on personnel and operations related to the firm, not broader policy

(*continued*)

Table 2.1 (continued)

	Pluralism	*Societal corporatism*	*State corporatism*	*Clientelism*	*Monism*
From firm's perspective	Firm lobbies directly, focusing on substantive policy issues of interest to firm and industry	Firm does not directly try to influence state policies	Firm does not try to influence state policies or receive orders directly from the state	Firm nurtures personal ties by providing material benefits to patron in exchange for preferential state policies	Firm contacts state to provide firm-related information and obtain personnel and production orders
Norms of interaction					
State-firm relationship	Competitive	Cooperative	Cooperative	Cooperative	Cooperative
Policy process transparency	High	High	Low	Low	Low

Source: Kennedy (2005: 6). Copyright © 2005 by the President and Fellows of Harvard College

Table 2.2 China in comparison with dominant models of state–business relations

	Pluralism	*Societal corporatism*	*State corporatism*	*Marxism*	*Clientelism*	*China*
State structure	Unified	Unified	Unified	Unified	Oligarchic power-holders and local bosses	Fragmented authoritarianism
Interests of the state	Neutral	Consensus building	Political control	Long-term capital accumulation	Spoils to officials	Varied (control, accumulation, spoils)
Business structure	Atomistic or diverse	Organized from below	Organized from above	Diverse	Atomistic	Diverse
Interests of business	Particularistic or sectoral; profit maximization	Collective; profit maximization	Collective; profit maximization	Class interests; capital accumulation	Particularistic; rent seeking	Particularistic; profit and rent seeking, political advancement
Forms of interaction	Competitive lobbying	Collective bargaining through peak associations	State order through peak associations	Business capture	Individual exchanges through patron–client relationship	Exchanges at both individual and institutional levels
Terms of exchange	Collective policy privileges for votes/support	Collective policy advantages for political consensus	Collective policy advantages for political acquiescence	Collective protection for regime support	Particularistic rents/privileges for spoils/loyalty	Particularistic rents for spoils or fulfilment of local economic targets
Nature of relationship	Arm's length; competitive	Cooperative	State licensing; cooperative	Symbiotic	Collusive	Collusive

the state is anything but a neutral policymaker acting in response to competing economic and social demands. The fragmented state in China has interests of its own, and these interests are varied and even contradictory between different bureaucratic sections and administrative levels. It is probably correct to say that market reform in China has given rise to a plurality of interests, but to imply that state–business interaction has become pluralistic is an overstatement.

Relatively speaking, China corresponds more closely to the clientelist model, in which collusion between officials and business interests is most common. Many observers have underlined the key role played by personal connections (*guanxi*) when officials offer discretionary privileges in terms of scarce resources, credit, access to market, and so on, to particularistic businessmen and enterprises in exchange for taxes, payoffs, employment, and personal rewards (Wank 1996; Zhou 2010). Yet there are subtle differences between cases in China and the patron–client networks found in many Southeast Asian countries. For a long time, observers have noted that state power in Southeast Asia was monopolized by competing political factions that were held together by networks of personalized patron–client relations. Business behaved as "pariah entrepreneurs" (Riggs 1966; Searle 1998) or "crony capitalists" (Hutchcroft 1991; Kang 2002) who sought patronage from individual officials. A revised version saw the prevalence of local power brokers who combined state-based resources with private proprietary wealth to form a kind of "bossism" (Sidel 1999). Viewed in this way, businesses are essentially rent seekers. Chinese business interests share many features of rent seekers striving to obtain political patronage. However, China differs from typical clientelist politics in that official patrons are not merely power brokers jockeying for personal gain through their control over resource allocation. Besides predicating on *personal* exchanges, state–business interactions in China also involve symbiotic alliance between *institutional* entities, that is, local state authorities and enterprises, and often exhibit a developmental dimension in which the local state offers protective privileges to local businesses not only for rewards and power but also for the sake of developing the local economy. Such state–business alliance has been labelled local state corporatism by Oi (1992). She refers to the arrangement by which local governments coordinated economic enterprises within their jurisdictions in a way that resembled a diversified business corporation. The developmental outcome of such arrangements thus defies the predatory tendency of clientelism.

Oi's label is misleading, however, since she is referring to a corporation-like arrangement of economic coordination rather than a corporatist mechanism of interest intermediation. The latter has been underlined by many studies analysing state–business relations in China (Dickson 2003; Kennedy 2005; Unger and Chan 2008). The distinctive corporatist element can be found in the top-down creation of state-sponsored associations for various business sectors, foreign investors, local entrepreneurs, and so on. Membership is compulsory, and the leadership is usually taken up by state or party officials. Many of these associations are housed in government compounds and rely on governmental support for their daily operation. In brief, if we look at the formal institutional arrangements, we can indeed find close resemblance to the state corporatist model.

However, we would warn against characterizing state–business relations in China as state corporatist. The corporatist structures are primarily used for political control. More precisely, they seek to pre-empt the emergence of organized interests outside the reach of the party–state. In practice, they play a very limited role in interest intermediation between the state and business, and an even smaller role in representing business sectors. In recent years, researchers have found evidence of some business associations (in particular, associations for Taiwanese investors, see Lee 2011) moving beyond their role as appendages of state agencies to become more autonomous. For instance, Unger and Chan (1995) believe that in the course of development, some groups have been shifting gradually but perceptibly in a "societal-corporatist" direction as they increasingly assert the interests of their constituencies. However, even with this gradual shift it would be a gross mistake to treat those corporatist institutions as a major channel of state–business interactions. Instead of going through business associations, most businesses in China communicate their demands via personal connections with state officials. The predominance of state-sponsored business associations in China in fact rules out formalized institutions for genuine interest representation and intermediation between the state and business. Like many post-socialist and authoritarian societies, effective interest intermediation is based on particularistic contacts rather than formalized channels.

Finally, we should briefly explain China's deviation from the developmental state model. Studies of East Asian political economy have highlighted the agential role of the state (Kohli 2004; Woo-Cumings 1999; Wade 1990). The behaviour of the East Asian states apparently differs from their Western counterparts in their readiness to intervene in the economy and to displace market mechanisms for the sake of long-term development. This idea of a developmental state challenges established thinking about the liberal political economy, in which the constitutive function of the state is limited to the provision of law and order, leaving the free market to maximize economic efficiency and growth. The East Asian experience—first typified by the rise of Japan and followed by South Korea, Taiwan, and the rest—suggests otherwise: that a "plan–rational state", to use Johnson's (1982) much-quoted term, can engineer growth.

The existence of a strong Leninist state intervening extensively in market operations has led some observers to liken China's rapid economic growth to a developmental state (So 2003). For them, China falls within the East Asian pattern of an active state with a strong desire to govern business and the economy, a state engaged not only in macro-economic planning but also in micro-economic intervention in specific business operations. Yet apart from a superficial resemblance, the Chinese party–state is a far cry from the socially embedded autonomous state staffed by meritocratic technocrats which typifies the developmental state in East Asia (Evans 1995; Wade 1990). Instead, the Chinese state is not only fragmented, incoherent, and dominated by parochial interests, but it also embraces state–business collusions that enforce developmental as well as predatory practices. It is true that the Chinese state, especially subnational states at local levels, has at times taken on a developmental role in fostering local economic development. However, a state that performs developmental functions is not equivalent to the developmental state which spearheaded the so-called East Asian miracle.

All in all, we find the existing models incapable of providing a nuanced understanding of state–business relations in China. If Kennedy's (2005) observation—that China fits into the existing models to varying degrees—is not just a blind-man-and-the-elephant exercise, we are obliged to explain why China exhibits different traits of state–business relations at the same time. And if the different traits confirm the heterogeneity of state–business relations in China, we still have to identify the structures and agencies which contribute to the variations across time and space.

The Fragmented Polymorphous State

To arrive at a more nuanced understanding of state–business relations in China, it is imperative to clarify what we mean by the state and business. This immediately opens a big can of worms because of the multiplicity of institutional forms and interests of different segments of the state and businesses. To disentangle the complexities, let us first deal with the nature of the Chinese state. We can separate the discussion into the state's roles and structures.

The roles of the state in a modern market economy have been aptly summarized by Wilson (1990: 16). First, the state exerts its agential role as an actor in formulating and implementing industrial policies, forging collaborative relations with business, and regulating market exchanges. Second, the state serves as an institutional arena in which competing economic interests seek to capture its influence and power. Third, the state is a structuring agent which shapes the forms and actions of societal actors, including business, through the enactment of laws, tax regimes, and property rights arrangements. We can take these three roles as the point of departure for our discussion.

First, let us deal with the agential role of the state. As discussed earlier, the Chinese state has played a prominent role in macro-economic planning, market regulation, and micro-economic intervention including actual business operations. As a result, observers have proposed various characterizations of the role of the Chinese state. Some see it as developmental (So 2003) or entrepreneurial (Duckett 2001). Others consider it purely predatory (Pei 2008). And as Saich (2002) puts it, the interpretations are likened to the blind man and the elephant because of the multi-faceted nature of the Chinese state. The situation is vividly described by Howell (2006: 278) who calls the Chinese state "a polymorphous state that reveals contradictory features of developmentalism and predation, rivalry and unity, autonomy and clientelism, efficiency and inefficiency, across time and space".

One of the causes of polymorphism is the fragmented structure of the state. Since the introduction of market reform three decades ago, the Chinese government has implemented numerous administrative and institutional reforms including major decentralization involving deconcentration, devolution, and delegation (Cheema and Rondinelli 2007). Regulatory and supervisory powers have been granted to regional bureaus of national ministries and departments for administering local affairs. At the same time, local governments have been given extensive fiscal and administrative power to meet the needs of their local population. The devolution of state power has enabled local authorities to direct their attention and resources to turning their subnational territorial units into a source of growth and competition. The immediate outcome of this was severe competition between localities, both in terms of actual benefits, such as access to resources and investments, and in symbolic achievements, such as higher ranking. At the same time, deconcentration and devolution created separate sets of jurisdiction, control, accountability, and interests. The vertical hierarchy of administrative responsibilities formed under deconcentration (usually referred to as the *tiao*) often encountered conflict with local governments which had gained extensive fiscal and administrative autonomy under devolution (usually referred to as the *kuai*). The result was a decentralized system characterized by multiple levels of administration across a vast number of regions. Bargaining and contention between sectional interests occurred along vertical hierarchies of functional administration and across horizontal levels of territorial government. The criss-crossing of various jurisdictions constitutes a complicated power matrix commonly known as the *tiao–kuai* system (Mertha 2005). The fragmentation of authority within such an administrative matrix has generated conflicting goals and responsibilities (Lieberthal and Oksenberg 1988).

Since the Chinese state is fragmented, the locus of agency rests not only on the central authorities but also on many of the substates. It is therefore difficult to speak of *the* state in China, regardless of whether it is developmental or predatory. The agential role has been played most noticeably by state institutions at the local level—in various provinces, cities, counties, and townships. Local authorities have been prepared to safeguard parochial interests vis-à-vis other locales and even at the expense of national objectives. As a result, when we explore state–business relations in China, it is imperative to look at "states-businesses" relations.

The centrality of substates under fragmented polymorphism has a number of implications. First and foremost, substates behave differently across regions. In comparing Shanghai and Beijing—both belonging to the same administrative level—Segal and Thun (2001) observe that Shanghai exhibited a much stronger developmental and interventionist stance towards business. The Shanghai government focused on strengthening the market positions of large state-owned enterprises at the expense of smaller non-state firms. In contrast, the Beijing government did not discriminate against small private business. Instead, infrastructural and investment projects were used to support private small firms that apparently did not have political connections. Segal and Thun argue that the difference in state–business relations in the two cities is attributable to two factors: the structure of the local bureaucracy and the dominant form of industrial organization. Accordingly, Shanghai has a unified municipal bureaucracy and a local economy dominated by large conglomerates, while Beijing has a more fragmented local bureaucracy with a market led by smaller firms. The unified municipal bureaucracy possessed more effective policy instruments and allowed city officials in Shanghai to control the head offices of corporate groups in the city. Similar institutional structures and incentives were lacking in Beijing. Likewise, Carney's study in this volume also highlights the distinctive differences between substates in Shanghai and Guangdong.

While regional variations in the behaviour of substates are well documented in the existing literature, another closely linked variation has been largely overlooked, that is, the multiscalar contentions arising from overlapping substatal jurisdictions within a single locality. Under the existing spatial order, a business enterprise is bound to face several substates at the same time. This does not just refer to functional bureaus responsible for taxation, environmental protection, business registration, and so on. Depending on the administrative status of its host city, a business enterprise is also under the overlapping jurisdictions of the provincial authorities and the prefectural, district (county), and even local township governments. For instance, an enterprise in the Hengqin New Area falls directly under the jurisdiction of the Hengqin Management Committee which administers the New Area on behalf of the Zhuhai government. The enterprise is also subject to regulation from the Guangdong provincial government, to which Zhuhai belongs. Since Hengqin is located within the Xiangzhou district, the enterprise is also dependent on the Xiangzhou government for infrastructural and social support. In short, in any location, numerous substates have varying jurisdictional powers over a business enterprise. Conflicts between substates along the scalar hierarchy within the same region are extremely common (Ngo et al. 2017). Polymorphism thus exhibits another dimension: from the point of view of an enterprise in a specific region, the provincial state may be regulatory, the prefectural state developmental, and the county/district state predatory. Another business located at a different development zone within the same city may have a different relation with the substates simply because the zone belongs to a different scalar level of administrative hierarchy.

The existence of regional and scalar differences means that the complexity of state–business relations in China has been largely underestimated. These are therefore the immediate questions that follow: Under what circumstances does the (sub)state take up a specific agential role? Are entrepreneurial, developmental, clientelist, and predatory roles contingent upon regional location, administrative level, or bureaucratic functions? Alternatively, is it possible that substates assume different roles at different periods of time? In other words, do they exert different agencies towards different actors/sectors at the same time, so that from one economic player's point of view the substate could be developmental, but from another it could be predatory? Is it possible that the role of the state is relational, temporal, and contingent, rather than fixed, as most existing studies have assumed? If so, we are back to the question of under what circumstances a substate assumes a specific role towards a business enterprise. Before we probe further into these questions, we first have to address the nature of business.

The Hybridity of Business

The typical modern state serves as an institutional arena where economic players—mainly businesses—compete for influence and power. Haggard et al. (1997) identify a number of conceptualizations of business in its relations to the state. One perspective conceives business as capital and examines the constraining effects of private investment decisions on public policies and the political process. Another perspective focuses on the sectoral interests of business and their contentions. The third perspective understands business as firms, and explores the influence of firm size, conglomeration, and oligopolistic position on the political process. The question of business capture looms large in this perspective. The fourth perspective underlines the role of business associations as collective actors. The fifth perspective highlights business as networks and explores the familial, regional, dialectal, or ethnic connections in which businessmen and state officials are embedded.

Regardless of the difference in emphasis between these perspectives on business, there is an underlying assumption of a distinguishable separation between the state (and substates) and business. In a neoliberal political economy, there is a clear distinction between the public and private sectors. The market is dominated by private firms with well-defined ownership structures engaging in mutual exchanges for the sake of profit maximization. That is why it is referred to as the private sector.

However, this assumption is somewhat problematic when applied to China. In the dominant literature, the firm is often seen as the main embodiment of capital. In China, however, companies are not the sole capitalist actors in the economy. A large variety of state actors, social actors, and individuals stand side by side with enterprises in business operations. As mentioned earlier, state actors, including the government bureaucracy, the ruling party, the military, and so on, have business connections; social actors such as universities, news agencies, and hospitals have business ties. It is an example of extreme commercialization and commodification, to the extent that religious bodies, rural villages, educational institutions, medical establishments, and so on, are run like profit-making enterprises. Furthermore, a very substantial proportion of economic activities is taken up by individuals or networks of individuals in underground finance, production and distribution of counterfeit products, trafficking, cross-border trade and exchanges, sex services, and so on. These are not necessarily illegal as huge volumes of parallel trade, Internet shopping, and so on, form a close symbiotic relationship with legitimate economic activities in the provision of daily products and services (Hung and Ngo 2015).

Even if we focus exclusively on firms, the case of China still defies our understanding of the conventional paradigm. Property rights in China are highly diffused, with different degrees of overlapping public and private ownerships, which is unlike a mixed economy where one can find both publicly owned enterprises and private firms with well-defined boundaries. Instead, there exist a vast number of companies in China which cannot be clearly categorized as either public or private. This wide spectrum of hybrid business includes state-owned enterprises, collective enterprises (mostly at the township and village level), share-holding enterprises with a mixture of public and private shareholders, public–private joint ventures, private companies disguised as state-owned or collective enterprises, crony enterprises which are politically connected to influential office bearers, relational enterprises which are linked to national or local monopolies and oligopolies, and so on.

There is a dearth of conceptual categories to describe this plurality of property rights regimes, even though the Chinese case is not the only exception. The blurring of the public–private divide and the fuzziness of enterprise boundaries are defining features of East European capitalism as well. Stark (1996: 1016) calls this recombinant property, where new forms of ownership emerge when the attributes of private and public are dissolved, interwoven, and recombined; and firms have exploited such ambiguity to their advantage. The collapse of the formal structures of socialist regimes in Eastern Europe did not result in an institutional vacuum. Instead, old practices, social ties, and organizational forms have been appropriated and recombined to become new assets and resources. Institutions have been rebuilt "not on the ruins but with the ruins of communism" (Stark 1996: 995). In this context, recombinant property is a strategy of organizational hedging with which market players spread risks in an uncertain environment by diversifying assets and recombining resources.

The emergence of recombinant property in China is the result of a number of parallel developments during market reform, including commercialization, corporatization, and privatization. From the outset, the administrative restructuring of the Chinese state has led to the commercialization of a substantial number of bureaucratic units into companies or professional social organizations, in addition to the vast number of state-owned enterprises. At the same time, state ownership takes on a new meaning under corporatization. During the period of the command economy, state ownership necessarily implied indivisible ownership of the state and total control by state bureaus. Under shareholding reform, many state-owned enterprises were transformed into shareholding companies, with the state holding a controlling, but not necessarily the majority, share.

Meanwhile, privatization has been undertaken in a rather uneven manner. Some localities aggressively sold state-owned enterprises under their control, while others adopted a lukewarm attitude towards privatized public enterprises. Zeng (2013) finds that local officials have played a crucial role in China's ownership reform. Instead of enforcing central policies and regulations uniformly, local authorities were selective in the implementation of privatization. The fragmentation of the state means that substates often acted opportunistically and in accordance with parochial interests in their pursuit of commercialization, corporatization, and privatization.

While the existence of a large state-owned sector is also found in other countries, several features underline the peculiarities of hybrid businesses with recombinant property forms in China. First, state-owned enterprises and quasi-state firms play an overwhelmingly dominant, if not monopolistic, role in most of the strategic economic sectors such as banking, energy, telecommunication, shipping, aviation, and railway. Second, recombinant businesses can be found in all major economic sectors, across different geographical regions, and at various levels of government administration. They are either supervised by certain ministerial bureaus, controlled by specific local authorities in host localities, or they maintain close relationships with relevant bureaucratic units. In other words, they merge into the *tiao–kuai* system. Third, compared with the 75 million companies registered with the

State Administration for Industry and Commerce in 2015, in absolute numbers, the size of this group of hybrid businesses pales in comparison. However, their economic significance is substantial. For instance, officially defined state-owned enterprises (with the state holding a majority share of over 50 per cent or a controlling share of over 30 per cent) alone constituted some 25 per cent of the total value of industrial production in 2011. Although this percentage has declined substantially from its high point in the 1990s when more than 50 per cent of industrial production was state-generated, this is still a very substantial proportion. And if we include those enterprises with minority state shares, the size of this hybrid sector is even more significant. It should be noted, however, that collective enterprises such as firms owned by townships and villages are not included in these statistics.

So far, we have just scratched the surface of business hybridity. Recombinant property deriving from the restructuring of ownership constitutes only one source of hybridity. Other sources of hybridity come from overlapping memberships as well as convoluted connections between the state, the party, and business. In his study of government–business relations in Poland, Schoenman (2005: 69) argues that post-socialist governments have created economic empires through forging alliances with firms whose owners depend on political support for economic success. This has led to the emergence of an economic class that is embedded in state politics. This finding, finds resonance in the case of China. Recent crackdowns on high-level corruption show that political power during the reform era has increasingly relied on direct control of public and private assets. Details of corruption allegations against prominent figures in the party, military, parliamentary bodies, state ministries, and state-owned enterprises reveal the personal involvement of high-ranking political leaders in business transactions, rent seeking, and the exchange of political office for personal and economic gains. Some vast business empires have been exposed as linking directly to top politicians.

Thanks to the doctrine of the "Three Represents" which allowed business elites to join the party and engage in an active political life, the Chinese Communist Party (CCP) has functioned as a networking mechanism that links business to the state and vice versa. It is the bridging apparatus, the transmission belt, between business and politics. Dickson (2003) underlines a number of ways with which the CCP forged a close relationship with the private sector. The first is the proliferation of state-sponsored associations which many observers have seen as corporatist arrangements.

The second is the large number of CCP members who quit official positions and became businessmen. The third is the recruitment of businessmen into the CCP.

It is difficult to tell whether overlapping interactions between the state and business represent business capture of the state or the other way around. But it goes beyond typical cronyism in which business clients seek political patronage from individual officials or power brokers for protection and special privileges. In our case, the patron and client are fused. A substantial number of influential business elites have emerged from the ranks of cadres and the *nomenklatura*. By virtue of their political capital, many veteran party members, former official bearers, and family members of influential cadres have become very successful economic players. They wear many hats, distribute name cards carrying a dozen titles, and change their roles easily between regulator and market player and between rent creator and rent seeker (Ngo 2009).

All in all, we find a variety of business actors, a diversity of organizational forms, and a plurality of property rights in China. In this unique constellation, the most prominent actors are not conventional private firms but new breeds of bureaucratic enterprises, politically embedded businesses, joint public–private ventures, and private firms disguised as collective enterprises. Various forms of ownership exist side by side, with property rights divided into components such as right of usage, claim to resource flow, and right of transfer, with different ownership structures commanding different combinations. Many of these businesses respond simultaneously to market signals and political incentives.

Interests of Substates and Hybrid Businesses

Understanding the fragmentation of the Chinese state and the hybridity of business is important because such insight allows us to re-examine the interests of the state and business. And locating the interests of the state and business is the first step towards mapping out state–business relations in China.

It has been taken for granted that the pursuit of profit is the defining interest of business enterprises. There are, however, certain qualifications. Profit making as the legitimate *raison d'être* of modern business was only gradually recognized and institutionalized in the course of market reform in China. In fact, before the 1990s, business activities aiming at increasing turnover and profit, such as sales promotion, trade, expansion of market share, and so on—activities which are part and parcel of normal business operations in a capitalist market—were frowned upon by the state. Businesses ran the risk of crackdown.

The legitimation of profit making is a process of selection and negotiation during which certain forms of returns (including economic rents) and certain ways of earning (including rent seeking) were eventually recognized as legitimate sources of business income. Yet the interest of business is not exclusively concerned with profit making. Other than profit making, social and political obligations are viewed as part and parcel of business activities.

Under the structure of recombinant property, many hybrid businesses are expected or obliged to undertake non-commercial functions. This is particularly so for hybrid businesses with the state as one of the stakeholders. Township and village enterprises are one obvious example. They belong to the so-called collective enterprises, with ownership resting (theoretically) in the hands of the village collective. Very often, a township or village enterprise is an administrative-cum-business-cum-social-cum-welfare entity. In some places, the whole village becomes an enterprise, with the party secretary-cum-village head as the enterprise manager. In such a setup, profit making is only one of the objectives of the enterprise. Social and welfare functions such as the provision of employment, infrastructural development, generation of village revenue, social security provisions, and so on, are equally important. Workers are less bound by "labour contracts" than by social ties in the village.

State-owned enterprises are another example. They are often entrusted with multiple tasks not necessarily related to profit making. Studies have found that local governments, especially those in inner regions with slow economic growth, often pressurized local state-owned enterprises to invest beyond their means in order to achieve higher gross domestic product growth. Regardless of their actual production capacity, some state-owned enterprises were required to take on more workers, especially in times of rising unemployment. More profitable state-owned enterprises have been forced to take over or merge with loss-making ones (Buckley et al. 2005).

Hybrid businesses, especially those with a substantial share of state ownership, respond simultaneously to market signals and political incentives because they are run by political managers. This is a group of technocratic cadres who manage state-owned enterprises and state-controlled hybrid enterprises. Almost without exception, this group of technocratic cadres come from the party ***nomenklatura*** but claim their achievement through the performance of the enterprises they run. The party retains controlling power over the appointment, rotation, and transfer of board chairmen and CEOs of these enterprises. As Jin Zhang points out in her contribution in this volume, these cadres or managers strive to use their corporate performance as springboards to higher political careers by growing their companies in ways that advance the interests of the party and the state.

In short, recombinant ownership leads directly to peculiar state interests and enterprise behaviours. On the one hand, profit making is not the sole concern of businesses in China. On the other hand, bureaucratic rivalry among substates and local governments is not exclusively limited to turf-fighting but is also connected to material benefits. The result is a logic of state–business interactions predicating upon alternative forms of rationality. This brings us to the central argument of this chapter: as a result of the peculiar forms of rationality arising from state fragmentation and business hybridity, state–business relations in China is characterized by differential closeness between different substates and hybrid businesses. Examining such differential closeness enables us to see the paradox of the polymorphous state and the heterogeneity of state–business interactions in a new light.

Differential Closeness Between Substates and Hybrid Businesses

Differential closeness signifies uneven interactions between the state and business. While Wilson (1990) reminds us that the modern state has become an institutional arena in which competing economic interests seek to capture its influence and power, we should qualify this proposition where China is concerned because the state is not a uniform institutional arena open to all competing economic interests. In other words, the Chinese state is not an impartial referee adjudicating conflicts arising from business competition. From the outset, certain business interests are more equal than the others.

State–business relations are graded in China, ranging from businesses serving as appendages of the state to symbiotic collusion, clientelist-dependent, and arm's-length relationships. This gradation is shaped by the interests of state and business actors. While existing studies have attributed regional variations in state–business relations to the institutional configurations of the local state and the market structure of the local economy, we augment this argument by exploring a micro-foundation of state–business relations: interests. The interests of (sub)state actors lie in fulfilling parochial departmental or local development priorities (as laid down in performance contracts) in order to advance their political careers, and/or to obtain personal benefits through bribes, kickbacks, and so on. The interests of business actors vary considerably, depending on the ownership structures of enterprises, and interests range from increasing the market share and profitability of companies to fulfilling policy targets. The degree of closeness is determined by the extent to which interests intersect.

In our attempt to disaggregate the state and business, we see that the interests of various substates and hybrid businesses vary. Because of this, a specific substate may protect one type of business while discriminating against another. In a similar vein, an enterprise may receive strong support from a local state in one area but meet with hostility in another area. Even within a single region, an enterprise may have the blessing of one level of government while encountering trouble with higher or lower levels of government.

In general, state actors embrace those businesses that can help them achieve their political and economic priorities or advance their personal interests. Most of the time, these priorities include policy goals such as high growth rate, low unemployment, steady taxation, technological upgrading, and policy targets set down by the national five-year plans and other politico-economic projects initiated by the country's top leaders. It is thus unsurprising that state-owned enterprises under the direct supervision of a particular substate enjoy the closest relationship with that substate because the latter sees such enterprises as appendages of the local state. Next to state-owned enterprises are local enterprises with substantial state or collective ownership. Strategic enterprises such as those that contribute substantially to local revenue and employment, those that are supported by national plans, or those that help raise the economic profile of their hosting locales also receive the official blessing of local states. They are usually large-scale enterprises with forms of recombinant property in the so-called pillar industries (Pearson 2005). Alongside types of enterprises whose links to substates are officially sanctioned, we can also find crony enterprises which are privately connected to individual party leaders or local officials. It is not uncommon to find crony enterprises classified as strategic local businesses under state sanction.

Businesses that are mainly privately owned and fail to cultivate personal *guanxi* with power-holding officials have a more distant relationship with the local state. Among such businesses are "outsider businesses" whose headquarters are located in other regions. Their relationship is even more distant. At the end of the spectrum are privately owned, small and medium-sized enterprises in non-strategic industrial sectors with headquarters in other regions and which have few *guanxi* connections. Their relations with the local state are the most distant.

Before we further analyse the factors shaping differential closeness, let us first answer a basic question: what does it mean to have close state–business relations? Concretely this is measurable by means of the preferential privileges that a business enjoys under official sanction. Differential closeness is often manifested by policy privileges or regulatory conveniences offered by substates to selected businesses. Put differently, privileged businesses benefit from the allocation of economic rents by substates. The closer a business is to the state, the more accessible it is to economic rents and/or the larger the amount of rents it can obtain.

As a matter of fact, a substantial proportion of economic resources in China is allocated not by market exchange but by state licensing. Given the extensive degree of state intervention and the shifting roles of the state as regulator-cum-investor, an enormous amount of economic rents is created and transacted. In retrospect, the creation and allocation of economic rents have been used by the Chinese state as a policy instrument for effecting industrial plans and development priorities. By controlling resources such as land, low-interest rate loans, foreign exchange, and so on, and by exercising its power to ration such resources to targeted industries or enterprises, the state, including its central and local institutions, has been the main creator of economic rents and particularistic benefits (Ngo 2008). Furthermore, in many sectors, the state controls market entry through various licensing arrangements and production catalogues (Yang 2004). Economic rents are again created by selective restrictions on market entry.

Local governments have relied on rent allocation to manoeuvre the development of local economies. Under the fragmented *tiao–kuai* system, the interests of substates do not necessarily match those of the central authorities. More often than not, substates are prepared to promote local development at the expense of the national economy. In particular, local states have colluded with local enterprises to overcome national entry barriers. This has led some observers to label the local state as developmental or entrepreneurial (Duckett 2001; Oi 1995). Others characterize the system as Chinese-style federalism (Montinola et al. 1995). The immediate consequence of local protectionism is severe competition between localities, both in terms of actual benefits, such as access to resources and investments, and symbolic achievements, such as higher ranking (Chien and Gordon 2008).

There exists a multiplicity of economic rents and rent-like transfers created by state policy and licensing in China. Elsewhere, I have discussed the nature of different types of rents and rent-like transfers and their implications on economic governance (Ngo 2009). Suffice it to say here that many of these have hitherto been sanctioned by the state as legitimate earnings. For instance, many observers have noted that the apparently impressive earnings of many giant Chinese conglomerates such as PetroChina, China Telecom, State Grid, Baosteel, and Haier were not derived from their market competitiveness or production efficiency but rather from the economic rents obtained from state subsidy or market protection. In fact, national and local businesses alike have depended upon the rents granted by state authorities in order to compete in the national market. And this is not the end of the story. The domination of state monopolies in the sectoral markets has created a long chain of subcontractors. These subcontractors can be wholly owned subsidiaries of the monopolies themselves, or companies with recombinant property such as joint ventures, or crony businesses with good connections. Given the position of state monopolies as the sole supplier or customer, they control the power of licensing when they choose subcontractors. The principle of differential closeness applies again to the selection of subcontractors, who in turn repeat the power exercise when looking for sub-subcontractors.

Factors Shaping Differential Closeness

Let us now return to the question of what determines the degree of closeness. We argue that differential closeness between substates and hybrid businesses is a result of the intersection between the interests of state and business actors, and is shaped by three factors, namely the ownership structures of hybrid business, the location and scalar position of substates within the *tiao–kuai* hierarchy, and the strategies of state and business actors. These three factors are interrelated. Since differential closeness to businesses shapes the priorities of the state and substates in the allocation of economic rents, manipulating such closeness becomes a major rent-seeking strategy pursued by business interests. On the face of it, this seems to conform to the commonly accepted idea that most businesses in China are engaged in the cultivation of personal networks. *Guanxi* cultivation has been a common strategy of seeking and receiving official attention, favouritism, bribes, cover-ups, and so on (Wank 1996). What has been overlooked is that *guanxi* cultivation represents only one form of rent seeking and one mode of state–business relations. Equally important is the manipulation of recombinant property. By mimicking, camouflaging, and adapting obscure ownership structures, businesses can increase their differential closeness to the state, hence claiming legitimate entitlement to selective privileges granted by the state. By the same token, some businesses also try to go local and/or adjust their scale of operation so that they fall under the jurisdiction of specific substates in the scalar hierarchy.

The earliest attempts of camouflaging can be found among the so-called *getihu* (individual household business) and private business during the nascent period of market reform. Many newly established private enterprises were seen to be competing for scarce raw materials with the public sector. They were also blamed for driving up inflation and causing market disorder. Private businesses were accused of blind investment, repeated establishment, overlapping construction, and disrupting the industrial plan of the government. To avoid persecution, many businesses disguised themselves as public enterprises. Some paid an annual "management fee" to townships and villages and were disguised as collective enterprises. Others sought local government affiliation and appeared as state-owned enterprises. The practice is commonly referred to as "wearing a red hat".

Even township and village enterprises, which are regarded as collective enterprises, have sought to form joint operations with state-owned enterprises. In this way, they become de facto subcontractors of state-owned enterprises. For state-owned enterprises, such cooperation allows them to lower their production and operation costs. In return, township and village enterprises receive skills and technological and capital support. They also gain access to raw materials and strategic goods exclusively reserved for use by state-owned enterprises. Most importantly, such cooperation allows township and village enterprises to enter a particular market reserved for state-owned enterprises only. By forming partnerships with state-owned enterprises, such township and village enterprises take on the guise of state-owned enterprises operating in the state-owned sector.

Mimicking a local state-owned enterprise has been a common strategy. It is a way of overcoming market closures or policy restrictions which prohibit private enterprises from operating in a certain market sector. Even in the absence of entry restrictions, such practice is still common because it is a handy way of legitimizing preferential policy treatment by local governments. For instance, in some cases, the paid-up capital comes from a private source, but through clientelist relations the enterprise is registered as an investment of a state organization. Other creative camouflaging strategies abound. One example is Huawei, which adapted its ownership structure to form joint ventures with local telecommunication bureaus in Tianjin and Shanghai and in the provinces of Sichuan, Shandong, Zhejiang, and Hebei. In this way, these local subsidiaries of Huawei became a kind of state-owned enterprise. This status allowed Huawei to monopolize local markets and become the sole supplier of telecom services to local governments in cities and provinces.

There have been attempts by the central authorities to weed out fake state and collective enterprises. For instance, a campaign was launched by the State Council in the early 1990s to purge disguised businesses in the public sector. In response to the campaign, some enterprises came up with a new strategy. They put in place a shareholding system, according to which a certain percentage, say 15 per cent, of the total assets of an enterprise was set aside as collective ownership, belonging to all workers of the enterprise. In this way, the enterprise was disguised as a collective enterprise.

It is in this sense that the state plays a structuring role which shapes the forms and actions of societal actors as Wilson (1990) reminds us. Business firms often restructure themselves in accordance with the local demand. Krug and Hendrischke (2008) find that businesses are shaped by the competition between local state institutions. Local businesses have to reorganize firms and industries in line with local institutions to facilitate their operation. They interact with local governments through networks that draw on cultural norms and traditions. Put differently, business enterprises adjust their organizations and operations in order to forge relations with substates at specific locations and scalar levels, as the Huawei case has shown.

It should be noted that not all businesses are equally keen on engaging in rent seeking. This is because rents come at a price. And the price varies, ranging from political risk (especially in periods of severe crackdown against corruption or during elite power struggles) to non-commercial commitments and social obligations, and sometimes unreasonable requests from the state or state officials. Rent-receiving enterprises are usually among the major taxpayers in a locality. They have to take an active part in social and political campaigns initiated by central and local governments. During the recent stock exchange meltdown in 2015, the central authorities forbade state-owned enterprises to sell stocks in order to prevent the stock exchange index from plunging further.

There is also no guarantee that those firms receiving rents will necessarily become successful market players. Nee and Opper (2012) note that there is no evidence to suggest that the success of enterprises in the Yangtze delta region depends on positional advantages and social privileges held by company founders. Even those cadre entrepreneurs who received the most favourable treatment from local governments lost their initial advantages within a couple of years. In the view of local governments, neither party membership nor cadre statues nor personal ties with government authorities can guarantee a superior firm performance.

Close relationships between substates and hybrid businesses also carry unintended consequences. Under administrative decentralization, the fragmentation of the state has created multiple layers of authorities with contentious jurisdictions and competing policy goals, with each of these power centres developing its own resource base and channelling resources to specific targets. At the same time, economic players at various levels and in different regions are caught up in attempts to link their own interests to those of the local authorities. The result is the creation of competing rent-generating and rent-seeking regulatory regimes. It is thus not surprising to find that even national state-owned enterprises do not exhibit similar degrees of closeness with the state. Since most national state-owned enterprises are giant undertakings, they have tens of dozens of provincial and local offices as well as subsidiaries. Most of these local establishments are nominally under the supervision of the national headquarters. In actual practice, the selection and appointment of local managers are often determined by either local governments or local branches of functional ministries. As a result, these local subsidiaries tend to act according to local interests rather than to the nation-wide plans set by their corporate headquarters. Intensive competition between various levels of local state authorities for jurisdiction, resources, incomes, and so on, can also occur between local subsidiaries of the same group. Intra-firm competition, duplicate investment, and mutual sabotage across local branches and subsidiaries are sometimes more cut-throat than between rival business enterprises.

Finally, how does this differential closeness revise our current understanding of state–business relations in China? Studies have highlighted market structure as a factor shaping regional variations in state–business relations. Earlier, we cited Segal and Thun (2001) who argued that Shanghai adopted a more interventionist stance towards business because the local economy was dominated by large conglomerates, in contrast with Beijing which adopted a more laissez-faire approach when faced with a local economy led by smaller firms. From our perspective, we can fully account for regional variations by looking at differential closeness. As we have argued, small private firms without strong strategic significance usually keep the furthest distance from the state. A local economy that is dominated by small private business will thus invite the least intervention from a substate. Put differently, a substate is least likely to actively extend selective privileges to business in a sea of small enterprises. The Wenzhou model is a typical case of limited state intervention (Parris 1993). In contrast, in local economies such as Shanghai where a large number of large state-owned enterprises can be found, substates share close relationships with these enterprises. Active state support for these enterprises thus makes these substates developmental. In the region of Sunan, the local economy was once dominated by township and village enterprises with collective ownership. Efforts of local substates to coordinate hybrid businesses earned them a reputation, the Sunan model, which was subsequently conceptualized as local state corporatism (Walder 1995).

It should be noted, however, that these characterizations are merely abstractions of the general situation. For instance, in places where local substates have been largely indifferent to small private enterprises, a few state-owned enterprises or strategic hybrid businesses continued to receive strong support from local authorities in the extension of economic rents and regulatory privileges. Such uneven treatment of businesses within the same region cannot be explained in terms of market structure but can be accounted for in terms of differential closeness. We can therefore see why Jili Auto had benefited from state support in laissez-faire Taizhou in Zhejiang Province, as had Jianlibao from the relatively poor Sanshui District in Guangdong Foshan and Tieben Steel in Changzhou in Suzhou.

Differential closeness also explains the abrupt downfall of some prominent enterprises such as Brilliance China, Tieben, and Jianlibao, which once enjoyed close state–business relations. As we have argued, differential closeness is shaped by the ownership structure, location and scalar position of the substates, and business strategies. Changes in these factors can radically alter existing state–business relations. In the case of Brilliance China, the first Chinese company to be listed on the New York Stock Exchange and once the recipient of unlimited support from the Shenyang government, its former chairman Yang Ron attempted to launch a huge project in Ningpo and to move the headquarters out of Shenyang. This ran against the interests of the Shenyang government, which decided to withdraw its support to the enterprise group: it would rather destabilize the whole business than to give it to another region. In the case of Jianlibao, the former number one sport drinks manufacturer in China, the CEO attempted to alter the status of state ownership and to arrange a management buyout. This angered the local Sanshui District authorities who subsequently withdrew support for the enterprise. The fall of Tieben Steel is even more dramatic and ironic. The enterprise was a well-managed private manufacturer. It was treated by the prefectural city of Changzhou as a strategic business under its jurisdiction. It received numerous privileges extended by the Changzhou government, local banks, and even the land bureau in Jiangsu Province. Ironically, the officially sanctioned expansion of manufacturing capacity by local substates was deemed to be against the national policy of reducing the investment capacity of heavy industries. The conflict between different scalar authorities eventually caused Tieben to go bankrupt, while the CEO was put in jail. These cases show how variations and alterations in the three factors can radically change micro state–business relations even when the broader socio-political circumstances remain stable.

Conclusion

Our discussions underline the micro-foundations of state–business relations in China. We have tried to give some initial characterization and conceptualization of the patterns which we have identified. We argue that the first step is to disaggregate the state and business since there is little uniformity underlying state fragmentation and business hybridity. Disaggregation enables us to understand the heterogeneity of interests across different state institutions in China's *tiao–kuai* matrix, as well as that among various hybrids of business enterprises. Once we have done this, we find that state–business relations are graded, in the sense that different types of business enjoy different degrees of closeness to the state and substates. Such differential closeness is determined, in general, by the ownership structures of business, the locations and scalar positions of the substates within the *tiao–kuai* hierarchy, and the strategies of substates and businesses. Close relations are manifested by the granting of economic rents by the state to a privileged few. State-owned enterprises thus have the highest priority in receiving state-sanctioned rents, followed by other hybrid businesses with recombinant property, crony enterprises, and so on. A consequence of this is the proliferation of rent-seeking activities, with businesses trying to manipulate their positions within the differential hierarchy in order to capture rents.

Our approach offers a new perspective to account for the long-existing puzzle of state polymorphism in China, in which the same state appears to be developmental and predatory at the same time. State–business relations seem to manifest corporatist, pluralist, and clientelist characteristics simultaneously, and different regions vary tremendously in terms of the degree of state intervention in market exchanges and business activities. Such paradoxical and contradictory perceptions derive from a gross oversimplification of state–business relations in China as being uniform or dominated by one specific form of interaction. While some studies have tried to locate regional variations in state–business relations, their disaggregation stops short of extending beyond regional analysis. Because of this, the heterogeneity of interactions between substates and businesses at the enterprise level has remained largely unproblematized. In trying to fill this gap, the idea of differential closeness offers a conception of state–business relations at the micro level. Once we understand that substates interact with different enterprises in an uneven manner, the paradox of state polymorphism can be explained.

This is, at best, a preliminary step towards a fuller theorization of state–business relations in China. Space limitations do not allow us to substantiate our argument with more case studies; we have also refrained from analysing uneven changes over time in order to avoid further complication. Nonetheless, we hope this provides an alternative perspective from which to probe the complex contours of state–business relations in China.

References

Buckley, P. J., Clegg, J., & Tan, H. (2005). Reform and restructuring in a Chinese state-owned enterprise: Sinotrans in the 1990s. *Management International Review, 45*(2), 147–172.

Cheema, G. S., & Rondinelli, D. A. (2007). From government decentralization to decentralized governance. In G. Shabbira Cheema & D. A. Rondinelli (Eds.), *Decentralizing governance: Emerging concepts and practices* (pp. 1–20). Washington, DC: Brookings Institution Press.

Chien, S.-S., & Gordon, I. (2008). Territorial competition in China and the West. *Regional Studies, 42*(1), 31–49.

Dickson, B. J. (2003). *Red capitalists in China: The party, private entrepreneurs, and prospects for political change*. Cambridge: Cambridge University Press.

Duckett, J. (2001). Bureaucrats in business, Chinese-style: The lessons of market reform and state entrepreneurialism in the People's Republic of China. *World Development, 29*(1), 23–37.

Evans, P. (1995). *Embedded autonomy: States and industrial transformation*. Princeton: Princeton University Press.

Haggard, S., Maxfield, S., & Schneider, B. R. (1997). Theories of business and business-state relations. In S. Maxfield & B. R. Schneider (Eds.), *Business and the state in developing countries* (pp. 36–60). Ithaca: Cornell University Press.

Howell, J. (2006). Reflections on the Chinese state. *Development and Change, 37*(2), 73–97.

Hung, E., & Ngo, T.-W. (2015). *Parallel trade in the Pearl River delta region*. Paper presented to the International Workshop on Cross-border Exchanges and the Shadow Economy, Leiden, 14–15 December 2015.

Hutchcroft, P. D. (1991). Oligarchs and cronies in the Philippine state: The politics of patrimonial plunder. *World Politics, 43*(3), 414–450.

Johnson, C. (1982). *MITI and the Japanese miracle*. Stanford: Stanford University Press.

Kang, D. C. (2002). *Crony capitalism: Corruption and development in South Korea and the Philippines*. Cambridge: Cambridge University Press.

Kennedy, S. (2005). *The business of lobbying in China*. Cambridge, MA: Harvard University Press.

Kohli, A. (2004). *State-directed development: Political power and industrialization in the global periphery*. Cambridge: Cambridge University Press.

Krug, B., & Hendrischke, H. (2008). Framing China: Transformation and institutional change through co-evolution. *Management and Organization Review, 4*(1), 81–108.

Lee, C.-Y. (2011). *Taiwanese business or Chinese security asset: A changing pattern of interaction between Taiwanese business and Chinese governments*. London: Routledge.

Lieberthal, K., & Oksenberg, M. (1988). *Policy making in China: Leaders, structures, and processes*. Princeton: Princeton University Press.

Mertha, A. C. (2005). China's 'soft' centralization: Shifting *Tiao/Kuai* authority relations. *China Quarterly, 184*, 791–810.

Montinola, G., Qian, Y., & Weigast, B. (1995). Federalism, Chinese style: The political basis for economic success in China. *World Politics, 48*(1), 50–81.

Nee, V., & Opper, S. (2012). *Capitalism from below: Markets and institutional change in China*. Cambridge: Harvard University Press.

Ngo, T.-W. (2008). Rent-seeking and economic governance in the structural nexus of corruption in China. *Crime, Law and Social Change, 49*(1), 27–44.

Ngo, T.-W. (2009). The politics of rent production. In T.-W. Ngo & Y. Wu (Eds.), *Rent seeking in China* (pp. 1–21). London: Routledge.

Ngo, T.-W., Yin, C., & Tang, Z. (2017). Scalar restructuring of the Chinese state: The subnational politics of development zones. *Environment and Planning C (Politics and Space), 35*(1), 57–75.

Oi, J. C. (1992). Fiscal reform and the economic foundations of local state corporatism in China. *World Politics, 45*(1), 99–126.

Oi, J. C. (1995). The role of the local state in China's transitional economy. *China Quarterly, 144*, 1132–1149.

Parris, K. (1993). Local initiative and national reform: The Wenzhou model of development. *China Quarterly, 134*, 242–263.

Pearson, M. M. (2005). The business of governing business in China: Institutions and norms of the emerging regulatory state. *World Politics, 57*(2), 296–322.

Pei, M. (2008). *China's trapped transition: The limits of developmental autocracy*. Cambridge: Harvard University Press.

Riggs, F. W. (1966). *Thailand: The modernization of a bureaucratic polity*. Honolulu: East-West Center Press.

Saich, T. (2002). The blind man and the elephant: Analysing the local state in China. In L. Tomba (Ed.), *East Asian capitalism: Conflicts, growth and crisis* (pp. 75–99). Milano: Fondazione Giangiacomo Feltrinelli.

Schoenman, R. (2005). Captains or pirates? State-business relations in post-socialist Poland. *East European Politics and Societies, 19*(1), 40–75.

Searle, P. (1998). *The riddle of Malaysian capitalism: Rent-seekers or real capitalists*. Honolulu: University of Hawaii Press.

Segal, A., & Thun, E. (2001). Thinking globally, acting locally: Local governments, industrial sectors, and development in China. *Politics & Society, 29*(4), 557–588.

Sidel, J. T. (1999). *Capital, coercion, and crime: Bossism in the Philippines*. Stanford: Stanford University Press.

So, A. (2003). Introduction: Rethinking the Chinese developmental miracle. In A. So (Ed.), *China's developmental miracle* (pp. 3–26). New York: M.E. Sharpe.

Stark, D. (1996). Recombinant property in East European capitalism. *American Journal of Sociology, 101*(4), 993–1027.

Unger, J., & Chan, A. (1995). China, corporatism, and the east Asian model. *Australian Journal of Chinese Affairs, 33*, 29–53.

Unger, J., & Chan, A. (2008). Associations in a bind: The emergence of political corporatism. In J. Unger (Ed.), *Associations and the Chinese state: Contested spaces* (pp. 48–68). New York: M.E. Sharpe.

Wade, R. (1990). *Governing the market: Economic theory and the role of government in East Asian industrialization*. Princeton: Princeton University Press.

Walder, A. (1995). Local government as industrial firms: An organizational analysis of China's transitional economy. *American Journal of Sociology, 101*(2), 263–301.

Wank, D. L. (1996). The institutional process of market Clientelism: Guanxi and private business in a South China city. *China Quarterly, 147*, 820–838.

Wilson, G. (1990). *Business and politics: A comparative introduction*. London: Chatham House.

Woo-Cumings, M. (Ed.). (1999). *The developmental state*. Ithaca: Cornell University Press.

Yang, D. (2004). *Remaking the Chinese leviathan: Market transition and the politics of governance in China*. Stanford: Stanford University Press.

Zeng, J. (2013). *State-led privatization in China: The politics of economic reform*. London: Routledge.

Zhou, X. (2010). The institutional logic of collusion among local governments in China. *Modern China, 36*(1), 47–78.

PART II

Changes and Variations in Business–Government Relations

CHAPTER 3

The Evolution of Government–MNC Relations in China: The Case of the Automotive Sector

Gregory T. Chin

Introduction

Important changes occurred in the relations between the Chinese government and the world's leading multinational corporations from the mid-1990s to the mid-2000s. In this period, consequential shifts occurred in

This chapter was completed during a Visiting Fellowship at the Institute for Advanced Study in Humanities and Social Sciences at Zhejiang University, Hangzhou, China, in June 2016, with the kind support of Institute for Advanced Study in Humanities and Social Sciences (IAS) Executive Dean Zhu Tianbiao and Ms. Wu Qi. I thank Louis Hughes, Stefan Messnann, Rudy Schlais and researchers at China's National Development and Reform Commission for their participant observations, and Loren Brandt, Ha-Joon Chang, Victor Falkenheim, B. Michael Frolic, Jeremy Paltiel, Louis Pauly, Margaret Pearson, Eric Thun, Robert Wade, Hongying Wang and Joseph Wong for their earlier comments. I thank Zhang Xiaoke and Zhu Tianbiao for their editorial suggestions. I thank Li Qingdong for the previous research support.

G.T. Chin (✉)
Department of Political Science, York University, Toronto, ON, Canada

X. Zhang, T. Zhu (eds.), *Business, Government and Economic Institutions in China*, International Political Economy Series,
DOI 10.1007/978-3-319-64486-8_3

the Chinese state's approach to regulating foreign multinational corporations (MNCs), especially in sectors that state planners deemed "strategic", with regard to attracting foreign investment, namely the energy, transportation, raw materials, and agriculture sectors. These regulatory changes led to the emergence of new trends and patterns of government–business relations.

This chapter examines the evolution of automotive industry, government–MNC relations in China's automotive industry from the mid-1990s to the mid-2000s, and the ensuing pattern of changing government–MNC relations that emerged henceforth in the automotive sector. The central argument is that, in China, the automotive industry witnessed especially dramatic changes in the governance of government–MNC relations that encouraged more full use of the capital, technology and know-how of the leading foreign MNCs for the modernization of this sector. In turn, the world leading foreign automotive MNCs responded to these regulatory changes, and the rapid growth of China's domestic auto market by making some of the largest ever investments in China. From a comparative perspective, the capital invested, and transfers of technology and know-how by the MNCs to China enabled Chinese domestic automotive corporations to absorb leading-edge global practices ("global best practices") and technology more rapidly than in other large developing countries such as India (Ray and Miglani 2016).

As a result of the pattern of *two-way trade-offs* between the Chinese government and foreign MNCs, global value chains were extended more fully to China, and the country has become a manufacturing hub for large cars, SUVs and minivans, and for smaller cars. In comparison, Indian scholars have argued that the relatively limited contributions of foreign MNCs to India's automotive industry, through technology transfers and imports (rather than production inside India), and India's much heavier reliance on its home-grown firms to propel its industry, are key factors in explaining the greater relative gains in automotive modernization that China achieved in this long decade, compared to India.[1] Although capable of end-to-end production, India has largely become an assembly hub for large cars and a manufacturing hub only for small cars (Ray and Miglani 2016). These comparative observations seem to confirm the argument by one scholar that "without the technology transfer from foreign firms, it is virtually impossible that the Chinese firms would have been able to achieve" the gains they made; that technology transfer from foreign companies enabled a complete transformation of China's automobile industry during the 1980s and 1990s (Gallagher 2006: 121). This chapter highlights that important changes in the *governance* of government–MNC relations *preconditioned* the waves of FDI and foreign know-how into China's auto sector from the mid-1990s to the mid-2000s. Regulatory changes were one of the main determinants behind the dramatic gains that China achieved in catch-up modernization, in the automotive sector, during this period.

Following the methodology to address cause and effect that has been developed by the co-editors of this book (see the Introductory chapter by Zhang and Zhu), this chapter takes the approach of aggregated effects of a range of causal factors on the changing varieties of interactions between state agencies, economic actors, and corporations; endogenous and exogenous causes; political and economic causes; and ideational and material causes—rather than try to provide a unified and parsimonious theory to account for changes in government-business relations, at this stage.

The chapter is divided into three main sections. The first details the main changes in the governance of government–MNC relations in the automotive sector, starting with the ideational shift that state planners made—whereby they came to accept that in order to attract higher quality and large-scale foreign investment from leading multinational automakers, they had to modify their regulatory approach to allow the logic of profits, markets, and competition to take effect. Limits had to be placed on state power, especially the state's direct invention in the day-to-day management of the corporation. Chinese regulators learned that they needed to reduce or avoid disincentives for MNCs to invest and transfer their capital, technology, and know-how.

The second section analyzes three dimensions of the institutionalized changes in government–business relations that were set in motion by the changes in governance arrangements, and by China's fast-growing domestic automotive market. The first is how the regulators modified their industrial policy—the 1993 Automotive Industrial Policy (AIP)—to target only the world's largest and most capable MNCs for investment into China; allowed the leading Chinese auto groupings to form more than one joint venture (JV) partnership; and then restrained themselves from intervening directly except to negotiate the terms of the JV partnership with the foreign MNC. The new regulatory approach and the 1993 AIP gave MNCs and the Chinese auto groupings more leeway to operate, after the founding negotiations were completed, and to make their own strategic and operational adjustments, as needed, amid the intensifying market competition.

The second dimension is that, although the national regulators may have limited their regulatory focus to negotiating the terms of entry of the leading foreign MNCs, the regulators exhibited substantial direct leverage in these negotiations. The critical case study was the deal with General Motors (GM) Corporation for the second JV with Shanghai Automotive Corporation (SAIC), and how GM responded to the demands of the Chinese regulators with major investment and technology-transfers for the formation of the new joint venture, Shanghai GM. However, GM also demanded that its quality, service, price (QSP) system for global purchasing of parts and components be used in the JV, that is, GM demanded more room from regulators to operate, day to day, and it was granted by the Chinese authorities.

The third dimension is that the changes in the governance of government–MNC relations also spurred some unintended outcomes. Toyota overcame its unwillingness to invest in automotive manufacturing inside China, and formed a JV in Tianjin, first with Tianjin Automotive Grouping (TAG), and when TAG was acquired by FAW, Toyota partnered with FAW to produce vehicles both in Changchun and Tianjin. Japan's leading automaker not only overcame its previous resistance to make substantial transfers of capital, technology and know-how to China. Rather it also responded to the Chinese leadership's national development campaign to develop China's Western region by opening a new compact bus production facility in Sichuan province. Toyota was also given more space to operate with its JVs. However, the pattern that emerged was *some* transfers of technology and know-how for the lower to medium value-added inputs in the value chain, but a *lack* of transfer of the highest value-added segments of the value chain. For the Chinese side, this was an unintended outcome.

In the third and concluding section of this chapter, we examine the longer-term consequences of the changes in the governance pattern of government–business relations that emerged in China's auto sector in the 1990s. We highlight how the pattern of two-way trade-offs between the government and the MNCs has continued to be the underlying pattern of relations between the Chinese government and the MNCs in the sectors, where, despite the growing emphasis to supporting homegrown brands, the government is still also targeting the leading foreign corporations to support the PRC's evolving national developmental goals. In the case of the auto sector, the contemporary developmental goals are lower polluting electric vehicle production inside China, and green financing of such production.

Ideational Shift

The mixed results from the first wave of utilizing foreign capital to modernize China's automotive industry through joint ventures (1984–1990) taught the second generation of national strategists that further attitudinal shifts, and regulatory adjustments were needed if China's automotive industry was to make a great leap in modernization.

Ideationally, the cases of failure in the first wave of automotive JVs that were formed in the mid-1980s—specifically Beijing Jeep and Guangzhou Peugeot—made Chinese state planners and regulators more aware than previously, of the scale of the challenge in turning China's automotive groupings into the "GMs" or "Toyotas" of China, and despite the partnering with *foreign* automakers. Beijing Jeep and Guangzhou Peugeot largely remained sites of final assembly for outdated "Third World" car models, and with most of their parts imported from outside of China. In contrast, Shanghai Volkswagen (SVW) became *the* model for creating a modern automotive supply network inside China, specifically in the Shanghai area, and especially from 1987 onwards (Chin 2010: 77–101; Thun 2006). Dr. Stefan Messmann, the former head of Volkswagen (VW) China and Asia said, in an interview with the author, that "a supply industry, in a modern sense, did not exist in China when VW started the JV project [in Shanghai] in the mid-1980s."[2] However, a preliminary local modern automotive parts supply and assembly network was built, in Shanghai, through the combined efforts of the Chinese state (central and local levels), the MNC (Volkswagen), the local corporate partner (SAIC), and local supply firms. Moreover, the Santana model that was produced at SVW was more advanced than what the other foreign automakers had offered to their Chinese partners. Despite the gains at Shanghai VW, it is tenable to suggest that none of the JVs in the PRC during the first wave—Shanghai VW, Beijing Jeep, or Guangzhou Peugeot—had achieved the capacity to produce the latest vehicle models, or to design and develop their own models, or to produce vehicles that were of a quality to be exported to foreign markets in the East Asian region. Japanese automakers and the rising Korean automotive companies held the upper hand. As such, the Chinese partners in these JVs still had a ways to go to catch-up, and that few gains had been made by local Chinese parts producers, except those associated with Shanghai VW.

The first decade of catch-up modernization confirmed to Chinese planners that the modernization of the automotive industry—a comparatively capital- and technology-intensive sector—required not only money, but also the intangibles required to keep up with rapidly changing and increasingly sophisticated global (industry) trends in technological innovation, computerization, systems-integration, and fast-evolving consumer tastes. The results proved that automotive manufacturing had different requirements from producing televisions, for example. For televisions, entire production lines could be imported and set up for domestic manufacturing, and then modifications and new products could be researched and developed, or their technology acquired, to allow for continuous modernization. This was the strategy that the Chinese authorities allowed for television manufacturers such as Hisense, Skyworth, and TCL. Foreign television manufacturers were not allowed to gain a production base inside China. However, it was reconfirmed to Chinese planners that a similar strategy of importing entire plants, assembly lines, equipment, and constantly investing to modernize, was not feasible for the automobile industry. Moreover, by the early 1990s, it had become apparent to Chinese industry watchers that the global spread of post-Fordist innovations in the auto sector made the challenge of catching-up, and then pushing further to innovate, even harder.[3]

The only sensible option, according to Chinese strategists, was to double-down on utilizing foreign capital, foreign technology, and foreign know-how, which only the foreign MNCs possessed; and then combine these elements together with technology imports and building homegrown capacity. This decision meant a continuation of the JV strategy. However, from the first phase of partnering with MNCs (1984–1990), Chinese planners learned that not any MNC would do as a JV partner. In order to achieve their modernization goals, China would need to target the world's leading (i.e. the most capable, most advanced) and biggest automakers for partnerships. From the case of Shanghai VW, they observed that only a very capable MNC would engage in localization of parts production, and the intensive international technology and know-how transfers. Neither AMC/Chrysler nor Peugeot were willing to take on parts localization during the first phase. As one industry insider, Perkowski, remarked, the downside of partnering with maverick firms, where the foreign managers were not in the "mainstream of the global automotive industry and weren't familiar with the latest trends in manufacturing, is that the foreign partner is not at the top of 'their game'" (Perkowski 2008: 123–5). For the next phase, the goal, according to Chinese planners, ought to be to "bring a complete end to CKD kits" and China only providing low value inputs.[4] This meant no more industry followers, and focusing instead on attracting industry leaders.

The positive results at Shanghai VW, and the successful negotiations (for the Chinese side) that led to creation of FAW-VW in Changchun in Northeast China, taught the Chinese strategists to "go big". According to the senior German negotiator for the FAW-VW deal, Stefan Messmann,[5] the Chinese side was not afraid of making large demands for transfers of technology, know-how, and capital, and the experience with VW taught the Chinese that "only strong multinationals were capable of dealing with China. The smaller ones were too afraid".[6] During the negotiations over what would become FAW-VW, Chrysler CEO Lee Iachocca offered to partner with FAW. However, he was unwilling to commit to the type of investment and technology transfer that the Chinese were asking for, and that VW was offering, which in addition to advanced technology, also included staff training for the Chinese workforce, and creating a research center in China.[7]

While the second generation of Chinese strategists had decided to go after the world's leading (and largest) automotive MNCs, it was still a tall order to *actually* attract them. The leading MNCs knew they had special capacity, and they could exert a lot of leverage in such negotiations. They could afford to be tough negotiators. They also wanted to protect their reputation ("brand") as *the* global leaders. They wanted the leeway or space to operate, and not to be regulated excessively or in unpredictable ways by state authorities. It had become apparent to Chinese industrial strategists and their planners that foreign automotive MNCs needed to be given more incentive to invest inside China. The second generation of automotive strategists observed that Chinese majority equity control had helped the Chinese partners to maintain control in the JV, but that having this degree of control likely came at the cost of securing more technology transfers from the foreign partner. Chinese planners also observed that the "one foreign partner only" rule, which prevented the Chinese auto grouping from creating a second JV, also had costs on the Chinese side in terms of securing more transfers. If the foreign partner was either uncommitted or unwilling to invest more in the JV, the Chinese partner had almost no leverage to "jostle" the foreign partner into increasing its investment. If the two sides had no other options which could be pursued, then the only other option was the drastic "threat of exit".

Behind the automotive sector-specific considerations, China's state planners were doing a broader rethink of their national industrial modernization strategy, especially for the national strategic sectors where they wanted to attract more targeted foreign investment. Chinese strategists had come to realize that they needed to place stricter limits on the exercise of state regulatory power, if the PRC was to attract more foreign investment, especially from the world's leading MNCs, and in the more complex and capital-intensive sectors. *Regulatory restraint* was needed in order for the foreign MNCs to want to invest; that boundaries (on state intervention) were needed in order to avoid creating disincentives for MNCs to invest, and on their day to day operations. It meant allowing regulations that facilitate the logic of profits, pricing that reflects supply and demand, competition, winners and losers, and extinction of the losers (i.e. market dynamics). These changes meant further loosening and eliminating command-type controls over the day-to-day operations in the JVs, in the strategic sectors, and allowing the Chinese auto groupings to form more than one JV partnership, in order to spur more competition between the foreign automakers so that they would vie more intensely for the attention of their Chinese partners. Regulatory restraint also meant related changes to the regulation of the overall automotive market, such as removing the restrictions on personal (private) car purchases, and no longer artificially suppressing the private car and small car market. Lifting government measures that had kept domestic car demand "artificially low" by the late 1980s and early 1990s, was seen as crucial to supporting domestic manufacturers, the JVs, and encouraging them to improve the quality of the vehicles that were produced locally.

The aforementioned changes in ideas and the mindset of key authorities and strategists paved the way for changes in the state's approach to regulating the auto industry that ran from the mid-1990s to the mid-2000s. In this period, the regulatory approach shifted from the 1980s' modified command-control protection from international competition to a more market-oriented regulatory approach that was increasingly geared toward supporting the shift to market dynamics of demand and supply within the sector. The regulatory approach also shifted to increasingly internationalized operations, with the Chinese auto sector integrated more fully into global value chains. However, it was not all loosening of state mediation and removing restrictions over foreign MNCs. Central regulators and their local representatives continued to press the foreign MNCs to pursue "joint" corporate objectives which supported the nation's development goals.

Counter-Trend

There was a key counter-trend, or an element of re-regulation, amid the de-regulation. It was not all about relaxing state controls. The early 1990s also saw a reassertion of centralized control measures by those who argued that the decentralization of the 1980s had generated economic distortions and irrationalities that were detrimental to the industrial modernization objectives of the nation. Initially, the push to reassert central control came from Chen Yun, Li Xiannian, Yao Yilin, and Li Peng. However, their call to restore the predominance of the planned economy was no longer viable, either socially or economically. With backing from the elder conservative reformers, Premier Li Peng and Vice Premier and State Planning Commission (SPC) Chair Zou Jiahua pushed for a recentralization agenda built on "pillar industries", that is, focusing investment on a select group of strategic industries, which would be the foundation for the nation's future growth and development. In so doing, they re-established the role for state planning at the core of the Party's normative agenda, though now mainly for pillar industries and the "commanding heights" of the economy, while accepting a different balance between state and market for the non-strategic sectors.

The new regulatory approach that emerged in the early 1990s was not a simple "either/or" choice of pro-market versus pro-planning. Older conservative reformers tried to restore the primacy of the planned economy, but failed, due in large part to the personal intervention of paramount leader Deng Xiaoping, who weighed in on the side of returning to rapid market reform and internationalization. However, a younger group of so-called economic neoconservatives, backed by the elder conservatives, did succeed in advocating for the state to continue as an "indispensable actor" in economic development and not simply a "passive actor", especially in the strategic industries. The neoconservatives called for a new synthesis, which has actually carried forward for more than two decades: to develop the scope and depth of the domestic market while recentralizing state authority over the strategic or pillar industries of the economy, and letting go of a range of controls in the non-strategic sectors. Chen Yuan, son of the elder leader Chen Yun, was one of the leading spokespeople who called for the creation of strong and strategic "pillar industries", the promotion of "national champions", and the use of state power to readjust the country's industrial structure. The neoconservatives believed that the nation's strategic development cannot be left to "whims of the market"; that market forces *alone* could not be counted on to bring about industrial transformation. Influenced by the experiences of the fast-developing economies in neighboring East Asia, the neoconservative reformers called for the Chinese government to use strong and clear industrial policy to direct resources to strategic industries (and, unlike the elder conservatives, in an increasingly market-oriented economy).

Sharing a similar mindset with Chen Yuan, He Guangyuan, the Minister of Machinery Industry, advocated that China needed to have a "modern and pillar" auto industry, and to ensure that it had its own national models and brands. He called for a two-stage strategy: in the first stage, from 1994 to 2000, the focus would be on building the foundations of the sector, and in the second stage from 2000 to 2010, the domestic auto industry was to have caught up with the most advanced international levels, developed indigenous R&D capacity, and fostered a group of internationally competitive national auto companies (He 1993).[8] State planners argued that the pillar industries were unlike labor-intensive, low-technology sectors or the new high-tech sectors because the former use production technologies that require major fixed investments including large capital and advanced technology and equipment. These are large "sunken" costs, and the country could not afford "blind investment" or duplication that could result from unregulated competition. Rather than a strategy of "growing out of the plan" as Naughton has suggested, the neoconservative economic reformers of the early 1990s drew selectively from Western economics, but combined it with a clear preference for strong state steering of industrial development in the strategic sectors.

When the new ideational synthesis was translated into the modified approach to regulating foreign capital utilization in the automotive industry, it featured, on the one hand, a loosening of regulatory control over the operational space within the JV, giving MNCs more room to operate in their day-to-day business. On the other hand, it also entailed focusing state mediation onto the MNC's terms of entry into the domestic market, which in turn, set some of the key parameters and priorities for the MNC's post-entry operations inside China. The regulatory goal became what I have elsewhere referred to as "improved mediation", not *laissez faire* (Chin 2010: 145–54).[9]

Institutional Outcomes

This section details two sets of intended institutionalized outcomes that emerged with the shift in regulatory approach outlined above, and a third combination of intended and unintended outcomes.

1994 AIP: Operational Space for the MNCs but Higher Industrial Development Requirements

The new thinking on the regulation of the leading automotive MNCs was institutionalized in the 1994 AIP. Embedded within the 1994 AIP was a new foreign investment strategy that brought changes in government–MNC relations. The clauses in the AIP that pertained to the use of foreign investment, *loosened* government oversight over the MNCs (and their Chinese JV partners) in the day-to-day operations of the JV, as long as the MNC was a world leading MNC, willing to abide by a set of conditions including forming a JV with a large Chinese automaker, willing to not hold more than 49% of the shares in the JV, willing to not be involved in distribution and sales, willing to commit to parts localization at set rates, and willing to establish R&D facilities with its Chinese partner inside China.

The 1994 AIP preserved the requirement that foreign automakers could only invest in assembly production inside China through a JV. However, it reflected the new thinking detailed above, in that the 1994 AIP granted MNCs the right to hold a larger ownership and equity share in the JVs, than previously. Clause 32 stated that the Chinese share could "not be less than 50% in a Sino-foreign JV that is assembling engines, complete cars, and motorcycles". The clause specifically stipulated that foreign automakers investing in China in complete car projects, or projects in three key components (motors, air bags, and anti-lock braking systems) could not exceed 50% equity holdings.

While the clause proscribed the limits, the new rules actually meant that the foreign partner could henceforth hold as much as 49% of the equity and shares in the JV, which marked a substantial increase for the foreign side. This decision reflected, on the one hand, the new ideational perspective on the part of the Chinese regulators, discussed above, that they needed to give the leading MNCs more incentive to investment, and thereby encourage the needed transfers of technology, know-how, and capital from the MNC to its China-based JV. On the other hand, the cap for the foreign partner at below 50% for equity holdings reflected the continuing desire on the part of the Chinese planners and regulators to maintain ultimate control on the Chinese side. Chinese regulators believed that giving up more than 50% ownership and control to the MNC would mean giving up the state's capacity to regulate the sector for the public good; and to ensure stable growth and meet the welfare needs of a sector (transportation) that is ultimately about the "needs of the common people".[10]

The 1994 AIP also maintained the exclusion of foreign participation in the distribution and sales of vehicles. As a result, the MNCs had to rely on their Chinese partners for distribution and sales, that is, their return on investment. The goal, for Chinese planners, was to forge a "serious developmental partnership" between large Chinese SOEs and the leading foreign automakers.

The 1994 AIP reflects a clear desire to target only "the best" and the "biggest" MNCs as partners for the next wave of JVs. Clause 28 states that, in utilizing foreign direct investment (FDI) to establish a new assembly facility, the Chinese auto group must choose a foreign automaker with the following characteristics:

1. Have its own product patent and trademark rights (read: famous brand)
2. Own product development and production technology, and have a product technology index that conforms with the current legislation in its country of origin (read: have world-leading and export-ready technology)
3. Own an independent international sales network (read: export-ready)
4. Have superior financing ability (read: no more cash-strapped firms, and capacity to raise more financing, as needed, for the JV)

The message of Clause 28 is that only world-leading automotive MNCs need apply for the JV bids in future.

The other important change in the governance of MNCs in the 1994 AIP was that it stipulated that the foreign automakers were allowed to partner with two Chinese automotive companies. This loosening of the JV partnership arrangements under the 1994 AIP opened the way for Chinese auto groupings to also form JV partnerships with more than one foreign MNC, although this decision was not stated explicitly in the AIP for the Chinese side. The benefit of not declaring the number of partnerships was that it allowed for open and flexible interpretation. According to one Chinese planner, "the Chinese government did not, and has not since, placed any formal limitations on the Chinese companies in finding multiple foreign partners. This encouraged, for example, SAIC to form numerous foreign partnerships, with VW and GM only being the largest and at the assembler level. SAIC has also formed numerous important partnerships with foreign parts producers".[11] Moreover, although the 1994 AIP loosened the JV partnering restrictions, the Chinese authorities did not allow the MNC to have unlimited partnerships. The same NDRC planner said, "the Chinese industrial structure for the auto industry was already too decentralized, too fragmented with small companies spread throughout the country, lacking in economies of scale. If we allowed the MNCs to establish JVs with three Chinese partners, for example, this would have resulted in 18 JVs, which is too many, since China already has over 100 companies involved in the assembly of automobiles at the time".[12] The regulator's objective was to encourage "managed [market] competition" in the domestic auto industry, while avoiding excess duplication and excess diffusion of technology.

The 1994 AIP gave stiffer parts localization requirements than in the previous AIP (1985), however, it also gave more preferential duty rates for the ventures that could meet the higher local parts requirements. The new JVs would need to start operations with 40% local content, and in so doing, would qualify for 37.5% import duties on the remaining imported parts. JVs that reached 60–80% local content rates were allowed to import parts at 30% and 20% import duties. Proposals to establish a new JV assembly project were required to include a localization plan for the first and second years of operations. For vehicles that were classified as "imported vehicles", the 1994 AIP also provided different tariff rates related to higher or lower local parts inputs, with lower tariffs if more local parts were used in the "imported", "completely knocked-down" or "semi-knocked-down" kits. Central regulators further supported the localization conditions in the 1994 AIP with local content policy in the 9th Five-Year Plan (FYP) (1996–2000), that stated that new passenger car projects should not be started unless the unit parts (engine and transmission) and related parts were locally available at the start of the project, and that the local content rate for the vehicle must exceed 40% at the launch of the JV. The 9th FYP also gave detailed statements about the types of support (financial, taxation, policy, and administrative) that the government would give to further develop the parts industry.[13] One state planner remarked that the goal behind the localization and JV requirements, and support, was, on the one hand, to encourage the MNCs to extend their value chains more fully to China; on the other hand, it was to deter the MNCs from establishing new links in their value chains outside of China, and to contain the desire of the MNCs to establish "their own" (wholly foreign-owned) production and assembly facilities inside China.[14]

Clause 31 in the 1994 AIP outlined the following upgraded requirements for foreign support in R&D:

1. A technological R&D center must be established within the new company, and the new center must be able to develop the designs for product changes and new models.
2. The JV must be able to make products equivalent to current technology standards (early 1990s).
3. The JV must intend to export products and achieve foreign currency balance.
4. Chinese parts producers should receive equal consideration as parts suppliers.

This section of the AIP also stated that the Chinese government would support joint R&D on vital projects. The AIP further stated that the JVs should hire and train local engineers. It should be noted that during the first wave of JVs, it was not only the foreign partner that tended to ignore R&D, but also the domestic Chinese assemblers who were focused instead on acquiring and applying the new technologies and were challenged enough with trying to meet higher production targets and quality standards.[15] Local governments, feeling pressured to spur local industrialization and growth, also funneled their financing support into machinery imports and integration, in order to drive output numbers and they also neglected R&D.[16] The onus on R&D requirements in the 1994 AIP was thus meant to remedy the neglegence on all sides, with the new JVs.

Give and Take for Global Purchasing at Shanghai GM

The changes in government–MNC relations that resulted from the shift in thinking about the regulatory approach—and with the implementation of the 1994 AIP—could also be seen in the outcome of the negotiations over the second JV for SAIC. General Motors Corporation eventually prevailed, and it agreed to a record-breaking investment deal. However, Ford and Toyota were also in the running. Chinese authorities pushed the three bidders to transfer comprehensive technology and know-how to China, in addition to capital, and GM decided it was in its long-term corporate interests to meet, and eventually even exceed the demands of the Chinese authorities in the negotiations. Their winning bid actually exceeded the demands when GM decided to work proactively with its network of key component suppliers to invest in China to build a modern supply network to feed the new JV with sophisticated and high value-added components manufactured inside China. Local state authorities in Shanghai also pressed GM to make the necessary final concessions in the negotiations, after they had coached the foreign automaker on how to engage central authorities.

GM agreed to a record-breaking investment of more than US $1.5 billion, for a 50/50 JV with SAIC—called Shanghai GM—that included a new US $1 billion state-of-the-art assembly plant, to produce cutting-edge luxury sedans at the new factory. In fact, the GM deal far exceeded the minimum requirements for foreign investment in the 1994 AIP, including an agreement to increase production capacity to 3,000,000 vehicles per year, production of a mid-range luxury car modeled on the Buick sedan, and production and soft technology for a full line of modern vehicles to be built on entirely new production lines. GM also agreed to customize vehicles for the Chinese market, exceed localization requirements, have GM colleagues at the JV work alongside Chinese engineers and managers, and establish a new R&D center (Faison 1998).

However, the concessions did not run only one way. GM also demanded, in exchange for agreeing to transfer the latest technology, that the Chinese government agree to build the highways and roads that would allow for the growth of the local car market, and support the development of a steady logistics and distribution network which was needed for GM to set up its modern just-in-time production systems in the new Shanghai facility. GM demanded more operational space than the previous MNCs, and the Chinese authorities agreed. The clearest empirical example of the increased space to operate was GM's request that Shanghai GM adhere to GM's "QSP system". GM executives were aware that the biggest start-up challenge in establishing the new Shanghai JV was meeting the localized parts requirements, of the 1994 AIP, at the start of operations. Louis Hughes, Senior Vice President International for GM, stated in a speech to the mayor and seven vice mayors of Shanghai that, at a minimum, the localization requirements meant that a company had to reach 40% local content overall, and reach 60% on three-of-five major subsystems: body, engine, transmission, front suspension, and HVAC (heating, ventilation, and air conditioning).[17] Hughes impressed upon China's national and Shanghai leaders that using GM's global QSP system was "essential for fostering a world-class automotive industry in China, in Shanghai".[18] The Chinese side agreed, and SAIC consented to GM's request to make it a contractual obligation for their new JV to abide by GM's QSP system. The

GM China team then went about implementing the purchasing system with their Chinese managerial counterparts at the JV. GM's QSP system was thus used to establish quality standards for the lean production system that GM introduced into China. With this system, the JV made purchasing decisions based on (global) standard procedures of supplier evaluation, with a specific budget for every component on the worldwide average price for the component. This sourcing system became the foundation for building the market competitiveness of Shanghai GM.

In exchange for the right to source globally using its QSP system, GM encouraged its affiliated parts suppliers such as Delphi Automotive Systems to increase their investment in China. Delphi, which had already employed around 3500 people in Shanghai, was the only foreign components supplier that was manufacturing mass original equipment inside China for export. Delphi increased its investment further, and its number of employees, and the two Delphi JVs (China-based) acquired QS9000 status (the globally recognized indicator of a high-quality supplier). Delco Electronics, which had merged with Delphi, established 11 JVs and 2 wholly owned manufacturing plants inside China. By 1997, Delphi's total investment in China exceeded US $250 million. Hughes remarked that Delphi's growing footprint inside China was a further indication of how the "GM group", as a whole, was assisting China's automotive modernization efforts.[19]

Unintended Outcome

A third institutionalized outcome, in terms of changing government–MNCs, involved Toyota. The Japanese automaker made a number of key shifts in corporate strategy in the mid- to late-1990s, when it finally decided to share its technology and know-how with the most privileged Chinese automaker, FAW. The 1994 AIP and GM's success in securing the JV deal with SAIC were crucial in forcing Toyota to finally invest large-scale in China, which led to its partnerships with FAW. The temporary freeze on investment in assembly projects that came prior to the 1994 AIP suggested that future investment freezes were a possibility. Also, it was unclear what the negotiations over China's accession to the World Trade Organization (WTO) would mean for foreign investors in the auto sector. These factors, combined with the speed and scope by which China's domestic auto market was growing by the late 1990s, spurred the Japanese latecomers to take action. Although Honda was actually the first to react, moving into Guangzhou in 1998, Toyota's first major moves occurred through its longtime alliance with Tianjin Xiali. Senior officials in Beijing delivered the message that they expected to see a shift in corporate strategy from Toyota, compared to its hesitancy about investing in China when it was approached by Chinese leaders in the past. Vice Premier Wu Bangguo, and SPC Chair Zeng Peiyan, emphasized that the Chinese government expected that any future investments from Toyota would contribute to China's national development and market transition.

From 1995 to 1999, Toyota and its affiliated suppliers made a number of investments, in new JVs with Tianjin Xiali Automotive Group (TAG) to produce parts and components such as universal joints, castings, and steering components. Toyota invested US $321 million into these ventures. Toyota helped to upgrade its existing parts JV, Tianjin Toyota Motor Engine Corporation (but did not transfer engine design or modification capacity), and it invested another US $132 million to create the Toyota China Technology Center in Tianjin, ostensibly to train Chinese suppliers and to build a network of dealers, service facilities, and vehicle repair centers (Chin 2010: 194). By 2000, over 30 of Toyota's Japanese suppliers had a presence in the Tianjin area. In May 2000, after seven years of negotiations, Toyota and TAG were given approval to establish a new JV, Tianjin Toyota Motor Corporation. Toyota then transferred a substantial portion of its technology and know-how to build the popular economy-sized Vios model, and set up several other JVs with Chinese parts suppliers to feed its assembly JV. In 2001, Toyota also invested US $67 million in Sichuan province to establish a new JV to produce compact buses (Chin 2010: 195). Toyota said that the decision to invest in the Western region was not only a business opportunity, but also a concrete demonstration of its support to the Chinese leadership's national goal of developing China's Western region. It appeared that, like VW and GM before, Toyota had come around to understanding how taking a longer-term business approach to China, that concurred with the national development interests of the Chinese state would be beneficial to its corporate interests over the longer-term.

In March 2002, FAW acquired TAG, in a move that surprised Toyota. For Toyota, FAW's acquistion meant that its Chinese partner was upgraded dramatically. Working with FAW, which Toyota had spurned in the 1980s and early 1990s, Toyota proceeded to jointly produce a line of vehicles, ranging from economy mini-cars to mid-sized luxury models to SUVs.[20] Toyota also shared its technology with FAW to build a new line of *Hongqi* (Red Flag) models. The Soviet-era limousine that had transported Mao Zedong and the most senior Chinese Communist Party leaders of that era was by then very outdated. Toyota's decision to allow FAW to produce a version of the Toyota "Crown Majesta" (Lexus GS in the United States), and not to charge management fees on purchases of spare parts, essentially saved the *Hongqi* brand. In 2006, Toyota helped FAW to add another model to the *Hongqi* fleet, a reworked model of the Mazda 6, which FAW named, "Besturn".

Toyota also partnered with FAW to produce a smaller *Hongqi* model, which was assembled on the same line as FAW-Toyota Vizi and Vela (adaptations of the Toyota Echo). However, the Japanese automaker did not achieve the success of Shanghai GM in localizing. In retrospect, one can question whether Toyota was actually fully commited to transferring the highest value-added segments of the value chain to China. Japanese researchers found that, even into the mid-2000s, domestic Chinese suppliers had made few inroads in supplying the more sophisticated components and higher value-added parts for the models assembled in Toyota's JV in Tianjin, even with FAW as its partner. According to Toyota management, the main reason was that Chinese suppliers could not meet the quality standards demanded by Toyota, and the Japanese management preferred to continue sourcing the key inputs from their traditional suppliers in Japan, within their *keiretsu* network. Chinese suppliers were only supplying the low-tech labor-intensive parts to the plant in Tianjin (Chin 2010: 207). The Chinese management responsible for purchasing was embarrassed by the limited local contribution. The fact that Toyota was able to operate to the extent even though it had created a pattern of limited transfers of the highest value-added segments of the value chain, that was observable by researchers, suggests that the Japanese automaker was also given substantial room (space) to operate, after the JV was negotiated and launched. That Toyota had responded to the Chinese government's demands by agreeing to substantial technology, know-how and capital transfers, and had received, in return, significant operational space for its day-to-day operations, are both intended outcomes. However, the lack of transfer of the highest value-added segments of the value chain was an unintended result for the Chinese side. After Chinese authorities highlighted the shortfall in parts localization at the Toyota JV, the Japanese automaker knew enough about the local political environment to issue statements to the Chinese media that Toyota intended to increase local inputs in its China-based JV projects in the future.

Concluding Remarks

The discussion above makes three main points. First, important changes in the relations between the Chinese government and leading multinational corporations occurred from the mid-1990s to the mid-2000s. Second, in this period, important shifts occurred in the Chinese state's approach to regulating foreign MNCs, especially in sectors that state planners deemed "strategic", in terms of attracting foreign investment, namely the energy, transportation, raw materials, and agriculture sectors. Third, these regulatory changes led to the emergence of new patterns of government–business relations.

In addition to holding relevance in the 1990s, one can also discern the longer-term resonance of the changes in the pattern of government–business relations that emerged in China's auto sector in the 1990s. Especially relevant is how the pattern of two-way trade-offs between the government and the MNCs, that was detailed above, has continued to be an underlying pattern in the governance relations between the Chinese government and the MNCs in the sectors where the government is still targeting the leading foreign corporations for special national developmental service for China. In the automotive sector, the MNCs continue to demand more room to operate, day to day, and the ability to organize their business and operations according to market dynamics or global business procedures. In turn, the leading MNCs have continued to respond relatively constructively to the government's latest national development demands, which in the auto sector, has shifted focus to the co-design and joint development of new vehicle models, especially environment-friendly vehicles and technology.

Buoyed by what the Chinese planners perceive as the relatively successful outcomes that resulted from the 1994 AIP, Chinese strategists formulated another AIP that was issued in 2004. This time, the 2004 AIP again targeted technology transfers from foreign partners, but placed more emphasis on developing the capacity for indigenous innovation. The government also highlighted the development of indigenous brands in the Eleventh FYP (2006–2010). Since 2004, there was also a subtle shift in the government's approach to further developing the automotive sector, shifting from high reliance on foreign capital, technology, and know-how to giving more support to nurturing domestic automakers, with greater consideration to productivity, efficiency, and economies of scale, and more willingness to support dynamic *private* Chinese automakers.

However, the government has continued to lean on the MNCs for some of its key developmental objectives. More recently, the Chinese government has "declared war" on pollution as part of its efforts to upgrade the economy, shift away from heavy industry, and improve living conditions in China. Automobiles are one of the major contributors to air pollution in the country, and the government has offered financial incentives to automakers to develop more environmentally friendly vehicles—especially electric-powered vehicles. In April 2014, the government announced a RMB 10 billion (US $1.61 billion) fund to support companies to develop new green and low-carbon technologies to cut fossil fuel use and reduce the use of non-renewables. The Chinese government is offering subsidies that reach as high as RMB 114,000 (US $17,500) per vehicle for highly electrified vehicles, and have exempted these vehicles from the license plate restrictions (traffic congestion control measures) in major cities.

VW, the first-mover in the 1980s, and the only successful case in the early lot, has stepped up again, promising initially that it would introduce more than 15 electric or plug-in hybrid vehicles to China by 2018, and that it would produce many of the models locally. It has subsequently said (October 2014) that it will launch more than 20 models of electric cars in China over the next period.[21] VW is, however, now in catch-up mode, inside China. As early as 2008, Build Your Dreams ("BYD") Company introduced its hybrid plug-in car, F3DM, and in 2009, Chery Automobile introduced its first electric car, the S18. Of the major foreign brands, Toyota was the first to unveil its FT-HT concept car, a four-door six-seat hybrid, designed for the Chinese market in 2013.[22] The model (also known as Yuejia in China), was designed for family trips, and features a powertrain, Yundon-Showanchin II, based on Toyota's latest hybrid technology and developed by Toyota Motor Engineering Corporation (in China). Even though Toyota's hybrids are not eligible for the customer incentives from the Chinese authorities, the Japanese automaker appears to have doubled-down on the hybrid models in the Chinese market.[23] In contrast, VW is taking a more conciliatory line with the Chinese authorities. VW said (in March 2014) that it had planned to develop and build a new, environmentally friendly vehicle with FAW, after talks between Chinese President Xi Jinping and German Chancellor Angela Merkel. In Shanghai, speaking to reporters, (October 2014) where the German automaker was launching a week-long campaign to promote e-mobility in China's financial hub, Jochem Heizmann, head of VW China said, "In the near future, Volkswagen will be offering Chinese drivers over 20 NEVs, from small cars to large-sized SUVs, from plug-in hybrids to pure electric cars".[24] In pursuing these goals, especially in offering pure electric cars in China, VW lags behind its global rivals BMW, Tesla Motors, and Nissan.[25] Daimler and its local partner BYD Corporation started selling their Denza electric vehicle in 2014. Europe's biggest carmaker is somewhat of a late starter in producing environmentally friendly cars in China, even though the country is its number one market, and accounted for one-third of its record 9.7 million global deliveries in 2013. Undeterred, VW is moving ahead by introducing a plug-in hybrid (combing a gasoline engine and electric motor) in China, with its Chinese partner FAW.[26] VW says that its hybrid can travel longer distances on battery power than ordinary hybrids, and the German automaker sees a large potential market given the desire of the Chinese leaders to fight hazardous levels of air pollution. According to *Reuters*, production of the FAW-VW hybrid is likely to be at their new assembly plant in Foshan, Guangdong province, in southern China. At Shanghai VW, the German automaker is also teaming up with SAIC to co-design and co-develop green cars, as VW's next generation of car models, globally. VW signed an agreement with SAIC in 2015 on e-mobility research, and Shanghai VW, their JV, is expanding its main plant in Anting to accommodate the production of new electric and plug-in hybrid models. In total, VW will introduce 15 plug-in cars in the four-year period of 2015–2019, and the first all-electric Volkswagen vehicle in China will be available for sale "in about four years" (2019).

The other leading market actor in China, GM, has taken a somewhat rocky road to e-cars in China. In autumn 2011, the American automaker seemingly promised,[27] and then un-promised to manufacture its newest electric car in China, stating that it had only agreed to produce new green car technology in China, implying its desire to protect its intellectual property.[28] However, in March 2016, GM announced that it would roll out more than 60 new or refreshed models in China in the next five years, and the GM President added in a briefing in Beijing, that the U.S. automaker would also introduce electric and hybrid models, and autonomous-driving technology.[29]

Although Toyota may be foot-dragging on pure e-vehicles, it is playing a pioneering role on the green finance front in China. In an important move that also corresponds to the pattern of relations between the Chinese government and the MNCs discussed above, foreign automakers are becoming active in the green bond market, and raised US $2.5 billion in 2016 to finance electric and hybrid vehicle production in China. In May 2016, Toyota's financing arm sold US $1.6 billion in green bonds to fund consumer purchases and leases of energy efficient Toyota and Lexus vehicles. This represented an especially bold move as the Japanese carmaker had originally intended to only sell US $1.2 billion in green bonds.[30] Chinese automaker Geely Group (headquartered in Zhejiang province) also raised US $400 million in May 2016, in a green bond sale, to finance the development of zero-emission black cabs for the UK. The demand for the bond was strong as the bond was six-times oversubscribed. According to green fund managers, such as TIAA-CREF Social Choice Bond Fund (which holds US $75 million of Toyota's green fund), other automakers are expected to come to market with green bonds in China.

In summary, the more market-oriented regulatory approach and the ensuring two-way trade-offs—between the government and MNCs—that emerged in the 1990s have continued to underlay the 2005 AIP and government–MNC relations in the automotive sector, into the contemporary period, where the much-needed push, now, is on designing and developing the technology and know-how for green cars. Future research can be directed to detailing the transformative impact of changing government-MNC relations in other industrial sectors, and during the same time period. The 1990s and the first decade of the 2000s also turned out to be a key period of catch-up modernization in other transport sectors such as aerospace and aircraft manufacturing, and railways and trains. Comparative analysis of the variations and similarities in Chinese government-MNC relations and evolving state-corporate governance patterns across these sectors should feature at the core of future research.

Notes

1. It should be noted that the reality of the Indian auto market as one of the largest markets worldwide for lower cost, small cars is another key factor for the limited capacity for large car manufacturing in the country.
2. Author's interview of Stefan Messmann.
3. On post-Fordist innovations see Bernard (2000).
4. *Zhongguqichebao* [China Automotive News], January 4, 1990, p. 3.
5. Stefan Messmann was also the former head of VW's China/Asia operations during the late 1980s.
6. Correspondence from Stefan Messmann with the author, August 2008.
7. For the details of the technology and know-how transfers in the FAW-VW deal, and the additional transfers from VW to FAW beyond the JV, that were associated with the deal, see Chin (2010: 149–150).
8. He, Guangyuan, "Mingque mubiao wanshan zhanlue tuijin jixie qiche chanye de zhenxing [Clarify goals, improve strategy, invigorate the mechanical and automobile industry], *Gongcheng jianshe yu sheji* [Project construction and design], 3, 1993, pp. 2–5.
9. This conceptual point builds on the thinking of Amsden (1989), Chang (1996), Johnson (1982), Katzenstein (1985), Kohli (2004) and Wade (1990) on the role of the state in national development.

10. Author's interview with NDRC automotive industry researcher, Beijing, January 2006.
11. Author's interview with a leading researcher at the Academy of Macroeconomic Research of the NDRC, Beijing, May 2006.
12. Ibid.
13. For details see (Chin 2010: 122).
14. Author's interview with NDRC automotive industry researcher, Beijing, January 2006.
15. Ibid.
16. Ibid.
17. Notes on the presentation by GM Executive Vice President Louis Hughes on "GM's Strategic Plans in China and Developing Shanghai's Automotive Industry", November 2, 1997.
18. Ibid.
19. Author's interview with Louis Hughes, September 2008.
20. For the details see Chin (2010: 197–98).
21. http://www.reuters.com/article/volkswagen-ecars-idUSB9N0ME02920141028
22. http://www.chinadaily.com.cn/business/motoring/2013-04/26/content_16452465.htm
23. http://www.bloomberg.com/news/articles/2016-04-24/toyota-doubling-down-on-hybrids-despite-china-s-subsidies-snub
24. http://www.reuters.com/article/volkswagen-ecars-idUSB9N0ME02920141028
25. http://www.reuters.com/article/volkswagen-ecars-idUSB9N0ME02920141028
26. http://www.d1ev.com/30260.html
27. http://www.reuters.com/article/us-gm-china-idUSTRE78J36U20110920
28. http://www.ictsd.org/bridges-news/biores/news/too-many-strings-attached-to-chinese-electric-car-subsidy-gm
29. http://www.wsj.com/articles/general-motors-gears-up-in-china-amid-shifting-demand-1458559757
30. http://greenautomarket.com/

References

Amsden, A. (1989). *Asia's next giant: South Korea and late industrialization*. New York: Oxford University Press.

Bernard, M. (2000). Post-Fordism and global restructuring. In R. Stubbs & G. Underhill (Eds.), *Political economy and the changing global order* (pp. 152–162). Toronto: Oxford University Press.

Chang, H.-J. (1996). *The political economy of industrial policy*. London: Macmillan.
Chin, G. T. (2010). *China's automotive modernization: The party-state and multinational corporations*. Basingstoke: Palgrave Macmillan.
Faison, S. (1998). GM opens Buick plant in Shanghai. *The New York Times, 18*, 1.
Gallagher, K. S. (2006). *China shifts gears: Oil, pollution and development*. Cambridge, MA: MIT Press.
He, G. (1993). Mingque mubiao wanshan zhanlue tuijin jixie qiche chanye de zhenxing [Clarify goals, improve strategy, and invigorate the mechanical and automobile industry]. *Gongcheng jianshe yu sheji [Project construction and design], 3*, 2–5.
Johnson, C. (1982). *MITI and the Japanese miracle: The growth of industrial policy, 1925–1975*. Stanford: Stanford University Press.
Katzenstein, P. J. (1985). *Small states in world markets: Industrial policy in Europe*. Ithaca: Cornell University Press.
Perkowski, J. (2008). *Managing the dragon*. New York: Crown Business.
Ray, S., & Miglani, S. (2016). *Innovation (and Upgrading) in the Automobile Industry: The Case of India*. ICRIER Working Paper No.320, May.
Thun, E. (2006). *Changing lanes in China: Foreign direct investment, local governments, and auto sector development*. Cambridge: Cambridge University Press.
Wade, R. (1990). *Governing the market: Economic theory and the role of government in east Asian industrialization*. Princeton: Princeton University Press.

CHAPTER 4

Regional Business Associations in China: Changes and Continuities

Juanfeng Liu and Jianjun Zhang

Introduction

If the remarkable growth of the private sector in China is one of the most striking socio-economic changes since the onset of market-oriented reforms in the late 1970s, burgeoning business associations have constituted another profound social and political development associated with the process. From less than 1000 associations in the early years of the reform, their number had soared to about 70,000 by 2015. The relationship between the Chinese state and business associations has been experiencing dramatic changes since the turn of the century.

In 2007, the State Council required business associations to be decoupled from the government. Several years later, the government also dispensed with the requirement that societal organizations be registered with and regulated by both the civil affairs authorities and state agencies in functional areas in which they operated. In 2015, it formulated a radical

J. Liu (✉)
School of International Relations, University of International Business and Economics, Beijing, China

J. Zhang
Guanghua School of Management, Peking University, Beijing, China

X. Zhang, T. Zhu (eds.), *Business, Government and Economic Institutions in China*, International Political Economy Series,
DOI 10.1007/978-3-319-64486-8_4

and far-reaching plan to transform the relationship between the state and business associations, particularly those that were affiliated with the government. According to the plan, associations were to be registered with the civil affairs authorities as independent organizations which would no longer receive any government funding in 2018 and, more importantly, would make personnel, financial, and managerial decisions on their own. This suggests that the state has been prepared to further relax its controls over business associations that can be expected to act as an increasingly important institutional linkage between government and private businesses and exert growing influence over public policy processes.

Despite these national-level regulatory and policy changes, business associations have displayed crucial variations across regions, in terms of their organizational structures and their interactions with state agencies. We argue that these regional variations have primarily derived from distinctive sub-national approaches to restructuring the local economy and governing development processes. To sustain this argument, we focus on Wuxi in Jiangsu Province and Wenzhou in Zhejiang Province that have varied significantly in state–business association relations and in the corresponding pattern of economic development.

In Wuxi, business associations that are largely funded and controlled by the local government have weakened the role of private entrepreneurs in influencing the evolution of business–state ties and socio-economic developments. By contrast, many grass-roots business associations initiated and led by private entrepreneurs themselves have emerged forcefully and played active roles in the process of local socio-economic changes in Wenzhou. These associations have helped enhance the economic power of private business, although they have remained relatively passive in political arenas. The different roles of business associations in these two cities are an important function of their divergent development patterns: government-led development in Wuxi and local entrepreneur-initiated development in Wenzhou. We argue that the growth of private entrepreneurship and the spread of market-oriented socio-economic relations, together with the willingness of state actors to allow societal groups and entities to operate in a relatively liberal political and policy environment, are the primary conditions for the emergence and development of strong business associations in China.

The balance of this chapter is divided into five sections. In the first section, we briefly review a few theoretical approaches to examining state–business relations and critically assess their applicability in the analysis of regional variations in business associations in China. We then explore major differences in the dominant pattern of local socio-economic development between Wuxi and Wenzhou and their connections with the changing variation of business associations' organizational structures and linkages with state actors in the second and third sections. Finally, we present a focused comparison of changing interactions between business associations and local governments in the two cities before discussing theoretical implications in the concluding section.

Theoretical Considerations

In this section, we provide a brief critique of extant theoretical approaches to examine state–business relations in China—corporatism, pluralism, and clientelism. The focus will be on how well each of these approaches can help us understand the changing variety of state–business association relations, particularly at the sub-national level of analysis.

Much of the existing scholarship tends to categorize state–business relations in China as a state corporatist system (Lee 1991; Pearson 1997; Dickson 2003; Kennedy 2005). A common understanding among China scholars is that the corporatist relationship has remained largely intact, despite the fact that business associations and other intermediary organizations have developed rapidly and extensively during the reform era (Yang 2013). According to the definition provided by Schmitter (1974), a corporatist system has at least four features: limited autonomy of associations, compulsory membership, hierarchical organization, and jurisdictional monopoly. Most business associations in China, especially those that are initiated or tightly supervised by the government, do not have an autonomous ability to manage personnel affairs, secure financial resources, and formulate policy directions. Memberships in few government-funded and controlled associations are compulsory. Some associations set up by government agencies are hierarchically structured with local and industrial branches. Moreover, the government requires that there should be only one association for each industry at each locale (*yi di yi ye yi hui*).

In China, many regulations on the operation of non-governmental organizations have been specifically directed toward business associations. State officials have often expressed concerns over the rising influence and role of business associations that have partly stemmed from the rapid growth of the private sector, especially after China's admission to the WTO. Both the central and local governments in China have played a key role in initiating, directing, and financing business associations. Dozens of national-level business associations (mainly industry guilds and entrepreneurs' associations) have come under the direct oversight of different ministries and commissions of the central government. Local governments have established many business associations that operate across industries and consist of firms of various ownership forms. Private businesspeople are encouraged persuaded, or even forced to join these associations. In this sense, China has both state and societal corporatist arrangements. The government has attached growing importance to the bridging role of business associations, as its ability to regulate the increasingly market-oriented economy has weakened. On the other hand, private entrepreneurs have used business associations as an important institutional mechanism to advance their policy and economic interests.

However, the corporatist model has failed to capture the full dynamics of changing state–business relations in China. Kennedy even suggests that "corporatism is a poor description of government-business relations in China" (2005: 44). The corporatist depiction of relations between the state and business associations have paid inadequate attention to the complexity of such relations. While business associations may generally lack operational autonomy from government, their membership is not completely compulsory, hierarchical structures may be weak in some sectors and regions, and jurisdictional monopoly has never been prevalent. For instance, associations at the higher administrative level do not have authority over those at the lower level, although their relationships are hierarchically ordered. Similarly, while sectoral associations are often required to join industry-wide business organizations, the former are not subordinate to the latter.[1]

In recent years, the role of business associations has been scrutinized and criticized by both government officials and business leaders. They have contended that associations should defend the interests of their members.[2] Several waves of administrative reforms have significantly weakened the traditional dirigiste approach to steering economic development associated with the central planning era. Business associations that once operated as "secondary government agencies" in the command economy have now been urged to become more autonomous. Furthermore, the rapid and sustained growth of more than three decades has fostered the emergence of numerous private entrepreneurs. They have had an inherent need to organize themselves to tackle various socio-economic problems and, more importantly, enhance their bargaining power vis-à-vis that of the government.

China might have strong corporatist arrangements in the past, but the country's growing integration with the world economy and sustained market-oriented reforms have weakened these arrangements. First, private entrepreneurs have often preferred to approach the government via personal networks since the beginning of the economic reform in the 1980s. The wealthiest and most successful business entrepreneurs usually have had multiple channels through which they solve their economic and political problems. Second, newly emerging business associations that are more independent of government controls have become increasingly influential both at home and abroad. As corporatism provides an inadequate analytical tool for examining and understanding changing state–business relations, scholars have turned to the pluralist perspective.

In a pluralist system, the characteristics of business associations are vastly different from those of their counterparts in a corporatist system. Associations are established and led by business actors themselves and compete in a free and horizontally structured society. They are free to articulate and defend their members' interests, even when these interests conflict with those of the state. In this sense, pluralism means a plurality of routes of access to the political system. Pluralism also suggests that the state has limited influence and control over business associations, as they are voluntary and independent. The growing variety of private businesses' access to policy-making processes, particularly at regional and local levels, suggests that the current configuration of state–association relations is increasingly tinged with pluralism. The number of business associations with increased operational autonomy has been growing over the past decades. The recent government plan to decouple business associations from state agencies has strengthened the pluralist tendencies.

While the pluralist perspective has revealed important changes in state–business relations in China, it has a number of theoretical and empirical weaknesses. In the first place, there are still significant political constraints on the autonomy of many business associations, particularly with regard to their ability to manage personnel and financial issues. Yang (2013) has argued that business associations would have to completely accept the leadership of the Chinese Communist Party (CCP) as a primary precondition for their existence. Furthermore, chairpersons or secretaries general of many business associations are de facto government officials or hold important positions in state agencies. This has allowed state policy-makers to continue exerting influence over the operation of associations, even though many are not affiliated with the government. Finally, private firms and their interest-representing organizations are still facing formal and informal obstacles to their participation in public policy processes; they are more capable of making policy proposals than influencing the actual formulation of policies themselves.

It is clear from the above that the reality of state–associations relations does not easily fit with the theoretical assumptions of the pluralist model. Leaders of business associations are acutely aware that their ability to promote the interests of member firms and influence policy processes is contingent on the continuation of close affiliation with government. As a result, they have been keen to operate under the auspices of political leaders, invite policy-makers to attend their meetings, and organize their activities collaboratively with state agencies. For a similar reason, business leaders have also had strong incentives to be delegates to local people's congresses or political consultative conferences. By the same token, private entrepreneurs know only too well that enhanced access to government is of great importance to the success of their businesses and sometimes even their survival. Many of them have thus spared no effort to establish and cultivate *guanxi* connections with government officials.

This last point suggests that clientelism may also provide a useful theoretical perspective for understanding government–business interactions in general and state–associations relations in particular. Direct and personal interactions have always been an important route of policy influence for private businesses in China. Private entrepreneurs have generally relied on informal and personalized mechanisms to pursue their business interests. In the early years of market reforms, they had to do so when the official status of the private sector was still politically controversial (Tsai 2007). The importance of such mechanisms has not significantly declined; if anything, private businesses have further strengthened their *guanxi* connections with state policy-makers, particularly at the sub-national level.

In this sense, the clientelist model appears to be a plausible analytical instrument to describe and explain the dynamics of state–business relations in the Chinese political economy. It is interesting to note that business associations that act as bridges between government and business have become crucial channels through which government officials and businessmen get acquainted with each other and develop patron–client relationships. An official from the Ministry of Commerce admitted that he had been frequently invited to attend meetings of business associations or even board meetings of specific companies (author interview). A leader from a national business association also opined that many firms were keen to join business associations, mainly because they knew that associations would provide them with a good opportunity to get to know and establish personal connections with government officials (author interview).

The prevalence of *guanxi* connections between state and business actors may be a major cause of corruption that has become rampant since the early 1990s.[3] However, national policy processes are not easily subject to clientelist influences. Officials from the central government are more cautious about interactions with the business community. An official from the Ministry of Commerce said that he always declined invitations from business associations or businesspeople except when he was explicitly permitted by his superiors to take part in these activities; but he did not deny that he had many good friends in the business community (author interview). *Guanxi* connections between state and business actors are instrumental in helping firms get their investment plans approved and obtain licenses, bank loans, land, and other resources, which are mainly regulated by local governments. However, at the national level, private entrepreneurs and business associations are less capable of gaining entrée into the government via patron–client relationships and influencing policy-making processes.

State corporatist structures, emerging pluralist relations, and clientelist practices thus have limited application to the comparative analysis of variations in the organizational configuration and external linkages of business associations in China. While limited in different ways, the three theoretical models have tended to adopt an aggregated approach to analyze state–business relations and paid inadequate attention to the causal importance of regional and sectoral differences (Kennedy 2005; Ngo this volume). This is particularly problematic when it comes to the analysis of business associations and their linkages with the state in a country as large and heterogeneous as China. The preceding critical review, in illustrating the limitations of these variables, suggests an alternative analytical framework for understanding regional variations in the development of business associations. The major propositions to be advanced in this chapter build on an integrated focus on the causal connection between local economic development, socio-political institutions, and state–business interactions.

Divergent Development Patterns in Wuxi and Wenzhou

In the late 1970s and early 1980s, decentralization in China created an opportunity for localities to adopt different development paths that reflected divergent resource endowments and government capacities (Oi 1992). There were thus many different local development patterns, among which the Sunan model (with which Wuxi was closely associated[4]) and the Wenzhou models were prominent ones.

Wuxi and Wenzhou have both witnessed fast industrialization and rapid development over the past three decades or so. Yet, the two regions have followed strikingly different paths. Wuxi was characterized by the predominance of collectively owned enterprises (so-called township–village enterprises or TVEs) and the active involvement of local governments in economic development until the late 1990s. As the TVE sector weakened significantly, local governments turned to the establishment of industrial parks and cluster as a new strategy to attract foreign capital and spur economic growth. In Wenzhou, private business was strong from the beginning of the reform and has been a major driving force behind local socio-economic development. When the private sector was dramatically weakened by the 2008–09 global financial crisis and the subsequent global recession, local entrepreneurs joined forces to urge the local government to resuscitate the local economy. Wuxi's development pattern can thus be regarded as government-led, while the Wenzhou development pattern is entrepreneur-initiated. In other words, Wuxi's early development was characterized by marketization without privatization but Wenzhou's development witnessed both marketization and privatization.

Government-Led Development in Wuxi

The 1990s represents a watershed of government-led development in Wuxi. Local governments acted as entrepreneurs in establishing and running enterprises in the 1980s and early 1990s. Oi (1992: 100) explains that "local governments have taken on many characteristics of a business corporation, with officials acting as the equivalent of a board of directors …" and argues that this "merger of state and economy characterizes a new institutional development" that she labels "local state corporatism." From the mid-1990s, local governments began to privatize TVEs and emphasized the development of industrial parks as an important strategy to sustain economic growth. The industrial output of private enterprises in Jiangsu was higher than that in the other provinces in 2011 (China Statistical Yearbook 2012). Local governments withdrew from TVEs as controlling shareholders when many of them got into financial troubles in the 1990s. However, they remained closely involved in the process of local socio-economic development.

The initial conditions for this arrangement included a high rate of collective accumulation from agriculture, a relatively strong industrial base developed during the pre-reform era and a historical legacy of government involvement in socio-economic development (Whiting 2001). With its higher level of agricultural development, strong industrial infrastructures, and geographical proximity to large industrial centers (especially Shanghai), Wuxi was in a strong position to industrialize more rapidly. At the same time, the concentration of resources in the hands of governments enabled them to actively direct the development process. Such historical legacies, together with the new incentive created by the fiscal reform that pushed local governments to generate revenues from local industrial development, stimulated the rapid growth of TVEs (Walder 1995; Li 2005).

Prior to the 1990s, TVEs were not delinked and did not enjoy operational autonomy from local governments. As de facto owners of these enterprises, local governments had a major say in important decisions about resource allocation, investment, profit distribution, management, and most critically, the selection and appointment of managers (Byrd and Lin 1990; Chen 2000). Local governments also acted as coordinators between different TVEs under their supervision, transferring managerial personnel from one enterprise to another and sometimes cross-subsidizing each other. Meanwhile, local governments protected TVEs against the predation from the upper levels of government. Under these circumstances, TVEs and their managers had limited autonomy and little incentive to take initiatives to shape the socio-political environment, including associational arrangements, in which they operated.

However, TVEs ran into difficulties in the mid-1990s (Li and Rozelle 2003; Ho et al. 2000). Local governments then decided to privatize them by first delinking them from government agencies (Yi and Zhao 2001; Zhang 2005). By the early 2000s, many TVEs had been privatized or transformed into shareholding companies. Meanwhile, barriers to the growth of private business were gradually removed (Wen et al. 2013: 222). Joint ventures between foreign and local private firms, many of which were mediated by state agencies, became a new strategic focus of local governments. The key feature of the new Sunan model was the active encouragement of foreign capital that was designed to enhance the vigor of local economic development.

Local governments in Wuxi have taken alternative measures to encourage the economy as the economic situation is changing, without relaxing its involvement and control. On the one hand, the strong legacy of government involvement left local governments and officials with the competence to maintain their heavy influence. On the other hand, foreign capital has become a more important substitute for TVEs, and it takes time for local private business owners to grow and to form its own interest groups. Therefore, government-led development in Wuxi resulted in social conditions that are unfavorable to bottom-up, autonomous associations. First, a dominant government left little room for societal actors to organize. Second, the embrace of foreign capital makes the scenario more complex and difficult for the local private business owners to act collectively.

Entrepreneur-Initiated Development in Wenzhou

By contrast, the Wenzhou pattern incorporates a prominent role for private business and entrepreneur-initiated development (see Nolan and Dong 1990; Forster 1990; Liu 1992a, b; Parris 1993; Whiting 2001; Yuan 1987; Shi et al. 2002). Compared with Wuxi, this was a remote and poor region. As a frontline province on the Taiwan Strait, Wenzhou received negligible state investment after the CCP took power in 1949 due to possible war (Shan 2000).

Consequently, the state sector was small and the collective economy was weak. Local government thus had limited opportunity to extract and control surplus resources from society. According to official statistics, fiscal income per capita in Wenzhou in 1980 was only 30 yuan, about one-tenth of the 286 yuan in Wuxi (Wenzhou Statistic Yearbook 2001; Wuxi Statistics Yearbook 2000). Local governments could barely maintain their basic functions, let alone develop collectively owned enterprises.

Under such circumstances, Wenzhou was forced to rely on people's initiatives for development. From the late Cultural Revolution period, Wenzhouese started to go out to seek opportunities or engage in underground industrial or commercial activities at home. Using Alan Liu's (1992a) phrase, Wenzhou's success can be summarized by "three Ms"—mass initiatives, mobility, and markets. Mass initiatives—initiatives from the people or entrepreneurs—are the essential feature of Wenzhou's development. Governments only played supportive or supplementary roles such as issuing official documents, helping entrepreneurs to get licenses, and so on.

Despite twists and turns due to political and ideological shifts, private business developed rapidly in Wenzhou. The number of private business grew significantly and the importance of the private sector in the local economy increased dramatically. In 2015, more than 96% of industrial enterprises were private (*Communiqué on Major Data of the Third Wenzhou Economic Census No. 3*).[5] According to Zhejiang Bureau of Statistics, in 2011, the private sector accounted for 81.9% of GDP, employed 92.9% of labor force, contributed 82.4% tax, and occupied 79.7% export in Wenzhou. In contrast with Wuxi, private businesses in Wenzhou are independent and autonomous economic entities, and private entrepreneurs are emerging as an independent and vigorous social force.

Market orientation is another important feature of Wenzhou's development. Wenzhou's business and industry all grew out of a market environment. Market competition is the primary mechanism that guides production. Due to Wenzhou's limited industrial base, it developed its labor-intensive consumer products including shoes, garments, cigarette lighters, and glasses (spectacles) as the main industries.

Success in such areas has seen others mimic them, and similar enterprises spring up. Consequently, there was a proliferation of hundreds or even thousands of firms producing similar products within each industry. Small and medium enterprises are prevalent. Among 315,816 industrial firms in 2014, only 4266 (about 1.3%) had sales exceeding five million yuan. By the end of 2010, small and medium enterprises make up for 99.7% of the total enterprises (*Wenzhou Statistical Yearbook*, 2010: 223–4). Such features, combined with imperfect market institutions and ineffective regulations at the early stage of market reform, caused intensive and even chaotic competition. Cut-throat competition, pirating, producing fake or low-quality commodities (the so-called market failure problem) plagued Wenzhou's early development. All these conditions called for new organizations and new mechanisms to coordinate and manage production and competition.

Compared to Wuxi, entrepreneur-initiated development in Wenzhou created favorable social conditions for autonomous associations to develop. First, its vibrant private business and once chaotic competition called for new organizations. Second, its independent and strong capitalist class had the capacity to take initiatives to organize collectively. Third, the historical legacy of "hands-off" government created space for these actors.

Divergent Development Patterns and Different Regional Associations

Different development patterns created different social space and imperatives for business associations to emerge. In Wuxi, associations manifest both state initiative and state will, while in Wenzhou they reflect a pattern of more independent and private initiatives where associations try to meet the needs of their constituents.

Top-Down Business Associations in Wuxi

In Wuxi, the dominant type of business association is that organized in a top-down manner by various government offices and representing the will of government to incorporate societal forces. These associations are essentially government organized non-governmental organizations (GONGOs). A few entrepreneur-organized associations have been overshadowed by GONGOs. During 1980s to 1990s, government agencies organized these associations not on their own initiative or from local necessity, but mainly out of bureaucratic necessity; if the upper levels of government have a particular organizational arrangement, then each subordinate level must have a similar arrangement. As the market economy expanded rapidly after 1990s, local governments help and support to establish business associations for administrative and economic necessity. Therefore, Wuxi has all of the main associations, including the Private Enterprises Association (PEA) and Self-Employed Laborers' Association (SELA), organized by Industry and Commerce Administration Bureau; guilds within some industrial sectors (hangye xiehui), organized by Economic Commission; various levels of Chambers of Commerce, organized by the Federation of Industry and Commerce (FIC); recent Entrepreneurs' Associations, organized by local governments. PEA and SELA are government-organized associations nationwide and are thus rather homogeneous (Unger 1996).

Before 2002, most business associations shared similar characteristics: they are government-organized, funded, and run organizations. When asked if there were any business associations initiated from below, a staff member in a county Industry and Commerce Administration Bureau frankly expressed his surprise, stating that "associations must be organized by the government. Otherwise, how can the people organize associations?" (Interview in Wuxi, May 2002). Apparently, government officials consider grass-roots initiative unimaginable. In addition, the heads and staff of associations were state officials, appointed and remunerated by the government.

Since 2002, complying with the central government policy, Wuxi embarked on a reform of business associations and guilds. In 2003, Wuxi issued the first city-level law—*Ordinance of Wuxi City to Promote the Development of Business Associations and Guilds*—which started the separation of government and business associations and guilds. The latter were required to detach from the former in personnel, office, and finance. The reform was completed by the end of 2006. In 2005, 327 government officials quit their part-time position in business associations and guilds. In 2007, all business associations and guilds were supervised by the Federation of Industry and Commerce of Wuxi. To help business associations and guilds survive and develop after independence from government agents, Wuxi introduced two measures. One is government purchase of services from business associations and guilds. The other is to have the latter undertake certain governmental functions which are considered redundant to government agents and suitable to business associations and guilds (Wang et al. 2012).

Paradoxically, in many towns, taking Wutao town as an example—not the real name of the town—where the director of the PEA is also the deputy director of the town's Industry and Commerce Administration Bureau and the director of SELA is a low-ranking town government official. The Town Entrepreneurs' Association, like other associations here, indicates government's dominance. The town government organized the Association in 2003, and formed the governing body. A deputy town head was appointed as the director of the Association, and a town government employee was responsible for the day-to-day operation as its secretary-general. Some prominent entrepreneurs serve in the standing committee of the Association, but they regard it more as an honor rather than a real commitment to an association that represents their interests. The Association currently serves as an elite club without substantial functions. Its funds are derived from both the town government and membership fees. Like other associations, its establishment was a response to higher-level government's requirement: "the district government asked us to do so," said the deputy party secretary of the town. "In places like ours, it is still impossible for entrepreneurs to organize since they are used to following government. Government has to take initiatives" (Telephone interview, August 2004).

The official purpose of setting up these organizations involves corporatist intentions such as incorporating the new social forces into the existing system, mobilizing business people to fulfill local development targets,[6] listening to their members' concerns and solving problems for them, creating a channel through which members can communicate, and the like. But in reality, such purposes are not achieved effectively. As a matter of fact, local governments pay little attention to associations in Wuxi. Many officials see associations as secondary departments (*er bumen*), subordinated and inferior to other government departments or branches.

Downplayed by government officials, even those heads and staff working in associations see their positions as marginal and try to move to more powerful and resourceful departments. Or more often, they were transferred from other government departments as surplus personnel during rounds of bureaucratic reform.

Entrepreneurs in Wuxi evidence an apathetic attitude toward associations. Almost all entrepreneurs I interviewed considered Wuxi's business associations useless, and had little interest in participating. One entrepreneur expressed his view, "associations are useless. I would rather spend time playing mahjong than attending their activities" (interviews, September 2001 and May 2002). But close scrutiny does find different attitudes. Big and influential businessmen—most of them were former TVE managers—usually looked down upon associations since they have their personal means to reach officials and achieve their purposes. Such personal means came from their close relations with government officials and are a historical legacy of the merger of state and economy, and the current mutual interest between the two groups—businessmen need support from officials for stable social order, public security, and protection from predation of upper-level governments; officials need businessmen to help them realize the target of economic development (Wank 1995).

By contrast, small and less influential businessmen do exhibit an intention to work with associations, hoping to get help and protection from them. But current official associations do not often meet their expectation.

In sum, predominant associations in Wuxi were organized by various government branches in a top-down process, following the administrative hierarchy. From the early years of the new century, local governments began to separate them from government agents. During 1980s to 1990s, they were overlooked by government and turned away from entrepreneurs. Currently, they are expected to survive on their own with little support from government. Most of them have no vitality. Foster pointed out that those associations were embedded in government and served as appendages to government. Nowadays, they are made autonomous with little competence to survive.

Bottom-Up Business Associations in Wenzhou

In contrast to Wuxi's government-organized associations, Wenzhou has a full spectrum of associations: from official government-organized associations, such as SELA and PEA,[7] to semi-official associations and independent associations (for a classification, see White 1993). Compared to official associations, these semi-official and independent business associations are new types of organization in China: they highlight societal initiative and serve their members' interests. Besides various economic functions, they have gradually begun to play some political roles. Their active role once attracted national and international attention in the first decade of this century.

Semi-official business associations mainly include those trade associations within industry (*hangye xiehui*) that were originally organized by government with the support of entrepreneurs. Despite their semi-official status at the outset, these associations became more autonomous over time. For example, *Hangye xiehui* emerged around 1988 when both entrepreneurs and government recognized the necessity for Wenzhou to take action over its low-quality products. As mentioned above, the early stages of Wenzhou's development revealed serious problems with product quality and counterfeiting due to Wenzhou's poor industrial base and ineffective regulation. This led to consumer resistance. For example, Hangzhou publicly burned Wenzhou-made shoes in 1987; Wenzhou produced low-voltage power appliances that caused a number of accidents, resulting in a central government investigation of all enterprises in the industry in 1990 (Hu and Wu 2002). Such problems hurt Wenzhou's reputation and damaged all enterprises. Some enterprises and entrepreneurs thus solicited government action. But government felt ill-prepared to act alone in dealing with numerous private businesses. It was under these circumstances that various industry associations came into being. Economic regulative agencies, such as the Economic Commission, Industry and Commerce Administration Bureau, with the support of leading companies, organized associations to regulate the relevant industry. Some associations were granted certain regulatory rights. Entrepreneurs took an active part in running associations. The emergence and evolution of this type of association will be discussed below in the context of the Lighter Producers' Association.

Independent business associations mainly include trade associations within an industry, and entrepreneurs' associations based on locality across an industry (such as enterprises located in the same town or same county), that were organized and governed by entrepreneurs. Such trade associations were identified as *tongye gonghui* at the beginning changing to *tongye shanghui* (chambers of commerce) later on.

Tongye gonghui appeared around the same time period as *hangye xiehui* and out of similar motives. The Federation of Industry and Commerce (FIC) played a role in encouraging, assisting, and supervising the emergence and activities of such associations. After separation reform in 2008, all business associations are under the supervision of FIC. But more often it was entrepreneurs who took initiatives to organize and then seek support and legitimacy from the FIC. As they have no official status, these associations do not have regulatory functions like semi-official associations. Their main function thus focuses on serving their member enterprises. In the discussion below, the Wenzhou Garment Chamber of Commerce will be used to illustrate this type of association.

As independent organizations, Wenzhou's associations have gained increased social recognition. In contrast with trade associations which focus on economic functions, entrepreneurs' associations have political roles, such as defending members' interests against government predation and the abuse of power and seeking group advantage. The Longgang Entrepreneurs' Association is an example that will be discussed further.[8]

From 2006 to 2008, just like Wuxi, Wenzhou completed the separation of business associations and government agents and all the business associations were affiliated with FIC by 2012 (Cai 2015: 28). Formally, it means all business associations and guilds are autonomous in Wenzhou at present. Many might be encouraged by the independence of business associations and expect a powerful future of them. However, the story is more intricate than expected after the 2008 global financial crisis and local debt crisis in Wenzhou in 2011. Before looking at the new development of business associations after 2008, we'd review the honored history of the autonomous business associations in Wenzhou.

In August 2002, there were 104 trade associations at the city level in Wenzhou (Chen et al. 2004). This number does not include those associations organized at county and township level.[9] Among the 104 associations, 22 were affiliated with the FIC; 31 were with the Economic Commission; others were affiliated with the organizations such as the Construction Bureau, the Science Commission and the Transportation Bureau. In general, associations affiliated with the FIC were all independent associations (tongye gonghui), while associations affiliated with other government branches were originally official or semi-official associations (hangye xiehui). Based on the research conducted by Chen et al. (2004: 142), among the 64 trade associations they studied, 24 were organized by private entrepreneurs, 15 were organized by leading firms in related industries, 24 were organized by the FIC or other government agencies with the involvement of entrepreneurs; only two were completely organized by government.

The Lighter Producers' Association: A Semi-official Association

The Lighter Producers' Association (*yanju xiehui*) was originally a semi-official association. Wenzhou's lighter industry started from the late 1980s. At the beginning, there were only four small enterprises in the industry. But soon after, numerous lighter factories were established and competition soared, resulting in ruthless price cutting, and product quality remained low. Some entrepreneurs were afraid that the industry would lose its market if these problems persisted, and they asked government to take action. The Lucheng district government was persuaded to launch a campaign to bring order to the industry. The Lighter Producers' Association was established to assist government remedial action and regulation of the industry. It is clear that the formation of the Association reflected the "dual impetus" of business and government.

Due to its semi-official status, membership of the Association was made compulsory. To make the Association more effective, the government granted four administrative rights to the Association: pre-screening license applications (effectively, acting as a gate keeper), quality control, setting the lowest price in the industry, and protecting the intellectual property rights of member enterprises. Among these functions, the last is the most effective and most interesting. The Association worked out an efficient and effective way to pursue such a patent-like task. According to the Association's "Code of Conduct" and "Measures to Protect Members' Rights," any member enterprise that wants to apply for protection must submit a sample of a new design to the Association. If the design is accepted as a new one, the Association will post an advertisement in the local Wenzhou Evening News newspaper, with the enterprise receiving a certificate at the same time. Then the enterprise has the exclusive right to use the design for six months. If copies are found, copied products will be confiscated and the producing equipment will be destroyed. For those who violate seriously or frequently, the Association will request the Industry and Commerce Administration

Bureau to suspend or even invalidate their licenses. In the ten years to November 2001, the Association granted 887 exclusive rights to member enterprises. State officials at the Patent Bureau appraised this innovation, viewing it as "an effective complement to the Patent Law," since it saves both time and money (interview in Wenzhou, November 2001).

What earned the Association nationwide reputation is a trade dispute with the EU. In June 2002, the EU decided to investigate dumping charges against Chinese-made cigarette lighters most of which were produced in Wenzhou. If tagged as dumping products, lighter producers in Wenzhou would be deadly damaged—then, the city exported more than 500 million lighters to the EU annually. When the Association and several leading companies in the industry turned to the city government for help, the city government declined it bluntly: "It is inappropriate for government to be involved. Those who benefit should be those who contribute [money to counter the EU action]." The Lighter Producers' Association and leading companies therefore shouldered the whole responsibility, such as collecting contributions from member enterprises, finding lawyers, lobbying the EU, and so on. By frequently consulting experts and state officials in Hangzhou and Beijing, together with their legal experts, the Association went to the EU and worked with their EU partners to lobby. After the EU officials went to Wenzhou in late 2002 to investigate Wenzhou companies, their trade practices and the role of government subsidies, the European Lighter Producers' Federation withdrew its litigation and the anti-dumping investigation was terminated in 2003. The Association had thus enhanced its reputation on the international stage. In all subsequent trade disputes, the Association played a critical role.

The originally semi-official association became more autonomous over time (see also Zhu 2003). The Association proclaims that it practices the principles of "self-discipline, self-governance, and self-funding" to fulfill its purposes of "self-service, self-coordination and self-supervision." Its response to the EU anti-dumping case demonstrates its relatively independent character especially when the overwhelming involvement of government in economic life in China is considered. Though the secretary-general of the Association was from Lucheng District Economic Commission, he receives his salary from the Association. All of the directors and deputy directors are entrepreneurs in the industry, and the Association raises all its own funds and makes its own decisions.

The Wenzhou Garment Chamber of Commerce: An Independent Business Association

The Wenzhou Garment Chamber of Commerce (*Wenzhou fuzhuang shanghui*) is a purely independent organization, initiated by private entrepreneurs, although it has been affiliated with the official Wenzhou Chamber of Commerce/Federation of Industry and Commerce as this is a requirement under the state regulation of social organizations.[10] The Chamber was founded in 1994. According to its former director Liu Songfu, the main motivation for organizing the Chamber was to raise the quality of the garment industry in Wenzhou (interview in Wenzhou, October 2001). The garment industry in Wenzhou started with primitive technology and could only produce low-quality garments. Many entrepreneurs were worried that Wenzhou's garment industry would be seriously damaged if quality could not be improved. The Garment Chamber of Commerce was thus born to promote quality control and regulate the industry.

The Chamber took measures, such as setting up a quality-testing center, training, distributing information, seeking cooperation with manufacturers outside Wenzhou, and developing research institutes, to improve product quality in the industry. Moreover, the Chamber received the administrative right to grant technical certificates to fashion designers and technical workers in the industry. It organized several sub-committees, offering technical assistance and expert advice to member enterprises. With the growth of the industry, the Chamber became more ambitious, and as well as serving its member enterprises. The Chamber, working closely with the city government, has been lobbying national authorities to have Wenzhou recognized as "China's Garment Capital." These activities raised the reputation of Wenzhou garments and promoted the local garment industry. The total sales of the industry rose from less than two billion yuan in 1993 (before the Association appeared) to more than 30 billion in 2002.

As a private business organization, the Chamber enjoys full autonomy: voluntary membership, elected leaders, self-employed staff, self-funding, and self-governance. The Chamber has established fairly democratic rules to choose its governing body: members elect the board of directors; then the board of directors elects standing members; and then standing members elect the director and deputy directors. The heads of its ten subcommittees are all chosen by election. Election could be highly competitive. Candidates should address the members and give their promises. The prosperity of the garment industry provided the Chamber with exuberant financial resource and made it the wealthiest and most influential association in Wenzhou.

General Features and Functions of Business Associations in Wenzhou

The examples cited indicate that business associations in Wenzhou share three characteristics. First, non-governmental initiative, organized from the bottom-up, played a critical role in the emergence and evolution of the associations. Even semi-official associations involved initiatives by entrepreneurs, as in the case of the Lighter Producers' Association. Second, these associations were organized according to market principles (contractual and horizontal) rather than hierarchical, administrative principles. Membership is voluntary, and members are free to join or quit; this results in great pressure for associations to serve their members' interests.[11]

Third, the associations are self-funded and self-governed entities, enjoying considerable autonomy. Using Hirst's (1994) concept, these associations are, to certain extent, practicing "associative democracy." Their self-governance can be demonstrated in their sources of funding, the way they choose leaders, and their decision-making. In the survey by Chen et al. (2004: 150), it was shown that only 4% of funding was from government, with the rest from membership fees (63%), donations by association leaders (17%), service income (1%), and other sources (15%). Most associations choose their leaders by elections. Among the 64 associations Chen et al. (2004: 146) studied, only one stated that its director was appointed by a supervisory government unit; 19 associations answered that their leaders were nominated by supervisory government unit, but elected by member enterprises or standing committees; and 44 associations answered that their leaders were elected by member enterprises without government intervention. Most associations establish their own rules for, and their areas of, decision-making, and usually government does not meddle with the internal affairs of associations. Indeed, even when an association seeks government help, government may be reluctant to become involved. As intermediate organizations, these business associations function as bridges between member enterprises, the market, and government.

There appear to be three reasons for the Association's autonomy. First, the government does not have the administrative capacity to undertake this regulatory work, and views the Association as shouldering the cost of the regulatory burden. Second, the Wenzhou state is situated in a highly marketized environment and is used to taking a hands-off approach in economic development. Third, officials view the Association as a helping hand rather than a challenge to government.

Weathering the Crisis

Once an economic trendsetter, the Wenzhou model has recently faltered into low-road development path (Anderlini 2011). Shrinking profit margins in local manufacturing and the proliferation of "underground banking" have driven investment into real-estate speculation. Worse still, slowing global demand for cheap Chinese exports, rapid appreciation of RMB, rising production costs, the tightening of monetary policy, and a stagnating real-estate market have combined to crush Wenzhou's most celebrated enterprises (Zhang and Peck 2016: 19). This has triggered nationwide anxiety and doubt about the Wenzhou model. Thus, the receding economy sees struggling business associations in Wenzhou. Once acclaimed as the "real civil associations" and well known for their success, all the independent business associations in Wenzhou have been cornered by the economic recession and closing down of companies since 2008. The situation has been compounded by de-bureaucratization of former semi-official and official business associations. In general, business associations are subsiding quickly. In Jiang's word (2008), just like the government and market, business associations also have the problem of failure. The failure of business associations in Wenzhou results from several reasons.

For those former official associations, bureaucratic reform and reorganization frequently put them in a position without immediate boss to report and to get approval, and more importantly without policing authority and necessary political resources to attract enterprises. When the once semi-official Lucheng Shoes Association was transformed into a completely independent civil organization, number of members shrank from 1800 to 400 in 2009, while Lucheng district had 1500 shoe companies by 2008. The coverage of the association's membership was less than 30% in the industry (Jiang and Zhang 2009: 83). Since the start of separation between business associations and government agents in Wenzhou in 2006, members are shrinking surprisingly, which leaves business associations struggling for survival.

Thanks to the global financial crisis and 2011 local debt crisis in Wenzhou, failure of business associations is prevalent since their members are weakened. Heavily dependent on international market, Wenzhou's economy has been badly hit by the global recession since 2008. Closing down of factories and vanishing of business owners are no news. According to a report of Longwan District Shoes Association in 2014, the loss or closing down of member companies reached a thousand within one year, about 50% of its entire members (Cai 2015: 29). Wenzhou Lighter Producers' Association has lost most of its members since less than 100 lighter producers survived, while Wenzhou was once proud of its more than 4000 lighter producers by the end of the twentieth century. Wenzhou Garment Chamber of Commerce has figured out a way to get rid of the trouble. It has established several companies in foreign countries to help its members get orders, warehousing, and selling in local markets. In 2013, the association established a company—Wenga Fashion Inc.—in the USA with 30 member companies contributing capital in the incorporation (Xu 2014). Wenzhou Metal Association organized 73 leading companies to set up a business group to construct a plaza in 2009 and 36 member companies gathered together to launch another project (Cai 2015: 27). It seems that business associations are ready to become enterprises and engage themselves in the market directly. Otherwise, they have no viable solution to the current problem.

Currently, the business associations in Wenzhou are suffering in the dead of winter. Nevertheless, it's still too early to have an assertive conclusion of failure. Some associations will die out with their members disappearing, and some definitely will go through the crisis because the necessity of associations is paradoxically rising in the crisis. Meanwhile, Wenzhou government is trying to help establish new business associations to stimulate the economy. For example, Wenzhou Electronic Commerce Association was established in the end of 2011 under the auspices of the city government in hope of bailing out medium- and small-sized manufacturers by transforming Wenzhou traditional trade based on wholesale supplies into electronic selling that is in heyday. To individual business association like the Lighter Producers' Association, it might fade into the past. However, the pioneering self-governance principle and arm's length away from government agents practiced by the business associations have far-reaching influence on the relations between business and government.

Changing State-Association Relations: A Focused Comparison

As explained above, Wenzhou's associations are voluntary, representative, and autonomous. Yet relationships between associations and government are intricate. In general, a twofold relationship can be observed. On the one hand, both sides have mutual interests and thus share an intention to come closer to each other. The collusion between the emerging entrepreneurial class and the state appears automatically. Such collusion is understandable given the overwhelming state power and China's gradualist approach to reform. Capitalists are more likely to engage with government officials to seek to protect their interests, and/or try to seek individual or group advantages rather than to challenge government. On the other hand, as some scholars have observed, confrontation and conflict between business and government also occur (see Ostergaard 1989; Gold 1990). Some associations have begun to put pressure on government, both directly and indirectly. In brief, both mutual attraction/collusion and conflict exist between associations and government.

In examining shared interests and mutual attraction, as already observed, both government and business associations are motivated to cooperate to manage the market. The proliferation of private enterprises and the intensification of market competition created crucial problems of economic coordination and government regulation. Old forms of coordination and regulation under command economy have proved inappropriate and ineffective. Thus, both state actors and market actors need to find new and effective ways of regulation and coordination. It is under these circumstances that associations (especially trade associations) became a collective response and institutional answer for both sets of actors. Occupying the niche between enterprises, market, and government, associations serve as bridges that link the three entities. Associations transmit government policies and rules to members and pass on grass-roots business opinion to assist the government to regulate enterprises and to help members to gain access to the state.

As explained, they also regulate their sector of the market, manage competition, and unite members to respond to market challenges. With shared interests, associations and government attempt to attract each other. Government agencies and officials find associations useful as an instrument to regulate and control the market economy, to promote the Wenzhou economy, and as a means to gain access to the wealth and power of the new entrepreneurs who are members of business associations.[12] Associations also want a powerful government patron in order to have access to political and administrative resources. For example, the Wenzhou Economic Commission wanted to use associations as a means to control relevant industries, and attempted to persuade some associations to shift their affiliation to the Commission. Some associations did try to switch affiliation, seeing the Commission as more powerful and resourceful than the FIC. This effort failed largely because the head of the FIC had a higher political status as the vice chairman of the city's People's Political Consultative Conference and he successfully prevented such a move (interview, FIC, Wenzhou, June 2002). Association leaders mention that it is important to keep good relations with government, since government is still the most important source of power, resources, and legitimacy in today's China.

At the same time, associations pose some challenges for the state. As representative of business interests, associations attempt to defend the rights and interests of members against government predation and the abuse of power. They also push for improved government performance and urge officials to abide by the law. This has an impact. According to an informant in the Longgang Local Tax Bureau, the Bureau had to be cautious when investigating enterprises that are members of the Entrepreneurs' Association. If the Bureau's officials did not have solid evidence or behaved improperly, there would be complaints from the Association (interview in Wenzhou, June 2002). Such pressures directly demand that government rationalize its bureaucracy and operations, and encourage the development of the rule of law.

Associations in Wenzhou may indirectly come into conflict with government and even promote future democratization. Fung (2003) summarizes the contributions associations make to democracy, including: the intrinsic value of associative life; fostering civil virtues and teaching political skills; offering resistance to power and checking government; improving the quality and equality of representation; facilitating public deliberation; and creating opportunities for citizens and groups to participate directly in governance. In Wenzhou, associations more or less fulfill the functions noted by Fung. Here, however, we summarize these into three categories drawn directly from Wenzhou's experience and the words of some informants.

First, the emergence of autonomous associations challenges the current organizational principle of government. Associations, being self-organized, self-funded, and self-governed entities, establish an autonomous arena in which entrepreneurs govern their own collective affairs. This phenomenon directs people's attention to an intermediate realm of organizational growth outside the realm of state-organized politics (see White et al. 1996). Due to different organizational principles and working styles, clashes between associations and their official supervisory bodies are seen. Staff in several associations expressed their frustration with their supervisory body, the Federation of Industry and Commerce. Accustomed to a new marketized way of working, the associations are increasingly dissatisfied with the inefficiency, bureaucratism, and arrogance of government supervisors. This clash is particularly acute when they work in the same building.

Second, associations are identified as "schools for democracy, at least for business people."[13] Leaders of associations are elected through a democratic procedure, and some elections have been highly competitive. This way of choosing leaders provides important learning opportunities for entrepreneurs, teaching them necessary skills for political action (organizing, running meetings, making speeches, lobbying, and so on). These practices are significant for a country such as China that does not have a history of democratic experience and they may help to lay a foundation for future democratization. Of course, business associations are an arena of elite experience and also permit some entrepreneurs to pursue personal power and reputations. But this does not negate the argument that associations can be an incubator for democratization.

Third, associations have the potential to evolve into interest and pressure groups. Associations provide channels of communication, foster horizontal links between entrepreneurs, improve flows of information, cultivate bonds of commonality, nurture a sense of group interest and identity, and sharpen the awareness of business people as tax payers. For example, one leader of the Longgang Entrepreneurs' Association expressed a members' perspective, stating, "We are tax-payers. We are not criminals. We deserve better treatment from government" (interview, Wenzhou, June 2002). Recognizing the strength of collective action in defending interests, entrepreneurs indicate solidarity, which reinforces associations as interest and pressure groups.

True as it is, entrepreneurs' associations in Wenzhou, which manifest an increasingly political dynamic, come to resemble interest and pressure groups and are becoming significant in the local economy and politics. It might well be a promising agent of political change in China. As a matter of fact, except for a few associations—and most especially the powerful entrepreneurs' associations—defending members' rights and lobbying is still a minor and difficult element of most associations' work. In contrast, policy consultation with government has no such embarrassing complexity. Overall, the main function of trade associations remains economic, and the "market dynamic" remains dominant (White et al. 1996).

Concluding Remarks

Successful practices of business association and deeper marketization entail the development of business associations. With the separation of business associations and guilds and government agents, the former is given institutional room and opportunity to prosper in the future. The significant role played by business associations in the market economy is highly recognized by the Chinese government.

China's economic reforms are creating the independent sources of wealth, power, and influence that could be key factors in political change. Thanks to the increasing economic and political clout of China's private entrepreneurs, scholars have become more and more interested in the way that they might promote political change.

The differing practices of business associations in Wuxi and Wenzhou are the social political consequences of different development patterns over several decades. The development of TVEs and attraction of foreign capital in Wuxi, with the dominant role of local governments, and thus limited the space for, and deterred the emergence of, societal organizations. Wenzhou's development, underpinned by the initiative of private entrepreneurs and the rapid growth of private business gave rise to the appearance of a new social force and changing state–society relations.

By comparing the different socio-economic contexts and analyzing the development of business associations in the two localities, we can conclude that the growth of the private sector and the spread of market relations, together with the willingness of government to leave space to societal actors, are critical structural requisites for bottom-up organizations.

Concretely, this development requires the following four conditions. First, the state has to be willing to allow space for entrepreneurs to organize. This space has been created everywhere in China following the economic reforms, but there is immense variation across regions, dependent on the role local government has chosen to play in economic development and the space it allows societal actors (Baum and Shevchenko 1999). In a similar vein, an interventionist and dominant government is more likely to seek to control associations, resulting in corporatist practices or downplaying the role of associations. Where local governments play a limited role in local economic development and other affairs, grass-roots initiatives are more likely. Of course, what kind of role local governments played in economic development is often not a matter of choice, but an outcome of historical legacies and resource endowments.

Second, and related to the first condition, the quality of the entrepreneurial class is significant. If entrepreneurs are not independent from government, or if they continuously rely on the government for coordination and help, they have neither capacity nor the motivation to adopt new ways to govern and coordinate business communities. Evidently, the development of TVEs did not create an independent entrepreneurial class that could act independently. Even so, as private business develops further, entrepreneurs appear to develop some capacity for relatively independent action. Wenzhou's self-reliant development nurtured an independent entrepreneurial class with both the capacity and the motivation to organize, while Dongguan's dependent development made capital-friendly government and an independent group of private entrepreneurs who can stay away from politics.

Third, the critical space required for the emergence and operation of associations appears to expand as market relations take root. Over time, individual enterprises become aware of collective needs to deal with the challenges of market and state. Trade associations sprang up and became strong in Wenzhou and Dongguan where the market economy developed earlier and more deeply than elsewhere.

Fourth, leadership is important. If the above three conditions are structural, then leadership is a relatively random factor. The evidence seems to be that a strong and committed leadership is a necessary condition for associations to emerge and operate effectively. The Wenzhou Garment Chamber of Commerce and Yiyang Chamber of Commerce in Dongguan is a good example, with its founder devoting so much time and energy to the Chamber that his own business failed (interview in Wenzhou, November 2001 and interview in Dongguan, July 2014).

Many places in Zhejiang, Fujian, and Guangdong provinces have also witnessed similar development of business associations. The common features these provinces share are that they have relatively developed private business with well-developed market relations. Thus, we may predict that the further growth of the entrepreneurial class and the deepening of market relations will increase opportunities for the development of business associations. This may well mean a loosening of government control and regulation, at least for business. Privatization of TVEs, encouraged private business, and the reform of SOEs in Wuxi since mid-1990s tend to support this proposition. Previous bond between government and enterprises has loosened and a relatively autonomous entrepreneurial class is growing, with intensifying market competition. Some business-organized associations have emerged since 1998, and by 2002, there were 18 business associations in Wuxi citywide, among which most are trade associations within industry (interviews with FIC officials, Wuxi, May 2002). They now function similarly to trade associations in Wenzhou, mainly managing competition within their industries.

Nonetheless, "the political significance of business associations in China is a question of the half-full glass. On the one hand and historically speaking, this is progress in the direction of democratization because more or less they must represent the interests of their members and voice their desire and concerns. On the other hand and prospectively speaking, it is difficult to see how far these associations can go in the direction of democratization. They are very wary of the potential consequences to their personal assets brought about by any political change. (Yang 2013: 111)" It's quite likely that Chinese state and private business owners with their business associations have reached two tacit principles. One is "keeping business to business" (Ibid: 106). Political demands and changes made by capitalists are still rare in China. A more rational strategy of survival in the party–state system is to befriend government officials and stay away from the government politically. The other principle is "to criticize individual official without attacking the government in general" (Ibid: 109) and to solve problems in the case-by-case style.

Moreover, economic recessions incurred by global financial crisis in 2008 have resulted in a more intricate situation. As numerous private businesses are susceptible to global economic fluctuation in Wuxi and Wenzhou, local governments had to step in to prevent the collapse of the entire industry and formation of a national business association. Business associations, such as the once prominent Lighter Producers' Association and Garment Chamber of Commerce in Wenzhou, are in agony because of the closing down of factories and the waning manufacturing in Zhejiang province as a whole. The government shares their agony but finds it painfully necessary to give a hand. In this way, relationships between business and government have become subtle and blurry. And the associations between them remain someway in limbo.

It might be exciting, for scholars believing in the proximity of entrepreneurs and democracy, to find that business associations play a significant role in China as Wenzhou's experience suggests a more assertive entrepreneurial class, seeking to protect its own interests, and thus making associations potential vehicles for interest and pressure group politics. However, based on the original survey data of 133 business associations in Zhejiang and Jiangsu Provinces, Yu et al. (2014) found that self-established business associations lobby less and those with consultant status lobby more frequently. Instead, the relationship between these two sides will go forward characterized by mutual attraction, accommodation, interest and, perhaps, sporadic conflict. It's safe to conclude that business associations are promising in helping the government regulate the economy, but still early to conclude the political significance since the transformation into a market economy is still ongoing and the subsequent political change lags far behind. What's more, the picture of business associations in China remains a mixed and variegated one.

Notes

1. The fifteen associations appointed by the State Economic and Trade Commission in early 2001 are transferred to the SASAC for management. These associations officially supervise the Party affairs, leadership appointments, creation of branches or sub-associations, and foreign-related activities. However, these associations still do not have subordinate relations. And in interviews, respondents deny "subordinate relationship". One respondent said that their branches have their own "responsible business department" and should comply with the local government at the same level.
2. An ambitious leader of a national-level business association said to me in the interview that in the end all government-managed business associations have to return to its original position which is to defend its members' interests, provide public goods for the whole industry, and act as a bridge between government and business community. Business associations

should autonomously compete for constituents and support by offering necessary and popular service for its members.

3. According to surveys by Transparency International (www.transparency.org), China is one of the most corrupt countries in the world.
4. Sunan, literally southern Jiangsu province, includes Suzhou, Wuxi, and Changzhou. These three prefectures have followed a similar pattern of development during the last several decades. Sunan was very famous for its TVE miracle in the 1980s and early 1990s (Zhou and Zhou 1996).
5. Several categories in the official statistics are essentially private, including shareholder cooperatives, limited liability companies, shareholder companies, private business, and self-employed industrial and commercial households.
6. The cadre evaluation system is a strong institution in this region. Each level of government is subject to certain development targets every year, issued from its upper-level government. Such institution affects the behavior of local cadres (Whiting 2001).
7. According to Parris's (1993) documentation, official associations in Wenzhou are not so different from other places. When conducting fieldwork I heard considerable criticism of SELA and PEA from entrepreneurs, and some entrepreneurs even publicly called for their abolition. However, it is clear that official associations do not have the significance of the private associations; this is why we pay more attention to the latter.
8. In total, since 1995, Wenzhou business people have organized 102 Wenzhou Chambers of Commerce in other cities, such as Kunming and Chengdu, to protect their interests (Chen et al. 2004). It is well known that, even before reform began, Wenzhou people have migrated all over China seeking opportunities. Nowadays, Wenzhou business people are numerous and influential in many cities. These associations are apparently independent. I do not discuss them in this article, since the focus is the link between the pattern of local economic development and the practices of business associations.
9. There is a hierarchy among associations based on the level of government organizations with which they are affiliated. In Wenzhou, there are city-level associations, county-level associations, and town-level associations. The number here only gives city-level associations.
10. The Chamber of Commerce and the Federation of Industry and Commerce were actually one organization with two titles. The former name reflects its non-governmental character, while the latter reflects its official status as a united front organization. Recently, the two have started to separate. A well-known entrepreneur replaced the previous government official to become the head of the Chamber of Commerce.

11. The semi-official associations began with compulsory membership. But it was difficult to achieve complete coverage of the industry since there were numerous enterprises and most of them were small. And governments did not have effective ways to punish those enterprises that did not participate. Under such circumstances, membership later became voluntary. Of course, low coverage of membership in industries causes difficulty for effective regulation and coordination since non-members do not obey the rules set by associations.
12. In interviews, some officials frankly expressed the idea that associations are a good way to get to know entrepreneurs.
13. The term used –"school for democracy"– comes from a conversation with Zhang Renshou, a Wenzhou expert. He used this term when discussing the functions of business associations in Wenzhou. Others have recognized the role of associations in promoting democracy (see Chen et al. 2004).

References

Anderlini, J. (2011, October 19). A workshop on the wane. *Financial Times* (Chinese). http://www.ftchinese.com/story/001041248/en

Baum, R., & Shevchenko, A. (1999). The 'state of the state'. In M. Goldman & R. MacFarquhar (Eds.), *The paradox of China's post-Mao reforms*. Cambridge: Harvard University Press.

Byrd, W., & Lin, Q. (Eds.). (1990). *China's rural industry: Structure, development and reform*. New York: Oxford University Press.

Cai, J. (2015). "Qu Xingzhenghua Hou de Kunjing yu Biange: Wenzhou Hangye Xiehui Shanghui Fazhan Xianzhuang Yanjiu" (Dilemma and reform after de-bureaucratization: Study on the development of Wenzhou business association). *Zhongguo Shehui Zuzhi, 19*, 28–29.

Chen, H. (2000). *The institutional transition of China's township and village enterprises*. Aldershot: Ashgate.

Chen, S., Wang, J., & Ma, B. (2004). *Zuzhihua, Zhizhu Zhili yu Minzhu (Organizing, self-governance and democracy)*. Beijing: Chinese Social Science Press.

Dickson, B. J. (2003). *Red capitalists in China: The party, private entrepreneur, and prospects for political change*. Cambridge: Cambridge University Press.

Forster, K. (1990). The Wenzhou model for economic development: Impressions. *China Information, 5*(3), 53–64.

Fung, A. (2003). Associations and democracy: Between theories, hopes and realities. *Annual Review of Sociology, 29*, 515–539.

Gold, T. (1990). The resurgence of civil society in China. *Journal of Democracy, 1*(1), 18–31.

Hirst, P. (1994). *Associative democracy: New forms of economic and social governance.* Amherst: University of Massachusetts Press.

Ho, S., Bowles, P., & Dong, X. (2000). *Letting go of the small: An analysis of the privatization of rural enterprises in Shandong and Jiangsu.* University of British Columbia Institute of Asian Research, Center for Chinese Research, Working Paper 00–02, Vancouver.

Hu, H., & Wu, X. (2002). *Wenzhou Xuannian (Wenzhou puzzle).* Hangzhou: Zhejiang Renmin Chubanshe.

Jiang, H. (2008). "Minjian Shanghui de Shiling jiqi Jiaozheng," (Failure and redress of grass-root business associations). *Jingji Tizhi Gaige, 1*, 164–167.

Jiang, H., & Zhang, J. (2009). "Minjian Shanghui de Daibiaoxing jiqi Yingxiang Yinsu Fenxi: yi Wenzhou Hangye Xiehui Weili," (Representativeness and causal analysis of civil business associations: Wenzhou trade associations). *Gonggong Guanli Xuebao, 6*(4), 78–88.

Lee, P. (1991). The Chinese industrial state in historical perspective: From totalitarianism to corporatism. In B. Womack (Ed.), *Contemporary Chinese politics in historical perspective* (pp. 153–179). New York: Cambridge University Press.

Li, H., & Rozelle, S. (2003). Privatizing rural China: Insider privatization, innovative contracts and the performance of township enterprises. *The China Quarterly, 176*, 981–1005.

Li, L. (2005). Understanding institutional change: Fiscal management in local China. *Journal of Contemporary Asia, 35*(1), 87–108.

Liu, A. (1992a). The 'Wenzhou model' of development and China's modernization. *Asian Survey, 32*(8), 696–711.

Liu, Y. (1992b). Reform from below: The private economy and local politics in the rural industrialization of Wenzhou. *The China Quarterly, 130*, 293–316.

Nolan, P., & Dong, F. (Eds.). (1990). *Market forces in China: Competition and small business – The Wenzhou debate.* London: Zed Books.

Oi, J. (1992). Fiscal reform and the economic foundations of local state corporatism in China. *World Politics, 45*, 99–126.

Ostergaard, C. (1989). Citizens, groups and a nascent civil society in China: Towards an understanding of the 1989 student demonstrations. *China Information, 4*(2), 28–41.

Parris, K. (1993). Local initiative and National Reform: The Wenzhou model of development. *The China Quarterly, 134*, 242–263.

Pearson, M. (1997). *China's new business elites: The political consequences of economic reform.* Berkeley: University of California Press.

Schmitter, P. C. (1974). Still the century of corporatism? *The Review of Politics, 36*(1), 93–94.

Shan, D. (Ed.). (2000). *Zhejiang fei Guoyou Jingji Nianjian (Zhejiang non-public economy yearbook)*. Beijing: Zhonghua Shuju.

Shi, J., Jin, X., Zhao, W., & Luo, W. (Eds.). (2002). *Zhidu Bianqian Yu Jingji Fazhan: Wenzhou Moshi Yanjiu (Institutional change and economic development: A study on the Wenzhou model)*. Hangzhou: Zhejiang University Press.

Tsai, K. S. (2007). *Capitalism without democracy*. Ithaca/London: Cornell University Press.

Unger, J. (1996). 'Bridges': Private business, the Chinese government, and the rise of new associations. *The China Quarterly, 147*, 795–819.

Walder, A. (1995). Local government as industrial firm: An organizational analysis of China's transitional economy. *American Journal of Sociology, 101*, 263–301.

Wang, H., et al. (2012). Hangye Xiehui Shanghui Guanli de Wuxi Moshi (Wuxi model of business associations and guilds management). In H. Mengfu (Ed.), *Zhongguo Shanghui Fazhan Baogao No. 3* 2011 (*Annual report on the development of China's chamber of commerce No. 3* 2011) (pp. 228–234) Beijing: Zhongguo Shehui Kexue Wenxian Chubanshe (Social Sciences Academic Press, China).

Wank, D. (1995). Private business, bureaucracy, and political alliance in a Chinese city. *Australian Journal of Chinese Affairs, 33*, 55–71.

Wen, T., et al. (2013). *Jiedu Sunan (Interpreting Southern Jiangsu)*. Suzhou: Suzhou Daxue Chubanshe.

Wenzhou Statistics Bureau. (2010). *Wenzhou statistics yearbook*. Beijing: China Statistics Press.

Wenzhou Tongji Nianjian. (2001). *Wenzhou statistics yearbook 2001*. Beijing: Zhongguo Tongji Chubanshe.

White, G. (1993). The prospects for civil society in China: A case study of Xiaoshan City. *The Australian Journal of Chinese Affairs, 29*, 63–67.

White, G., Howell, J., & Shang, X. (1996). *In search of civil society: Market reform and social change in contemporary China*. Oxford: Clarendon Press.

Whiting, S. (2001). *Power and wealth in rural China: The political economy of institutional change*. Cambridge: Cambridge University Press.

Wuxi Tongji Nianjian. (2000). *Wuxi statistics yearbook 2000*. Beijing: Zhongguo Tongji Chubanshe.

Xu, Q. (2014, December 11). Wenzhou You Yigu Xiehui Liliang (Wenzhou has strength from associations). *Zhejiang Daily*.

Yang, K. (2013). *Capitalists in communist China*. Basingstoke: Palgrave Macmillan.

Yi, S., & Zhao, X. (2001). "Sunan Yuyan" (Sunan story). *Caijing (Finance), 5*, 33–50.

Yuan, E. (Ed.). (1987). *Wenzhou Moshi Yu Fuyu Zhi Lu (Wenzhou pattern and the road to rich)*. Shanghai: Shanghai Shehui Kexue Chubanshe.

Zhang, J. (2005). "Zhengfu Quanli, Jingying Guanxi, he Xiangzhen Qiye Zhuanzhi" (State power, elite relations, and privatization of Chinese rural industry). *Shehuixue Yanjiu (Sociological Research)*, *5*, 92–124.

Zhang, J., & Peck, J. (2016). Variegated capitalism, Chinese style: Regional models, multi-scalar constructions. *Regional Studies*, *50*(1), 1–27.

Zhou, H., & Zhou, D. (1996). *Su Xi Chang Fazhan Tese Yanjiu (Research on the developmental characteristics of Suzhou-Wuxi-Changzhou region)*. Beijing: People's Daily Press.

Zhu, K. (2003). *Laizi Diceng de Biange (Change from the below)*. Hangzhou: Zhejiang Renmin Chubanshe.

CHAPTER 5

Trapped into Collusion: The Under-Institutionalized Taxation System and Local Business–State Relations in China

Changdong Zhang

Introduction

On March 8, 2013, during the secessions of the 12th National People's Congress (NPC), Xi Jinping, the general party secretary and new president, joined the NPC deputies in panel discussions and gave a speech. In his speech, Xi urged government officials to have a moral baseline and keep steady (communist) belief, especially when dealing with businesses. "There are too many temptations and traps around power (holders) now days," Xi said, "the government official should keep their distance from the businesses and treat the later according to rules, do not collude with them (goujian dabei) to lose the boundary between public and private." Xi suggested that the healthy relationship between government officials and businessmen should be characterized as "clean (qing) and close (qin)."[1] However, journalists commonly use the idea of collusion to explain state–business relationships in China, while scholars apply such concepts as "commercialized communism" (Wank 1999), "crony communism," "integrated

C. Zhang (✉)
School of Government, Peking University, Beijing, China

X. Zhang, T. Zhu (eds.), *Business, Government and Economic Institutions in China*, International Political Economy Series,
DOI 10.1007/978-3-319-64486-8_5

wealth and power" (Dickson 2008; An Chen 2002; Alpermann 2006; Chen and Dickson 2008), and "clientelist local state" (Ong 2012) to the relationship between businesses and local governments. If these terms accurately describe the relationship between the state and business, they identify a significant problem. Prior to the early 1990s, scholars often used concepts such as the "local state corporatism" (Oi 1992, 1999), "(local) entrepreneur state" (Duckett 1998), and "local developmental state" (Blecher and Shue 1996) to describe a collaborative relationship that had existed by then. Collaborative state–business relationships are even more important today because they are a precondition for industrial transformation and upgrading (Evans 1995; Chen 2014). Why have collusive relationships become more dominant? This chapter investigates the nature of state–business relationships in China and the forces that have shaped them.

In a comprehensive theoretical discussion of the political economy of state–business relationships, Haggard et al. (1997) identify five perspectives of business in its relations to the state: business as capital, sectors,[2] firms,[3] associations, or networks. Firms are an institutional factor, capital and sectors are structural, and associations and networks are dependent variables that measure the state–business relationship, which the structural and institutional variables conjointly determine.[4] While China's regional political economies display both similarities and variations in the configuration of state–business relationship, the current chapter will use the method of agreement to study similarities rather than variations. The variations are issues for future research; a single chapter could not examine them fully. In other words, I take state institutions, especially the taxation institution, as its independent variable. The dependent variable is state–business relationships, which the chapter categorizes as predatory, collusive, collaborative, or regulatory. Structural factors, including the level of economic development, industrial sectors, and capital mobility, are control variables based on this study's use of the method of agreement, and factors like firm size will be discussed when relevant.

Alexander Gerschenkron (1962) discusses the different development strategies and the roles states played in countries started industrialization under different world historical times. Different development strategies mean different types of state–business relationships, ideologies, and political regimes. For some East Asian late developers, his academic tradition was later developed into the developmental state theory for East Asia (White and Gray 1988), while for Latin American countries dependent development dominates.[5] Eva Bellin finds that in late-industrializing countries, the capitalist class is fragmented and divided into many groups with different interests. Because the state plays an important role in economic development in these countries, many capitalists are dependent on the state for government resources, including, but not limited to, financial aid and government permits (Bellin 2000).

Like other comparative political economy scholars who focus on institutional factors, China studies scholars have investigated the state–business relationship using institutional analysis.[6] Scholars who argue for a collaborative state–business relationship focus on institutions like fiscal decentralization (Oi 1992; Montinola et al. 1996), which, combined with the cadre evaluation system, gives priority to regional economic development and revenue increases (Huang 1996; Whiting 2001, 2004; Edin 2003; Shih et al. 2012). Scholars who see the state–business relationship as collusive also argue that party–state institutions determine the nature of that relationship. Based on Peter Evans's analytical framework of embedded autonomy and a review of local state–business relationships in China, Ong argues that market liberalization has reduced local governments' control of (financial and raw material) resources and thus rendered them less autonomous from businesses. At the same time, privatization has reduced local governments' institutional capacity. Ong argues that businesses are acquiring more autonomy and even gaining power over local governments and that local governments have degenerated into clientelist states since the mid-1990s (Ong 2012).

In his seminal work, *Embedded Autonomy*, Evans argues that embedded autonomy is the "underlying structural basis for successful state involvement in industrial transformation." Autonomy refers to a Weberian bureaucracy that has a highly selective meritocratic recruitment and long-term career rewards that create commitment and corporate coherence, while embeddedness or connectedness refers to "a concrete set of social ties that binds the state to society and provides institutionalized channels for the continual negotiation and renegotiation of goals and policies" (Evans 1995: 12). Based on Evans's concept of embedded autonomy, I develop a typology of state–business relationships in Table 5.1.

This typology departs from Evans, who focuses on three typologies: developmental, intermediate, and predatory states.[7] This chapter introduces the regulatory state as the fourth type to create a two-by-two matrix and redefines the intermediate state as the collusive state–business relationship. Collaborative state–business relationships have both strong embeddedness and autonomy, whereas collusive state–business relationships have

Table 5.1 Typologies of state-business relationships

		Embeddedness/connectedness	
		Strong	*Weak*
Autonomy	Strong	Collaborative/developmental	Regulatory state
	Weak	Collusive: clientelism/captured	Predatory state

strong embeddedness but weak autonomy. Collusive state–business relationships could be clientelist or crony (Kang 2002) if the state is stronger than business, or it could be captured if business is stronger.[8] In a regulatory model, the regulator is independent from and impartial to business it regulates, and high degree of transparency is vital (Pearson 2005: 299–300). The predatory state lacks the ability to prevent individual incumbents from pursuing their own goals; therefore, they extract at the expense of society (Evans 1995: 12).

Like Johnson (1982), Evans finds that institutional factors or the "internal structure of the state" are of prominent importance when studying state–business relationships.[9] Evans argues that state internal structure and policies shape the characteristics of business community. Without the state's autonomy and internal coherence, collusive state–business relationships or predatory states prevail. Many studies specify the "state" as the "pilot agency" to make the argument more convincing.[10] The taxation institution, which is a very important state institution, however, is often neglected in the study of state–business relationships. The consequence for neglecting taxation is that the power balance between the state and business is misperceived, as I will elaborate in the next section. This chapter focuses on the taxation institution to make an institutional argument on state–business relationships. I argue that the under-institutionalized taxation system reflects limited state coherence on the one hand and weakens the businesses and pushes them to build patron–clientelist ties with government on the other.

This chapter contributes to the state–business relationships debate by placing it in the context of the taxation institution, especially tax administration. It builds on the wide recognition that the property rights institution plays a crucial role in shaping business's interests and the central role of the taxation institution in the property rights institution (Acemoglu et al. 2002; North 1990; North and Thomas 1974). While scholars accurately recognize the role of fiscal institutions in regional development, most have focused on the central–local fiscal relationships (Oi 1992; Landry 2008; Whiting 2001; Wong 2009) rather than the state's taxation practices, or the implementation of tax policies.

This chapter begins by reviewing the literature regarding taxation politics (or fiscal sociology) and links it with state–business relationships. A description of data sources and research design follows. The second section provides an in-depth analysis of formal dimensions of the current taxation system in China, and the third section introduces and discusses the informal practices of China's taxation system. The fourth section analyzes and discusses the impact of an under-institutionalized taxation system on the private entrepreneurs' interests and survival strategies. The fifth and final section concludes the chapter.

State-Business Relationships and Taxation Politics

Scholars have long regarded war and taxation as dynamics of modern state-building in Western Europe (Schumpeter 1991; Ertman 1997; Mann 1993; Tilly 1990). They also recognize taxation as playing a crucial role in shaping state–society relationships, including state–business nexuses, in today's developing and transitional countries. It rebuilds the state, as well as the society (Besley and Persson 2009, 2011; Brautigam et al. 2008; Levi 1988; Migdal 2009).[11]

Taxation can be a bargain or a coercive practice. Fiscal contract theory describes taxation as an exchange relationship between tax payers and the government in which taxpayers pay taxes because they want the government to provide public goods. In other words, businesses do not simply minimize their tax burden but also maximize the public goods and tax burden ratio (Ross 2004; Timmons 2005). However, most of these studies de-embed taxpayers from institutional contexts and put them in an ideal world—in other words, a completely competitive (political) market without the presence of power. The coercive perspective view of taxation, on the contrary, emphasizes the power and punishment for noncompliance. Putting taxpayers into the institutional context, which includes the taxation system, makes it possible to undertake comparative institutional studies of capitalists' interests and strategies of survival and state–business relationships.

In his study of developing countries, Waterbury finds that business groups and investors, though not innately democratic, are particularly important in a modern political system because of their share of tax revenue.

They can either bargain with the government to protect and advance their business activities or exit, and this can make the government accountable to the business therefore build collaborative state–business relationships. Accountability is not necessarily democratic, and democracy is a largely western phenomenon, but does lead to social corporatism (Waterbury 1997). Other research reveals that in most developing countries, taxation is not a consensual practice but a coercive practice that strengthens the authoritarian state. Mick Moore specifies the conditions for coercive taxation.[12] Duara and Bernstein and Lü find coercive taxation in rural China in the 1940s and 1980s to 1990s, respectively, and discuss its destructive consequences for state-building in Republic China and the P.R. China (Duara 1988; Bernstein and Lü 2003). However, Scott Gehlbach argues that taxation offers accountability in some post-communist countries that are geographically close to Western Europe and have high asset mobility (Gehlbach 2008).

Private enterprises are the most important source of tax revenue for most local governments in China, which could provide some types of representation therefore to build collaborative state–business relationships. Through examining the current taxation system, especially its on-the-ground practices, and discussing how it shapes the state–business relationships in local China, this chapter can also contribute to this debate.

Data Sources and Research Design

This chapter's empirical data comes from three sources: the author's interviews, published and unpublished local government and Local People's Congress (LPC) documents, and media reports. In the course of fieldwork from 2007 to 2013, the author collected data on taxation and related issues through interviews with dozens of tax officers and other government officers, private entrepreneurs, and trade association leaders in seven counties in four provinces and municipalities (Zhejiang, Shanxi, Hunan, and Chongqing).[13] The counties vary from two relatively underdeveloped agriculture counties in Hunan and Chongqing, to three top 100 counties (*Baiqiangxian*) in Hunan and Zhejiang. They vary significantly on the level of economic development and major industries' asset mobility (from light industry to heavy industry and coal mining). Therefore, the data provides enough variations for the control variables for a method of agreement research design. The author read the government documents broadly and intensively to investigate the taxation system at the county

Table 5.2 Basic facts of seven counties

County	*Province*	*Economic development (2009 GDP per capita, Unit: Yuan)*	*Industry*	*Government business relationship*
County A	Zhejiang	Medium (28,200)	Light industry	Mainly collusive, some collaboration
County B	Shanxi	Medium (28,035)	Coal mining	Collusive and predatory
County C	Zhejiang	Very high (40,893)	Light industry	Collusive, also with collaboration
County D	Shanxi	Medium (21,544)	Coal mining	Collusive and predatory
County X	Hunan	Low (14,424)	Agriculture	Collusive and predatory
County Y	Zhejiang	Very high (41,933)	Light industry	Collusive, also with collaboration
County Z	Chongqing	Low (9820)	Light and heavy industry	Collusive and predatory

and township levels. In-depth media reports act as complementary sources to cross-validate other data sources used here to avoid the inherent bias of media sources.[14] The primary research this chapter presents contributes to a very small area of literature on China's taxation system (Table 5.2).[15]

Formal Dimensions of the Taxation System

A taxation system includes two aspects, official rules and actual practices, which could be very different from the rules on the paper. Taxation systems in different countries differ in terms of tax types and rates and legislation and administration, which in turn reflect the governance of a country. China has a high nominal tax rate and two parallel independent bureaus. However, the practice of taxation is under-institutionalized: tax officers have high discretional power, and the taxation system is deeply embedded in local politics and therefore has limited autonomy. This section will describe the formal side of the system.

High Nominal Tax Rates

While studies of taxation politics in developed countries mostly focus on the rule-making process (Campbell 1993; Steinmo 1993), in China, a strong authoritarian state, the legislation and rule-making are closed systems, and the State Council drafts the tax laws. In 1985, the National

People's Congress (NPC) standing committee delegated the power of taxation to the State Council and has not taken it back.[16] Thus, private entrepreneurs and interest groups have little opportunity to lobby for tax policy-making.[17] The Local Taxation Bureau (LTB) has limited power to set and adjust tax rates at the provincial level. The Chinese government relies heavily on indirect taxes like VAT and sales tax, and the nominal tax rates are very high (VAT 17%, corporation income tax rate 33%). High tax rates make it difficult for private entrepreneurs to make any profit if they pay their taxes honestly; most are in low profit rate industries because of government regulation, as well as low capital and technology barriers. Therefore, tax evasion is rampant. As a senior tax officer told me, in his 30 years of tax administration, he came across only one enterprise in which he failed to identify any tax evasion behavior.[18] Most of my informants disclosed that it's impossible for a company to make money without evading taxes.

While a private enterprise has virtually no opportunity to influence the process of setting the tax rate, entrepreneurs, as well as other taxpayers, can influence tax implementation. The next section describes this process and its vulnerability to influence.

Institutional Framework of the Current Taxation Regime

Tax administration in China has two vertically managed systems: the State Administration of Taxation (SAT) and LTB.[19] The State Council vertically manages the SAT; it is institutionally independent from the local government. The higher-level LTB and the local government share leadership of the LTB. The higher-level LTB has most of the power, including appointing and supervising the directors and determining the size and organization of lower-level LTBs.[20]

The independent structure of SAT and LTB helps improve the autonomy of the tax bureaus, which gives them greater ability to resist the intervention of local officials. In one interview, a senior tax officer told me several stories about the tax bureau's autonomy and its limitations. In one case, the county SAT director overrode the county party secretary's request to protect a private entrepreneur who had evaded taxes.[21]

The tax bureaus' enhanced autonomy, however limited, along with the tax policy reform, helped to significantly enlarge the government's tax revenue and the central government's share of total tax revenue. Separating SAT and LTB essentially doubles the cost of tax administration in that it requires two sets of staff, buildings, and equipment. If the LTB and SAT fail to share information with each other, this raises costs further. Taxpayers also need to deal with two organizations instead of one. What's more, tax bureaus overspend because there's no budgetary check on their power.[22]

Informal Practices: An Under-Institutionalized Taxation System[23]

Though it has many defects, the formal taxation institution appears to be independent and autonomous from the local government. However, a close examination of the practice of taxation reveals that the tax bureaus have limited inner coherence.[24] This section examines two important aspects: operation of tax collection and the tax target system.

Practices of Tax Administration

The 1994 Tax Share reform changed the methods of tax collection. Before 1993, the so-called "One Person-in-Charge-of-All System" (*shuishou zhuanguanyuan zhidu*) was the dominating system of tax collection. The 1994 Reform changed this system into the Concentrated Administration System (*jizhong zhengguan zhidu*). In 2001, China introduced a new system, the Tax Administrator System (*shuishou guanliyuan zhidu*). By institutionalizing the taxation system, these reforms helped, with limited success, retain the tax officer's discretional power.

The institutional reform enacted in 1994 was designed to limit the power of tax officers by separating the authority to inspect from collection and assessment. This new system, the Centralized Administration System, is based on tax declaration and improved taxation service. It uses the computers and intranet, centralizes the tax collection, and inspects selectively. Reform merged widespread small taxation offices into large Tax Service Halls. Tax officers no longer needed to go out to the entrepreneurs to collect taxes. Taxpayers were required to declare their taxes, have them approved by the tax officer, and then pay their taxes in the Tax Service Hall. As a method of enforcing compliance and checking the power of the tax assessment, the tax inspection officers inspected taxpayers selectively. China set up a "Tax Inspection Team" which it later upgraded to a "Tax Inspection Bureau," which became the most powerful subunit in the tax administration.

As no specific tax officer was responsible for monitoring particular jurisdictions, centralized enforcers had little opportunity to obtain new information about enterprises, especially newer enterprises. Tax evasion grew several years after the reform was implemented. In the early 2000s, another reform returned the tax officer to the field, but with dramatically decreased power. Their job duties now are now limited to "management" tasks, such as monitoring the tax base, daily checking, cross-validating the account, and evaluating taxes, rather than "collecting" tasks.

This administrative reform helps curtail the power of tax officers to a degree. However, the effectiveness of the taxation is limited because tax officers found that violating laws and rules receive only mild punishments. Adequate reasons exist to explain why enterprises have difficulty assessing tax liability: the common use of cash transactions, incomplete or even non-existent accounting systems, intentional false accounting, and so on. Large enterprises are easier to monitor as they have modern accounting systems, but medium and small enterprises conduct most transactions in cash and often do not keep any transaction records.[25] Due to these constraints, the tax bureau has two established methods of assessing tax liability: assessing through estimation (*heding zhengshou*)[26] and assessing through auditing (*chazhang zhengshou*).[27] However, both methods of tax collecting empower tax officers with discretional power.

To sum up, the tax administration reforms have significantly changed the implementation of tax policies, improved the tax bureau's autonomy by giving it more independence, and constrained the officers' discretionary power to some degree. The state's institutional extraction capacity also improved significantly.[28] However, these reforms have only achieved limited success. The taxation system is still highly under-institutionalized, and tax evasion remains rampant.

The Tax Target System Against Rule-of-Law

Besides the defects of the formal taxation institution, the taxation regime, like other institutions, is embedded in the local political institution. This embeddedness weakens the autonomy of the tax administration and further deinstitutionalizes it as a rule-by-law regime. What's more, like any individual, the tax officer is embedded in social networks that shape his or her interests. Especially in a county where people know each other well, tax officers have many concerns beyond simply collecting more taxes for the state.

As the ruling party of a unitary authoritarian state, the CCP has developed a somewhat effective cadre evaluation system. Many criteria, including economic development, tax revenue, social stability, and population control, are used to evaluate the local political leaders' performance. This performance-driven system is also called the "pressure-based system" (*yalixing tizhi*), which is defined as a system in which "in order to achieve the economic 'catch-up' plan and meet the targets set by the supervisors, the county and township-level political organizations assign targets, which can be measured quantitatively, to lower level organizations and individuals who must meet reach their assigned targets in a given time. Cadre's ability to meet these targets will be awarded or punished both economically and politically."[29]

This "pressure-based system" also applies to the tax administration system. In practice, taxes are not collected according to the law or tax liability (*yifa zhengshui, yingshou jinshou*), but according to tax targets set by tax collectors' supervisors and local government. All the tax collection agents have specific targets (*shuishou renwu*), which typically increase at specified rates. The higher-level tax bureau and the county government set specific tax targets for both the county SAT office and the LTB. Since leaders in the county government view meeting the tax target as critical politically, they seek to intervene.[30] Lacking power to appoint or promote the tax bureau directors, they typically set higher tax targets and share the increase with the tax bureau and township governments.[31] The tax bureaus set the targets for their branches and for every tax officer based on the target the county government sets. In most counties, even the tax inspection bureau, which is in charge of investigating tax evasion, has a target.

Local governments want the tax growth rate to keep constant (if not to increase) because of increasing public expenditure.[32] If the tax revenue target (or tax revenue growth rate) keeps step with economic growth, as it did in most regions in China before 2000, the tax target system achieves this without undue strain on the economy.[33] However, economic fluctuation imperils the system. As one media report finds:

> In Sept. 9, 2009, a local newspaper of Ouhai county of Wenzhou, Zhejiang, published the county LTB's "List of the Tax Arrears Enterprises." The highest amount is RMB 0.5 million Yuan (USD 74,000) and the lowest is only RMB 54 Yuan (USD 8). This list signals that the tax bureaus are serious in improving tax collection in this economic crisis era, and it is just an epitome of a national wide movement of improving tax collection.[34]

Two government officers mentioned that the tax bureaus of one county also required the enterprises to pay much higher taxes in 2010 than they had in 2009 and that meeting the tax target during economic crises would be difficult without this. "The enterprises must pay the extra taxes because they had benefited from the loose tax collection practices in the past years. Now it's the time for them to pay back and help the tax officers to meet the tax revenue target). They cannot complain but must comply." This also happened in counties in Shanxi.[35]

A more common way to meet a tax target is to collect the taxes for the next year, a practice called "Eat May's Grain in April" (*Yin chi mao liang*). This is regarded as illegal, and SAT headquarters and the Ministry of Finance formally forbid it, but local SATs and LTBs still do it under harsh fiscal pressure.[36]

The broader context in which the tax administration operates also limits the tax bureaus' independence and coherence. Tax officers live in the county in which they work and may have many opportunities to enjoy favors from the county government. Therefore, officers seek to maintain positive relationships with powerful, local officials.[37] As a tax officer of county C summarizes other statements he's made to me, "we collect taxes for the state; that's our job. But what is the state? After all, the state is composed of real people (cadres). The state is the people. So, after all, we, including myself, are working for these people." He implicitly admits to sacrificing the formal rules for personal relationships.[38]

Like personal networks, other institutions with which the tax bureaus must work limit the tax officers' autonomy. Though the tax bureau is vertically administrated, it faces serious horizontal constraints. The Party Committee and its departments and subcommittees (especially the Commission of Discipline) limit the tax bureau's power and autonomy. As one of my informants described, tax officers are afraid of the Party's disciplinary power because most, if not all, have allowed some level of tax evasion or taken some bribe.[39]

To sum up, although several rounds of taxation reform have strengthened the taxation system and achieved some degree of success in institutionalization, improving both its autonomy and capacity, China's taxation system is still under-institutionalized. It has three characteristics: high nominal tax rates, tax officers' strong discretionary power (both of which lead to rampant tax evasion), and a tax target system. The broader political system and the system's design defects weaken institutionalization efforts and reduce the taxation system's autonomy. This under-institutionalized taxation system is not a rule of/by law system. This has several important implications for the capitalists' interests and strategies of survival and, therefore, the collusive state–business relationships.

The Under-Institutionalized Taxation System and Local State-Business Relationships

China's businesses typically have a network, and therefore collusive rather than collaborative relationship with the state, although elements of associational relationships exist in few cases.[40] I argue that this is partially caused by the under-institutionalized taxation system. Rampant tax evasion by the enterprises, rampant rent-seeking by tax officers, and deinstitutionalization of taxation as a rule-by-law system lead to vulnerable private entrepreneurs who prefer to build patron–client relationships to gain personal benefits instead of demanding institutional change. Besides the similarities, different types of businesses vary, mostly by size. While small enterprise owners have hard time dealing with tax officers, large enterprise owners may enjoy privileged connections with local political leaders, as well as tax officers, and make institutional arrangements.

Tax officers can help an entrepreneur to reduce his or her tax burden, and other government officers can patron a tax officer to perform the same function. This offers many opportunities to extract rent from enterprises. While tax administration reform has constrained rent-seeking in some regions, it has had limited success. The resulting rampant tax evasion and rent-seeking leads to the deinstitutionalization of state–business relationships. The best strategy for a private entrepreneur is not to demand a good taxation institution or lower tax rates, but to build a good relationship with the tax officers or a higher-level patron in the government.

Apart from reducing government's fiscal income, rampant tax evasion has two effects: it promotes economic development and makes entrepreneurs criminals who can be charged, and severely punished, by the government at any time. Entrepreneurs can invest more in their businesses through withholding money from the government, but they live under threat of very severe punishment for tax evasion (Articles 201 and 211 of China's criminal law). Serious tax evasion can be punished with a fine that ranges from one to five times the amount of evaded taxes and less than three years of imprisonment. Tax evasion that exceeds 30% of the total liable taxes can incur three to seven years of imprisonment and a fine valued as high as five times the amount of taxes evaded.[41] Private entrepreneurs therefore have limited ability to achieve representation or demanding for a more service-oriented government through taxation. Challenging the government may lead to an audit and a severe penalty, so it makes more sense for private entrepreneurs to be free riders on the system of bribes than to seek political change. Besides, personal connections with government officers offer business opportunities as well as protections for tax evasions.

There are many ways to build political connections. With the leverage of their increasing role in generating tax revenues after three decades of market reform, private entrepreneurs have become increasingly politically active. Some become deputies in the LPC, members of the Local People's Political Consultant Congress (LPPCC), or join the local party committee. These positions can provide political, social, and economic privileges as well as opportunities to meet and befriend government officials. They can also lead to positions in local government. Private entrepreneur deputies have become the second largest group in the LPC, after Party and government cadres, in many regions.[42] According to various sources, including the authors' interviews in six counties in Zhejiang and Shanxi provinces in 2010, 20–30% of LPC deputies at the county level are private entrepreneurs.

Being an LPC deputy has become very attractive to private entrepreneurs. Some even spend substantial amount of money to buy votes. But they seek personal benefits rather than public interests. Challenging the state or demanding for institutional reform is too risky. A private entrepreneur told me that discussing policy issues in the LPC would draw a tax audit.[43] Another informant told me about a private entrepreneur who spent half million USD to purchase votes to become a municipal LPC deputy, but resigned when the county LPC director threatened to audit him.[44] Xin Sun et al. provide quantitative data showing that LPC is a platform for the organizational clientelism between private entrepreneurs and government officials (Sun et al. 2014).

While capitalist personal connections have social and political causes, the level and intensiveness of personal connections are in general correlated to their enterprises' size, as well illustrated in Table 5.3. Owners of large enterprises, especially those who are major taxpayers, can build connections with local political leaders or even higher-level government officials. The owners of smaller enterprises try to build connections with tax officers or simply evade taxes; if they fail to do so, they will be predated by the government by charging high taxes and fees. The practice of local government leaders of keeping close contact with major enterprises, contacting large

Table 5.3 Entrepreneurs with different levels of political connection and their enterprise sizes

PC and PPCC title levels		*Enterprise's sale amount in 2007 (10,000 Yuan)*	*Enterprise's tax paid in 2007 (10,000 Yuan)*
No	Mean	2516.236	105.839
	N	2105	2043
Township level (PC only)	Mean	6300.256	247.665
	N	78	78
County level	Mean	6603.435	285.162
	N	904	889
Prefecture level	Mean	6,118,509.144	477.345
	N	573	567
Province level	Mean	25,734.690	1128.872
	N	113	109
National level	Mean	79,583.840	3218.318
	N	25	22
Total	Mean	927,477.872	257.163
	N	3798	3708
F test		1.128	126.170***

Data Source: Private Enterprise Survey 2007 (By All-China Federation of Industry and Commerce)

***Significance level 0.000

enterprises frequently, listening to their concerns, and helping them resolve difficulties (like providing easy and cheap bank loan), also suggests the importance of firm size under a system that local governments compete with each other in attracting large investors.

Since private entrepreneurs prefer to seek specific clientelist protection, it prevents them from collectively lobbying for tax bargaining. For example, the general secretary of a large trade association told me that "The tax bureau is the big boss; they never care about us [the association]." Further, he said that the relationships larger enterprises have with the tax bureau allow them to bargain for a tax reduction and that this depresses their investment in the trade association.[45] In another county, the tax bureau head told me, "yes, the largest trade association [the coal washing association] in our county did bargain with us for a lower effective tax rate. We agreed to reduce it to a reasonable level because they provided good reasons." Later on, he disclosed that the primary reason for lowering taxes was that the trade association hired the retired director of the county PC's standing committee, who holds a considerable amount of influence in the county, as the secretary of the association.[46]

If private entrepreneurs are afraid of the government because they are criminals, how can the tax protests occurred in county A[47] and in other places like the town of Zhili[48] be explained? Furthermore, why would private entrepreneurs act collectively and demonstrate for cancelling new taxes? If we examine these tax riots closer, we find that the majority of demonstrators were non-residents rather than local people, were small workshop owners rather than narrowly defined private entrepreneurs. In county A, local businessmen (both workshop owners and private entrepreneurs) were warned by the government not to take any serious actions against the new taxes weeks before they implemented; otherwise they would face criminal prosecution for a host of crimes including, but not limited to, evading taxes, illegal land use, and violating pollution laws. Therefore, most local private entrepreneurs do not participate in tax resistance, but mobilize their connections in order to reduce their current tax burden or help them move to a region with lower taxes. However, the non-residents were not afraid of these kinds of punishment since they could exit without getting serious punishments.[49]

To sum up, the under-institutionalized taxation system gives the local government weak autonomy, which leads to clientelist or collusive state–business relationships. Capitalists choose to collude with the state actors by building networks, rather than act collectively through tax riots or associational behaviors. The low level of institutionalization of the state–business connection makes collaboration unlikely.[50] For example, the selective uses of tax break, which the developmental state theorists consider as an important tool for industry policies, is distorted in China. According to the national audit report, tax break policies were mis-implemented and caused a 36.31 billion RMB tax loss to the government in 2008.[51]

Discussion and Conclusion

An under-institutionalized taxation system, characterized by high nominal tax rates, high discretional power of the tax officer, and a tax target system, along with other institutions (also characterized by the absence of rule of law), reveals that the Chinese local states have weak state autonomy (coherence). The "fragmented authoritarianism" (Liberthal 1992) literature supports these findings in general. On the other hand, the system encourages private entrepreneurs to evade taxes, often through illegal methods, which leads to collusion between the state and businesses. In theory, tax evaders are taking great risks, but in reality, the current taxation system benefits well-connected private entrepreneurs and imposes heavy tax burdens and fees on those less well-connected. Entrepreneurs have little incentive to demand institutional change. Even those who suffer heavy tax burdens cannot undertake collective action to encourage formal institutional reforms of tax administration.[52]

While the literature has analyzed network or *Guanxi* style Chinese capitalism in many respects (Hamilton 1996; Lo and Otis 2003; McNally 2012; Wank 1999), this chapter adds nuance to our understanding of China's local state–business relationships by revealing the importance of the under-institutionalized taxation regime. While acknowledging that some regions and sectors exhibit collaboration, it clarifies the asymmetry in power balance between local state and business in clientelist relationships. While Ong (2012) argues that market liberalization and privatization have changed the power balance between local state and business in favor of the former, this chapter reveals that as business has become more resource-rich and powerful, local political leaders collude with these resource-rich economic elites. However, the businesses are still vulnerable to the local government, not only because of the limits of market liberalization[53] but also because transforming resources into power requires working through political institutions. In China, the under-institutionalized taxation system makes the entrepreneurs criminals and significantly reduces their bargaining power. Local government and business form collusive relationships that represent institutional hostage or interdependence, but the local government is a more powerful player; and some government officials, including tax officers, play the role of patron for the businesses. This finding is consistent with Tianbiao Zhu's chapter in this book, which argues a state domination of business. While another recent study by Lee and Zhang on "bargained authoritarianism" in China argues patron–clientelism has decreasing importance in grassroots states because of marketization (Lee and Zhang 2013), this chapter finds that marketization may also strengthen patron–clientelism when the market institutions are not rule-of-law institutions and make the private entrepreneurs vulnerable in front of the government. As this chapter shows, this partial and unfinished market reform, which includes the under-institutionalized taxation system as an important institution, has neither generated an autonomous state nor institutionalized embeddedness that Evans calls for; as a result, collusive state–business relationships dominate.

Notes

1. Xinhua News Agency, "Xi Jinping: The government office should keep distance from the business and have a clear boundary between public and private," http://www.china.com.cn/news/2013lianghui/2013-03/09/content_28181490_4.htm, accessed on September 1, 2015.
2. See Kennedy (2005) for a good example.
3. See Kang (2002) for a good example.
4. As this chapter will discuss in detail, the network/connectedness can be collusive or collaborative, and associational governance represents collaborative network through collective action.
5. There are many literatures on this topic; for a classic explanation, see Evans (1979). For comparative studies of state–business relationships in developed countries, borrowing some concepts from the historical institutionalism generated the varieties of capitalism debate in the last decade; see Hall and Soskice (2001).
6. Given the method diversity, some scholars do not use institutional argument. Network or *Guanxi* is used to analyze economic development under a society that lacks rule of law. For example, see Walder (1996).
7. Intermediate state has limited degree of autonomy and connectedness (Evans 1995).
8. For China's failure to build a regulatory state, see Pearson (2005).
9. Maxfield and Schneider (1997) put state characteristics and collective business action as two conditions for collaborative state–business relationships. Evans argues the latter is partially influenced by the former. Also collective business actions are shaped by the structural factors. See Evans (1995, 1997). Also see Kohli (2004).
10. For example, Johnson (1982) on MITI; Woo (1991), Wade (1990), and Amsden (1989) on Korea.
11. Schumpeter called for treating tax policy as both a symptom and a cause of large-scale changes in the economy and society. But most scholars "with rare exception" heeded only on the symptom. See Martin et al. (2009: 2). This chapter takes taxation as the causes.
12. Coercive taxation "appears to be associated with the following combination of factors: (a) poor agrarian environments; (b) revenue raising for local governments; (c) the existence on paper of a wide variety of potential taxes charges; and (d) the lack of any effective regulation of the process by higher levels of government" (Moore 2008).
13. Taxation is a sensitive topic, for both government officials and private entrepreneurs, which meant that valid information and reliable access required a good deal of patience and persistence.

14. Some media reports actually provide more thorough reports, with broader coverage and deeper investigation, than an academic can conduct, given time, fiscal, and access constraints and training. In recent years, as public budget and taxation reform become a more important public topic, there has been a corresponding increase in the number of in-depth reports on this issue in media in China.
15. The literature provides only very limited introductions and analysis of China taxation system, especially its practice, in the Chinese or English language. OECD (2013) has a chapter on China's taxation system, which describes some of its important characteristics. This chapter enriches important details as well as finds some new practical aspects of the taxation system.
16. Only three types of tax (out of 18) were approved by the NPC and its standing committee. See "No Time-table for Getting Taxation Legislation Power back to NPC," http://news.xinhuanet.com/politics/2013-03/10/c_114969944.htm?prolongation=1
17. Tax policy-making was a highly politicized issue in the 1950s, and at the early stage of the "anti-right" movement, Mao Zedong described the strife as a symbol of "class struggle within the Party."
18. Author's Interview, June 13, 2010, Hunan. Interviewees were promised anonymity.
19. Before the 1994 Tax Share Reform, the Tax Administration Bureaus, under the direct leadership of local government, at the corresponding level, were in charge of collecting most taxes in their jurisdiction.
20. The province government manages the province-level LTB directors and organization.
21. Author's interview, July 13, 2010, Hunan.
22. My informants told me that the LTB and SAT offices are the "best" government bureaus to work for, as they provide high salaries and good benefits (including housing, kids' education, bonus for holidays). A 2007 report by the National Audit Office, which included an audit of the costs of taxation for 236 tax bureaus, across 18 provinces, also pointed to excessive spending. See Liu, Jiayi, "Audit report on the central government budget implementation and other fiscal income and expenditure of year 2007," report on the NPC standing committee, August 27, 2008.
23. This section and "High Nominal Tax Rates" section are revised from the author's another paper; see Zhang (2017). Some papers are also valuable: Yu 2007.
24. Skocpol defines state autonomy by two characteristics: independent from social forces and inner coherence; see Skocpol 1985. Besides the reasons relating to embedding I discuss here, grassroots tax officials have very lim-

ited chances of promotion, which typically does not depend on merit or performance.

25. If they do keep records, they keep it for their own reference and have a fake one for the tax officer; tax officers know this and the enterprises know that the tax officers know it.
26. Assessing through estimation applies to the small enterprises that lack accounting systems or for which it is difficult to calculate the profit and costs. Thus, there are no reliable records to assess tax liability.
27. Assessing through auditing is a more advanced method, but it can only be applied to the large- and medium-sized enterprises that have good accounting systems. Different types of taxes, that is, the VAT, enterprise income tax, individual income tax, business tax, are collected based on accounting information.
28. The growth rate of national tax revenue has been much higher than the economy in recent years.
29. Rong (1998).
30. Tian and Zhao (2008) provide many details as to local governments' tax pressure and their crazy coping strategies, including tax purchasing.
31. Author's interviews: July 13, 2010, Hunan; June 13, 2010, Shanxi; February 21, 2013, Zhejiang.
32. For the importance of tax revenue growth for local government, see Landry and Lu (2014).
33. See Whiting (2001) for how the local government intentionally set low tax rates to encourage development of private enterprises in Wenzhou municipal of south Zhejiang province.
34. "The tax audit storm in Wenzhou, where the private enterprises were originated the earliest, may lead to another wave of enterprise moving out," *Jingji Guancha* (*The Economic Observation*), September 11, 2009.
35. Author's interview B, April 23, Zhejiang; June 22, 2010, Shanxi; June 23, 2010, Shanxi.
36. See a report in *Huaxia Times* (*Huaxia Shibao*), "Local Non-tax Revenue Increases Significantly against the Economy Decline, Chaos Fees Reappear" (defang feishui shouru nishi gao zengzhang, luanshoufei chongxin taitou), http://finance.qq.com/a/20121027/001582.htm, accessed October 28, 2012. Another way to meet the target is through fees and fines.
37. Author's interview A, June, 11, 2010, Shanxi; June 20, Shanxi.
38. Author's interview A, June 11, Shanxi.
39. Author's interview, June 13, 2010, Hunan.
40. As discussed above, Haggard et al. (1997) describe two competing state–business relationships: business as association or network.

41. The original statute specified the amount incurring the strongest punishments to be RMB 0.1 million Yuan; in 2008 it was revised and no specific amount was listed in the revised tax law.
42. Since there are no statistics for how many deputies are private entrepreneurs in LPCs, it is hard to decipher accurate numbers and percentages. In the LPCs, private entrepreneurs have no specific category and are categorized into other "social groups," like workers, peasants, intellectuals, and cadres. The LPPCC has a category called economical group (*Jingji jie*), but there are still many private entrepreneurs who get their position in other groups (like technology, cadre, etc.).
43. Author's interview, April 27, 2010, Zhejiang.
44. Author's interview, March 11, 2011, Zhejiang
45. Author's interview, March, 18, 2010, Zhejiang.
46. Author's interview, July 14, 2010, Shanxi.
47. In March 2011, hundreds of people gathered in front of the county government buildings and demanded that the government halt the implementation of a new taxation policy, designed to collect taxes from the factories and family workshops producing handcrafts.
48. The Zhili anti-tax riot evolved into a violent conflict and got extensive media attention; it ended with stopping the implementation of tax policy. For English media reports, a good example is "Chinese Town Cancels Tax That Sparked Riots", *Wall Street Journal*, http://online.wsj.com/article/SB10001424052970204505304577003503223216724.html, accessed December 3, 2011.
49. Author's interview, August 27, 2011, Zhejiang.
50. Hard but not impossible to achieve, there are many successful as well as failed cases of state–business collaborations.
51. The National Office of Audit Report, 2008.
52. Another feature of the current tax system that empowers the state against the capitalists is that tax revenue only provides part local government's total fiscal revenue. Besides various types of fees and fines, another big share is land transfer fees which comprise one-third to one-half of local government revenue. For a discussion of the evolution of the extra-budgetary fund and land transfer fees as a major source of local government, see Whiting (2011).
53. While catching many important aspects of the local state–business relationships, Ong neglects other important facts. For example, many local governments monopolize the supply of land (an important input) and still have good access to bank system through the financing platform (*Rongzi Pingtai*), and, therefore, the local governments still have enough resources to keep autonomy or leading *power* of regional economic development (*jingji fazhan zhudaoquan*), as Cao and Shi (2009) find.

References

Acemoglu, D., Johnson, S., & Robinson, J. (2002). Reversal of fortune: Geography and institutions in the making of the modern world income distribution. *Quarterly Journal of Economics, 117*(4), 1231–1294.

Alpermann, B. (2006). 'Wrapped up in cotton wool': Political integration of private entrepreneurs in rural China. *The China Journal, 56*, 33–61.

Amsden, A. H. (1989). *Asia's next giant: South Korea and late industrialization.* New York: Oxford University Press.

Bellin, E. R. (2000). Contingent democrats: Industrialists, labor, and democratization in late-developing countries. *World Politics, 52*(2), 175–205.

Bernstein, T. P., & Lü, X. (2003). *Taxation without representation in contemporary rural China.* Cambridge/New York: Cambridge University Press.

Besley, T. J., & Persson, T. (2009). The origins of state capacity: Property rights, taxation, and politics. *American Economic Review, 99*(4), 1218–1244.

Besley, T., & Persson, T. (2011). *Pillars of prosperity: The political economics of development clusters.* Princeton: Princeton University Press.

Blecher, M., & Shue, V. (1996). *Tethered deer: Government and economy in a Chinese county.* Stanford: Stanford University Press.

Brautigam, D., Fjeldstad, O., & Moore, M. (Eds.). (2008). *Taxation and state-building in developing countries: Capacity and consent.* Cambridge/New York: Cambridge University Press.

Brys, B. et al. (2013). *Tax policy and tax reform in the People's Republic of China* (OECD taxation working papers, no. 18). Paris: OECD Publishing.

Campbell, J. (1993). The state and fiscal sociology. *Annual Review of Sociology, 19*, 163–185.

Cao, Z., & Shi, J. (2009). Seizing the initiative in economic growth: A theoretical hypothesis and case study of the Chinese local governments strategies responding to the reformation of market economy (in Chinese). *Shehuexue Yanjiu (Chinese Sociology Review), 4*, 1–27.

Chen, A. (2002). Capitalist development, entrepreneurial class, and democratization in China. *Political Science Quarterly, 117*(3), 401–422.

Chen, L. (2014). Varieties of global capital and the paradox of local upgrading in China. *Politics & Society, 42*(2), 223–252.

Chen, J., & Dickson, B. (2008). Allies of the state: Democratic support and regime support among China's private entrepreneurs. *The China Quarterly, 196*, 780–804.

Dickson, B. (2008). *Wealth into power: The Communist Party's embrace of China's private sector.* Cambridge/New York: Cambridge University Press.

Duara, P. (1988). *Culture, power, and the state: Rural North China, 1900–1942.* Stanford: Stanford University Press.

Duckett, J. (1998). *The entrepreneurial state in China: Real estate and commerce departments in reform-era Tianjin.* London/New York: Routledge.

Edin, M. (2003). State capacity and local agent control in China: CCP cadre management from a township perspective. *The China Quarterly, 173*, 35–52.

Ertman, T. (1997). *Birth of the leviathan: Building states and regimes in medieval and early modern Europe*. Cambridge/New York: Cambridge University Press.

Evans, P. (1979). *Dependent development: The alliance of multinational, state, and local capital in Brazil*. Princeton: Princeton University Press.

Evans, P. (1995). *Embedded autonomy: States and industrial transformation*. Princeton: Princeton University Press.

Evans, P. (1997). State structures, government-business relations and economic transformation. In S. Maxfield & B. Schneider (Eds.), *Business and the state in developing countries*. Ithaca: Cornell University Press.

Gehlbach, S. (2008). *Representation through taxation: Revenue, politics, and development in postcommunist states*. Cambridge/New York: Cambridge University Press.

Gerschenkron, A. (1962). *Economic backwardness in historical perspective, a book of essays*. Cambridge: Belknap Press of Harvard University Press.

Haggard, S., Maxfield, S., & Schineider, B. R. (1997). Theories of business and business-state relations. In S. Maxfiel & B. R. Schneider (Eds.), *Business and the state in developing countries*. Ithaca: Cornell University Press.

Hall, P., & Soskice, D. (2001). *Varieties of capitalism : The institutional foundations of comparative advantage*. New York: Oxford University Press.

Hamilton, G. G. (Ed.). (1996). *Asian business networks*. Berlin: Walter de Gruyter.

Huang, Y. (1996). *Inflation and investment controls in China : The political economy of central-local relations during the reform era*. Cambridge/New York: Cambridge University Press.

Johnson, C. (1982). *MITI and the Japanese miracle: The growth of industrial policy, 1925–1975*. Stanford: Stanford University Press.

Kang, D. C. (2002). *Crony capitalism: Corruption and development in South Korea and the Philippines, Cambridge studies in comparative politics*. Cambridge/New York: Cambridge University Press.

Kennedy, S. (2005). *The business of lobbying in China*. Cambridge: Harvard University Press.

Kohli, A. (2004). *State-directed development: Political power and industrialization in the global periphery*. Cambridge/New York: Cambridge University Press.

Landry, P. F. (2008). *Decentralized authoritarianism in China: The Communist Party's control of local elites in the post-Mao era*. Cambridge/New York: Cambridge University Press.

Lee, C. K., & Zhang, H. (2013). The power of instability: Unraveling the microfoundations of bargained authoritarianism in China. *American Journal of Sociology, 118*(6), 1475–1508.

Levi, M. (1988). *Of rule and revenue*. Berkeley: University of California Press.

Liberthal, K. (1992). Fragmented authority (chapter 2). In K. Lieberthal & D. Lampton (Eds.), *Bureaucracy, politics, and decision making in post-Mao China*. Berkeley: University of California Press.

Lo, M., & Otis, E. (2003). Guanxi civility: Processes, potentials, and contingencies. *Politics & Society, 31*(1), 131–162.
LÜ, X., & Landry, P. (2014). Show me the money: Interjurisdiction political competition and fiscal extraction in China. *American Political Science Review, 108*(3), 706–722.
Mann, M. (1993). *The sources of social power* (Vol. 2). Cambridge/New York: Cambridge University Press.
Martin, I. W., Mehrotra, A. K., & Prasad, M. (2009). *The new fiscal sociology: Taxation in comparative and historical perspective*. Cambridge/New York: Cambridge University Press.
Maxfield, S., & Schneider, B. (1997). *Business and the state in developing countries*. Ithaca: Cornell University Press.
McNally, C. A. (2012). Sino capitalism: China's reemergence and the international political economy. *World Politics, 64*(4), 741–776.
Migdal, J. S. (2009). Researching the state. In M. I. Lichbach & A. S. Zuckerman (Eds.), *Comparative politics: Rationality, culture, and structure* (2nd ed.). Cambridge/New York: Cambridge University Press.
Montinola, G., Qian, Y., & Weingast, B. (1996). Federalism, Chinese style: The political basis for economic success. *World Politics, 48*(1), 50–81.
Moore, M. (2008). Between coercion and contract. In D. Brautigam, O.-H. Fjeldstad, & M. Moore (Eds.), *Taxation and state-building in developing countries: Capacity and consent*. Cambridge/New York: Cambridge University Press.
North, D. C. (1990). *Institutions, institutional change, and economic performance*. Cambridge/New York: Cambridge University Press.
North, D. C., & Thomas, R. P. (1974). *The rise of the western world: A new economic history*. Cambridge: Cambridge University Press.
Oi, J. C. (1992). Fiscal reform and the economic foundations of local state corporatism in China. *World Politics, 45*(1), 99–126.
Oi, J. C. (1999). *Rural China takes off: Institutional foundations of economic reform*. Berkeley: University of California Press.
Ong, L. H. (2012). Between developmental and Clientelist states: Local state-business relationships in China. *Comparative Politics, 44*(2), 191–209.
Pearson, M. (2005). The business of governing business in China: Institutions and norms of the emerging regulatory state. *World Politics, 57*(2), 296–322.
Rong, J. (Ed.). (1998). *From the pressure-based system to democratic cooperative system: Political reform at the county and township level (in Chinese)*. Beijing: Zhongyang Bianyi Press.
Ross, M. (2004). Does taxation lead to representation? *British Journal of Political Science, 34*(2), 229–249.
Schumpeter, J. A. (1991 [1919]). The crisis of the tax state. In J. A. Schumpeter & R. Swedberg (Eds.), *The economics and sociology of capitalism*. Princeton: Princeton University Press.

Shih, V., Adolph, C., & Liu, M. (2012). Getting ahead in the Communist Party: Explaining the advancement of central committee members in China. *American Political Science Review, 106*(1), 166–187.

Skocpol, T. (1985). Bringing the state back in: Strategies of analysis in current research. In P. Evans, D. Rueschemeyer, & T. Skocpol (Eds.), *Bringing the state back in*. Cambridge/New York: Cambridge University Press.

Steinmo, S. (1993). *Taxation and democracy: Swedish, British, and American approaches to financing the modern state*. New Haven: Yale University Press.

Sun, X., Zhu, J., & Wu, Y. (2014). Organizational clientelism: An analysis of private entrepreneurs in Chinese local legislatures. *Journal of East Asian Studies, 14*(1), 1–29.

Tian, Y., & Zhao, X. (2008). *Taxiang zhi Shui: Yige Xiangzhen de Sanshinian, yige Guojia de 'Yinmi' Caizhengshi (in Chinese)*. Beijing: Zhongxin Chubanshe.

Tilly, C. (1990). *Coercion, capital, and European states, ad 990–1990*. Cambridge, MA: Blackwell.

Timmons, J. (2005). The fiscal contract: States, taxes and public services. *World Politics, 15*(4), 530–567.

Wade, R. (1990). *Governing the market: Economic theory and the role of government in east Asian industrialization*. Princeton: Princeton University Press.

Walder, A. (1996). Introduction. In A. Walder (Ed.), *China's transitional economy* (pp. 1–17). Oxford: Oxford University Pres.

Wank, D. L. (1999). *Commodifying communism: Business, trust, and politics in a Chinese city*. Cambridge/New York: Cambridge University Press.

Waterbury, J. (1997). Fortuitous by-products. *Comparative Politics, 29*(3), 383–402.

White, G., & Gray, J. (1988). *Developmental states in East Asia*. New York: St. Martin's Press.

Whiting, S. H. (2001). *Power and wealth in rural China: The political economy of institutional change*. New York: Cambridge University Press.

Whiting, S. H. (2004). The cadre evaluation system at the grassroots: The paradox of party rule. In B. Naughton & D. Yang (Eds.), *Holding China together*. New York: Cambridge University Press.

Whiting, S. (2011). Values in land: Fiscal pressures, land disputes, and justice claims in rural and Peri-urban China. *Urban Studies, 48*(3), 569–587.

Wong, C. (2009). Rebuilding government for the 21st century: Can China incrementally reform the public sector? *The China Quarterly, 200*, 929–952.

Woo, M. (1991). *Race to the swift: State and finance in Korean industrialization*. New York: Columbia University Press.

Yu, H. (2007). From Zhuanguanyuan to Shuiguanyuan: The evolution of China's tax administration (in Chinese). *China Taxation (zhongguo shuiwu), 4*, 15–16.

Zhang, C. (2017). A fiscal sociological theory of authoritarian resilience: Developing theory through China case studies. *Sociological Theory, 35*(1), 39–63.

CHAPTER 6

Chinese Private Entrepreneurs' Formal Political Connections: Industrial and Geographical Distribution

Jiangnan Zhu and Yiping Wu

Introduction

Business–government relations have generated keen research interests among many scholars. At the global level, the development of multinational enterprises (MNEs) in sovereign states after the Second World War reveals a new trend of international business–government relations. MNEs have shown the ability to alter industry policies both in major trading countries and within their own countries through working collaboratively

J. Zhu (✉)
Department of Politics and Public Administration, The University of Hong Kong, Hong Kong, China

Y. Wu
School of Public Economics and Administration, Shanghai University of Finance and Economics, Shanghai, China

X. Zhang, T. Zhu (eds.), *Business, Government and Economic Institutions in China*, International Political Economy Series,
DOI 10.1007/978-3-319-64486-8_6

with government (Ramamurti 2005). Mutual benefits between local governments and MNEs are an important impeller of emboldening international government–business ties (e.g. Meyer and Jensen 2005), though tensions between sovereign state governments and MNEs also emerge due to the rise of new actors, issues, and ideologies (e.g. Boddewyn 2016). At the domestic level, private firms and their political stakeholders are more interdependent in developing countries with reforming markets (Meznar and Johnson 2005). Corporate success depends on both its internal capabilities and external environment favorable for their performance. A solid relationship with governmental actors helps firms to create an advantageous environment to gain profits, as shown by cross-country studies (e.g. Cruz and Keefer 2015; Shami 2012).

Chinese private entrepreneurs' political connections share similarities with those of their counterparts in other developing countries. The existence and consequences (i.e. both positive and negative) of political connections actually reflect the politico-economic institutions in China during the reform era. This chapter explores the formal political connections of Chinese private entrepreneurs from a less studied perspective: how those formal connections are distributed across industrial sectors and geographical regions. In other words, which sectors and geographical regions tend to have more private entrepreneurs who are delegates of people's congresses and/or political consultative conferences? This perspective is inspired by studies in other countries, such as Latin America and Pakistan, which have shown that the patron–client ties between government and business can vary across industrial sectors because of the sectoral features, for example, the major resources and capital market that an industry relies on (Shami 2012; Schneider 2008). However, little scholarly effort has been made to bring this perspective to bear on the Chinese case.

In the following, we will first review the concept of *guanxi*, because business–government relation in China is often referred to as *zhengshang guanxi*. Then we briefly introduce the Chinese legislature, the people's congress and political consultative conference, as the institutional background. This is followed by the empirical exploration of the sectoral and regional distribution of private entrepreneurs based on surveys conducted over years. Interestingly, we find that the sectoral and regional concentration of formal political connections greatly overlaps with the distribution of sectoral corruption uncovered by our previous research (Zhu and Wu 2014). The final section concludes the chapter with a discussion of the potential consequences of such business–government relations.

A Review of the Concept "Guanxi"

Guanxi is a frequently used term in the Chinese society. Instead of merely referring to interpersonal relationship, *guanxi* has a profound meaning in the Chinese context. Based on a cultural approach, Nan Lin (2001) defines *guanxi* based on its nature of instrumentality and sentimentality rooted in the Chinese culture. He defines a good *guanxi* as "the ability to reach direct or indirect social ties that can provide help in achieving an instrumental goal" (p. 156). The dominant power of *guanxi* in the Chinese society, according to Lin, is embedded in transactions of resources in economic exchanges and maintenance of ties in social exchanges. He argues that the major purpose of developing *guanxi* is to explore broader social connections by which individuals can obtain access to more resources. In addition, the sentimental elements contribute to the asymmetric and nonreciprocal feature of *guanxi*. A favor which is not repaid immediately enables future transactions in *guanxi* networks.

Beyond viewing *guanxi* from a cultural perspective, Mayfair Yang (2002) redefines *guanxi* as an institutional mechanism in the context of China's reforming market economy. Yang argues that the major practitioners of *guanxi* have shifted from ordinary people to private entrepreneurs, state managers, and officials in the business and urban industry realm. Under incomplete marketization, *guanxi* becomes a type of political networks and an institution for private entrepreneurs to obtain resources, favorable policies, and market information controlled by state officials. Yang defines the phenomenon as "*Guanxi* capitalism", a "personal network for small flexible firms which provides access to new markets and supplies" (p. 473). In accordance with Yang's study, scholars have shown that entrepreneurs with more political *guanxi* networks bring more benefits to their business (Li et al. 2011; McNally et al. 2007; Peng and Luo 2000; Wank 2002).

While many studies have focused on the new trend of *guanxi*, limited efforts have been made to differentiate dimensions of political *guanxi* networks. The study of 15 Chinese private firms by McNally et al. (2007) identifies two components of political *guanxi* networks between private entrepreneurs and state officials: formal networks as positions taken by private entrepreneurs in political institutions such as local People's Congresses (LPCs) and People's Political Consultative Conferences (PPCCs) and informal ties with state officials established through personal relationship such as family backgrounds. Their study shows that despite taking formal positions in the legal, political, and market institutions, informal personal ties are becoming crucial for business success in the private sector. David Wank (2002) also makes distinctions between the two types of political *guanxi* networks and provides a different conclusion. He argues that, in China's new market economy, formal *guanxi* networks based on reputation, status, and bureaucratic rank are overriding the traditional type of *guanxi* networks based on informal, personal ties. He finds that formal *guanxi* networks become more important for a private firm when its business scale increases and concludes that *guanxi* practices are transforming from a highly personalistic to an organizational basis. In addition, Peng and Luo (2000) investigate the impact of managerial *guanxi* with government officials on firm performance by differentiating firms into service and manufacturing industries and find that the positive impact on service sector is more salient. However, the data used in that study are of the late 1990s, and other industrial sectors are not included. Thus, more substantive investigation into the dynamics of formal political *guanxi* networks across different regions and industries is needed.

The Institutional Context: The Chinese Legislature

A large majority of authoritarian regimes, regardless of types (i.e. hegemonic/single party regimes, monarchies, and personalist regimes, or military regimes), have legislative institutions. Malesky and Schuler (2010) point out that in terms of nomination procedures, electoral competitiveness, and professionalism of these institutions, authoritarian regimes display significant variations. In some countries, such as Malaysia, elections for legislative seats can be quite competitive. The elected members of parliament in Malaysia are also more like professional legislators in western democracies, who meet on a regular basis. In contrast, the People's Congress, the major legislature in China, is made up mainly of part-time delegates, who are elected through less contested elections and meet rarely each year (O'Brien 1994). For decades, the People's Congresses were considered the "rubber stamp" of decisions made by the Chinese Communist Party (CCP) and the government. However, the Chinese legislature has played an increasingly active role in the past years with its expanded jurisdiction, capacity, and assertiveness (Manion 2008).

The People's Congresses in China, following the party and government hierarchies, exist at every administrative level, from the central, to provincial, prefectural, to county and township levels. At the central level, as stipulated by the Chinese Constitution, the National People's Congress (NPC) is considered the highest organ of state power in China. Theoretically, like the parliament in democracies, the NPC enacts laws, makes policies, and elects top government officials of the central government. LPCs emulate the NPC, electing chief officials at their respective administrative levels, drafting and approving local laws and policies. They even have the power to impeach government officials if necessary.

Recent research shows that LPCs are more energetic than commonly thought and are closer to the local power center than the NPC (Cho 2009; Xia 2007). Along with the administrative reform, the LPCs have emerged as partners in governance providing a new arena for interested parties to work out differences. Responding to the principle of "lawmaking in advance", LPCs actively step into areas not legislated by the central government, making local statutes and creating test points. Most of the locally made laws concern the economy, especially market creation, such as promoting private enterprises, restructuring state sectors, and regulating the stock market. Moreover, local lawmaking has become a more pluralized policy process in which the originally strong impact of the party committees and government departments has increasingly been limited and indirect, and multiple players have opportunities to provide policy inputs (O'Brien 2009).

In addition to a stronger capacity of lawmaking, LPCs also strengthened their oversight of government performance through organized inspection tours, appraisal of local officials' work, approval of local leaders, and examination of work reports of the government. For instance, the LPCs once vetoed a court work report in Shenyang, and refused to ratify the appointment of several bureau directors in Guangdong (Cho 2009, p. 1–2). These striking cases are probably unable to represent the common practices across the country, but they do show the rising assertiveness of LPCs in China.

Finally, LPC delegates have also tried to reflect more public opinions than they did in the past (Cho 2009, p. 4–5). With the influx of younger and better-educated deputies, LPCs are energized. Many congresses have developed into forums for outspoken members, such as intellectuals and entrepreneurs, to speak up for groups or localities, to nudge policy in a preferred direction, and to win government support. Many deputies even spend private time replying letters and making visits, doing fieldwork, and acting as ombudsmen (O'Brien 2009).

A consultative body parallel to the PC is the PPCC, which is "somewhat analogous to an advisory legislative upper house" (Li et al. 2006, p. 7). Since the invention of the PPCC in 1949, the CCP has consistently used it to solicit social support by intentionally incorporating influential non-Communist and social elites. Therefore, the PPCC has a much smaller party representation than PC, and PPCC members' average education level is also higher than that of PC members. The PPCC is responsible to hold political consultations with the party-state on major social, political, and economic policies in the decision-making process and provide feedback during the implementation of these policies. The PPCC also exercises democratic supervision over the performance of party corps and state employees, the enforcement of laws and regulations, and the implementation of government policies, through taking inspection tours and making proposals and criticisms at regular meetings with party and government officials. The government also needs to respond to the proposals raised by PPCC members within a certain time, making the PPCC a platform for policy discussions and deliberations (Yan 2011).[1]

It should be clear that the Chinese legislature has played a more vigorous and binding role in the process of local governance. However, this development should not be exaggerated. Confrontation between LPCs and other political institutions is still limited. The dominant pattern of lawmaking is described as "active consultation, voluntary cooperation, and intentional pre-emption of conflict" (Xia 2007, p. 174). Popular preferences have remained under-represented in the lawmaking process. This limitation, among all the reasons, is largely due to the election process of legislative members.

While the selection of both PC deputies and PPCC committee members are nominally subject to some democratic voting procedures, local governments can often exert very strong influence, if not complete control, on the process and outcome of such selection. For PC members, the Electoral Law of NPC and LPCs of the People's Republic of China (the Electoral Law henceforth) stipulates that all administrative units, companies, residential committees, schools, political parties, social organizations, or even ten ordinary voters as a group have the right to recommend preliminary candidates for PC deputies at the county level. After preliminary candidates are nominated, each electoral district determines the final list of candidates in the last round of the election through "deliberation (*yunniang*), discussion (*taolun*), and negotiation (*xieshang*) by voter groups in the electoral district". However, the Electoral Law does not specify who those "voter groups" should be and how the procedure of deliberation, discussion, and negotiation should be conducted, which leaves local governments with plenty of room for interference and manipulation. The party committees can utilize the strict Communist Party discipline to direct votes of party-member delegates and controlled contestation to guarantee their designated candidates to win congress elections (Manion 2008). To ensure the party-state's influence in the legislative process, all major party and government officials are also placed in the LPCs and NPC as delegates. Although the party control of the PPCC is less tight, candidacy for the county PPCC is "overwhelmingly determined by the Communist Party's evaluation of each candidate's loyalty to and identification with the regime" (Yan 2011, p. 61).

Thus, local party committees retain a tight grip on the election of local Chinese legislators from vetting to final candidate selection. Although local delegates are more vocal in sessions, the party still ultimately determines who will take the representative seats. This party control weakens the connection between the elected and the public, who only nominally elect the deputies (Xia 2007, p. 101).

For private entrepreneurs, delegate status has shown to be an advantage for firms. In addition to voicing out policy preferences mentioned previously, more importantly there are material benefits, especially in terms of obtaining bank loans and preferential policies (Li et al. 2006). Various political positions, such as party members, delegates of the PCs and PPCCs, and former government officials, are taken up by private entrepreneurs for obtaining resources and overcoming redundant regulations for scaling up business (Kung and Ma 2016). However, Sun et al. (2014) suggest that private firms with formal political connections also need to help local government bear policy burdens, such as making donations and taking over ailing state-owned enterprises (SOEs). In other words, local governments also need private firms to carry out policies and reach targets assigned by their superiors. Given this mutually dependent relationship, it is worth examining how formal political connections distribute across industrial sectors and regions to further understand interactions between state and business actors in China.

Gauging Chinese Private Entrepreneurs' Formal Political Connections

We use the survey of private firms conducted jointly by the All-China Federation of Industry & Commerce (ACFIC), a semi-governmental organization for Chinese industrialists and businesspeople, and other organizations. This survey has been conducted every two to three years since 1991 among firms in all the provincial units in China. Since 2000, the following two questions have appeared on the questionnaire: (1) "Are you a PC member?" and (2) "Are you a CPPCC member?" We take the *PC and CPPCC membership* surveyed between 2000 and 2012 to measure two types of formal political connections and explore their distributions across industrial sectors and provinces.

Method

First, we classify firms by sectors and provinces, respectively. The main sectors from 2000 to 2012 include agriculture (i.e. farming, forestry, livestock husbandry, and fishing), mining, manufacturing, energy (i.e. electricity and gas), construction, infrastructure, transportation, restaurant and retail, finance and insurance, real estate, social services (e.g. resident services, renting), science and technology, and culture, education, public health, and sports (CEHS). However, the finance and insurance and infrastructure sectors usually include no more than three firms per survey, as these sectors are largely beyond the reach of private enterprises. We therefore omit these sectors, which leaves 11 sectors in the study. Table 6.1 provides more detailed information on the data set, the number of firms classified by industries; and Table 6.2 groups firms by provinces.

Second, we aggregate the number of *PC delegates* and *CPPCC members* for each sector and province in each of the seven years. These political connections are represented by the variables LPC_{it} and $CPPCC_{it}$, respectively, where i is the ith sector or province and t is the year.[2]

Third, for each of these two indicators, we use two approaches to generating final political connections indices across sectors and province. In the first approach, we first calculate the average political connections across industries or provinces in each year (see Tables 6.5, 6.6, 6.7, and 6.8 in Appendix). We then take the frequency with which each sector or

Table 6.1 Number of firms classified by industries in the sample

Industry	*Number of firms in the whole sample*	*Number of firms reported PC information*	*Number of firms reported CPPCC information*
Agriculture	1665	437	733
Mining	484	143	169
Manufacturing	9936	2448	3137
Energy	269	61	108
Construction	1612	370	508
Transportation	674	107	218
Social services	1932	180	441
Restaurant and retail	5700	634	1592
Real estate	498	115	158
Science and technology	377	36	106
CEHS	530	52	163
Sample size	23,667	4583	7333

province falls into the above-average political connection level across the seven years. Frequency captures the consistency or stability of political connections for a sector or province. High frequencies of above-average levels of political connection mean that political connection in these sectors or provinces is constantly strong, not accidental, and that it results from systematic, rather than random, factors. Appendix illustrates sectors and provinces with above- and below-average political connection levels year by year during this period. In the second approach, we examine the average of LPC_i and $CPPCC_i$ for each sector or province across the seven years and denote them as $AVELPC_i$ and $AVECPPCC_i$. Using $AVECPPCC_i$ as an example, we calculate it as follows:

$$AVECPPCC_i = \frac{\sum CPPCC_{it}}{7}, t = 2000, 2002, 2004, 2006, 2008, 2010, 2012.$$

i is a certain industry or province.

If frequency measures which sector own political connections most often, AVEPC gauges which sector or province own the most political connections on average during the seven years. It measures the extent of

Table 6.2 Number of firms classified by provinces in the sample

Industry	*Number of firms in the whole sample*	*Number of firms reported LPC information*	*Number of firms reported CPPCC information*
Beijing	1212	123	387
Tianjing	572	78	165
Hebei	1091	181	375
Shanxi	466	121	199
Inner Mongolia	386	72	101
Liaoning	1128	256	296
Jilin	655	166	227
Heilongjiang	755	127	231
Shanghai	2224	241	390
Jiangsu	2824	573	731
Zhejiang	1885	413	336
Anhui	691	166	244
Fujian	667	174	285
Jiangxi	536	94	202
Shandong	1944	405	564
Henan	814	207	351
Hubei	1239	197	338
Hunan	568	144	191
Guangdong	2199	372	743
Guangxi	423	64	184
Hainan	388	29	129
Chongqing	772	135	254
Sichuan	907	265	413
Guizhou	595	93	242
Yunnan	431	70	139
Tibet	81	19	39
Shannxi	804	161	316
Gansu	488	66	142
Qianghai	246	49	76
Ningxia	205	43	67
Xinjiang	360	46	105
Sample size	27,556	5150	8462

formal political connection in a sector or province. For comparison, we also check the standardized $AVELPC_i$ and $AVECPPCC_i$ to determine how many standard deviations a sector or province's political connection level is above or below the average. If a sector or province is substantially above average, this indicates that political connections in this sector or province are widespread. For both approaches, we roughly categorize sectors into high-, medium-, and low-level political connection. Combining both methods helps balance out the possible bias caused by the limited number of years observed in this sample.

Understanding Industrial Distribution of Political Connections

Table 6.3 reports the AVELPC and AVECPPCC of each sector and their respective standardized values, as well as the frequency with which each sector is above the yearly cross-sectoral average over the seven years. In each of the two categories of political connections, we classify sectors with both high average values of political connections and high frequencies above the yearly political connection average as high-level political connection sectors (shaded in dark gray). Several sectors also have low values and frequencies; we categorize these as low-level political connection sectors (shaded in light gray). Sectors in the middle have medium-level political connections (not shaded).

Table 6.3 shows that agriculture, energy, and mining have the highest overall level of formal political connections. For example, 32% and 40% of private entrepreneurs in the mining industry own LPC and CPPCC mem-

Table 6.3 Average level of political connections across sectors

Rank	Sector	LPC average	LPC frequency above yearly average	CPPCC average	CPPCC frequency above yearly average	Total frequency above yearly average (LPC+CPPCC)
1	Agriculture	0.2846 (1.0574)	7	0.4757 (1.8698)	7	14
2	Mining	0.3291 (1.6130)	7	0.4034 (0.8355)	6	13
3	Manufacturing	0.2663 (0.8290)	7	0.3440 (–0.0143)	4	11
4	Energy	0.2362 (0.4532)	4	0.4269 (1.1717)	6	10
5	Construction	0.2534 (0.6679)	6	0.3464 (0.0200)	4	10
6	Real estate	0.2131 (0.1648)	5	0.2402 (–1.4993)	4	9
7	Transportation	0.1714 (–0.3558)	1	0.3547 (0.1388)	5	6
8	Restaurant and retail	0.1217 (–0.9763)	0	0.3136 (–0.4492)	3	3
9	CEHS	0.1064 (–1.1673)	0	0.3263 (–0.2675)	3	3
10	Science and technology	0.1144 (–1.0674)	0	0.3071 (–0.5422)	2	2
11	Social services	0.1025 (–1.2160)	0	0.2569 (–1.2604)	0	0

bership per year on average between 2000 and 2012. This figure is about one standard deviation higher than the industrial average of all the 11 sectors. Furthermore, the mining industry falls into the above-average political connections level seven times in the seven surveys. The construction, energy, manufacturing, and agriculture also fall into the above-average political connections level five times in the seven surveys, indicating that these sectors also have quite strong political connections. In contrast, CEHS, restaurant and retail, and social services industries have lower density of political connections.

Interestingly, the levels of formal political connections in the sectors shown in Table 6.3 are largely in consistency with the sectoral distribution of corruption demonstrated in our earlier research (Zhu and Wu 2014), in which real estate, agriculture, mining, construction, and energy are found to be sectors involving high levels of corruption. It is worth to point out that even though the strength of formal political connections in the real estate sector is ranked in the middle of all sectors surveyed as shown in Table 6.3 here, many large private enterprises extend their business in the real estate sector. Six of top ten companies in real estate are private enterprises in 2017.[3] Thus, formal political connections in private real estate firms should not be overlooked. The high correlation of the current finding and our previous finding probably means that the account for sectoral corruption may also help to explain sectoral ranking of formal political connections.

On the one hand, private firms in industries that rely more on government support, policies, or state-controlled resources are more likely to be actively engaged in formal politics, so as to build stronger ties with government officials and also to influence favorable formal policies. For example, agriculture ranks as the highest politically connected sector. Agricultural firms actually depend heavily on government support for resources, such as land and bank loans, and policy support. While the land market is still in its formative stage, the capital market in China is even less developed; enterprises, especially private ones, must pay extensive costs, including bribes, to obtain loans from state-controlled banks.[4] Agricultural enterprises are more disadvantaged in terms of securing bank loans. The agricultural sector is highly labor intensive with low skill requirements. Firms need to rent land to grow or process products and to purchase seeds and fertilizer, which require large amounts of initial capital. Moreover, agricultural production is vulnerable to climate change, often needs relatively long investment cycles, and thus faces more business risks. This low-technology, high-risk feature makes it more difficult for agricultural firms to procure bank loans than others. The 2002 ACFIC survey shows that agricultural firms, on average, spent 57% more money than other sectors to obtain bank loans. Agricultural firms also need to overcome various internal trade barriers caused by local protectionism when trying to sell products across regional borders. These particularly high demands for more support, better services, and protections from government have likely also increased agricultural entrepreneurs' desire for political participation. The ACFIC survey shows that during the five years, more than 63% of sampled agricultural entrepreneurs reported that they were representatives of LPCs and PPCCs. This ratio is higher than all other sectors, which is 47% on average. This kind of political titles can bring benefits, such as low-interest rate bank loans and other preferential policies, which small- to medium-sized enterprises cannot get.[5]

Another example is the mining industry. The inherent scarcity of mines has increased along with the rising demand for energy and various scarce minerals. Local governments, as the de facto owner of local mines, have the actual right of disposal. It also determined how state-owned mines were privatized in the early 2000s, when systems of property rights exchange and state property management were poorly developed. This corresponds to the pattern shown in Appendix, which indicates that the level of overall formal political connections in the mining industry began to increase in 2004. This suggests that entrepreneurs in the sector have been more eager to participate in the government decision-making process to make their voices heard through formal political channels. Positions, such as PC representatives, also provide private entrepreneurs with the opportunities to cultivate and enhance their relationships with government officials and, by doing so, significantly benefit their businesses.

As discussed in Zhu and Wu (2014), the degree to which a sector relies on the scarcity and mobility of government provisions, such as state-controlled natural resources, services and support, very likely determines how much that sector is willing to and/or must enter into politics. Considering the politically densely connected industries together, land, mine, and energy resources are not only scarce but also immobile between different localities. Immobility and scarcity of state-controlled resources can give local governments more bargaining leverage over enterprises, mainly because these firms have fewer choices when selecting investment destinations in these sectors. Thus, enterprises enter into politics to facilitate their competition for scarce and/or immobile basic productive factors, mainly land, natural resources, and capital. In comparison, sectors that rely less on scarce state provisions face this kind of competition to a lesser degree. For example, in the restaurant and retail sector, although enterprises also need government-approved licenses, these licenses usually are not provided in a competitive way. As long as an enterprise meets the requirements, the licenses are approved.

On the other hand, as Dickson (2003) argues, absorbing private entrepreneurs into the CCP and its formal institutions is the CCP's "cooptation" strategy. The government is also more likely to co-opt industries that are strategic for national economic growth. Mining, construction, energy, and manufacturing industries are among China's primary economic engines and contribute more than 50% of its GDP annually. Compared with many other sectors with low-level political connections, these sectors involve greater capital investment. Profits gained by private firms in the manufacturing, mining, and agricultural product and by-product processing sectors were the highest among private firms, which respectively accounted for 52.25%, 8.72%, and 7.96% of total profits of the private sector in 2012.[6] Government assigning private entrepreneurs of these sectors political representative identities may indicate the degree of government's policy and fiscal reliance on the high profit sectors. As Sun et al. (2014) find, private firms whose owners have local legislative representative identities show more support to local governments by voluntarily contributing to public goods and services, reimbursing government purchase, assisting ailing SOEs, and increasing local employment.

Understanding Geographical Distribution of Formal Political Connections

Based on the average value of political connections across provinces (Table 6.4), we illustrate the geographical distribution of formal political connections in maps (Figs. 6.1 and 6.2). In Figs. 6.1 and 6.2, provinces with darker colors have more private entrepreneurs who are delegates of PC or PPCC. Browsing the two maps, we find that provinces with more extensive formal political connections tend to be either

Table 6.4 Average level of political connections across provinces

	LPC average	LPC frequency above yearly average	CPPCC average	CPPCC frequency above yearly average
Beijing	0.1243 (–1.4594)	0	0.3569 (–0.3029)	4
Tianjing	0.1505 (–1.0582)	2	0.3131 (–0.7573)	1
Hebei	0.1845 (–0.5375)	0	0.3835 (–0.0270)	2
Shanxi	0.2971 (1.1868)	4	0.5657 (1.8631)	7
Inner Mongolia	0.1767 (–0.6570)	2	0.2944 (–0.9512)	2
Liaoning	0.2455 (0.3966)	4	0.2901 (–0.9959)	1
Jilin	0.3333 (1.7412)	6	0.4346 (0.5031)	4
Heilongjiang	0.1907 (–0.4426)	3	0.4426 (0.5861)	4
Shanghai	0.1254 (–1.4426)	0	0.1718 (–2.2230)	0
Jiangsu	0.2039 (–0.2404)	3	0.2761 (–1.1411)	1
Zhejiang	0.2518 (0.4931)	5	0.1971 (–1.9606)	0
Anhui	0.2558 (0.5544)	4	0.3850 (–0.0114)	3
Fujian	0.3407 (1.8545)	6	0.4730 (0.9015)	7
Jiangxi	0.2077 (–0.1822)	4	0.4004 (0.1483)	2
Shandong	0.2197 (0.0015)	3	0.3007 (–0.8859)	0
Henan	0.3141 (1.4472)	6	0.4927 (1.1058)	6
Hubei	0.1742 (–0.6953)	0	0.2874 (–1.0239)	2

(continued)

Table 6.4 (continued)

Hunan	0.2792 (0.9127)	5	0.4243 (0.3963)	2
Guangdong	0.1827 (–0.5651)	5	0.3693 (–0.1743)	3
Guangxi	0.2054 (–0.2175)	4	0.4990 (1.1712)	6
Hainan	0.0904 (–1.9786)	0	0.3468 (–0.4077)	2
Chongqing	0.2001 (–0.2986)	4	0.3953 (0.0954)	3
Sichuan	0.3353 (1.7718)	7	0.5077 (1.2614)	7
Guizhou	0.1786 (–0.6279)	3	0.4395 (0.5539)	5
Yunnan	0.1979 (–0.3323)	3	0.3867 (0.0062)	3
Tibet	0.2667 (0.7213)	4	0.5855 (2.0685)	6
Shannxi	0.2298 (0.1562)	5	0.4172 (0.3226)	4
Gansu	0.1667 (–0.8101)	1	0.3177 (–0.7095)	2
Qianghai	0.2292 (0.1470)	4	0.4095 (0.2427)	5
Ningxia	0.2972 (1.1884)	5	0.4629 (0.7967)	4
Xinjiang	0.1533 (–1.01	1	0.3433 (–0.4440)	3

regions with rich natural resources, such as Shanxi which is famous for its rich coalmines, or inland provinces with weaker institutional environment, such as Ningxia and Guangxi Ethnic Autonomous Regions which are largely rural and economically underdeveloped in comparison to national average. This pattern actually verifies the explanation provided in industrial distribution of formal political connections, because the major industries in those places tend to be mining or agriculture.

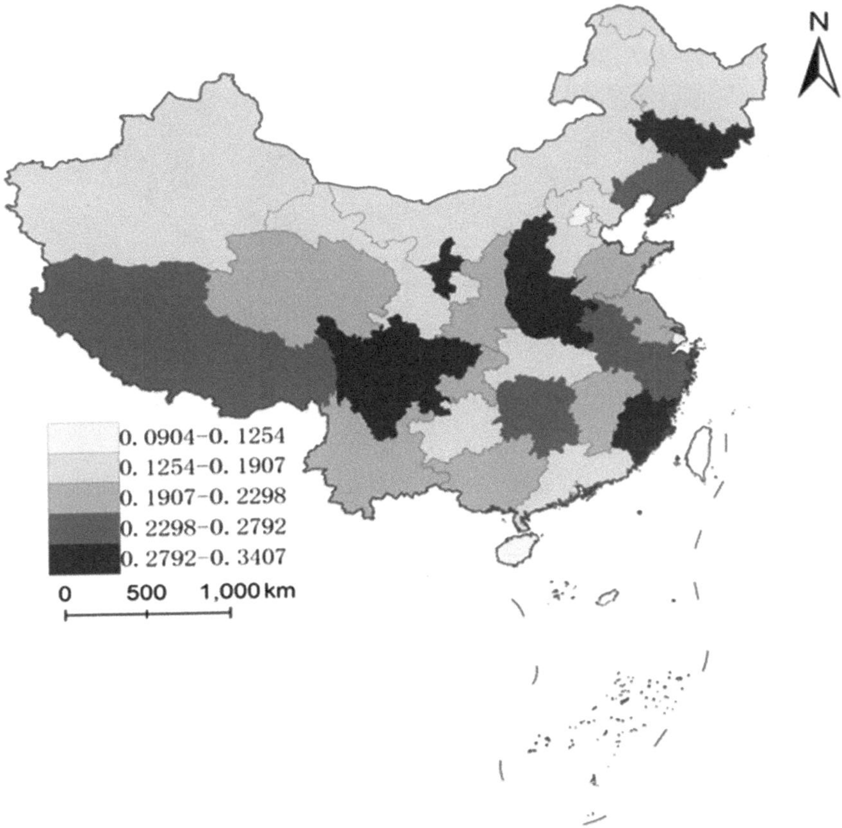

Fig. 6.1 The distribution of LPC across provinces

For resource-rich provinces, because the allocation of scarce resources is highly concentrated in the hands of government in China, entrepreneurs with close relationship with the government can be prioritized in obtaining those resources, which is vital to the development of private enterprises. Entrepreneurs being the LPC or CPPCC members can have more opportunities to meet and network with government officials. This relationship can facilitate these entrepreneurs to obtain priority in resources distribution.

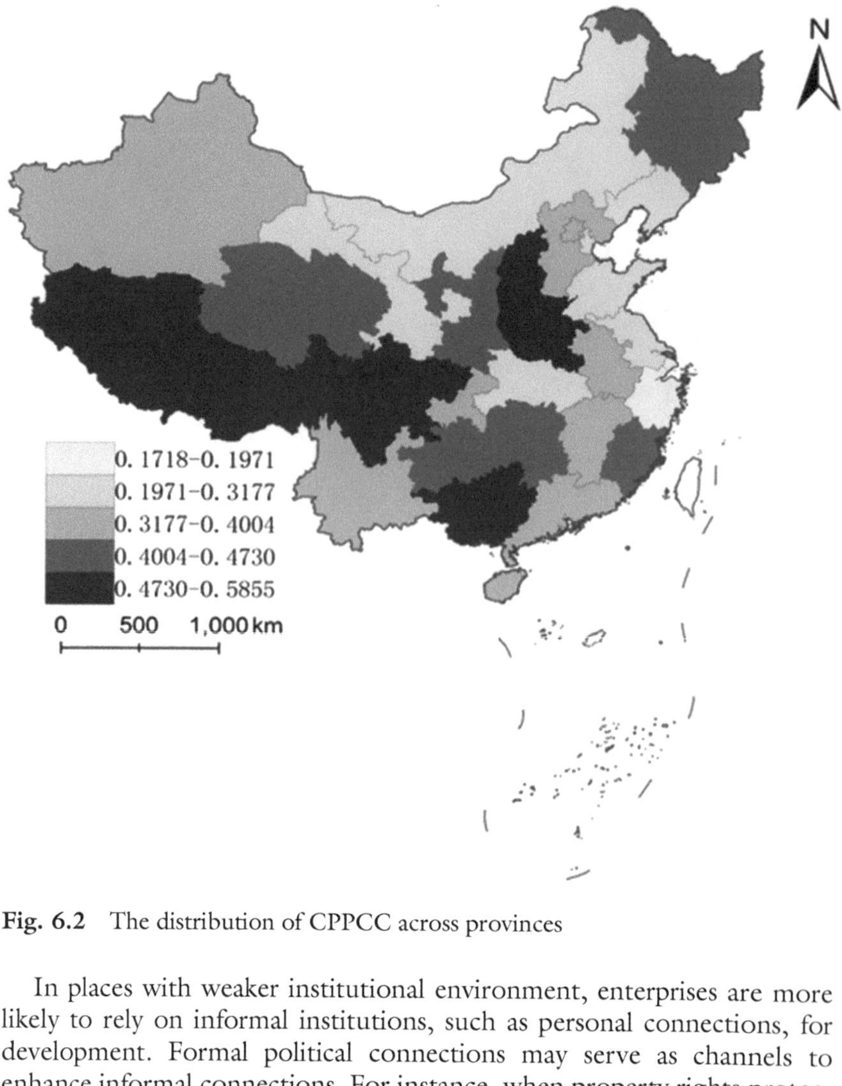

Fig. 6.2 The distribution of CPPCC across provinces

In places with weaker institutional environment, enterprises are more likely to rely on informal institutions, such as personal connections, for development. Formal political connections may serve as channels to enhance informal connections. For instance, when property rights protection is not ensured, private enterprises tend to lack incentive to invest. However, if they have maintained a close personal relationship with local government officials, it may be easier for entrepreneurs to acquire support and protection from the government, and therefore worry less about the infringement of their property right.

Conclusion

This chapter shows that the sectoral and regional distributions of formal political connections of private entrepreneurs demonstrate strong patterns overlapping with the sectoral distributions of corruption discovered by Zhu and Wu (2014). This coincidence may indicate the potential relationship between formal political connections and corruption. However, future research may need to explore whether established formal political connections are by-products of corruption or seeds breeding corruption. What can be concluded based on the current research is that the government and industrial sectors with high formal political connections are deeply interdependent, despite the ongoing market reform.

Thus, this study sheds new light on the limitations of China's market reform. Intensive formal political connections between private enterprises and government in some sectors reveal that the government intervention is still extensive in the current Chinese market economy system. Since the implementation of the open-door policy in 1978, China has initiated marketization which first started with product markets by introducing market competition and was then followed through restructuring SOEs and encouraging the establishment of non-SOEs, with government controls over land, natural resources, capital, and factors. As the sectoral analysis shows, marketization is insufficient and the major factor markets are intertwined with local business and government interests. Without competitive and effective factor markets, the government dominates the process of allocating scarce resources. Government officials can utilize their privilege of allocation to create and extract rents from private firms. Firms that successfully secure these factors and resources from the government are more likely to make profits and succeed in the marketplace, whereas those that fail to do so are struggling to survive. As a result, entrepreneurs consistently seek opportunities to establish connections with government by obtaining an LPC or CPPCC membership.

The sectoral and regional distributions of political connections may have potential impacts on China's political economy. First, connections between business and government through LPC and CPPCC memberships can give rise to corruption. Establishing connections with the government officials by legislative membership, private entrepreneurs may seek private gains through their legislative power or bribe state officials in absence of adequate supervision. Second, through the political connections, some private enterprises are able to obtain abundant factors, resources, and favorable policies and develop their business rapidly in spite of the imperfect market. Nonetheless, due to the structural defects in the Chinese market, these seemingly privileged private enterprises are often in a disadvantage in innovation and competition in the international market in the long term. Finally, formal political connections between business and government can help stabilize the current Chinese political regime. A key question is whether Chinese marketization and privatization will lead to transformation of Chinese political regime with the rise of private sectors and entrepreneurs. Formal political connections built through PC and CPPCC memberships demonstrate both the willingness of entrepreneurs to collude with the state power and the government's eagerness to co-opt private sectors. As Dickson (2007, p. 828) argues "China's capitalists have a stake in preserving the political system that has allowed them to prosper", and instead of posing a threat, they are "among the Party's most important bases of support". Therefore, politically, the formal connections between government and private entrepreneurs can contribute to the resilience of the Chinese Communist regime.

Acknowledgment The authors thank John Liu and Xiaoming Zhong for their excellent research assistance.

Appendix

*grey shade means high political connections.

Table 6.5 Overall LPC distribution across sectors

Rank	2000	STD	2002	STD	2004	STD	2006	STD	2008	STD	2010	STD	2012	STD
Agriculture	0.1894	0.5380	0.2011	0.5999	0.2844	0.8955	0.3349	1.3366	0.3862	0.8609	0.3962	1.0504	0.2000	0.6611
Mining	0.2647	1.8123	0.2250	0.9353	0.4375	2.1594	0.2273	0.2987	0.5179	1.9283	0.4194	1.2440	0.2121	0.8625
Manufacturing	0.2009	0.7326	0.2496	1.2810	0.2417	0.5429	0.2583	0.5975	0.3719	0.7448	0.3214	0.4245	0.2201	0.9949
Energy	0.1613	0.0624	0.0870	−1.0062	0.1579	−0.1495	0.3889	1.8572	0.2581	−0.1787	0.3864	0.9679	0.2143	0.8984
Construction	0.1910	0.5653	0.2240	0.9219	0.2340	0.4793	0.2444	0.4643	0.3533	0.5939	0.3333	0.5241	0.1938	0.5589
Transportation	0.1563	−0.0228	0.1282	−0.4261	0.1974	0.1765	0.1059	−0.8719	0.2182	−0.5022	0.2645	−0.0522	0.1293	−0.5141
Social services	0.0983	−1.0040	0.0977	−0.8551	0.0779	−0.8103	0.1135	−0.7981	0.1127	−1.3579	0.1250	−1.2192	0.0921	−1.1311
Restaurant and retail	0.1026	−0.9305	0.0831	−1.0607	0.1176	−0.4826	0.0931	−0.9951	0.1538	−1.0240	0.1889	−0.6845	0.1126	−0.7908
Real estate	0.2000	0.7174	0.2500	1.2869	0.0000	−1.4533	0.1928	−0.0340	0.3026	0.1827	0.3248	0.4526	0.2215	1.0186
Science and technology	0.0694	−1.4916	0.0781	−1.1305	0.0779	−0.8099	0.1020	−0.9090	0.2727	−0.0598	0.1379	−1.1110	0.0625	−1.6229
CEHS	0.1000	−0.9746	0.1200	−0.5415	0.1096	−0.5484	0.0984	−0.9444	0.1333	−1.1903	0.0795	−1.5996	0.1042	−0.9308
Average	**0.1576**		**0.1585**		**0.1760**		**0.1963**		**0.2801**		**0.2707**		**0.1602**	

Table 6.6 Overall CPPCC distribution across sectors

Rank	2000	STD	2002	STD	2004	STD	2006	STD	2008	STD	2010	STD	2012	STD
Agriculture	0.4167	0.2525	0.4425	0.8630	0.4978	1.4418	0.4387	1.7068	0.6162	1.9372	0.5493	1.8117	0.3688	3.4978
Mining	0.4706	0.8494	0.4000	0.5396	0.4375	0.9864	0.2879	–0.1665	0.5424	1.2242	0.4130	0.2836	0.2727	1.3996
Manufacturing	0.4063	0.1373	0.3474	0.1393	0.3634	0.4267	0.2645	–0.4571	0.3840	–0.3063	0.3710	–0.1872	0.2712	1.3668
Energy	0.5484	1.7110	0.5217	1.4658	0.3684	0.4645	0.4444	1.7776	0.3438	–0.6947	0.5000	1.2590	0.2619	1.1638
Construction	0.3876	–0.0698	0.3661	0.2816	0.2894	–0.1322	0.3056	0.0534	0.4136	–0.0203	0.4008	0.1469	0.2615	1.1550
Transportation	0.4531	0.6556	0.3077	–0.1629	0.3684	0.4645	0.2471	–0.6733	0.4426	0.2599	0.3920	0.0482	0.2721	1.3865
Socialservices	0.3006	–1.0332	0.2816	–0.3615	0.2213	–0.6465	0.2664	–0.4335	0.2523	–1.5787	0.2738	–1.2769	0.2026	–0.1310
Restaurant and retail	0.4052	0.1251	0.3278	–0.0099	0.3348	0.2107	0.2069	–1.1727	0.3497	–0.6377	0.3237	–0.7175	0.2471	0.8406
Real estate	0.2000	–2.1473	0.0000	–2.5046	0.0000	–2.3180	0.3373	0.4472	0.4167	0.0097	0.4554	0.7590	0.2722	1.3886
Science and technology	0.3611	–0.3632	0.2656	–0.4833	0.2208	–0.6503	0.2041	–1.2075	0.4857	0.6763	0.3000	–0.9832	0.3125	2.2686
CEHS	0.3833	–0.1174	0.3600	0.2352	0.2740	–0.2485	0.3115	0.1267	0.3261	–0.8657	0.2857	–1.1435	0.3438	2.9520
Average	**0.3939**		**0.3291**		**0.3069**		**0.3013**		**0.4157**		**0.3877**		**0.2806**	

Table 6.7 Overall LPC distribution across provinces

	2000	STD	2002	STD	2004	STD	2006	STD	2008	STD	2010	STD	2012	STD
Beijing	0.1026	−0.7577	0.1034	−0.9796	0.1626	−0.6165	0.0485	−1.8923	0.1667	−1.0179	0.1846	−0.6968	0.1019	−0.6263
Tianjing	0.0800	−1.0248	0.1111	−0.8817	0.0506	−2.0825	0.2895	0.7301	0.1279	−1.2747	0.1522	−0.9156	0.2424	1.2031
Hebei	0.1313	−0.4184	0.1328	−0.6056	0.1489	−0.7958	0.2086	−0.1502	0.2640	−0.3739	0.2652	−0.1526	0.1410	−0.1172
Shanxi	0.1316	−0.4149	0.1800	−0.0051	0.3571	1.9293	0.3784	1.6975	0.2982	−0.1476	0.5000	1.4328	0.2347	1.1029
Inner Mongolia	0.2667	1.1820	0.1400	−0.5140	0.3500	1.8364	0.0667	−1.6942	0.1111	−1.3858	0.1778	−0.7427	0.1250	−0.3255
Liaoning	0.1486	−0.2139	0.1724	−0.1018	0.2566	0.6139	0.1270	−1.0381	0.3902	0.4613	0.3450	0.3862	0.2784	1.6719
Jilin	0.3750	2.4622	0.3333	1.9453	0.2375	0.3639	0.4000	1.9325	0.5517	1.5301	0.2736	−0.0959	0.1623	0.1602
Heilongjiang	0.2079	0.4870	0.2000	0.2494	0.2222	0.1636	0.1295	−1.0109	0.1935	−0.8405	0.2397	−0.3248	0.1419	−0.1055
Shanghai	0.0667	−1.1820	0.0710	−1.3919	0.0588	−1.9751	0.0930	−1.4081	0.2569	−0.4209	0.2171	−0.4774	0.1146	−0.4609
Jiangsu	0.1254	−0.4882	0.2222	0.5318	0.1821	−0.3613	0.2557	0.3624	0.2695	−0.3375	0.1933	−0.6381	0.1792	0.3802
Zhejiang	0.2000	0.3936	0.2795	1.2608	0.2250	0.2003	0.1900	−0.3526	0.3714	0.3369	0.2852	−0.0176	0.2117	0.8034
Anhui	0.1282	−0.4551	0.1772	−0.0407	0.2066	−0.0406	0.2692	0.5092	0.3827	0.4116	0.3368	0.3309	0.2899	1.8216
Fujian	0.0952	−0.8452	0.3291	1.8919	0.2660	0.7369	0.2923	0.7606	0.7586	2.8994	0.4468	1.0736	0.1965	0.6055
Jiangxi	0.1967	0.3546	0.1951	0.1870	0.2405	0.4031	0.1401	−0.8955	0.4490	0.8504	0.2128	−0.5064	0.0196	−1.6979
Shandong	0.2120	0.5355	0.1304	−0.6361	0.1827	−0.3534	0.2073	−0.1643	0.3404	0.1317	0.2329	−0.3707	0.2322	1.0703
Henan	0.2517	1.0047	0.2267	0.5891	0.3010	1.1950	0.3768	1.6801	0.5089	1.2469	0.4167	0.8704	0.1172	−0.4271
Hubei	0.0960	−0.8357	0.1591	−0.2710	0.1222	−1.1453	0.2188	−0.0392	0.2615	−0.3905	0.2323	−0.3747	0.1298	−0.2630
Hunan	0.1719	0.0615	0.0750	−1.3410	0.2889	1.0367	0.2177	−0.0511	0.5577	1.5698	0.3854	0.6590	0.2581	1.4076
Guangdong	0.1658	−0.0106	0.1169	−0.8079	0.1844	−0.3312	0.2108	−0.1262	0.1579	−1.0761	0.3207	0.2221	0.1226	−0.3568
Guangxi	0.1064	−0.7128	0.2326	0.6641	0.2571	0.6204	0.2692	0.5092	0.3333	0.0847	0.1475	−0.9473	0.0920	−0.7552
Hainan	0.1296	−0.4385	0.1200	−0.7684	0.1000	−1.4359	0.1176	−1.1404	0.1250	−1.2939	0.0274	−1.7583	0.0130	−1.7839
Chongqing	0.2165	0.5887	0.1930	0.1603	0.2574	0.6243	0.2500	0.3003	0.1959	−0.8246	0.2016	−0.5820	0.0861	−0.8320

(*continued*)

Table 6.7 (continued)

Sichuan	0.2833	1.3783	0.2283	0.6094	0.2816	0.9411	0.3043	0.8912	0.5686	1.6420	0.4595	1.1594	0.2216	0.9323
Guizhou	0.2273	0.7163	0.1489	–0.4008	0.1077	–1.3351	0.2273	0.0533	0.1774	–0.9471	0.1909	–0.6543	0.1709	0.2721
Yunnan	0.0732	–1.1052	0.2653	1.0802	0.1803	–0.3848	0.2571	0.3776	0.2581	–0.4130	0.3014	0.0918	0.0500	–1.3021
Tibet	0.4000	2.7577	0.0000	–2.2952	0.2000	–0.1270	0.3333	1.2068	0.3333	0.0847	0.5000	1.4328	0.1000	–0.6510
Shannxi	0.0965	–0.8298	0.2133	0.4186	0.1491	–0.7932	0.2653	0.4668	0.4026	0.5433	0.2929	0.0344	0.1892	0.5104
Gansu	0.1111	–0.6572	0.2069	0.3372	0.1630	–0.6113	0.0734	–1.6213	0.2632	–0.3792	0.2542	–0.2269	0.0952	–0.7135
Qianghai	0.0909	–0.8960	0.3000	1.5216	0.2105	0.0105	0.2000	–0.2437	0.3333	0.0847	0.2388	–0.3309	0.2308	1.0521
Ningxia	0.2000	0.3936	0.2500	0.8855	0.2857	0.9948	0.2857	0.6888	0.2353	–0.5639	0.8000	3.4585	0.0238	–1.6432
Xinjiang	0.0784	–1.0437	0.0784	–1.2977	0.2647	0.7199	0.1915	–0.3362	0.2927	–0.1840	0.0882	–1.3477	0.0794	–0.9193
Average	**0.1667**		**0.1804**		**0.2097**		**0.2224**		**0.3205**		**0.2878**		**0.1500**	

Table 6.8 Overall CPPCC distribution across provinces

	2000	STD	2002	STD	2004	STD	2006	STD	2008	STD	2010	STD	2012	STD
Beijing	0.3590	−0.5658	0.3161	−0.8404	0.4146	0.0445	0.2335	−0.8137	0.4146	0.0445	0.4362	0.3110	0.3241	0.6226
Tianjing	0.3900	−0.3392	0.4815	0.3538	0.2658	−0.8498	0.2895	−0.4813	0.2658	−0.8498	0.3372	−0.3525	0.1616	−0.9339
Hebei	0.3838	−0.3845	0.4141	−0.1329	0.5000	0.5577	0.3374	−0.1970	0.5000	0.5577	0.3504	−0.2641	0.1987	−0.5785
Shanxi	0.5132	0.5614	0.5600	0.9206	0.7500	2.0601	0.6216	1.4896	0.7500	2.0601	0.4487	0.3948	0.3163	0.5479
Inner Mongolia	0.3333	−0.7537	0.3000	−0.9567	0.4750	0.4075	0.2000	−1.0125	0.4750	0.4075	0.1702	−1.4719	0.1071	−1.4559
Liaoning	0.1351	−2.2025	0.5517	0.8607	0.3009	−0.6388	0.2381	−0.7864	0.3009	−0.6388	0.3750	−0.0992	0.1289	−1.2471
Jilin	0.5500	0.8304	0.5641	0.9502	0.3125	−0.5691	0.6667	1.7573	0.3125	−0.5691	0.4375	0.3197	0.1990	−0.5757
Heilongjiang	0.5545	0.8633	0.5667	0.9690	0.6667	1.5595	0.1511	−1.3027	0.6667	1.5595	0.2764	−0.7601	0.2162	−0.4109
Shanghai	0.2944	−1.0380	0.1923	−1.7343	0.1038	−1.8233	0.0698	−1.7852	0.1038	−1.8233	0.2348	−1.0389	0.2038	−0.5297
Jiangsu	0.2724	−1.1988	0.2381	−1.4036	0.3266	−0.4844	0.1758	−1.1561	0.3266	−0.4844	0.3079	−0.5489	0.2851	0.2490
Zhejiang	0.2485	−1.3735	0.1223	−2.2397	0.2208	−1.1202	0.1636	−1.2285	0.2208	−1.1202	0.2314	−1.0617	0.1726	−0.8285
Anhui	0.6410	1.4956	0.4304	−0.0152	0.2727	−0.8083	0.3846	0.0831	0.2727	−0.8083	0.4327	0.2875	0.2609	0.0172

(*continued*)

Table 6.8 (continued)

Fujian	0.5238	0.6389	0.5570	0.8989	0.5000	0.5577	0.4000	0.1745	0.5000	0.5577	0.5588	1.1327	0.2717	0.1207
Jiangxi	0.6230	1.3640	0.6098	1.2801	0.3418	−0.3930	0.3248	−0.2718	0.3418	−0.3930	0.3462	−0.2922	0.2157	−0.4157
Shandong	0.4000	−0.2661	0.2657	−1.2043	0.2879	−0.7169	0.2694	−0.6006	0.2879	−0.7169	0.3512	−0.2587	0.2427	−0.1571
Henan	0.5175	0.5928	0.4800	0.3430	0.5340	0.7620	0.3623	−0.0493	0.5340	0.7620	0.5526	1.0912	0.4688	2.0086
Hubei	0.2080	−1.6696	0.4773	0.3235	0.2167	−1.1448	0.2969	−0.4374	0.2167	−1.1448	0.2984	−0.6126	0.2981	0.3736
Hunan	0.5938	1.1506	0.4000	−0.2347	0.5333	0.7578	0.3468	−0.1412	0.5333	0.7578	0.3261	−0.4269	0.2366	−0.2155
Guangdong	0.4663	0.2186	0.2540	−1.2888	0.3582	−0.2945	0.3213	−0.2926	0.3582	−0.2945	0.4948	0.7038	0.3324	0.7021
Guangxi	0.6596	1.6316	0.6512	1.5791	0.4714	0.3858	0.5385	0.9964	0.4714	0.3858	0.3333	−0.3787	0.3678	1.0412
Hainan	0.4074	−0.2120	0.5400	0.7762	0.2333	−1.0451	0.5294	0.9424	0.2333	−1.0451	0.3026	−0.5845	0.1818	−0.7404
Chongqing	0.4948	0.4269	0.5088	0.5509	0.3663	−0.2458	0.5250	0.9163	0.3663	−0.2458	0.3071	−0.5543	0.1987	−0.5785

(*continued*)

Table 6.8 (continued)

Sichuan	0.5333	0.7083	0.5870	1.1155	0.5243	0.7037	0.4957	0.7424	0.5243	0.7037	0.5000	0.7386	0.3892	1.2462
Guizhou	0.6667	1.6835	0.5213	0.6412	0.1538	−1.5228	0.7273	2.1169	0.1538	−1.5228	0.5370	0.9866	0.3162	0.5469
Yunnan	0.3902	−0.3377	0.4082	−0.1755	0.4426	0.2127	0.5429	1.0226	0.4426	0.2127	0.3553	−0.2312	0.1250	−1.2845
Tibet	0.5000	0.4649	0.3000	−0.9567	0.8000	2.3606	0.5833	1.2623	0.8000	2.3606	0.6154	1.5121	0.5000	2.3075
Shannxi	0.4298	−0.0482	0.4467	0.1025	0.4037	−0.0210	0.4286	0.3442	0.4037	−0.0210	0.5106	0.8097	0.2973	0.3659
Gansu	0.3889	−0.3472	0.4138	−0.1350	0.2609	−0.8792	0.1743	−1.1650	0.2609	−0.8792	0.4154	0.1716	0.3095	0.4828
Qianghai	0.4545	0.1323	0.6000	1.2094	0.4561	0.2939	0.4000	0.1745	0.4561	0.2939	0.2687	−0.8117	0.2308	−0.2711
Ningxia	0.3000	−0.9971	0.3750	−0.4152	0.5714	0.9868	0.5000	0.7680	0.5714	0.9868	0.8750	3.2520	0.0476	−2.0259
Xinjiang	0.2941	−1.0402	0.2745	−1.1408	0.5588	0.9111	0.1915	−1.0629	0.5588	0.9111	0.0968	−1.9638	0.4286	1.6236
Average	**0.4364**		**0.4325**		**0.4072**		**0.3706**		**0.4072**		**0.3898**		**0.2591**	

Notes

1. For a more systematic discussion of the PPCC's policy-making process and its relationships with the CCP and the government, see Li et al. (2006).
2. For example, for LPC_{it}, the PC of the real estate sector (RE) in 2000 is $LPC_{RE,2000} = (PC_{REFirm1,2000} + PC_{REFirm2,2000} + \ldots + PC_{REFirmN,2000})/N$, where N is the number of firms in this sector. The PC of the Jiangsu Province(JS) in 2000 is $LPC_{JS,2000} = (PC_{JSFirm1,2000} + PC_{JSFirm2,2000} + \ldots + PC_{JSFirmN,2000})/N$ where N is the number of firms in this province.
3. "2017 Top 100 Enterprises of Real Estate Research Report", NetEase Finance, March 20, 2017, accessed March 31, 2017, http://money.163.com/17/0320/10/CFVD9AUK002580S6.html
4. In a survey of 29 cities, nearly 82% of respondents reported that rent-seeking during capital allocation in Chinese banks was prevalent or very common, indicating the high cost beard by firms.
5. For example, see "Xi nongwei: guanyu yinfa wuxishi 2010 niandu nongye chanyehua longtou qiye fuchi zijin guanli banfa de tongzhi" ["Wuxi Agricultural Committee: About the notice of financial sponsorship management of leading firms in agricultural sector in Wuxi in 2010"] (http://www.wxagri.cn/web101/pages/nlzx/tzgg/423119.shtml)
6. "Indicators of Private Industry by Sector", Chinese Statistics Yearbook 2013.

References

Boddewyn, J. J. (2016). International business–government relations research 1945–2015: Concepts, typologies, theories and methodologies. *Journal of World Business, 51*(1), 10–22.

Cho, Y. N. (2009). *Local people's congresses in China: Development and transition.* Cambridge: Cambridge University Press.

Cruz, C., & Keefer, P. (2015). Political parties, clientelism, and bureaucratic reform. *Comparative Political Studies, 48*(14), 1942–1973.

Dickson, B. J. (2003). *Red capitalists in China: The party, private entrepreneurs, and prospects for political change.* Cambridge: Cambridge University Press.

Dickson, B. J. (2007). Integrating wealth and power in China: The communist party's embrace of the private sector. *The China Quarterly, 192*, 827–854.

Kung, J. K., & Ma, C. (2016). Friends with benefits: How political connections help to sustain private enterprise growth in China. *Economica.* http://dx.doi.org/10.1111/ecca.12212

Li, H., Meng, L., & Zhang, J. (2006). Why do entrepreneurs enter politics? Evidence from China. *Economic Inquiry, 44*(3), 559–578.

Li, S. X., Yao, X., Sue-Chan, C., & Xi, Y. (2011). Where do social ties come from: Institutional framework and governmental tie distribution among Chinese managers. *Management and Organization Review, 7*(1), 97–124.
Lin, N. (2001). Guanxi: A conceptual analysis. *Contributions in Sociology, 133*, 153–166.
Malesky, E., & Schuler, P. (2010). Nodding or needling: Analyzing delegate responsiveness in an authoritarian parliament. *American Political Science Review, 104*(03), 482–502.
Manion, M. (2008). When communist party candidates can lose, who wins? Assessing the role of local people's congresses in the selection of leaders in China. *The China Quarterly, 195*, 607–630.
McNally, C.A., Guo, H., & Hu, G. (2007). *Entrepreneurship and political Guanxi networks in China's private sector*. Working Papers.
Meyer, K., & Jensen, C. (2005). Foreign direct investment and government policy in Central and Eastern Europe. In G. Robert (Ed.), *International business and government relations In 21st century*. Cambridge: Cambridge University Press.
Meznar, M. B., & Johnson, J. H. (2005). Business-government relations within a contingency theory framework: Strategy, structure, fit, and performance. *Business & Society, 44*(2), 119–143.
O'Brien, K. J. (1994). Agents and remonstrators: Role accumulation by Chinese people's congress deputies. *The China Quarterly, 138*, 359–380.
O'Brien, K. J. (2009). Local people's congresses and governing China [Book review]. *China Journal, 61*, 131–141.
Peng, M. W., & Luo, Y. (2000). Managerial ties and firm performance in a transition economy: The nature of a Micro-Macro link. *Academy of Management Journal, 43*(3), 486–501.
Ramamurti, R. (2005). Global regulatory convergence: The case of intellectual property rights. In G. Robert (Ed.), *International business and government relations in the 21st century* (pp. 341–360). Cambridge: Cambridge University Press.
Schneider, B. R. (2008). Economic liberalization and corporate governance: The resilience of business groups in Latin America. *Comparative Politics, 40*(4), 379–397.
Shami, M. (2012). Collective action, clientelism, and connectivity. *American Political Science Review, 106*(03), 588–606.
Sun, X., Zhu, J., & Wu, Y. (2014). Organizational clientelism: An analysis of private entrepreneurs in Chinese local legislatures. *Journal of East Asian Studies, 14*(01), 1–30.
Wank, D. (2002). Business-state clientelism in China: Decline or evolution. In T. Gold, D. Guthrie, & D. Wank (Eds.), *Social connections in China: Institutions, culture, and the changing nature of Guanxi*. New York: Cambridge University Press.

Xia, M. (2007). *The people's congresses and governance in China: Toward a network mode of governance*. London: Routledge.

Yan, X. (2011). Regime inclusion and the resilience of authoritarianism: The local people's political consultative conference in Post-Mao Chinese politics. *The China Journal, 66*, 53.

Yang, M. M.-H. (2002). The resilience of Guanxi and its new deployments: A critique of some new guanxi scholarship. *The China Quarterly, 170*, 459–476.

Zhu, J., & Wu, Y. (2014). Who pays more 'tributes' to the government? Sectoral corruption of China's private enterprises. *Crime, Law and Social Change, 61*(3), 309–333.

CHAPTER 7

International Context and China's Business–Government Relations

Tianbiao Zhu

Introduction

Like most of the other concepts in social sciences, government–business relations are complex. Scholars attempt to simplify them into three models of interaction, which have also been examined by the literature on China's government–business relations (e.g., Pearson 1997; Kennedy 2005). The three models are corporatism, clientelism, and pluralism. Corporatism emphasizes the role of the government in managing government–business relations through its interaction with business representatives (e.g., business associations and large business groups). Clientelism points to formal and informal organizational structures linking political and business elites, especially the informal ties that hold the officials and their non-state clients together. Pluralism, on the other hand, emphasizes the power of civil society, in particular the role of business in getting the government to do what it wants.

As many China scholars have argued, it is difficult to fit China into any one model. Clearly, China is both unique and complex. Barry Naughton

T. Zhu (✉)
Institute for Advanced Study in Humanities and Social Sciences, Zhejiang University, Hangzhou, China

X. Zhang, T. Zhu (eds.), *Business, Government and Economic Institutions in China*, International Political Economy Series,
DOI 10.1007/978-3-319-64486-8_7

(2010: 438–9) believes that China's uniqueness rests on the combination of its large size, a relatively healthy and well-trained labour force as a comparative advantage, and a hierarchical authoritarian political system. Dan Breznitz and Michael Murphree (2010: 64) witnessed the complexity of the Chinese bureaucracy and wrote:

> The Chinese bureaucracy is not only vast and complex, but it is also steeped in numerous cross-allegiances and lines of authority. ... Not surprisingly, it is unclear which organization has final authority over specific domains and it is not even clear who is in charge of whom at every level of the bureaucratic structure. This unwieldy construction is then further muddled by the CCP (*the Chinese Communist Party*, added by author) infusion into every nook and cranny of both the bureaucratic system and industry.

Jude Howell (2006: 278) calls the Chinese state "a polymorphous state that reveals contradictory features of developmentalism and predation, rivalry and unity, autonomy and clientelism, efficiency and inefficiency, across time and space." Of course, this is not to say that it is either impossible or undesirable to find regular patterns in the Chinese case. Arjan de Haan (2011: 23) argues that China's land reform, strategies of industrialization, export promotion, and newly emerging global financial and soft power are all not necessarily unique characteristics of China, but "[w]hat makes China fairly unique—but its explanations not exceptional—is the commitment and ability to address existing and emerging development problems." China scholars have created a number of combined notions to explain this unusual commitment and ability, such as "fragmented authoritarianism" (Lieberthal and Oksenberg 1988), "decentralized authoritarianism" (Landry 2008), "fragmented influence" (Kennedy 2011), "fragmented integration" (Brødsgaard 2012), and "fragmented control" (Fu 2017).

The fact that China scholars have to modify standard concepts and combine them (often with opposite meanings) to describe China and its government–business relations reveals both the complexity of the Chinese case and the possibility of identifying general patterns within it. Thus, it is not surprising to discover traces of corporatism, clientelism, and pluralism in all of China's government–business relations, as pointed out by Margaret Pearson (1997) and Scott Kennedy (2005). The central task is therefore just to elucidate the general patterns that link them together. Following the tradition of combining standard ideas, some recent studies (e.g.,

McNally 2012; Zhu 2012) suggested understanding China's development model along the central–local divide, that is, "top-down state-led development with bottom-up entrepreneurial private capital accumulation" (McNally 2012: 744). This is certainly not a new way to study China, since central–local relations have been a focus of the existing literature for many years. However, it does provide a structural method for examining the Chinese political economy.

The aim of this chapter is not only to find systematic features of China's government–business relations, but more importantly to link those features to an international context. In other words, this work constitutes an attempt to study the international conditions of China's government–business formation and transformation. This study can be placed under the theoretical frameworks of late development, and examines how the motive of surviving and competing in international systems drives the Chinese state and businesses to confront changing conditions of international development, and therefore to form and transform government–business relations in China. Given the immense size of China, a claim that international factors have determined such relations seems untenable. However, this study will show the importance of the international context in shaping China's government–business relations, and in particular, how the features of corporatism, clientelism, and pluralism are linked in this context.

Late Development and the Extreme Form of Government–Business Relations

The international system that developed out of Western Europe is marked by the interaction between nation-states and capitalism. Military competition among nation-states forces their political elites to seek continuing financial support from the wealthy, which helped to strengthen business power and subsequently contributed to the rise of the most efficient production system in the world so far—capitalism. With the support of capitalism, nation-states began to wage even larger wars against each other. This state–capitalism interaction also drove the European international system to expand into other parts of the world. In order to win in both military and economic competitions inside of the system, nation-states and capitalism worked hand in hand to achieve external expansion to extract ever more and cheaper resources. When the relatively undeveloped areas were forced into the system, they immediately encountered the problem of development. Without development, they could not guarantee their survival, let alone prosper, in the system.

By examining the developmental experiences of Germany and Russia in the late nineteenth century, Alexander Gerschenkron (1962) observed a general tendency in economic development: the later that a country began the process of industrialization, the more organizational power was needed to mobilize limited capital to target the industries and industrial structures that had proved successful for early industrializers. Thus, while England utilized firms to industrialize, Germany used banks to coordinate its industrialization, and the more undeveloped Russia turned to the state. Gerschenkron also discussed the survival and competition motive behind late development. In particular, he pointed to military imperatives behind Russia's industrialization (1962: 17).

The particular structure of the international system after the Second World War was marked by the confrontation between the Soviet Union and its allies on the one side and the United States and its allies on the other. While the pattern of late development was present throughout the international system, it was particularly apparent along the confrontational line of the Cold War, from communist Eastern Europe to capitalist East Asia, although the pattern varied from region to region and country to country. Communist countries pushed organizational power to the extreme in the form of central planning systems, whereas East Asian late developers stressed government–business cooperation governed by the developmental states. Moreover, the political confrontation occurring during the Cold War period was accompanied by economic confrontation. While the Soviet bloc closed its market and replaced it with a central planning system of production, the United States and its allies engaged in so-called embedded liberalism, subordinating free trade and the free market to domestic conditions and needs, and the world market became more managed by domestic authorities. Thus, on both sides, the building of a vertically integrated industrial structure was the norm.

With this background, we now turn to China. Imperial China was gradually incorporated into the European international system after the 1840s. It was a typical late developer—economically backward and politically humiliated by the West. Generations of political elites in China sought to change this situation by striving for late development. During this process, they became increasingly radical, first being the Chinese nationalists and then the communists. Given the size of China (in terms of both its geographical area and population) and its geographical position, it would be quite difficult for it to avoid the fate of a front-line position during the Cold War, regardless of whether it was a nationalist China or a communist one. The Japanese invasion in the 1930s and 1940s, another international factor, accidentally helped to revive the communist forces from total defeat by the nationalists, and the communist engagement in the anti-Japanese war paved the way for its eventual victory over the nationalists in 1949.

In this way, China ended up on the Soviet side of the Cold War front-line. However, "leaning to one side" in the 1950s was not simply an ideological choice of the Chinese Communist Party (CCP). Mao Zedong had a long fight against Stalin's representatives inside the CCP before 1949. Mao once told a visiting American official in the mid-1940s that "China must industrialize. This can be done—in China—only by free enterprise and with the aid of foreign capital. Chinese and American interests are correlated and similar. They fit together economically and politically. We can and must work together" (Yahuda 1983: 54). On 28 June 1949, Mao made effort to approach the Americans by sending his message to John Stuart, the US ambassador, inviting him to attend the Yenching University reunion in Beijing. Stuart did not visit Beijing in the end, but after his trip to Shanghai in June 1949, he reported to the Secretary of State that: "[t] he trip to Shanghai gave me ample evidence local CCP authorities very anxious develop international trade and make utmost use Shanghai for promoting industry, communications, production, reconstruction. To this end, they especially want friendly relations with USA." (Rea and Brewer 1981: 332) However, the Cold War structure was already established globally by that time, and it was difficult for the United States to cross the divide of ideological orientation and domestic politics. The outbreak of the Korean War in 1950, the first war involving both sides of the Cold War, pushed the United States and China further apart.

Thus, the particular structure of the international system in the Cold War played a fundamental role in placing China into the Soviet bloc, and one consequence of this was the extreme form of government–business relations. Like all other communist countries, China copied the central planning system of the Soviet Union. The basis of operating this system is the overwhelming power of the state over both land owners and private business owners. The former were eliminated by land reforms in the 1950s (and even before), and the latter gradually disappeared in the process of nationalization in the 1950s and 60s. This resulted in a kind of government–business relations that was completely dominated by the former.

China has a long history of state domination over society and the economy; however, with the central planning system, this domination became extreme. Clearly, the international system of nation-states and capitalism in general, and the Cold War structure in particular, contributed greatly to the formation of government–business relations under the central planning system, which has a long-lasting impact even today. The start of this causal mechanism is the incorporation of China into the European international system in the nineteenth century. The motive of survival and competition then worked to create radical forces of salvation, and when the new state was established by such forces, it began to engage forcefully in late development. Finally, the Cold War structure of the international system shaped this late-development experience into an extreme form of government–business relations.

Obviously, the international system alone could not cause all of the above-mentioned changes. For one thing, the motive of survival and competition should work for all late developers, but not so many of them have become like China. An autonomous state in the developing world, which was able to eliminate both land and business owners, was rare at that time and also today. China has a tradition of strong state, which facilitates the process of state building in the modern era (Zhao 2009; Yang and Zhao 2015). The size and geographical position of China also played an important role. The large size of China made it impossible for any Western power to conquer it alone, and dividing China among those powers created opportunities for the rise of alternative political centres. Highly organized radical groups, first the nationalists and then the communists, not only had space to grow but were also able to gain substantial foreign support. When they came into power, the new state was able to dominate society and the economy, especially after 1949. Of course, the geographical position along the front line of the Cold War strengthened state power even further in China.

The international system was also essential in China's move towards reform in the late 1970s and early 1980s. Deng Xiaoping did not make a grand plan for reform in the beginning. It all started with a particular problem of late development, that is, the campaign of so-called leap forward by foreign means (*yang yue jin*). In 1976, the Cultural Revolution ended when Mao passed away and the new leadership under Hua Guofeng put extreme leftists (e.g., the "gang of four") into prison. The welcome political change temporarily stimulated economic growth, for example, the growth rate of total output of agricultural and industrial production in

1977 and 1978 went up 11.5 per cent annually and government revenue increased 44 per cent. Hua then campaigned for a "new leap forward in national economy" with an even higher growth rate. The Ten Year Plan made in 1978 aimed to construct and complete 120 large development projects, including 10 large iron and steel establishments, 10 large oil fields, 8 large coal establishments, 6 new railroads, 5 large ports, and 30 large electricity plants. To pay for them, China relied on oil sales. However, towards the late 1970s, few new oil fields were found, and the long-term productivity of many existing fields was damaged by a rapid expansion of petroleum output. Since the government was unable to fund these large development projects with foreign currency earned from oil sales, it had to assume a large amount of foreign debt, which is why Hua's campaign for rapid growth is often called the "leap forward by foreign means." The direct result was the China's largest deficit since 1949 (Jin 1990: 141; Gao 1993: 93). By 1980, the government had to put the whole plan on hold.

This economic crisis created an opportunity for reformers, such as Deng, to step into the process of economic decision-making and change economic strategy, which led to the open-door policy in the early 1980s. Thus, the open-door policy was created at a particular point in time to successfully cope with the problem of late development. While the "leap forward by foreign means" attempted to push for rapid growth by importing modern technology and equipment, only to generate a disastrous deficit, the open-door policy aimed at promoting exports and obtaining foreign currency in order to finance late development.

The particular structure of the Cold War also played an important role in this process. Under this structure, the break-up between the Soviet Union and China in the 1960s meant that the United States and China had a mutual interest in coming together, and this had important economic implications. Bruce Cumings (1989: 222) wrote:

> If there had been only a strategic content to the China card, then the United States would have been happy with China's 1976-1978 program of heavy industry, as it fuelled China's war machine and tied down the USSR in the Far East. .... But by the mid-1970s, there was a complementary economic logic as well, which sought not simply an anti-Soviet China but also a China that would be, for the foreseeable future, enmeshed with and dependent upon the US-managed world economy. Today, it is this economic logic that stands out, the strategic logic having lost its earlier luster for both China and the United States.

He argued that the United States mobilized its political and economic forces to influence China to choose the path of export-led development, even under the Reagan administration, which downgraded China's strategic importance (1989: 222–29).

With the open-door policy, China officially embarked on the path of economic reform, which has also transformed its government–business relations since then.

Open-Door Policy and the Power Balance Between the State and Business

The open-door policy and economic reform weakened China's state power by dismantling the central planning system, bringing in foreign investment, and cultivating private business (Zheng 2004; Feng 2006). In his study of China's textile and shipbuilding industries, Thomas Moore (2004) argued that the world market played a disciplinary role in reducing non-competitive behaviour in the two industries and placing immense pressure on state control. He noted that "the emergence of an externally driven buyers' market was crucial in both industries. In this way, moderate economic closure in world markets was instrumental in breaking (or at least weakening) the long-noted affinity in state socialist systems between bureaucrats and bureaucratic forms of economic coordination" (2004: 312–13).

A particular logic existed that linked the open-door policy to the decline of state power in China. The open-door policy promoted foreign trade and introduced international economic forces into the Chinese domestic economy, which shook the very foundation of China's central planning system. Naturally, there was initially strong resistance to the reform. Given this, Susan Shirk (1993) suggested a political logic behind the reform, linking the open-door policy to other reform programmes, including the household production responsibility system and economic decentralization. In order to overcome this resistance, the reformers adopted a gradual, particularistic, and decentralized approach—in Naughton's words, "growing out of the plan" (1996). By slowly turning the wheels of reform, by targeting reform areas individually, and by benefiting local communities with decentralization experiments, the reform coalition was established and became stronger. This succeeded in keeping reform at the top of the government's agenda.

However, the reform programmes turned against state power later on by weakening its primary foundation, that is, the central planning system. The household production responsibility system raised agricultural procurement prices in several stages, and it became more difficult for the state to transfer resources from the agricultural sector to the industrial sector at a low price. Economic decentralization provided an incentive for local governments to promote township and village enterprises (TVEs), which began to challenge the dominance of state-owned enterprises (SOEs) in the Chinese economy. The entry of TVEs and urban collectives into the domestic market broke the state monopoly over industry and drove down its profits (Naughton 1992: 28).

The reduction in the profitability of SOEs meant a reduction in the total resources controlled by the state (before the reform, about 80 per cent of government revenues came from the state sector). Government revenue, expenditure, and investment all experienced a significant decline in the 1980s (Hussain et al. 1991: 156). According to Shaoguang Wang and Angang Hu (1994: 36–38), the fiscal situation of China's central government was particularly tenuous. While its revenue as a percentage of GNP was 6.9 per cent in 1989—a very low rate by international comparison—the ratio for expenditure decreased sharply from about 20 per cent in 1972 to about 7 per cent in 1989. Thus, the dismantling of the central planning system led to a serious decline in state power, as it had been traditionally based on the centralization of economic resources for late development.

While the international context served to reduce the power of the Chinese state, it contributed directly to the development of foreign-invested enterprises (FIEs) and the private sector in general. China has become the largest recipient of foreign investment in the world for some years. In the 2000s, FIEs have already produced more than half of China's total trade (Xing 2010: 310), and the FIE-led private sector comprised about half of the Chinese economy, which also constitutes the most dynamic and efficient part of the economy (Dougherty et al. 2007). It is reported that the private sector nowadays has accounted for more than 60 per cent of China's GDP and about 99 per cent of total number of enterprises (Tu 2016: 7). Yasheng Huang (2008) argued that private sector estimates based on official counts are much smaller than they are in reality. For example, street vendors and small-scale enterprises are often not included in official statistics, and many collectively owned enterprises (COEs) are privately held in nature.

Leaving aside the debate about what exactly caused China's success, the discussion so far has revealed how the international context has contributed to the decline of state power and the rise of the private sector in China, which clearly points to the pluralist model of government–business relations. However, although the Chinese state may have lost its monopoly power over the economy, the government–business relations are still far from being dominated by the latter. In fact, almost of all recent major works on government–business relations in China tend to suggest that business as a whole has not yet come anywhere close to successfully challenging state power, and government–business relations are still very much dominated by the former (e.g., Pearson 1997; Dickson 2003, 2008; Kennedy 2005; Tsai 2007; Chen and Dickson 2010).

Regarding business, however, collective action presents a major problem. Kellee Tsai (2005) argued that private entrepreneurs have diversified employment backgrounds and social networks and therefore have very different identities and interests; thus, it would be difficult to view them as a "middle class." Although business associations do get formed, whether they can represent their members is frequently unclear, since the level of government intervention is quite high, and many of the associations are simply created by governments on different levels. Kennedy (2011: 118) noted that "[t]he consequence of such intervention is not to eliminate industry's voice but to fragment it." So, he called the business influence over the state's policy-making process the "fragmented influence." Although the internal strength of business associations varies across regions (Zhang 2007), fragmented influence ensures that none of them are powerful enough to pose a viable challenge to the state on a national level.

The attitudes of individual private entrepreneurs towards authority lie behind the collective action problem. There have been numerous discussions on the issue of "red capitalists." In a series of studies on this issue (Dickson 2003, 2007, 2008; Chen and Dickson 2010), Bruce Dickson contended that private entrepreneurs are very much incorporated into the CCP, since the former depends on the latter for resources and policy favours. By developing formal and informal connections, many private entrepreneurs have come to share the interests and views of government and party officials. Other studies confirmed that political connections helped private entrepreneurs in terms of tax disputes, legal support, bank loans, employment growth, and even increase in productivity (Chen et al. 2008; Li et al. 2008; Choi 2009; Du and Girma 2010; Wang et al. 2014; Wang 2016; Zhang 2017).

China's economic reform in general and the open-door policy in particular have also made FIEs a potential challenger to state power, especially the entry of multinational corporations (MNCs) into China and China's entry into global value chain (GVCs) of production. As noted before, China has been a top recipient of foreign capital for some years. The dependency theory has long argued that foreign capital played a powerful role in post-war Latin America, which in the long run had a negative impact on local development. In a comparison of the post-war development experience between Latin America and East Asia, Peter Evans (1987) suggested that in the former, foreign capital dominated local capital and the state, whereas, in the latter, the state dominated the other two parties, and this difference separated the two regions in terms of economic performance. From this perspective, China clearly belongs in the East Asia category. Kennedy (2007) shows that on the whole, MNCs still have nowhere near the ability to successfully challenge the state, but he did argue that forming alliances with local companies would increase the chance of lobbying success. By investigating the state's role in promoting the automobile industry, Gregory Chin (2010 and this volume) elucidated the reason behind the state domination. He showed that a small group of top leaders had a clear agenda for managing foreign capital in the automobile industry and was able to supervise its enforcement by mobilizing the Leninist arrangements linking different government agencies.

GVCs represent a strong challenge to the vertically integrated national economies (Coe and Yeung 2015), and certainly a potential change to any state which aims at controlling its own economy. If different parts of one product are produced in different countries, then it would be impossible for the state to promote it as a "national" product. By focusing its effort to promote manufacturing production, the Chinese state clearly faces the challenge of GVCs. However, the Chinese industrial structure to a large extend has been preventing international business from becoming a dominant partner of the Chinese state through controlling GVCs. In China, SOEs dominate the upper stream of production process by producing most of capital goods in heavy and chemical industries, while small private enterprises engage in manufacturing production, which connect GVCs. Thus, the relationship between the state and SOEs rather than GVCs holds the key to Chinese political economy (which I will discuss in next section).

In general, the central planning system has not been replaced by a free market economy, and the state has been struggling to guide the process of economic development. A study on the *lishu* system provides an apt illustration of the government's control over business in the reform era (Tan et al. 2007). *Lishu*, in Chinese, means "belonging or subordinate to" or "directly controlled by." The study points out that all firms, regardless of size and ownership, are controlled by hierarchically structured governments, including the central government, provincial governments, municipal or prefectural governments, county governments, and township governments. From imposing administrative fees to providing administrative guidance, governments at each level exercise various degrees of administrative control over the firms in their jurisdiction. The study noted that the *lishu* system "has become a basic fabric constituting the hierarchy of firms and government agencies as well as other institutions in the Chinese economy" (2007: 787).

The motive of survival and competition in the international system drives the dominant role of the state over business. Although China's development strategy has changed from self-reliance to open-door, the basic struggle among nation-states in the system has not changed; in fact, it may even have been intensified by globalization. With the decline of communist ideology, the original goal of making China into a thriving and powerful force in the world continues to be pursued by the CCP, and has almost become its only claim to legitimacy in the minds of the Chinese people. Overall, the motive of survival and competition guarantees the basic internal cohesion of the Chinese state, which helps it to become the more powerful player in the government–business relations balance.

Globalization poses new challenges to the Chinese state. The spread of different social and political values and ideas means that the possibility of social risk and unrest has risen tremendously, and increasing economic interdependence among countries makes individual economies more vulnerable to crises in the world market. For example, the idea of economic security, which focuses on threats of globalization to the national economy, such as economic crises and uncertainties, was first debated among Chinese intellectuals in the 1990s, especially after the Asian financial crisis in 1997, and then moved to the domain of policy (Yeung 2008). It has been argued that economic growth and national security have become the single logic informing Chinese leadership after the mid-1990s (Wang 2004). Those particular challenges and survival issues under globalization motivate the Chinese state to continue managing and even actively controlling the process of economic development, and therefore maintain its power over business. However, the state did not do this by re-claiming its monopoly power from the past.[1] Rather, it maintained the decentralization programme and allowed different levels of government to deal with the challenges of globalization according to local conditions. Consequently, we find different forms of government–business relations across China.

Economic Decentralization and Various Forms of Government–Business Relations

While late development in pre-1979 China was very much based on SOEs, the post-1979 development has been accompanied by multiple forms of ownership, that is, not only SOEs but also COEs, FIEs, privately owned enterprises (POEs), and TVEs, which consist of both COEs and POEs. According to the most recent comprehensive economic survey conducted by China's State Statistical Bureau in 2013, the shares of state capital, collective capital, legal entities' capital, individual capital, and foreign investor capital (including that from Hong Kong, Macau, and Taiwan) in total paid-in capital for all industrial enterprises are 20.0, 1.9, 35.1, 22.3, and 19.9 per cent, respectively[2] (Zhang et al. 2015: 6–7).

Economic decentralization, as a key reform programme of China's economic reform, made it possible for governments at different levels to adapt to local conditions. Multiple forms of enterprises and adaptive governments would naturally lead to multiple forms of government–business relations. This is shown most obviously along the east coastal line. In the north, state capital continues to dominate the economy, and the most important government–business relation here is between the central government and large SOEs or groups of them. In the middle of China, TVEs dominate. In Jiangsu Province, for example, most TVEs are COEs with a strong presence of local governments—which were even at times directly involved in running the operations of these enterprises, especially in the 1980s. Further south, in Zhejiang Province, COEs operated largely autonomously from local governments, embedded in an environment of many small private enterprises. Even further south, in Guangdong Province, local governments took a back seat as foreign capital established itself as a dominant economic force. In general, moving from north to south, the presence of the state in the economy weakens, and the role of the private sector grows in importance. The above-mentioned three provinces also happen to be the richest in China.

The open-door policy and economic decentralization opened China's closed economy in the 1980s as previously mentioned. SOEs faced tremendous challenges from newly developed TVEs and began to make massive losses as the state gradually relinquished its control over prices. In the 1990s, the state began to re-organize SOEs. The key strategy was the so-called grasping the large and letting go of the small, which aimed to push small-sized SOEs into domestic market competition via different ownership experiments (especially private ownership), and also to re-organize large-sized SOEs into enterprise groups in order to enlarge their economies of scale and therefore enhance their international competitiveness. The central government targeted 1000 SOEs to form the core of China's new SOE system and selected 512 enterprises to form the basis of enterprise groups. At the same time, the government re-organized the banking system to support these enterprise groups. One recent study of China's SOEs describes the size and power of SOEs as the following:

> The relatively low share of state-owned companies in national industrial output compared to the past should not be mis-interpreted as the demise of their economic importance in China. In terms of total sales revenue of China's top 100 enterprises in 2011, the SOEs accounted for around 90%. The state sector remains the driving force behind economic development in China. All the big commercial banks in China are SOEs. More importantly, given the fact that township and village enterprises (TVEs) owned by local governments belong to the state sector but are not regarded as SOEs, and a large number of entities operating inside and outside of China are actually owned or controlled indirectly via SOEs' subsidiaries, the true size of the SOEs is unknown. Their influence is far greater than official statistics suggest. (Yu 2014: 165)

Putting aside the debate over whether it has made SOEs more competitive (e.g., Chen 2010; Guest and Sutherland 2010; Johansson and Feng 2016), the strategy of "grasping the large and letting go of the small" is clearly one of "picking winners" and making "national champions." It is neither a free-market strategy nor a strategy of total state control since, on the one hand, a large number of small SOEs were taken over by the market and, on the other, the state continued to control a number of enterprise groups made by large SOEs. By investigating six strategic industries, Pearson (2005) argued that the emerging Chinese regulatory state differed greatly from how a regulatory state was traditionally understood in the West. She further pointed out the following four features of the Chinese regulatory state: "continued state ownership of strategic assets; continued dominance of state and party 'comprehensive' institutions with authority over economic development; the bureaucratic origins of regulators in the former line ministries; and the fragmented, ambiguous authority of the regulator" (2005: 297).

This argument is confirmed by Yukyung Yeo's study of the telecommunications service industry (2009 and this volume), in which she argued that the primary goal of the state was not to push for a free market, but to protect state assets. Just as there is a distinction between small and large SOEs made by the state, there is also a distinction between strategic and non-strategic industries. Roselyn Hsueh (2011) found that state control was more relaxed in the textile industry, but tighter in the telecommunications industry as they possess different strategic values. This practice of strategic planning has led some scholars to argue that it is not necessarily a transitional feature of China's development, but may rather constitute a structural characteristic of Chinese market socialism (Gabriele 2010).

Enterprise group managers, in both strategic and non-strategic industries, do make independent decisions regarding business, and they and their companies do become powerful in terms of affecting governments' economic decisions (Downs 2008). In his research on business lobbying, Kennedy (2005) identified company size as a decisive factor in shaping its relative ability to influence public policy. If this is correct, then enterprise groups are perhaps the only domestic business power which has the potential to become a more equal partner of the state. Yet, the state continues to play a dominant role in its relation to enterprise groups. This is not only because state ownership is firmly instantiated there, but perhaps more importantly, the CCP controls the appointment of the managers of these enterprise groups and uses a cadre transfer system or rotates business leaders to fill positions in government and party agencies (Brødsgaard 2012; Li 2016; Lin 2017). In other words, enterprise group managers are free to make day-to-day business decisions, but their careers are always controlled by the state. Kjeld Brødsgaard (2012) characterized this situation as "fragmented integration." In this way, the state's domination over enterprise groups is secured.

We now consider government–business relations at the local level. It has been long argued that local development holds the key to China's overall economic success (e.g., Montinola et al. 1995). Local governments, accounting for more than 70 per cent of total government expenditures around the turn of the twentieth century (Caulfield 2006: 253), played a crucial role in promoting national development. Again, the key to its power was economic decentralization, which created an adaptive state at the local level by giving local officials more power to respond to local needs. Adam Segal and Eric Thun (2001: 558) argue that "local governments do not simply try to reproduce and catch up with development efforts initiated by the central government, but are often the actual architects of growth, designing and implementing development policies that are conducive to local institutional frameworks and specific development needs." They went on to assert that even at the local level, there is no "one size fits all" development policy in China and that local governments have to pay attention to the specific needs of the industrial sectors that dominate the local economy.

Tsai's studies (2006 and 2007) on the rise of the private sector in China showed that it began with informal interactions between local state and economic actors, and over time, government institutions adapted to the situation until finally the private sector was officially promoted. The informal interaction here points to an important source of adaptation. Clearly, although different endowments of physical resources affect how the local state adapts to local conditions (Zhan 2013), social resources are even more important. Personal relationships, trust, and other informal institutions linking local officials and private entrepreneurs make successful adaptation possible (Chang 2011; McNally 2011; Zhang and Liu 2013; Chan et al. 2015).

Adaptation to local situations created different models of government–business relations at the local level. For example, there was the local corporatist model, in which local governments engage in selective support for the key local industrial sectors. There was also the entrepreneurial state model, in which local governments themselves become money-making organizations. In addition, there was the free market model, in which local governments take a back seat to private firms, and only play a facilitating role (Blecher 1991; Oi 1992; Duckett 1998, 2001; Thun 2004; Mulvad 2015). The entrepreneurial state model was an early phenomenon, and it has greatly declined in acceptance, if not disappeared, as the central government rejected it and private business began to spread in the 1990s.

The 1994 tax reforms, which formalized the tax revenue sharing between the central government and local governments, weakened both the local corporatist model and the free market model, since it became less profitable for the local state to promote COEs. However, at the same time, the burden of local government's spending increased due to the continued decentralization of spending responsibilities pushed down from the central government, and local governments began to use public ownership of land as a leverage to build industrial parks and attract manufacture business[3] (Su and Tao 2017). Many local governments even began to seek foreign investment as a source of new revenue and simultaneously began to cultivate alliances between foreign and local companies for purposes of technological improvement (Chen 2014). The massive inflow of foreign capital also introduced international market competition, which forced China to open further and reshape local government–business relations (Thun 2004; Brandt and Thun 2010; Krug 2004). As COEs declined and POEs began to spread, local governments had to increasingly balance domestic private business, on the one hand, and international business on the other.

It should be noted that local governments not just walk around the rules set up by the central government, sometimes they went directly against the rules. Wanwen Qu (2009) used the automobile industry as an example. She argues that specific agencies of local governments have supported the development of local automobile industries since the mid-1980s, in particular the Geely Company in Wuhu (a region in Anhui Province). Their efforts were directed explicitly against the stated development strategy of the central government, which sought to encourage the establishment of joint ventures with foreign automakers. When local automobile programmes proved to be a success, the central government changed its strategy and endorsed local initiatives. Local governments, which successfully promoted COEs in the 1980s and therefore contributed greatly to China's overall development in that decade, have also played a key role in supporting private capital accumulation since the mid-1990s. As Fubing Su and Ran Tao (2017: 237) noted, "[i]nstead of one developmental state coordinating industrial policies, thousands of local governments in China have embraced developmentalism since the mid-1990s."

Clearly, a five-level hierarchy from the central government to township governments is a stretch for top-down control, and incompetence and deliberate disobedience frequently cannot be differentiated, which leaves space for free action at the local level (Wedeman 2001, 2003). The notions of "fragmented authoritarianism," "decentralized authoritarianism," and "fragmented control" are all used to describe the situation in which policy implementation is a process of redefining policy content by various vertical agencies and spatial regions. Central–local interaction in terms of policy implementation leads to different results. There are cases of complete breakdown, for example, the industrial policy for the development of solar photovoltaic industry (Chen 2016b); there are also cases of effective policy implementation, for example, the "building a new socialist countryside" programme (Schubert and Ahlers 2012; Ahlers 2014; Ahlers and Schubert 2015). Most of the cases probably belong to a "median category," in which "local agents bend central policies to local political or social advantage (perhaps, though not necessarily, enriching or empowering themselves personally in the process)" (Hurst and Teets 2014: 176). It seems that the effectiveness in implementing central governments' policies depends on how local officials judge whether those policies help local development or not. Margaret Pearson (2016: 18) suggests that local bureaucrats sometime even ignore the centre's punishment of certain local behaviour just to set an example for the others since those local bureaucrats don't always know whether the threatened ad hoc punishments will be enforced.

In fact, bureaucratic fragmentation may characterize the day-to-day business of the Chinese state. Given this situation, local governments generally have more freedom and become more adaptive to local conditions. This is why the capacity of the central government to govern China's economy through formal institutions is often in question.[4] However, the central government always has a priority enforcement capacity. In other words, it does not possess the capacity to do everything, but it can always concentrate its power and resources to accomplish a few things, for example, to focus its efforts on regulating foreign capital in a certain strategic industry, such as the automobile industry, or to respond to extraordinary challenges presented by high associated costs, such as the Asian financial crisis and domestic bad loan problem in the 1990s. As Naughton (2007: 198) put it, "[o]nce the alarm bells are ringing, the system has an ability to respond and put out fires." Vivian Zhan (2009: 462) argued that "the central government's agenda-setting power and bargaining tactics allow it to initiate reforms that address the problems, sometimes in experimental, micro steps, before they turn into disasters that threaten the political and economic regime."

Then what renders the central and local governments committed towards a common goal of development in China? There have been a number of studies suggesting that the CCP, especially its personnel department, has played the key role in disciplining government officials and therefore keeping their behaviour in line with the party's objectives

(Shevchenko 2004; Li and Zhou 2005; Yang 2004; Landry 2008; Sheng 2007, 2010; Lin 2012). For example, a key criterion for career promotion is economic growth targets associated with local officials (Chen et al. 2017). In addition, informal control from the top also exists, which is exercised through personal relationships and factionalism (Cai and Treisman 2006; Hillman 2010). Ben Hillman (2014) suggests that local patronage network often works with the party-state to discipline local officials since underperforming cadres would weaken the network. Although the central state is incapable of supervising the day-to-day operation of the local governments, and it is even more difficult for the former to put an effective control over policy implementation down to the local level, it has been able to control the overall direction towards development.

This is not to say that all local governments in China are development oriented and capable. There is a view that local governments since the mid-1990s have become predatory and rent-seeking institutions (Ong 2012; Chen 2016a). Daniel Koss and Hiroshi Sato (2016) argue that the extractive power of local states in China varies with geographical distance. In other words, the reach of local states is uneven. Corruption and development did go hand in hand in many places, and economic growth did lead to critical problems like pollution, but predatory and rent-seeking local states cannot explain the consistent high growth rates on both local and national levels. As argued before, local developmentalism is still widespread after the mid-1990s, and the key is the public ownership of land used by local governments as an effective tool for development, which is out of reach for local social elites.

It is certainly true that the autonomy and capacity of local state vary across China, and even development-oriented local states are not completely free from predatory and rent-seeking features. But the central state's priority enforcement capacity and internal control linkage, as argued above, has been able to keep local states geared towards a common goal of development. Various surveys (from 1987 to 2015) have showed that the central government enjoyed high popular support in China (Dickson 2016a, b; Tang 2016; Dickson, Shen and Yan 2017), and the legitimacy of the regime comes from its economic performance among other things, so the central government has to continuously push for development. What is behind this performance legitimacy is the struggle for survival and competition in the international system, which is both a historical legacy and a constant concern of the CCP and Chinese state.

Conclusion

Since China was incorporated into the European international system in the mid-nineteenth century, the motive of survival and competition has gradually come to dominate the political practices of the Chinese elites, and this is especially the case after 1949 when an autonomous state was finally created. However, a particular international context often induces a corresponding state reaction. The Cold War structure and conditions of late development pressed the Chinese state to centralize its power and engage in forceful industrialization through a central planning system. This system, in turn, created an extreme form of government–business relations, with overwhelming power granted to the former. Later on, after China moved closer to the United States in terms of world politics, and when the Cold War structure was replaced by a multi-polar structure characterized by American hegemony, coinciding with the rapid expansion of the world market, the Chinese state engaged in economic liberalization and decentralization. This then modified the power balance between the state and business and gave rise to various forms of government–business relations.

Regarding the general models of corporatism, clientelism, and pluralism, the chapter found traces of all three in China. Firstly, the state continued to play a powerful role in managing the Chinese economy, and the balance of power between the government and business favours the former on both central and local levels. This makes China more closely fit a corporatist model. Secondly, various forms of government–business relations in the post-1979 era are very much based on informal institutions, in particular the personal connections between local officials and economic actors, which definitely exhibit some characteristics of clientelism. Finally, the open-door policy and economic decentralization have reduced state power in absolute terms, and economic liberalization gave rise to an ever-stronger private sector. It still does not have the power to challenge the state; however, from a pluralist perspective, the power of business and civil society is definitely increasing.

In this chapter, I have tried to link the above features of China's government–business relations to an international context. As argued in the beginning, however, an international context alone cannot elucidate the formation and transformation of China's government–business relations. In order to accomplish this, we need to link international and domestic factors through further study.

Notes

1. There has been renewed academic and government interest in planning. See, for instance, a special issue on Development "Planning" in Present-Day China—System, Process, and Mechanism, *Modern China*, 39(6), November 2013.
2. "Paid-in capital" refers to capital received from investors when the business is registered, and it shows the nature of the ownership when the business starts. Legal entities' capital in simple term is a mixture of individual and state capital.
3. Value added tax generated from manufacture business is the largest source of local revenues.
4. For example, see the special-issue discussion on state capacity building in China, *Public Administration and Development* 29, 2009.

References

Ahlers, A. L. (2014). *Rural policy implementation in contemporary China: New socialist countryside*. London/New York: Routledge.

Ahlers, A. L., & Schubert, G. (2015). Effective policy implementation in China's local state. *Modern China, 41*(4), 372–405.

Blecher, M. (1991). Developmental state, entrepreneurial state: The political economy of socialist reform in Xinji municipality and Guanghan county. In G. White (Ed.), *The Chinese state in the era of economic reform*. London: Macmillan Press.

Brandt, L., & Thun, E. (2010). The fight for the middle: Upgrading competition, and industrial development in China. *World Development, 38*(11), 1555–1574.

Breznitz, D., & Murphree, M. (2010). *Run of the red queen: Government, innovation, globalization, and economic growth in China*. New Haven: Yale University Press.

Brødsgaard, K. E. (2012). Politics and business group formation in China: The party in control? *The China Quarterly, 211*, 624–648.

Cai, H., & Treisman, D. (2006). Did government decentralization cause China's economic miracle? *World Politics, 58*, 505–535.

Caulfield, J. L. (2006). Local government reform in China: A rational actor perspective. *International Review of Administrative Sciences, 72*(2), 253–267.

Chan, K. S., Xu, X., & Gao, Y. (2015). The China growth miracle: The role of the formal and the informal institutions. *World Economy, 38*(1), 63–90.

Chang, K.-C. (2011). A path to understanding Guanxi in China's transitional economy: Variations on network behavior. *Sociological Theory, 29*(4), 315–339.

Chen, X. (2010). Modes of state intervention and business group performance in China's transitional economy. *Journal of Socio-Economics, 39*, 619–630.

Chen, L. (2014). Varieties of global capital and the paradox of local upgrading in China. *Politics and Society, 42*(2), 223–252.

Chen, K. (2016a). Two China models and local government entrepreneurship. *China: An International Journal, 14*(3), 16–28.

Chen, T.-J. (2016b). The development of China's solar photovoltaic industry: Why industrial policy failed. *Cambridge Journal of Economics, 40*, 755–774.

Chen, J., & Dickson, B. J. (2010). *Allies of the state: China's private entrepreneurs and democratic change*. Cambridge, MA: Harvard University Press.

Chen, Z., Lu, M., & He, J. (2008). Power and political participation of entrepreneurs: Evidence from Liuzhou, Guangxi, China. *Journal of the Asia Pacific Economy, 13*(3), 298–312.

Chen, J., Luo, D., She, G., & Ying, Q. (2017). Incentive or selection? A new investigation of local leaders' political turnover in China. *Social Science Quarterly, 98*(1), 341–359.

Chin, G. (2010). *China's automotive modernization: The party-state and multinational corporations*. Basingstoke/New York: Palgrave Macmillan.

Choi, E. K. (2009). The politics of fee extraction from private enterprises, 1996–2003. *China Journal, 62*, 79–103.

Coe, N. M., & Yeung, H. W.-C. (2015). *Global production networks: Theorizing economic development in an interconnected world*. Oxford: Oxford University Press.

Cumings, B. (1989). The political economy of China's turn outward. In S. S. Kim (Ed.), *China and the world: New directions in Chinese foreign relations* (2nd ed.). Boulder: Westview Press.

Dickson, B. J. (2003). *Red capitalists in China: The party, private entrepreneurs, and prospects for political change*. Cambridge/New York/Melbourne/Madrid/Cape Town/Singapore/Sao Paulo: Cambridge University Press.

Dickson, B. J. (2007). Integrating wealth and power in China: The Communist Party's embrace of the private sector. *The China Quarterly, 192*, 827–854.

Dickson, B. J. (2008). *Wealth into power: The Communist Party's embrace of China's private sector*. Cambridge/New York/Melbourne/Madrid/Cape Town/Singapore/Sao Paulo: Cambridge University Press.

Dickson, B. J. (2016a). The survival strategy of the Chinese Communist Party. *Washington Quarterly, 39*(4), 27–44.

Dickson, B. J. (2016b). *The dictator's dilemma: The Chinese Communist Party's strategy for survival*. New York: Oxford University Press.

Dickson, B. J., Shen, M., & Yan, J. (2017). Generating regime support in contemporary China: Legitimation and the local legitimacy deficit. *Modern China, 43*(2), 123–155.

Dougherty, S., Herd, R., & He, P. (2007). Has a private sector emerged in China's industry? Evidence from a quarter of a million Chinese firms. *China Economic Review, 18*, 309–334.

Downs, E. S. (2008). Business interest groups in Chinese politics: The case of the oil companies. In C. Li (Ed.), *China's changing political landscape: Prospects for democracy*. Washington, DC: The Brookings Institution Press.

Du, J., & Girma, S. (2010). Red capitalists: Political connections and firm performance in China. *Kyklos, 63*(4), 530–545.

Duckett, J. (1998). *The entrepreneurial state in China: Real estate and commerce departments in reform era Tianjin*. London/New York: Routledge.

Duckett, J. (2001). Bureaucrats in business, Chinese-style: The lessons of market reform and state entrepreneurialism in the People's Republic of China. *World Development, 29*(1), 23–37.

Evans, P. (1987). Class, state, and dependence in East Asia: Lessons for Latin America. In F. C. Deyo (Ed.), *The political economy of the new Asian industrialism*. Ithaca/London: Cornell University Press.

Feng, Y. (2006). Sources of political capacity: A case study of China. *International Studies Review, 8*, 597–606.

Fu, D. (2017). Fragmented control: Governing contentious labor organizations in China. *Governance, 30*(3), 445–462.

Gabriele, A. (2010). The role of the state in China's industrial development: A reassessment. *Comparative Economic Studies, 52*, 325–350.

Gao, B. (1993). *Hou Wenge Shi: Zhongguo Ziyouhua de Chaoliu [A history of post-cultural revolution: The trend of China's liberalization]*. Taipei: Lian Jing.

Gerschenkron, A. (1962). *Economic backwardness in historical perspective: A book of essays*. Cambridge, MA: Harvard University Press.

Guest, P., & Sutherland, D. (2010). The impact of business group affiliation on performance: Evidence from China's 'national champions'. *Cambridge Journal of Economics, 34*, 617–631.

Haan, A. (2011). Will China change international development as we know it? *Journal of International Development, 23*, 881–908.

Hillman, B. (2010). Factions and spoils: Examining political behavior within the local state in China. *China Journal, 64*, 1–18.

Hillman, B. (2014). *Patronage and power: Local state networks and party-state resilience in rural China*. Stanford: Stanford University Press.

Howell, J. (2006). Reflections on the Chinese state. *Development and Change, 37*(2), 273–297.

Hsueh, R. (2011). *China's regulatory state: A new strategy for globalization*. Ithaca/London: Cornell University Press.

Huang, Y. (2008). *Capitalism with Chinese characteristics: Entrepreneurship and the state*. Cambridge: Cambridge University Press.

Hurst, W., & Teets, J. (2014). Conclusion: Compliance, resistance, innovation, and involution. In J. Teets & W. Hurst (Eds.), *Local governance innovation in China: Experimentation, diffusion, and defiance*. London/New York: Routledge.

Hussain, A., Stern, N., Burda, M., & Newbery, D. (1991). Effective demand, enterprise reforms and public finance in China. *Economic Policy, 6*(12), 1–86.

Jin, Z. (1990). *Cong Mao Zedong Dao Deng Xiaoping [From Mao Zedong to Deng Xiaoping]*. Hong Kong: Tian Di.

Johansson, A. C., & Feng, X. (2016). The state advances, the private sector retreats? Firm effects of China's great stimulus programme. *Cambridge Journal of Economics, 40*, 1635–1668.

Kennedy, S. (2005). *The business of lobbying in China*. Cambridge, MA/London: Harvard University Press.

Kennedy, S. (2007). Transnational political alliances: An exploration with evidence from China. *Business & Society, 46*(2), 174–200.

Kennedy, S. (2011). Fragmented influence: Business lobbying in China in comparative perspective. In S. Kennedy (Ed.), *Beyond the middle kingdom comparative perspectives on China's capitalist transformation*. Stanford: Stanford University Press.

Koss, D., & Sato, H. (2016). A micro-geography of state extractive power: The case of rural China. *Studies in Comparative International Development, 51*, 389–410.

Krug, B. (Ed.). (2004). *China's rational entrepreneurs: The development of the new private business sector*. London/New York: Routledge Curzon.

Landry, P. F. (2008). *Decentralized authoritarianism in China: The Communist Party's control of local elites in the post-Mao era*. Cambridge/New York/ Melbourne/Madrid/Cape Town/Singapore/Sao Paulo: Cambridge University Press.

Li, C. (2016). Holding 'China Inc.' together: The CCP and the rise of China's *Yangqi*. *China Quarterly, 228*, 927–949.

Li, H., & Zhou, L.-A. (2005). Political turnover and economic performance: The incentive role of personnel control in China. *Journal of Public Economics, 89*, 1743–1762.

Li, H., Meng, L., Wang, Q., & Zhou, L.-A. (2008). Political connections, financing and firm performance: Evidence from Chinese private firms. *Journal of Development Economics, 87*, 283–299.

Lieberthal, K., & Oksenberg, M. (1988). *Policy making in China: Leaders, structures, and processes*. Princeton: Princeton University Press.

Lin, K.-C. (2012). Politics and the market in twenty-first-century China: Strategies of authoritarian management of state-society relations. *Political Studies Review, 10*, 73–84.

Lin, L.-W. (2017). Reforming China's state-owned enterprises: From structure to people. *The China Quarterly, 229*, 107–129.

McNally, C. A. (2011). China's changing *Guanxi* capitalism: Private entrepreneurs between Leninist control and relentless accumulation. *Business and Politics, 13*(2), 1–29.

McNally, C. A. (2012). Sino capitalism: China's reemergence and the international political economy. *World Politics, 64*(4), 741–776.

Montinola, G., Qian, Y., & Weingast, B. R. (1995). Federalism, Chinese style: The political basis for economic success. *World Politics, 48*(1), 50–81.

Moore, T. (2004). *China in the world market: Chinese industry and international sources of reform in the post-Mao era*. Cambridge: Cambridge University Press.

Mulvad, A. (2015). Competing hegemonic projects within China's variegated capitalism: 'Liberal' Guangdong vs. 'Statist' Chongqing. *New Political Economy, 20*(2), 199–227.

Naughton, B. (1992). Implications of the state monopoly over industry and its relaxation. *Modern China, 18*(1), 14–41.

Naughton, B. (1996). *Growing out of the plan: Chinese economic reform, 1978–1993*. Cambridge: Cambridge University Press.

Naughton, B. (2007). Reframing China policy: The Carnegie debates. *Journal of Chinese Economic and Business Studies, 5*(3), 193–202.

Naughton, B. (2010). China's distinctive system: Can it be a model for others? *Journal of Contemporary China, 19*(65), 437–460.

Oi, J. C. (1992). Fiscal reform and the economic foundations of local state corporatism in China. *World Politics, 45*(1), 99–126.

Ong, L. H. (2012). Between developmental and Clientelist states: Local state-business relationships in China. *Comparative Politics, 44*(2), 191–209.

Pearson, M. M. (1997). *China's new business elite: The political consequences of economic reform*. Berkley/Los Angeles/London: University of California Press.

Pearson, M. M. (2005). The business of governance business in China: Institutions and norms of the emerging regulatory state. *World Politics, 57*, 296–322.

Pearson, M. M. (2016). Local government: Friend or foe of the market. In S. Kennedy (Ed.), *State and market in contemporary China: Toward the 13th five-year plan*. Lanham/Boulder/New York/London: Rowman and Littlefield.

Qu, W. (2009). Ganchao Gongshi Xiandu xia de Zhongguo Chanye Zhengce Moshi: Yi Qiche Chanye Weili [The Chinese model of industrial policy under the catch-up consensus: The case of the automobile industry]. *Jing Ji Xue [China Economic Quarterly]*, 8(2), 501–532.

Rea, K. W., & Brewer, J. C. (1981). *The forgotten ambassador: The reports of John Leighton Stuart, 1946–1949*. Boulder: Westview Press.

Schubert, G., & Ahlers, A. L. (2012). County and township cadres as a strategic group: 'Building a new socialist countryside' in three provinces. *China Journal, 67*, 67–86.

Segal, A., & Thun, E. (2001). Thinking globally, acting locally: Local governments, industrial sectors, and development in China. *Politics & Society, 29*(4), 557–588.

Sheng, Y. (2007). Global market integration and central political control foreign trade and intergovernmental relations in China. *Comparative Political Studies, 40*(4), 405–434.

Sheng, Y. (2010). *Economic openness and territorial politics in China*. Cambridge: Cambridge University Press.

Shevchenko, A. (2004). Bringing the party back in: The CCP and the trajectory of market transition on China. *Communist and Post-Communist Studies, 37*, 161–185.

Shirk, S. (1993). *The political logic of economic reform in China*. Berkeley/London: University of California Press.

Su, F., & Tao, R. (2017). The China model withering? Institutional roots of China's local developmentalism. *Urban Studies, 54*(1), 230–250.

Tan, J., Li, S., & Xia, J. (2007). When iron fist, visible hand, and invisible hand meet: Firm-level effects of varying institutional environments in China. *Journal of Business Research, 60*, 786–794.

Tang, W. (2016). *Populist authoritarianism: Chinese political culture and regime sustainability*. Oxford/New York: Oxford University Press.

Thun, E. (2004). Keeping up with the Jones': Decentralization, policy imitation, and industrial development in China. *World Development, 32*(8), 1289–1308.

Tsai, K. S. (2005). Capitalists without a class: Political diversity among private entrepreneurs in China. *Comparative Political Studies, 38*(9), 1130–1158.

Tsai, K. S. (2006). Adaptive informal institutions and endogenous institutional change in China. *World Politics, 59*, 116–141.

Tsai, K. S. (2007). *Capitalism without democracy: The private sector in contemporary China*. Ithaca: Cornell University Press.

Tu, X. (2016). Guanyu Jiakuai Minying Jingji Fazhan de Jidian Sikao [Considerations on how to accelerate the development of private economy]. *Gaige yu Kaifang* [*Reform and Opening*], *13*, 7–14.

Wang, Z. (2004). Conceptualizing economic security and governance: China confronts globalization. *The Pacific Review, 17*(4), 523–545.

Wang, Y. (2016). Beyond local protectionism: China's state–business relations in the last two decades. *China Quarterly, 226*, 319–341.

Wang, S., & Hu, A. (1994). *Zhongguo Guojia Nengli Baogao [A report on China's state capacity]*. Hong Kong: Oxford University Press.

Wang, C., Ye, J., & Franco, J. C. (2014). Local state corporatism or neo-*Guanxilism*? Observations from the county level of government in China. *Journal of Contemporary China, 23*(87), 498–515.

Wedeman, A. (2001). Incompetence, noise, and fear in central local relations in China. *Studies in Comparative International Development, 35*(4), 59–83.

Wedeman, A. (2003). *From Mao to market: Rent seeking, local protectionism, and marketization in China*. Cambridge: Cambridge University Press.

Xing, Y. (2010). Facts about and impacts of FDI on China and the world economy. *China: An International Journal, 8*(2), 309–327.

Yahuda, M. (1983). *Towards the end of isolationism: China's foreign policy after Mao*. London/Basingstoke: Macmillan Press.

Yang, D. (2004). *Remaking the Chinese leviathan: Market transition and the politics of governance in China*. Stanford: Stanford University Press.

Yang, H., & Zhao, D. (2015). Performance legitimacy, state autonomy and China's economic miracle. *Journal of Contemporary China, 24*(91), 64–82.

Yeo, Y. (2009). Between owner and regulator: Governing the business of China's telecommunications service industry. *The China Quarterly, 200*, 1013–1032.

Yeung, B. (2008). China in the era of globalization: The emergence of the discourse on economic security. *The Pacific Review, 21*(50), 635–660.

Yu, H. (2014). The ascendency of state-owned enterprises in China: Development, controversy and problems. *Journal of Contemporary China, 23*(85), 161–182.

Zhan, J. V. (2009). Decentralizing China: Analysis of central strategies in China's fiscal reforms. *Journal of Contemporary China, 18*(60), 445–462.

Zhan, J. V. (2013). Natural resources, local governance and social instability: A comparison of two counties in China. *The China Quarterly, 213*, 78–100.

Zhang, J. (2007). Business associations in China: Two regional experiences. *Journal of Contemporary Asia, 37*(2), 209–231.

Zhang, C. (2017). Reexamining the electoral connection in authoritarian China: The local people's congress and its private entrepreneur deputies. *The China Review, 17*(1), 1–27.

Zhang, Q., & Liu, M. (2013). The political economy of private sector development in communist China: Evidence from Zhejiang province. *Studies in Comparative and International Development, 48*, 196–216.

Zhang, W., et al. (Eds.). (2015). *Zhongguo Jingji Pucha Nianjian* [*China economic census yearbook*] Dier Chanye Juan – Shang (Volume on secondary industry – Part 1). Beijing: Zhongguo Tongji Chubanshe [China Statistics Press].

Zhao, D. (2009). The mandate of heaven and performance legitimation in historical and contemporary China. *American Behavioral Scientist, 53*(3), 416–433.

Zheng, Y. (2004). *Globalization and state transformation in China*. Cambridge: Cambridge University Press.

Zhu, T. (2012). Compressed development, flexible practices, and multiple traditions in China's rise. In P. Katzenstein (Ed.), *Sinicization and the rise of China: Civilizational processes beyond East and West* (pp. 99–119). London/New York: Routledge.

PART III

Institutional Consequences of Changing Business–Government Relations

CHAPTER 8

Business–Government Relations and Corporate Governance Reforms

Richard W. Carney

Introduction

Corporate governance reforms generally seek to solve one of two basic problems. The first regards the capacity for a manager to act in a way that differs from what the owner(s) wants or agency costs (Berle and Means 1932). This problem occurs most commonly in firms with diffuse shareholding, as in the United States. The second problem regards the power of one or more owners to expropriate wealth from minority shareholders, or tunnelling, and often referred to as principal–principal problems (La Porta et al. 1997 and 1998). This is more common when there is one dominant owner. In China, listed firms tend to have concentrated ownership with either the state or a private person/family as the ultimate owner. Thus, tunnelling is more of a problem although agency costs can also exist when, for example, there are multiple government agencies with jurisdictional claims over an SOE or when there are multiple shareholders with large positions.

I would like to thank Pan Rongfang for helpful research assistance.

R.W. Carney (✉)
China Europe International Business School, Shanghai Shi, China

X. Zhang, T. Zhu (eds.), *Business, Government and Economic Institutions in China*, International Political Economy Series,
DOI 10.1007/978-3-319-64486-8_8

A variety of mechanisms both internal and external to the firm can help to resolve these problems. Such corporate governance measures are best seen as coming from the national government, and applied to all firms that list on the country's stock exchanges. However, their success in solving agency and principal–principal problems has varied depending on whether firms are state- or privately owned. For privately owned firms, the absence of effective solutions to these problems magnifies the cost of raising capital (since investors do not want to invest in firms in which a manager can act differently from their objectives or in which other investors could expropriate their invested funds), which often leads them to search for solutions outside the Chinese market. For state-owned firms, access to capital has been less of a problem, although they have still faced pressures to find more while minimizing its cost (hence the development of China's stock markets). The demand for capital coupled with varying access to its supply has led to divergent solutions that depend not only on a firm's owner, but also on the structure of local business–government relations.

Guangdong and Shanghai offer contrasting examples of China's corporate governance reform dynamics. These regions have differed systematically along three business-state dimensions: (1) centre–local relations, (2) the institutional structure of the state, and (3) the organizational configuration of business actors. Guangdong can be characterized as having maintained weaker ties to Beijing, with a more fragmented and less cohesive bureaucracy, and private firms that are better organized through localized networks and entrepreneur-initiated and led associations. Shanghai, by contrast, has kept stronger ties to Beijing, with a more cohesive and centralized state apparatus that connects relatively poorly organized private business actors through the subordination of economic action to centralized authority via a vertical socio-political structure. To map the implications of these business-state dimensions for corporate governance reforms, I examine two firms in the automotive industry: Shanghai Automotive Industry Corporation (SAIC) and BYD. The former is a state-owned enterprise located in Shanghai; the latter is a private firm in Guangdong. In both cases, a major source of corporate governance reforms has occurred through their international links, though local business–government relations have exerted a critical mediating effect. For SAIC, joint ventures with Volkswagen and General Motors contributed to higher quality accounting standards; but favouritism by the state has ensured SAIC could continue to access much-needed capital, dampening the call for further corporate governance reforms by minority investors. For BYD, the need for capital led it to list on the Hong Kong Stock Exchange, which in turn led to a series of important corporate governance reforms that have strengthened its competitiveness.

To detail China's divergent corporate governance reform dynamics, I begin by surveying the specific internal and external governance tools that are often used to address agency and principal–principal problems, and their effectiveness in the context of China. These are national-level issues. But the absence of effective reforms that would ease access to capital by privately owned firms has led to a bifurcated response, depending on the dominance of state- or privately owned business to the local economy. The three dimensions of business-state relations that have shaped these reform trajectories will be surveyed in the third section. The fourth section presents an analytic narrative of BYD and SAIC to illustrate the interplay of business-state relations and corporate governance reforms in the context of Guangdong and Shanghai, respectively. The final section summarily concludes.

Internal and External Governance Tools

To understand the state of corporate governance reforms in China, we must begin by examining their effectiveness at the national level before turning to the divergent efforts at the local level to compensate for their weaknesses. Potential agency and principal–principal (tunnelling) costs can be addressed either through internal or external governance tools.

Internal Governance Tools

Outside China, a variety of internal governance tools are commonly used to mitigate corporate governance problems, including (1) independent directors, (2) the use of debt in a firm's capital structure, (3) dividends, (4) incentive-based, (5) bank monitoring compensation, and (6) ownership structure. The first four primarily address agency costs; the last two concern both agency and tunnelling costs.

First, boards of directors with more independent directors are widely regarded as better at monitoring managers on behalf of shareholders and thereby reducing agency costs (e.g., Fama 1980; Fama and Jensen 1983). However, the evidence from China indicates that outside directors are not usually appointed for monitoring reasons; rather, they tend to be appointed to assist with poor property rights protections and/or to facilitate government access (Chen 2015). This deviation from their monitoring role is not surprising since most Chinese firms have concentrated ownership rather than the diffuse ownership problems that independent directors can address.

Second, the use of debt in a firm's capital structure can also discipline managers to regularly generate sufficient cash flows to service the debt and thereby moderate the agency costs of free cash flow (Jensen 1986). However, it is highly unlikely that debt is a disciplinary mechanism in China because (1) owners exercise strong oversight due to concentrated ownership, (2) bankruptcies are extremely rare due to weak creditor rights (Allen et al. 2005), and (3) large firms and SOEs can usually count on local and/or national government aid to prevent them from going bankrupt in order to preserve employment levels and maintain social stability (Bai et al. 2000).

Third, dividends may act as another source of managerial discipline if minority shareholders are concerned that profits will be diverted for private consumption or overinvestment (Rozeff 1982; Easterbrook 1984; Jensen 1986; La Porta et al. 2000). However, the evidence from dividend payouts of Chinese firms indicates that they are low in comparison to similar firms in other countries and therefore not used to reduce agency costs. This may occur either because minority shareholders in China are unable to pressure firms to pay out their earnings due to weak shareholder rights (Allen et al. 2005) or because investors act more like speculators and instead pursue capital gains. The high turnover rate on China's stock markets is consistent with this (Jiang and Kim 2015).

A fourth internal governance tool used to reduce agency costs occurs with incentive-based compensation contracts that reward good managerial performance with financial gains such as stocks, options, raises, and bonuses. But the effectiveness of this tool varies between SOEs and non-SOEs (usually family-owned firms). For family firms, the effectiveness of incentive-based compensation depends on whether the family has control of the firm. Cheng et al. (2015) find that when families have control, incentive-based compensation is effective; but when families are not in control (such as when there are multiple blockholders), incentive-based compensation is relatively less effective because agency costs can resurface due to coordination problems among owners. For SOEs, the China Securities Regulatory Commission (CSRC) encourages the use of incentive-based pay, however, Jiang and Kim (2015) report that such compensation arrangements are ineffective for two reasons. First, because managers of SOEs are civil service employees, their salary is capped at a certain multiple of average workers' pay to preserve social harmony within the firm. Second, the primary incentive for SOE managers is to be promoted to a high-level government position, thereby undermining the need for incentive-based compensation (Firth et al. 2006, 2007; Chen et al. 2010). Hence, the existing literature has not identified a relation between managerial compensation and firm performance in SOEs (Firth et al. 2006; Kato and Long 2006b; Conyon and He 2011).

A fifth internal governance tool may occur through banks monitoring managers (Fama 1985; Sharpe 1990; Diamond 1984, 1991). In China, however, because both banks and the firms that they primarily lend to are state-owned, banks do not act as effective monitors. For example, Qian and Yeung (2015) find that banks continue to lend to firms even when firms' controlling shareholders are known to be tunnelling from their minority shareholders. Hence, these authors argue that for capital markets to develop in a way that effectively permits the reduction of agency and tunnelling costs, the banking system needs to become more effective at disciplining borrowers.

The sixth internal governance tool regards firms' ownership structure. Because Chinese firms are dominated by large shareholders (families or the state), this could either lead to these large shareholders monitoring their firms and making them profitable by reducing agency costs (Berle and Means 1932; Jensen and Meckling 1976; Demsetz and Lehn 1985), or this could enable them to expropriate wealth from minority shareholders, or tunnelling (La Porta et al. 1999).[1] Prior work has found evidence for both the former (Xu and Wang 1999; Chen et al. 2009) and the latter (Liu and Lu 2007; Peng et al. 2011). Jiang and Kim (2015) argue these conflicting findings are due to the non-linear nature of the relation between firm performance and large shareholders.

In conclusion, the existing literature has found that the only internal governance tool to demonstrate consistently effective results is incentive-based compensation for managers of family-owned firms. The capacity for other internal governance tools to be effective, such as independent directors, depends on whether the firm faces specific listing rules, but such rules tend to apply only for foreign listings. This will be discussed further below, but to identify alternative corporate governance mechanisms that may effectively reduce corporate governance problems, I now turn to external governance tools.

External Governance Tools

I cover seven external governance tools, six of which are commonly used in high-income economies to reduce agency and tunnelling costs. The six include (1) a strong legal system, (2) institutional investors, (3) an active managerial labour market, (4) an active takeover market, (5) product market competition, and (6) cross-listing on a foreign stock exchange. The seventh offers a mechanism for firms in emerging economies to improve their corporate governance arrangements via a partnership with a foreign corporation—joint ventures or investment by a firm that follows a higher corporate governance standard.

The first, and potentially most effective, external governance mechanism is the legal system and its capacity to protect shareholders. But despite all of the new company laws and securities regulations that have been issued over the past decade, China's legal system remains ineffective at protecting investors (Allen et al. 2005; Pistor and Xu 2005; Liu 2006; Zou et al. 2008). When the quality of China's legal system is compared to that of 49 other countries around the globe (as compiled by La Porta et al. 1998), Allen et al. (2005) find that it falls below the average and that enforcement in particular is significantly below average. Kato and Long (2006a) likewise contend that China has neither a comprehensive set of legal rules necessary to protect minority shareholders nor the capacity to enforce existing laws. However, the Chinese government recognizes that its laws and enforcement are weak, and has begun taking steps to improve them (Jiang and Kim 2015).

A variety of other external mechanisms can, to some degree, compensate for a weak legal system, such as powerful institutional investors. As large long-term shareholders of firms, institutional investors may engage in shareholder activism or monitoring (Gillan and Starks 1998). In China, however, institutional investors are neither large shareholders at the firm level in comparison to controlling owners (families or the state), nor do they have long-run horizons (Chen et al. 2007). The capacity for institutional investors to exert influence over firms in other countries arises when the firm's ownership is diffuse, but diffuse ownership does not exist in China. Moreover, the evidence indicates that the turnover rate of institutional investors is very high (Jiang and Kim 2015). Hence, institutional investors lack the incentive to exert oversight over firms in which they own shares for the short term.

A third external mechanism by which to reduce governance problems is via an active managerial labour market. The potential to be hired by another firm can incentivize managers to improve their reputation by demonstrating a commitment to act in the best interests of shareholders, thereby minimizing agency costs (Fama and Jensen 1983; Jensen and Meckling 1976). In China, however, an active market for managers does not exist either for SOEs or for family-owned firms. SOEs are prevented from competing among themselves because an Organization Department maintains an exhaustive list of government employees at the central, provincial, municipal, and county levels, and it decides all of the state's important personnel assignments including SOEs managers (Kato and Long 2006a). But this may change as SOEs become increasingly focused on profits; SASAC, for example, has already increased its activity in recruiting top managers (Jiang and Kim 2015).

Chinese family firms, by comparison, generally hire managers from within the firm and/or family.[2] Over time, however, the labour market for non-SOE managers may also become more active for two reasons. First, as companies become larger and more complex, the need for professional managers increases (e.g., see Dalton and Kesner 1983; Jiang et al. 2013a). Second, China's one-child policy has severely limited the ability to keep the management team within the family, so owners may have no choice but to hire professional managers at some point.

A fourth external governance mechanism is the existence of an active takeover market.[3] In this situation, the manager of a weak firm is often fired soon after a takeover occurs, thereby motivating managers to work hard to prevent such an incident. However, a takeover market is almost non-existent in China because of the highly concentrated ownership of SOEs and non-SOEs. Moreover, even family firms that stand to gain significant financial wealth if they sell their firms are almost always unwilling to sell. The lack of investor protections reduces the attractiveness of selling off assets and diversifying them across investment classes in comparison to retaining control over a business in which diversification can occur across product categories.

Product market competition is a fifth external mechanism by which to discipline managers (Hart 1983; Scharfstein 1988; Schmidt 1997). In China, this can be a powerful corporate governance tool (Niu and Li 2005; Bai et al. 2004; Liu 2006; Jiang and Kim 2015). For example, SOE managers are incentivized to work hard to ensure that their firms do not underperform (or fail) because they do not want to be negatively appraised by the Organization Department and damage their political careers. For non-SOE managers, the nonexistence of a managerial labour market motivates managers to prevent their firms from failing since they may not find another job.[4] To assess performance, Chinese firms will often compare themselves to the industry leader and/or use that firm as a role model.[5] This practice has been widely adopted partly because the State Council has explicitly advocated this practice since January 2001.

A sixth external mechanism by which to improve corporate governance is through cross-listing on a stock exchange in a country that has a stronger legal environment. Firms voluntarily do this to "bond" themselves to a higher governance standard which can lead to higher firm valuations and lower costs of capital (Ferris et al. 2009). Cross-listings can be an effective way for Chinese firms to improve their corporate governance and thereby strengthen their competitiveness, as will be discussed in more detail below (Jiang and Kim 2015; Lit et al. 2015).

Finally, partnering with a foreign corporation can allow for modern practices to be transferred to the Chinese firm (Child and Rodrigues 2004; Child and Yan 2001; Guthrie 2005). A joint venture, in particular, can enable a Chinese firm to build an ongoing operational and organizational relationship with a multinational enterprise that can lead to the transfer of competencies and knowledge not just in production, but also in other areas where internationally competitive standards need to be achieved, such as corporate governance (Inkpen 1995; Simonin 2004; Child and Rodrigues 2005).

In summary, three external mechanisms are likely to strengthen Chinese firms' corporate governance practices: (1) product market competitiveness; (2) cross-listing on a foreign stock exchange; and (3) joint ventures with a foreign corporation that adheres to a higher corporate governance standard. Whether a firm meets the listing requirements of a foreign stock exchange depends on its financial health, and this in turn depends on the firm's product market competitiveness (in addition to the exchange's listing requirements). While product market competitiveness can be achieved without the assistance of a foreign corporation, firms that participate in a joint venture may gain a competitive advantage and implement corporate governance reforms in the process. Hence, competitiveness acts as a first step by which to improve corporate governance practices, and this may be aided by a joint venture which yields some corporate governance reforms. Enhanced competitiveness can then lead to even better corporate governance practices after listing on a foreign exchange, further strengthening the firm's competitiveness via access to cheaper capital. Hence, the key question concerns firm competitiveness. The answer to this question differs between SOEs and non-SOEs and depends on China's varying business–government relations at the local level.

Local Business–Government Relations

In the absence of effective national-level internal and external mechanisms to address corporate governance problems that impede access to capital, firms will search for alternative solutions. These solutions will depend on the local business–government relations in which they're located. Three dimensions of business–government relations are of particular salience, including (1) centre–local relations, (2) the institutional structure of the state, and (3) the organizational configuration of business actors. Whether these arrangements privilege SOEs or privately owned firms will have important ramifications for ongoing corporate governance reforms. Table 8.1 presents the three business–government dimensions, their relevant characteristics, the corporate governance implications, as well as identifying which region manifests these dichotomous arrangements—Shanghai or Guangdong.

Centre–Local Relations

Starting from China's economic reform in the 1980s, Guangdong and Shanghai embarked on distinct paths to tap into the wide range of reform possibilities. While Guangdong has enjoyed a relatively high level of autonomy from the central government in managing economic activities, Shanghai largely surrendered to Beijing due to a legacy of centralized planning based on the development of heavy industries. This divergence is reflected in Guangdong's smaller share of state-owned enterprises in comparison to Shanghai as displayed in Fig. 8.1.

Strong Centre–Local Relations: Shanghai

Starting in the 1980s, the ultimate goal of Beijing was to build Shanghai into an "industrial engine" that would attract capital and initiate industrial growth in other parts of the country. Shanghai was therefore constrained by Beijing's mandates to focusing on investments in light industry or services. This led to Shanghai becoming "an industrial workhorse" of the country,

Table 8.1 Business–government relations and their corporate governance implications

Business–government dimensions	*Characteristics*	*CG implications*	*Example*
Centre–local relations	Strong ties to Beijing	State ownership dominates and SOEs retain privileged access to finance and other state-sanctioned benefits	Shanghai
	Weak ties to Beijing	Privately owned firms more common	Guangdong
Institutional structure of the state	Cohesive	Preserve benefits of concentrated state ownership and privileged access to finance; long-term collaborative relationships nurtured	Shanghai
	Fragmented	Lack of state guidance for development of long-term collaborative relationships (including access to bank lending)	Guangdong
Organizational configuration of business associations	Poorly organized	SOEs dominate market and deny opportunities to private firms	Shanghai
	Well organized	Facilitates mutual assistance and information sharing (e.g., benefits, costs, and requirements to list overseas)	Guangdong

and contributing the largest fraction of any jurisdiction to the central revenue system (Yusuf and Wu 1997). It was reported that before 1980 Shanghai remitted as much as 86% of its revenue to the central government, accounting for approximately one sixth of overall government revenue (Yusuf and Wu 1997, 77). Because of its prominent role as an industrial centre and revenue generator, Shanghai was tightly regulated by Beijing and missed the opportunities brought about by the first round of reforms. Because of the support it received from the central government, including the entitlement of provincial status, land expansion, state-funded projects, supply of low-priced raw materials, and guaranteed market access, Shanghai was heavily taxed in the 1980s (Huang 2008). It was not until the mid-1980s that the central government started to loosen its control. Following

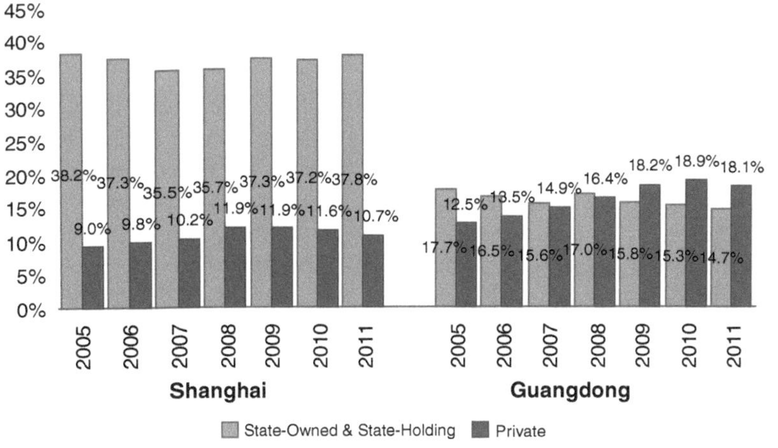

Fig. 8.1 The contribution of SOEs and private firms to the industrial output of Shanghai and Guangdong, 2005–2011 (Source: China Statistical Yearbook, 2012) (Note: The numbers do not add up to 100% because of the existence of other types of firms such as foreign-invested enterprises, township–village enterprises, and small enterprises below the designated size for inclusion in the sample)

Deng Xiaoping's Southern Tour in 1992, Shanghai was given greater authority to make decisions regarding investments. But due to historically close ties to Beijing in conjunction with its legacy of a planned economy, Shanghai evolved into a highly interventionist developmental state with SOEs dominating economic activity.

Weak Centre–Local Relations: Guangdong (Guangzhou)

At the initial stage of economic reform, the central government decided to make Guangdong (along with Fujian) an experimental zone because it made few contributions to central revenue, and it was safer to give more freedom in making experimental reform policies to a province located on China's periphery. It was believed that Guangdong could develop without the financial burden being borne by central funds because of its proximity to Hong Kong and historically close ties to international markets. This is why Guangdong and some of its municipal governments were able to pursue a "free-wheeling market-oriented" approach to reform (Thun 2006, 140). "New fiscal independence came in the form of a fixed tax payment—negotiated for five years—instead of a certain percentage of revenue sent to central government" (Goodman and Segal 2002, 180–1).[6] The Guangdong provincial government received little central supervision and was granted the right to retain all revenue exceeding the base amount, but in exchange it could not receive support as Shanghai did from the central government. Because of its fiscal independence, Guangdong leaders had greater bargaining power with Beijing and asked for special policies and favourable terms. Guangdong's provincial power was also decentralized to the sub-provincial levels, where Guangzhou could also enjoy liberty to promote economic development and have a fiscal relationship with Guangdong similar to that between Guangdong and Beijing. This has contributed to the relatively greater reliance on private firms as compared to SOEs, as seen in Fig. 8.1.

Institutional Structure of the State: Cohesive (Shanghai) Versus Fragmented (Guangdong)

To effectively maintain and leverage its relationship with the centre, the Shanghai government centralized decisions through a super municipal agency headed by the Shanghai mayor, which was set up based on a development programme in the mid-1980s (Huang 2008, 214). The unified bureaucratic structure helped coordinate and monitor developmental efforts effectively, and played a pivotal role with respect to capital accumulation and investment (Thun 2006, 107–8). It insured that top leaders in the local government were both informed about and involved in development decisions.

For example, the municipal government targeted the local auto industry to become one of the six pillars of Shanghai's economy and to make it one of China's three primary bases of sedan production (Thun 2006, 111–2). In order to achieve this goal, the municipal government set up a bureaucratic apparatus that is unified and coordinated at every level to guide the development of the industry. Directly under the mayor's office, the Auto Industry Leading Small Group was created to coordinate various government agencies and provide solutions when problems came up. Under the Leading Small Group, a localization office was also set up to supervise the auto industry on a daily basis—"it was in a sense the head office for the local industry" (Thun 2006, 112). The centralized bureaucratic structure working closely with hierarchical business groups (e.g., SAIC) helped extend the reach of local government into every aspect of firm operations (Thun 2006, 134). These institutional arrangements were very helpful in the initial stages of auto sector development when learning and economies of scale were particularly important.

By comparison, the autonomy that Guangzhou has enjoyed from central power has led to different incentive systems for political officials. Because the municipal government was not under great pressure of fiscal remittance to the central government, it had less incentive to collect revenue and coordinate economic activity. Bureaucratic organization in Guangzhou has therefore been fragmented, leading inter-firm relations to be decided via market coordination. The provincial government did not have strong institutions to align the competing interests of local cadre and weak business groups toward the pursuit of well-defined developmental goals (Thun 2006, 140). For example, the authority of auto firms was splintered over several government agencies and not fully controlled by the head office. This is described as "the loose, market-based relationships between firms" (Thun 2006, 147). In most cases, the Guangzhou government did not take up the role of accumulating and channelling investment capital into supply firms, and the business groups were not able to foster investment in supply firms and collaborative relationships between firms. Because the municipal head office was not assured of returns from investment, it did not have the incentive to nurture and promote learning among firms, and there was no attempt to create "long-term collaborative relationships" with supply firms. As assembly plants switched suppliers easily, commercial competition among firms impeded the development of technical and manufacturing skills. This has led Thun (2006) to label Guangzhou a "laissez-faire" local state (Thun 2006, 30).

Organizational Structure of Business Associations: Poorly Organized (Shanghai) Versus Well Organized (Guangdong)

By comparison, business associations in Guangdong are better organized via localized networks and entrepreneur-initiated and led associations. They generally exhibit three common traits. First, they are non-governmental initiatives, organized by business members from the bottom-up. Second, their organization mirrors that of the market; that is, firms engage in contractual and horizontal relationships rather than abiding by hierarchical, administrative principles. Because membership is voluntary and members are free to join or quit, associations face pressure to serve their members' interests.[7] Third, the associations are self-funded and self-governed entities, with considerable autonomy from the government.

A large proportion of associations' funds come from the associations themselves rather than government, and most associations choose their leaders by elections. Most associations establish their own decision-making rules, and the government does not usually meddle in their internal affairs.

Because the authority of auto firms was splintered over several government agencies and not fully controlled by the head office, the Guangzhou government did not take up the role of accumulating and channelling investment capital into supply firms, and the business groups were not able to foster investment in supply firms and collaborative relationships between firms. Because the head office was not assured of the returns from investment, it did not have the incentive to nurture and promote learning of firms, and there was no attempt to create "long-term collaborative relationships" with supply firms. As assembly plants switched suppliers easily, commercial competition of firms impeded the development of technical and manufacturing skills. Because the municipal government was not under great pressure of fiscal remittance to the central government, it faced fewer incentives to collect revenue. It had been active in the promotion of non-state firms. As seen in other industries, lack of capital has long been an impediment to development in Guangzhou's auto industry. Compared to Shanghai, firms in Guangzhou tended to be small, relatively separated and privately owned. This led firms to seek financing from elsewhere, such as foreign stock exchange listings. But to do so, they would first need to meet their listing requirements, which often required adhering to higher corporate governance standards and auditing requirements. Information sharing about the benefits and costs of overseas listing, in addition to the specific regulatory requirements, was transmitted relatively easily via the relatively strong organizational structure of business associations.

Cases

To illuminate the interplay of business–government structures and corporate governance reforms, I examine two automobile companies: (1) BYD, a private auto firm in Guangdong; and (2) SAIC, a state-owned auto firm in Shanghai. Gaining access to capital is at the heart of why firms list on a stock exchange, and the problems that arise with investors trying to protect their investments are what give rise to corporate governance problems (the agency and principal–principal problems discussed earlier). Hence, it is useful to focus on firms that engage in capital-intensive production, such as auto firms, since it is these companies that face the greatest pressures to find solutions to corporate governance problems.

Case 1: BYD

To list on the HKSE, a company must meet numerous criteria. In addition to a minimum size threshold as well as several financial health checks,[9] the HKSE requires that firms have adequate systems of internal control covering financial and compliance matters (Huang and Yeung 2014). Of particular importance are independent non-executive directors and the audit committee. Listing firms must appoint at least three independent non-executive directors, and at least one of them must have appropriate professional qualifications or accounting or related financial management expertise. Additionally, issuers must establish an audit committee comprising non-executive directors only. Finally, the HKSE requires that reporting accountants are properly qualified and independent of the issuer, to the standards of independence issued by the International Federation of Accountants. In Hong Kong, there is a concern with Chinese accounting standards; hence, this standard is higher than what is commonly found in Chinese firms.

To meet these requirements, BYD set up a board of directors that included two executive directors, one non-executive director, and two independent non-executive directors whose qualifications indicate that they are genuinely qualified and independent of BYD. Their experience and qualifications are fully disclosed in BYD's annual reports.[10] BYD also established several committees that report to the board of directors, including an audit committee, a remuneration committee, a nomination committee, and a strategy committee.[11] Committee members, their responsibilities, and their attendance at committee meetings are presented in BYD's annual reports. Finally, BYD hires an independent international auditor, Ernst & Young, to review and audit its financial statements.

Following its listing on the HKSE, BYD entered the auto business by purchasing a bankrupt state-owned auto manufacturer, the Tsinchuan Automobile Company (now BYD Auto), in 2003. During the subsequent 5 years, BYD's revenue grew dramatically, from USD0.5 billion in 2003 to approximately USD4 billion 5 years later.

BYD's success is partly attributable to two key innovations. The first is labour-intensive manufacturing. BYD successfully converted the capital-intensive Japanese battery production process into a labour-intensive one suitable to China's low-cost labour market. When BYD entered the automobile industry, the company applied the same model to the production process for cars (Huckman and MacCormack 2007). The second key innovation has been a high level of vertical integration in comparison to other car makers. This production model of high vertical integration is also similar to that of BYD's battery business. BYD's different business units produce at least 70% of the components for its own vehicles. BYD believes this model helps quality control and reduces the time to market. Lin Hongye, Director of the Integrated Business Office, Central Research Institute, explained: "The costs of in-house small volume production are equivalent to the price of external purchasing. However, the significant advantage is the speed of reaction. If we buy from the outside, the coordination costs will be higher, and we may miss some market opportunity" (Gong 2007).

BYD's remarkable growth and commercialization of electric vehicles and battery technology led to Warren Buffett acquiring a 10% stake in BYD in September 2008. The transaction occurred via MidAmerican Energy Holdings, a subsidiary of Buffett's Berkshire Hathaway. As part of the deal, MidAmerican would nominate a non-executive director to the board, and proposed David Sokol, MidAmerican Chairman, for the role. BYD stood to benefit in several ways from Buffett's investment. First, it would strengthen BYD's financial position and signal to other potential lenders/investors the strength of BYD's business model. Second, BYD would be able to draw on the experience and counsel of a world-renowned business conglomerate with extensive and diversified business experience as a strategic investor. Third, the entry of MidAmerican would facilitate BYD's reach to the global market with its rechargeable batteries and electric vehicles. In the year following Buffett's investment, BYD became one of China's top ten car producers, and in the year 2013, BYD ranked tenth in passenger vehicle sales and eleventh in total sales, covering both passenger and commercial vehicles delivered in China.[12] It has also partnered with Uber in the leasing of electric cars and aims to sell autos to the U.S. market.[13]

Finally, reflecting the alignment of managerial compensation with BYD's financial and share price performance, BYD's CEO, Wang Chuanfu, earned the highest annual salary of all listed carmakers in China from 2008 to 2010.[14]

Summary

BYD's rise to stardom in the Chinese automobile sector is unlikely to have occurred in the context of Shanghai. The local business–government relations of Guangdong formed a critical backdrop to BYD's success and have shaped its corporate governance reforms, with implications for other private firms in the region. Guangdong's weak ties to Beijing have granted more market opportunities to privately owned firms since state-owned enterprises do not crowd out local investment. At the same time, the lack of a cohesive institutional state structure creates space for entrepreneurs to succeed due to fewer impediments that might arise from state management of the economy's local development. The flip side of the absence of state coordination and weak ties to Beijing is the lack of capital for private firms. Capital scarcity poses a significant problem for capital-intensive industries, such as auto manufacturing. BYD successfully avoided this problem due to its reliance on labour-intensive production for batteries—it only entered the automotive sector after an infusion of capital from listing on the HKSE. But this is highly instructive for the implications for corporate governance reforms. To overcome capital constraints inherent to regions which lack strong ties to Beijing, firms must find ways to satisfy outside investors that their funds will not be expropriated (i.e., agency and tunnelling costs). This requires implementing corporate governance reforms more in line with those of the west. Finding out about the benefits and costs of proceeding down this path, as well as the specifics about how to implement these reforms, can come from other privately owned business owners; and this information is more readily transmitted through the business community via well-organized business associations.

Thus, the weak ties to Beijing coupled with a fragmented state structure force private firms to search for investors in order to expand. These problems are especially acute in capital-intensive industries. But once one firm learns how to solve this problem and demonstrates the benefits of proceeding down this path, others are likely to quickly follow. Consequently, Guangdong's business–government characteristics have played a critical enabling role to the rise of corporate governance reforms that more closely resemble those of the west insofar as they offer stronger protections to minority shareholders due to firms being bonded to a high corporate governance standard by listing on a foreign stock exchange.

Case 2: SAIC

SAIC is one of China's oldest carmakers, tracing its origins back to the 1950s. Despite its long historical standing, SAIC only became a leader in the Chinese auto industry in recent years. It has been the largest auto manufacturer by sales volume in China since 2010, most of which is due to its joint ventures with General Motors and Volkswagen.

SAIC's success is largely attributable to state support of the auto industry in Shanghai. The key hurdle to its successful development was not so much its lack of access to capital, but the establishment of a supplier network. The Shanghai government had the bureaucratic capacity, financial resources, and resolve to address this problem. But by the late 1990s, after the supplier network had been fully established, new problems arose—the need to lower costs. Thun (2006) notes that the president of VW Asia-Pacific, Bernard Leissner, estimated that it cost VW 18% more to produce a car in China than in Germany in 2003, primarily due to the high cost of components.

The main problem was the inability to objectively evaluate supplier performance. This problem was composed of two parts (Thun 2006, 251). First, suppliers lacked competitive pressures because of the Shanghai Municipal Localization Office's drive to ensure that there was no duplication of manufacturing capability within the supply network so as to maximize economies of scale. This led to Shanghai becoming the largest components manufacturing centre in China with around 10% of total production in 2002 (Oliver et al. 2009). Second, it was difficult to identify which firms were strong performers and which ones were weak. Efforts to bolster development of the supplier network would undercut efforts to improve firm-level efficiency. Firms that were seen as displaying strong performance would be handicapped by being paid a lower price for their components (weakening their balance sheets) and might be forced to take on new workers from other weaker firms, thereby adding to their labour costs. The Shanghai government was more interested in development than competitiveness.

The resolve to improve supplier performance was further hampered by the interests of its dominant owner—the state. The links between SAIC and the local government were highly entangled, going far beyond the straightforward principal–agent arrangements that characterize owners and managers in typical western firms. For example, until 1995, the SAIC president served as the director of the Municipal Localization Office (Thun 2006, 253). This position not only granted him control over the massive Localization Fund of around 5 billion USD (in addition to easing the process by which SAIC firms applied for funds), but also put him in charge of the government bureaucracy that oversaw the auto industry. Additionally, SAIC managers were appointed by the municipal government and the rotation of leaders between SAIC and high-level municipal posts helped to preserve conformity of views within the leadership of Shanghai's auto industry. The hierarchical structure of SOE business groups eased the pursuit of the local government's development objectives among SAIC's group firms, once a common development objective was agreed upon.

The Shanghai municipal government was developing the auto sector principally because it provided a large number of people with employment and social welfare benefits. Political control therefore led SAIC firms to employ excess workers. Such arrangements and political imperatives undercut efforts at cost-cutting and improving the competitiveness of group firms, including suppliers. SAIC bore the financial costs of workers' salaries, housing, and the provision of social services that would normally be paid for by the government in the west. Additionally, the prioritization of employment led to the expansion of the group in ways that would increase the number of workers, and prevent the introduction of technologies that would enhance competitiveness if it reduced the need for workers. It also stymied the introduction of new managerial governance techniques and incentive-based pay that might enhance competitiveness.

In 2003, restructuring efforts were introduced in order to separate the commercial and governmental role of the state by placing firms under the control of independent asset management offices. At the national level, SASAC has been charged with this new responsibility. The equivalent organization in Shanghai is the Shanghai Municipal Asset Management Committee, of which the Mayor is head, and the Shanghai Municipal Asset Management Office, which is the actual operating office. The office is responsible for approving new investment projects and ensuring that they conform to government regulations; management responsibilities would stay with SAIC. The new structure was intended to strengthen firms' corporate governance arrangements so as to permit the possibility of a public listing. But Thun (2006, 262) observes that the changes did not meaningfully change SAIC's governance arrangements. For example, the "outsiders" on the board of directors are government officials who do not have a detailed knowledge of the auto industry (and consequently cannot challenge the views of SAIC board members), the party committees within holding companies continue to heavily influence appointments, salaries are not linked to performance, and perhaps most importantly, the sole shareholder is still a local government with political interests. Nevertheless, the SAIC Group restructured itself and established a new holding company, SAIC Motor Corporation Ltd, in December 2004 in order to be listed on the stock markets in New York and Hong Kong (Yeo 2007, 104–11).[15] However, the overseas listing was delayed due to a sharp downturn in the country's auto sector, and never pursued afterwards.[16]

In addition to pursuing the often conflicting objectives of political and commercial priorities, SAIC competitiveness was further hobbled by its ability to objectively evaluate supplier performance. But foreign firms, via their equity stakes in joint ventures, introduced governance reforms that were more in line with commercial objectives. One manifestation of this occurred with the introduction of proper accounting and financial management for the simple reason that it would be impossible to divide profits and losses according to equity shares without effective accounting (Thun 2006, 262). Additionally, GM introduced mechanisms for evaluating suppliers from across China so as to introduce competitive pressures on Shanghai-based suppliers to reduce costs and boost quality.

In 2008, SAIC listed on the Shanghai stock exchange. While the Shanghai Stock Exchange listing introduced some market discipline, politics remain influential due to the state's dominant ownership position. Government policies also continue to be a source of major competitive advantage to SAIC despite the removal of many of the protective measures following WTO accession in 2002, including local content mandates, foreign exchange controls, and import tariffs that had to be significantly lowered (Ahrens 2013). Of particular importance are government procurement policies.

The Ministry of Industry and Information Technology publishes a product catalogue that lists the types of autos eligible for government procurement (Ahrens 2013). The 2012 catalogue did not include any foreign cars due to two specific procurement requirements: (1) government vehicles must have an engine smaller than 1.8 litres and cost than USD180,000; and (2) only companies that have spent 3% or more of their revenue on R&D qualify for a listing in the procurement catalogue. These requirements offer a way to avoid an explicit ban on foreign cars while privileging domestic auto makers. The government's procurement programme for cars is worth around USD12.7 billion, or 4.5% of all auto sales in China. In 2010, the Chinese government bought about 900,000 autos, making it a very significant market. Government officials have frequently chosen Audis in the past, so the shift to domestic brands has benefited SAIC Motor.[17]

Summary
The case illustrates that the Shanghai government played a central role in the development of SAIC into a national car champion. Historically, this was due to the strong ties that Shanghai maintained with Beijing, granting the latter considerable influence over the former and in turn creating inordinate privileges for state-owned enterprises, such as SAIC. But SAIC's success has also been attributable to the institutional structure of Shanghai's local government, which has centralized authority over local development as manifested by the Municipal Localization Office and its control over a massive Localization Fund. The local government's political priorities occasionally led to cross-purposes with those of SAIC, such as when Shanghai privileged development of the local supplier network over competitiveness. However, the long-term benefits of local state support have far outweighed these costs, as with preferential access to credit and preferential consideration for the government's procurement programmes. Indeed, these financial benefits have been of particular importance to SAIC due to the capital-intensive nature of automobile production. While it prepared to list on the NYSE and the HKSE, these efforts were ultimately scrapped and SAIC listed instead on the Shanghai Stock Exchange. This has enabled the state to retain disproportionate influence over the firm, not only because of its dominant ownership stake, but also due to less stringent information disclosure requirements and other standards designed to protect minority shareholders.

SAIC's dominance is also due, in part, to the weak organizational structure of private business associations. This was manifested by SAIC's efforts to improve the quality of supplier inputs following on its joint venture with GM. The inability of private firms to effectively lobby the local government or to coordinate among themselves enabled SAIC to implement the new supplier programme that forced many of them into bankruptcy.

Altogether, the strong ties between SAIC and the Shanghai local government has benefited both parties handsomely, despite occasional problems arising from the government's tending to political priorities ahead of commercial concerns. These benefits have arisen against the backdrop of historically close ties to Beijing, which incentivized Shanghai's officials to closely monitor and manage industrial upgrading, and further contributed to weak private-sector business associations. Ultimately, these arrangements have preserved SAIC's concentrated state ownership, with few internal or external remedies for outside shareholders.

Conclusion

China has initiated a range of initiatives with implications for corporate governance reforms, including the creation of SASAC in 2003 which aided the separation of commercial and political objectives for SOEs, the 2005 split-share reform which introduced a stronger focus on share price performance for SOEs, the 2002 corporate governance guidelines, and efforts to reduce corruption and strengthen the legal system. Nevertheless, their effectiveness remains open to question. The cases indicate that the major sources of corporate governance reform have come from international sources—either joint ventures in the case of SOEs or listing on a foreign stock exchange for both SOEs and private firms. Both of these were motivated by the effort to improve product market competition.

For BYD, the key challenge has been a lack of capital. This led it to develop innovative processes for manufacturing batteries and later automobiles by utilizing more labour-intensive production methods. Additionally, BYD became more vertically integrated with regard to the manufacture of components, which helped it be more agile in responding to market opportunities. These innovative solutions emerged as a result of Guangdong's weak ties to Beijing; the local government did not have the same motivation to coordinate activity so as to pay a high tax to the central government. As a consequence, the development of the auto industry was weakly coordinated by the local government, forcing firms to find innovative solutions to overcome the lack of a supplier base and a lack of capital.

BYD's stellar growth in battery manufacturing enabled it to list on the Hong Kong Stock Exchange. But this required several corporate governance reforms in order to meet the exchange's listing requirements and to assuage investors of the soundness of the company's finances. The infusion of capital due to BYD's listing on the exchange allowed it to purchase a state-owned auto company and begin developing electric cars. Its continuing growth led to Warren Buffett's purchase of a 10% stake in the company, not only granting BYD access to additional capital but also to additional market opportunities.

That BYD is listed on the Hong Kong Stock Exchange and must meet a higher accounting standard than Chinese firms listed on the Shanghai or Shenzhen Stock Exchanges indicates that investors can have greater confidence in the financial performance of BYD. In other words, BYD's higher level of corporate governance grants it access to cheaper capital than it would otherwise have access to, as well as to additional market opportunities which in turn strengthen BYD's product market competitiveness.

In Shanghai, the local government made a commitment to building up the automobile industry and provided adequate financing to fund its development. The strong links between the local government and the SAIC business group enabled the rapid development of the auto industry in order to build economies of scale for auto suppliers. The key challenge for SAIC was therefore not access to capital, but technology. Hence, SAIC created joint ventures with Volkswagen and GM. In addition to improving production quality, these partnerships introduced a higher standard of accounting and corporate governance, necessary to ensure each partner contributed the appropriate amount of financial resources to the joint venture as well as to appropriately allocate responsibilities and earnings. The drive to enhance the cost competitiveness of suppliers further forced improvements in corporate governance as supplier firms had to become more efficient with their resources and more effective in their allocation and management.

Despite these improvements, politics continue to influence firm strategy as the state remains the dominant owner. While commercial objectives have become relatively more important, SAIC is not immune from the state's influence. This is a double-edged sword in that it not only diverts attention from a strict focus on the firm's commercial pursuits, but also gives it access to government programmes that can offer a major source of revenue.

These cases clearly illustrate the divergent paths that corporate governance reforms have taken in China, which critically depend on the structure of local business–government relations. Nevertheless, the growing success of private firms across all regions of the country will increase pressure on local governments as well as Beijing to not simply pass more corporate governance reforms, but to follow through on enforcing them. While the courts are subject to political influence, the state also has the capacity to force itself to refrain from interfering in them in cases regarding commerce if the state perceives the protection of investor rights as in its best interests. This is likely to take considerable time, but it has begun to occur as recent court rulings in favour of investors indicate. Only if and when the CCP sees its best interests aligned with those of investors will meaningful corporate reforms be widely implemented. There is reason for optimism as the CCP's legitimacy primarily depends on economic performance, and this is increasingly due to successful private firms.

Notes

1. Using the 20% share ownership threshold employed by La Porta et al. (1999) to identify the existence of controlling shareholders means that most listed firms have at least one controlling owner. With this control, an owner can expropriate from minority shareholders via outright theft and fraud or through more subtle means such as intercorporate loans, loan guarantees for related companies, favourable transfer pricing for related companies, and via the dilution of new shares.
2. This is a common practice among family-owned firms in general (Bennedsen et al. 2007; Morck et al. 2000; Perez-Gonzales 2006).
3. See Kim et al. (2010) chapter 8 for a discussion of how takeovers act as an external governance tool.
4. Because bankruptcies (financial failure) are unlikely, as mentioned earlier, the type of failure that managers fear is liquidation (economic failure).
5. For example, the Korean firm, POSCO, is often regarded as a role model in the steel industry.
6. "Beginning in 1980 it was agreed that Guangdong would remit only a small and fixed amount of its revenues for five years to central government given the low level of Beijing's expected investment and expenditure in the province. In effect this was a financial contract between the PRC and Guangdong Province: Guangdong guaranteed to supply Beijing with a certain amount of revenue, and had full use of any surplus it could generate" (Goodman and Segal 2002, 187).
7. The semi-official associations began with compulsory membership. But it was difficult to achieve complete coverage of the industry since there were numerous enterprises and most of them were small. And governments did not have effective ways to punish those enterprises that did not participate. Under such circumstances, membership later became voluntary. Of course, low coverage of membership in industries causes difficulty for effective regulation and coordination since non-members do not obey the rules set by associations.
8. Gunther, Marc. 2009. "Warren Buffett Takes Charge," *Fortune*, 13 April.
9. The issuer must normally have a trading record of not less than three financial years under substantially the same management. The expected total market capitalization at the time of listing must be at least HK$200 million

and the total capitalization of securities held by the public must be at least HK$50 million. The issuer must also satisfy the profit test, the market capitalization/revenue/cash flow test, or the market capitalization/revenue test.

10. BYD annual reports, various years.
11. For their roles and duties, see BYD "Annual Report 2008," p. 24.
12. CPCA, China Auto Sales Hit Record High of 21.98 Million in 2013.
13. He, Laura. 2015. "Uber enters electric-car market in tie-up with BYD" *MarketWatch*, 16 March. Tian, Ying and Ho, Chua Kong. 2014. Buffett-Backed BYD Says Chinese Cars to Debut in U.S. *Bloomberg Business*, 7 January.
14. This is according to annual reports from 25 listed Chinese carmakers. China Daily—Hong Kong Edition, 27 June 2011. "Short Torque."
15. AFX Asia, "China's SAIC to set up holding company for overseas listing – report," 28 December 2004.
16. Francesco Guerrera, "Downturn may hit SAIC listing," 10 January 2005, Financial Times.
17. FAW and Guangzhou Automobile Group (both SOEs) also benefited. Ran, Yu. 2013. "Govt departments purchasing more locally made cars," *China Daily USA*, 21 March.

References

Ahrens, N. (2013). *China's competitiveness: Myth, reality, and lessons for the United States and Japan; case study: SAIC Motor Corporation*. Washington, DC: CSIS.

Allen, F., Qian, J., & Qian, M. (2005). Law, finance, and economic growth in China. *Journal of Financial Economics, 77*, 57–116.

Bai, C., Li, D. D., Tao, Z., & Wang, Y. (2000). A multitask theory of state enterprise reform. *Journal of Comparative Economics, 28*, 716–738.

Bai, C., Liu, Q., Lu, J., Song, F. M., & Zhang, J. (2004). Corporate governance and market valuation in China. *Journal of Comparative Economics, 32*, 599–616.

Bennedsen, M., Nielsen, K. M., Perez-Gonzales, F., & Wolfenzon, D. (2007). Inside the family firm: The role of families in succession decisions and performance. *Quarterly Journal of Economics, 122*, 647–691.

Berle, A., & Means, G. (1932). *The modern corporation and private property*. New York: Macmillan.

China Statistical Yearbook. 2012. National Bureau of Statistics of China. *China Statistical Yearbook*.

Chen, T., (2015). Institutions, board structure, and corporate performance: Evidence from Chinese firms. *Journal of Corporate Finance, 32*, 217–237.

Chen, X., Harford, J., & Li, K. (2007). Monitoring: Which institutions matter? *Journal of Financial Economics, 86*, 279–305.

Chen, G., Firth, M., & Xu, L. (2009). Does the type of ownership control matter? Evidence from China's listed companies. *Journal of Banking and Finance, 33*, 171–181.

Chen, J. J., Liu, X., & Li, W. (2010). The effect of insider control and global benchmarks on Chinese executive compensation. *Corporate Governance International Review, 18*, 107–123.

Cheng, M., Lin, B., & Wei, M., (2015). Executive compensation in family firms: The effect of multiple family members. *Journal of Corporate Finance, 32*, 238–257.

Child, J., & Rodrigues, S. B. (2004). Corporate governance in international joint ventures: Toward a theory of partner preferences. In A. Grandori (Ed.), *Corporate governance and firm organization* (pp. 89–112). Oxford: Oxford University Press.

Child, J., & Rodrigues, S. B. (2005). The internationalization of Chinese firms: A case for theoretical extension? *Management and Organization Review, 1*(3), 381–410.

Child, J., & Yan, Y. (2001). National and transnational effects in international business: Indications from Sino-foreign joint ventures. *Management International Review, 41*, 53–75.

Conyon, M. J., & He, L. (2011). Executive compensation and corporate governance in China. *Journal of Corporate Finance, 17*, 1158–1175.

Dalton, D. R., & Kesner, I. F. (1983). Inside/outside succession and organizational size: The pragmatics of executive replacement. *Academy of Management Journal, 26*, 736–742.

Demsetz, H., & Lehn, K. (1985). The structure of corporate ownership: Causes and consequences. *Journal of Political Economy, 93*, 115–1177.

Diamond, D. W. (1984). Financial intermediation and delegated monitoring. *Review of Economic Studies, 51*, 393–414.

Diamond, D. W. (1991). Monitoring and reputation: The choice between bank loans and directly placed debt. *Journal of Political Economy, 99*, 689–721.

Easterbrook, F. H. (1984). Two agency-cost explanations of dividends. *American Economic Review, 74*, 650–659.

Fama, E. (1980). Agency problems and the theory of the firm. *Journal of Political Economy, 88*, 288–307.

Fama, E. F. (1985). What's different about banks? *Journal of Monetary Economics, 15*, 29–40.

Fama, E., & Jensen, M., (1983). Separation of ownership and control. *Journal of Law and Economics, 26*(2), 301–325.

Ferris, S. P., Kim, K. A., & Noronha, G. (2009). The effect of cross-listing on corporate governance: A review of the international evidence. *Corporate Governance International Review, 17*, 338–352.

Firth, M., Fung, P. M. Y., & Rui, O. M. (2006). Corporate performance and CEO compensation in China. *Journal of Corporate Finance, 12*, 693–714.

Firth, M., Fung, P. M. Y., & Rui, O. M. (2007). How ownership and corporate governance influence chief executive pay in China's listed firms. *Journal of Business Research, 60*, 776–785.

Gillan, S. L., & Starks, L. T. (1998). A survey of shareholder activism: Motivation and empirical evidence. *Contemporary Financial Digest, 2*, 10–34.

Gong, X. (2007). BYD: The kangaroo model of car manufacturing. *World Business Report*, Available at http://oxford.icxo.com/htmlnews/2007/01/05/986451_1.htm. Accessed 11 Apr 2015.

Goodman, D. S. G., & Segal, G. (2002). *China deconstructs: Politics, trade and regionalism*. London/New York: Routledge.

Guthrie, D. (2005). Organizational learning and productivity: State structure and foreign investment in the rise of the Chinese corporation. *Management and Organization Review, 1*, 165–195.

Hart, O. (1983). The market as an incentive mechanism. *Bell Journal of Economics, 14*, 366–382.

Huang, Y. (2008). *Capitalism with Chinese characteristics: Entrepreneurship and the state*. Cambridge/New York: Cambridge University Press.

Huang, F. X., & Yeung, H. (2014). *Chinese companies and the Hong Kong Stock Market*. Oxon: Routledge.

Huckman, R. S., & MacCormack, A. D. (2007). BYD Company Ltd., Case 9-606-139, Harvard Business School.

Inkpen, A. C. (1995). *The management of international joint ventures: An organizational learning perspective*. London: Routledge.

Jensen, M. (1986). Agency costs of free cash flow, corporate finance, and takeovers. *American Economic Review, 76*, 323–329.

Jensen, M. C., & Meckling, W. (1976). The theory of the firm: Managerial behavior, agency costs, and ownership structure. *Journal of Financial Economics, 3*, 305–360.

Jiang, F., & Kim, K. (2015). Corporate governance in China: A modern perspective. *Journal of Corporate Finance, 32*, 190–216.

Jiang, F., Huang, J., & Kim, K. A. (2013a). Appointments of outsiders as CEOs, state-owned enterprises, and firm performance: Evidence from China. *Pacific Basin Finance Journal, 23*, 49–64.

Kato, T., & Long, C. (2006a). CEO turnover, firm performance, and enterprise reform in China: Evidence from micro data. *Journal of Comparative Economics, 34*, 796–817.

Kato, T., & Long, C. (2006b). Executive compensation, firm performance, and corporate governance in China: Evidence from firms listed in the Shanghai and Shenzhen Stock Exchanges. *Economic Development and Cultural Change, 54*, 945–983.

Kim, K. A., Nofsinger, J. R., & Mohr, D. (2010). *Corporate governance* (3rd ed.). Upper Saddle River: Pearson Prentice Hall Publishers.

La Porta, R., Lopez-de-Silanes, F., Shleifer, A., & Vishny, R. (1997). Legal determinants of external finance. *Journal of Finance, 52*, 1131–1150.

La Porta, R., Lopez-de-Silanes, F., Shleifer, A., & Vishny, R. (1998). Law and finance. *Journal of Political Economy, 106*, 1113–1155.

La Porta, R., Lopez-de-Silanes, F., & Sheilfer, A. (1999). Corporate ownership around the world. *Journal of Finance, 54*, 471–517.

La Porta, R., Lopez-de-Silanes, F., Shleifer, A., & Vishny, R. (2000). Agency problems and dividend policy around the world. *Journal of Finance, 55*, 1–34.

Lit, S., Brockman, P., & Zurbruegg, R. (2015). Cross-listing, firm-specific information, and corporate governance: Evidence from Chinese A-shares and H-shares. *Journal of Corporate Finance, 32*, 347–362.

Liu, Q. (2006). Corporate governance in China: Current practices, economic effects and institutional determinants. *CESifo Economic Studies, 52*, 415–453.

Liu, Q., & Lu, Z. J. (2007). Corporate governance and earnings management in Chinese listed companies: A tunneling perspective. *Journal of Corporate Finance, 13*, 881–906.

Morck, R., Stangeland, D., & Yeung, B. (2000). Inherited wealth, corporate control, and economic growth? In R. Morck (Ed.), *Concentrated corporate ownership*. Chicago: University of Chicago Press.

Oliver, N., Holweg, M., & Luo, J. (2009). The past, present and future of China's automotive industry: A value chain perspective. *International Journal of Technological Learning, Innovation and Development, 2*(1–2), 76–118.

Peng, W. Q., Wei, K. C. J., & Yang, Z. (2011). Tunneling or propping: Evidence from connected transactions in China. *Journal of Corporate Finance, 17*, 306–325.

Perez-Gonzales, F. (2006). Inherited control and firm performance. *American Economic Review, 96*, 1559–1588.

Pistor, K., & Xu, C. (2005). Governing stock markets in transition economies: Lessons from China. *American Law and Economic Review, 7*, 184–210.

Qian, M., & Yeung, B., (2015). Bank financing and corporate governance. *Journal of Corporate Finance, 32*, 258–270.

Rozeff, M. S. (1982). Growth, beta and agency costs as determinants of dividend payout ratios. *Journal of Financial Research, 5*, 249–259.

Scharfstein, D. (1988). Product market competition and managerial slack. *RAND Journal of Economics, 19*, 147–155.

Schmidt, K. M. (1997). Managerial incentives and product market competition. *Review of Economic Studies, 64*, 191–213.

Segal, A. (2003). *Digital dragon: High-technology enterprises in China*. Ithaca: Cornell University Press.

Sharpe, S. A. (1990). Asymmetric information, bank lending, and implicit contracts: A stylized model of customer relationships. *Journal of Finance, 45*, 1069–1087.

Simonin, B. L. (2004). An empirical investigation of the process of knowledge transfer in international strategic alliances. *Journal of International Business Studies, 35*, 407–427.

Thun, E. (2006). *Changing lanes in China foreign direct investment, local government, and auto sector development*. New York: Cambridge University Press.

Xu, X., & Wang, Y. (1999). Ownership structure and corporate governance in Chinese stock companies. *China Economic Review, 10*, 75–98.

Yeo, Y. (2007). *Regulating China's industrial economy: A comparative case study of auto and telecom service sectors* (pp. 104–111). Manuscript. College Park: University of Maryland.

Yusuf, S., & Wu, W. (1997). *The dynamics of urban growth in three Chinese cities*. New York: Oxford University Press.

Zou, H., Wong, S., Shum, C., Xiong, J., & Yan, J. (2008). Controlling-minority shareholder incentive conflicts and directors' and officers' liability insurance: Evidence from China. *Journal of Banking and Finance, 32*, 2636–2645.

CHAPTER 9

The Changing Business–State Relations in China: The View from Socialist Corporatism

Yukyung Yeo

Introduction

When corporate power is defined as the ability of business entities to influence state policy-making by means of political and professional resources,[1] how does it explain the changing relations between government and business in China? Since the mid-2000s, as the profits of large state firms in the leading sectors have increased, the view of the rising corporate power of those large state-owned enterprises (SOEs) is shared by scholars of Chinese political economy (Kennedy 2005; Naughton 2008; Downs 2008). For example, Erica Downs holds that national oil corporations are "becoming more autonomous and less influenced by the party-state, seeing as kind of monopolistic interest groups" (Downs 2008, p. 125) that place much more emphasis on maximizing their own commercial interests at the expense of social welfare.[2] Taking the civil aviation industry as an example, Barry Naughton also notes that central state firms have become strong enough to bypass the regulatory authorities' policies by using market

Y. Yeo (✉)
College of International Studies, Kyung Hee University, Seoul, South Korea

X. Zhang, T. Zhu (eds.), *Business, Government and Economic Institutions in China*, International Political Economy Series,
DOI 10.1007/978-3-319-64486-8_9

forces, such as shareholders (Naughton 2008). Yet, as the economic power of large state firms grows, the state also retools its regulatory capacity with somewhat different objectives and means of control. This is perhaps the most evident in China's strategic industries whose share of state assets is central to the national economy and security. Therefore, the growing economic and political capitals of large state firms do not necessarily lead to the substantial change in government–business relations as argued, at least in the top-tiered leading sectors.[3]

What is more, both internal and external challenges since the 2008 global financial crisis have brought about a shift in the nature of regulatory regime. As will be discussed later, the mounting wealth of state firms over the last decade has arguably slackened the reins of SOE reform, which is partly responsible for the failure of the nominal owner and regulator of SOEs, the State-owned Assets Supervision and Administration Commission (SASAC). In the meantime, the strong demand for rebalancing the economy and social policy, along with the massive infrastructure projects from the 4 trillion stimulus program, have actually led to empower the National Development and Reform Commission (NDRC) as a leading state agency. In examining the changing balance of power within those major economic institutions in China, I employ a rather broader concept of "regulation," which denotes aggregate efforts by state agencies to steer the economy beyond the conventional notion of "a set of authoritative rules accompanied by some administrative agency to monitor and enforce compliance" (Jordana and Levi-Faur 2004, pp. 2–5). In exploring how the changing interactions between government and business actors shaped the emergence and development of major economic institutions in China, we can posit that the discretion of state firms in the market is limited by the newly empowered comprehensive economic commission, the NDRC. To this end, the chapter first introduces socialist corporatism as a theoretical window for examining how China's resilient Leninist institutions, such bureaucratic status of big business and planning bureaucracy, constrain substantial change between government and business. It then discusses the government restructuring and economic downturn stemming from the 2008 global financial crisis onward as internal and external sources of emerging statist policy ideas, respectively. A discussion on how socialist–corporatist institutions, such as bureaucratic rank/status of the firms or the deeply seated party organizations in both government and business, prevent China's large state firms and business associations from acting as societal forces then follows. Institutionally, the changing balance of power in the state structure is emphasized in order to explain how China's market regulation is shifting to a more inclusive one. The case of the recent anti-monopoly probing against the telecom giants is examined to support these arguments. The study concludes with a brief reflection on the nature of regulation in the Chinese political economy.

Socialist Corporatism: The Concept Revisited

Often the subject of government–business relations is largely approached from the theoretical perspectives of state–society relations such as pluralism, corporatism, and clientelism (Solomon 1983; Wilks and Wright 1987; Katzenstein 1985; Pearson 1997; Kennedy 2005). However, other efforts have been also made, particularly focusing on the government–business relations in developing countries, by disaggregating "business" into five entities—capital, sector, firm, association, and network (Haggard et al. 1997, pp. 36–60). This specific kind of "theory of business" emerged partly due to the lingering concerns with "competing and sometimes contradictory ways in which business is theorized" (Haggard et al. 1997, p. 36), which causes empirical research on business–government relations to remain theoretically diffuse. While each approach to business is different, they all commonly emphasize that "market outcomes, investment, and growth are heavily influenced by the relationship between governments and private sectors" (Haggard et al. 1997, p. 36). When business is taken as the structure of capital, sectors, or firms, the behavior and preferences of the state can be constrained by private control of resources, the contending interests of different sectors, and the relative size of major firms and their internal diversification within firms. On the other hand, seeing business as an association or network enables us to look into "the political organization of business or the institutions that mediate business interests" (Haggard et al. 1997, p. 37). Among those approaches, the business-as-firm approach, which pays attention to the *political* consequences of corporate organization, and the business-as-individual-managers-and-owners approach that goes beyond formal institutional channels appear to have some benefits in studying the case of China's leading sectors. Nevertheless, due to its limited scope of business to the *private* sector, theoretic utility can be questioned in accounting for the dynamics between government and business in China's strategic industries where state ownership is predominant. More importantly, the deficiency in considering *socialist contexts*,[4] which play the primary roles in shaping government–business relations in China, adds another barrier to examining the case of China. Socialist contexts here refer to the resilient comprehensive state commissions (such as the NDRC or the SASAC), the continued pursuit of state-owned economy (国有经济), and the deeply penetrated party organizations in government and business. Given such inherent constraints, socialist corporatism may offer better analytic tools to examine how the resilient socialist political–economic institutions influence on shaping the government–business relations and their impacts on economic institutions, which is the core subject of this book project.

In general, corporatism can be defined as "a specific form of political exchange between the state and social interests, particularly of an economic nature" (Yep 2000, p. 550).[5] On the one hand, as state power is devolved to the concerned social interest, the latter is allowed to play a role in policy formulation or implementation and have some access to the state's material and symbolic resources. In return, the state obtains a promise of consensus or co-operation, which consists of useful social resources for the maintenance of legitimacy, efficiency and effectiveness of state action (Yep 2000, p. 551). As a result, each actor's autonomy comes to be limited, but they are willing to accept self-restraint (Yep 2000, p. 551). As a variant of statist corporatism that emphasizes "the dominant role of the state" in forming social organizations (including business groups) and controlling their leadership selection and interest articulation, socialist corporatism adds elements of the socialist structure, such as state planning agency or the party organizations, to statist corporatism (Pearson 1997, p. 39). In doing so, the socialist structure as a key aspect of the institutional structure in socialist corporatism plays the leading role in controlling the growth and autonomy of economic interests that have risen from the reforms. The socialist structure here refers to the state planning agency and the party-state organizations. In other words, although both statist corporatism and socialist corporatism assume the dominant role of the state in dealing with social forces, an oversight of socialist elements reveals the limits of statist corporatism as a theoretical framework. The predominance of the state planning agency and the party organizations inside the government tends to generate the hierarchically organized and coercive state structure.

Moreover, while state corporatism seeks to "gather in social forces in order to increase national power in the world economy, socialist corporatism emphasizes a dispersion of power to extra-state bodies even though the government itself holds an authority to create them" (Pearson 1997,

p. 39). In this way, the autonomy of economic interests and its growth in socialist corporatism is ***managed*** by the party-state rather than ***captured*** by state-formed organizations (i.e., business groups) in statist corporatism. In particular, socialist corporatism offers more appropriate guidance on explaining the concrete institutional results of shifts in state–business relations if there are any, in that socialist corporatism takes into account significant but often dismissed elements of Leninist background, such as the resilient powerful planning bureaucracy and historically weak social forces (or institutions). In this regard, the subject of government–business relations, particularly in the case of China's leading sectors, calls for taking into account the influence of "socialist contexts" on making the behavior and interests of business and ultimately on the changes of state–business relations. As will be discussed later, this chapter pays particular attention to the role of the former planning bureaucracy, the NDRC, and its power relations with other state agencies, despite the growing economic strength of large state firms in China's leading sectors. However, it should be also noted that the overall government–business relations in China can be hardly understood through the socialist–corporatist lens alone (Pearson 1997, p. 40).

Regime Shift: From Market-Enhancing to Market-Steering

In this chapter, I suggest that when the primary goal of state regulation is to encourage the active function of market-oriented rules, policies, and competition even though they are orchestrated by the state, then the regulatory regime can be characterized as market-enhancing. In other words, these are the state's robust efforts to establish the market mechanism in governing the economy, normatively, and institutionally. A range of regulatory authorities that were established by regulatory reforms between the early 1990s and the mid-2000s (such as the China Securities and Regulatory Commission, the China Bank and Regulatory Commission, the Ministry of Information Industry, etc.) are good examples for the market-enhancing regulatory regime (Yeo 2009; Yang 2004).[6] On the other hand, a market-steering regime here implies that the primary concern of the state is not monitoring the activities of market actors (i.e., competition and business management), but rather developing the markets and economy in general. In this process, sector-specific regulatory authorities were dismantled or merged, while the past planning bureaucracy has come to be empowered with the authorities for effective resource distribution and investments. Moreover, as discussed later, the weak corporate power of large state firms results from the limits of business associations in defense of commercial interests of the firms. Therefore, the empowerment of the planning bureaucracy, the NDRC, and the weakness of business associations together raise a theoretical utility of socialist corporatism to understand the changing government–business relations in China's leading sectors. The following discussions focus on the driving forces that bring about this shift in the regulatory regime. They include internal and external changes that facilitate the creation of statist policy ideas, the weak corporate power of state firms, and the changing balance of power among major state commissions. In other words, the rise of a powerful NDRC and the waning of the SASAC as supra-regulatory commissions, as well as the historically weak business association as a societal institution, show how China's rising economic capitals of state firms do not necessarily lead to declining state regulation; rather, a more *inclusive* regulatory regime that not only monitors market actors' compliance with rules but also steers the economy through direct and interventionist means of control.

Policy Ideas, Business, and State Structure

This section examines how three major forces are remaking Chinese system of regulation from market-enhancing to market-steering: statist ideas, expansive state in business, and a powerful state planning agency. More importantly, the inherently limited role of business associations in bringing about a meaningful change in government–business relations is addressed from the view of the socialist corporatism that ties business with the state.

Emerging Statist Ideas

Despite the state's efforts to deepen market reforms, statist ideas have arisen from both internal and external contexts/conditions. Internally, the Chinese leadership rolled out the so-called "super-ministry reform" (*dabuzhi gaige* 大部制改革), which was designed to restructure government functions and systems in order to deepen the administration reform (Yeo 2009b, p. 730). This 2008 government restructuring placed great emphasis on two issues: "strengthening macroeconomic regulation of key areas and promoting scientific industrial development; and improving public administration and services so as to enhance the building of social security system" (The Central People's Government of the People's Republic of China 2008; Yeo 2009b, p. 731). What is important to note is that this super-ministry reform in 2008 signaled a more interventionist state engagement in the markets for coordinating the sectors of information technology and manufacturing for scientific industrial development, as well as affording social services. As a result, the creation of the Ministry of Industry and Information Technology (MIIT), subordinating the previous telecom regulator, the Ministry of Information Industry, indeed reflects the state's efforts to strongly push for industrial development rather than building up the level of the playing field and enhancing de facto competition (Yeo 2009a). Moreover, unlike its original goal of focusing on macroeconomic issues, since the 2008 super-ministry reform, the NDRC is referred to as "the most powerful incarnation of it to date" (Weng et al. 2008). Externally, the 2008 global financial crisis provided the Chinese leadership with an opportunity to justify the state's direct intervention in the economy, both normatively and institutionally. The crisis from external causes (i.e., the global financial system), in fact, has generated a kind of internal/domestic atmosphere such that economic stability and sustainable development actually do need strong and active regulatory authorities to revive the economy. Because China's integration into the global economic system is already extensive, the accumulated problems in the global system will certainly affect the growth and stability of the Chinese economy (Naughton 2013, p. 61). A similar response to economic crisis during the 1980s was observed when the domestic market in the early stage of economic reform had suffered from endemic inflation and corruption. The internal economic crisis had helped conservative party leaders who resisted the reform to consolidate their ruling power in the name of macroeconomic stability. Rather than extensive changes to the old and inefficient system, this conservative leadership preferred to adopt a micro-managing state for the sake of stability and development. Responding to the global economic downturn in 2008, the Chinese government decided on "the RMB 4 trillion stimulus program, an amount equal to 12.5 percent of 2008 GDP" (Naughton 2009, p. 1). This RMB 4 trillion stimulus package comprises three components: "a large (infrastructure) investment plan, a set of funding mechanisms primarily through the banking system, and a series of strategic and rejuvenating industrial policies" (Naughton 2009, p. 1). What should be noted here are not the details of the Chinese stimulus package itself, but how these stimulus efforts directly and indirectly influenced on shaping and reshaping the scope and means of state regulation over the markets. Clearly, this signals that the primary purpose of regulation is shifting toward revitalizing the market through a strong state presence in the economy.

State in Business

Often, state–society relations in liberal market economies are measured by the rising influence of business associations on the government. However, state–business relations in transition economy, such as China, are shaped not by the forces of business associations, but by the state's efforts to prevent the autonomy and its growth of business interests though acknowledging the autonomy of business and its pursuit of economic interests. In other words, the changing state–business relations in the Chinese political economy can be better approached by focusing on the departure from the past highly penetrated Leninist party-state system toward a market-oriented economy with resilient socialist elements. State efforts to separate government from business (*zhengqi fenkai*) or to allow markets to play a decisive role in resource distribution are applied to here.[7] This is particularly valid in China's leading sectors whose ownership is predominated by the central government.

In the case of large SOEs in the leading sectors, as the bureaucratic rank of large state firms indicates, the deeply penetrated state in business, despite the reform over more than three decades, limits the substantive separation of the government from business. In other words, a remarkable change in state–business relations in China's leading strategic sectors is not likely to occur as long as they remain state-owned. Large state firms in China's leading sectors have grown out of the plan and remained *bureaucratic*, not business interest groups (Naughton 2008, p.). In effect, although there are no documented classifications with respect to the bureaucratic rank of central SOEs, scholars and officials in state research institutions commonly share this point.[8] Some of them (e.g., NOCs or Telecom giants) are equally ranked with the ministry,[9] and their managers are directly appointed by the Chinese Communist Party (CCP) Organization Department and ultimately approved by the Standing Committee of the Politburo (Yeo 2012). In this regard, the central SOEs with strong political capitals are capable of not only preventing the actual separation of government from business but also making it difficult for regulatory authorities, such as the SASAC, to effectively supervise their performance and enforce their compliance with rules that are against their commercial interests. Taking the NOCs as an example, Erica Downs finds that these firms become less constrained by the government in making business decisions that prioritize their own commercial interests over social welfare concerns (Downs 2008). Barry Naughton also makes a similar observation about the civil aviation industry; the SASAC has failed to bring in Singapore Airlines as a strategic investor in China Eastern Airlines, partly due to Air China's strong resistance to the deal, which was approved in advance by the authorities (Naughton 2008). That is, those large SOEs in the leading sectors attempted to challenge the authorities and advance their business interests by leveraging the high bureaucratic rank of central state firms, not by societal institutions, such as business associations. So why then, despite the mounting financial power of large state firms, do business associations remain weak?

Indeed, both the massive SOE reform (*zhuada fangxiao* 抓大放小) that began in the mid-1990s and the creation of the SASAC in 2003 as "the ultimate owner and guarantor of SOE assets" (Batson 2014, p. 10) have steadily contributed to enhancing the performance of state companies in China. In 2003, the profits of central SOEs were estimated as more than 200 billion RMB; these firms earned one trillion RMB in profits in 2007, slightly over 4% of the total Chinese GDP (see Fig. 9.1) (Naughton 2008, p. 2). Despite the increasing corporate profits, however, business associations in the leading sectors have remained weak in terms of representing commercial interests of the sectors and taking collective action to influence the government's policy-making.[10] Perhaps, since organized and monitored by the government, the behavior of business associations is inherently constrained by the state's control, which ultimately aims to preventing them from articulating and advancing economic interests. For example, there are two leading business associations in China's telecom industry: the Chinese Association of Communication Enterprises (CACE, *zhongguo tongxin qiye xiehui*) and the Chinese Association of Internet Network (CAIN, *zhongguo hulianwang xiehui*). However, both are closely guided and monitored by the MIIT (Zheng 2012). In other words, CACE's task and authority are assigned by the MIIT, and as it consists of government officials, telecom firms, scholars, and experts, one of its main responsibilities is to play a "mediator role" among them when necessary (Shi 2007). On the other hand, CAIN, though its work is also under the supervision of the MIIT, is distinguished from CACE in that it is a non-profit organization formed by Internet-associated companies on a

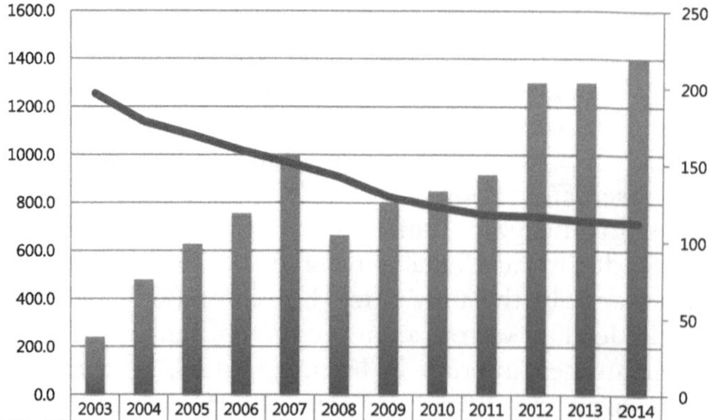

	2003	2004	2005	2006	2007	2008	2009	2010	2011	2012	2013	2014
Profit of Central SASAC Firms	240.5	478.4	627.6	754.6	996.8	665.2	797.7	848.9	917.3	1300	1300	1400
Number of Central SASAC Firms	196	178	169	159	151	142	129	122	117	116	113	112

Fig. 9.1 Profits and numbers of central state firms, 2003–2014 (Sources: SASAC's official webpage, "Yangqi minglu" (List of central state-owned enterprises), http://www.sasac.gov.cn/n1180/n1226/n2425/index.html; *Beijing Xinjing Bao*, 2010, various issues. Notes: unit of profits—100,000 million RMB; Yukyung Yeo. Revisiting China's economic regulatory reform. *Korean Journal of International Studies*, Vol. 10, No. 2 (December 2012), p. 263)

volunteer basis (*Zhongguo hulianwang xiehui* 2011). CAIN is responsible for delivering various demands from Internet companies to the government, as well as for organizing conferences and forums to promote better communication among membership firms (*Zhongguo hulianwang xiehui* 2011). As the case of anti-monopoly probing against telecom giants will later demonstrate, such "socialist–corporatist associations" that link business to the state serve the party-state's political interests, which is in line with preventing the rise of more autonomous business groups, rather than reflecting the business interests of the firms. Moreover, the predominance of state ownership also tends to create highly murky boundaries between "state interests" and "business interests," even though business interests exist.

Changing Balance of Power

While socialist corporatism shares the idea that the state remains central in mediating social forces with statist corporatism, it combines socialist structure with statist corporatism in approaching state–business relations.

Particularly, the resilient state planning agency over the market-oriented reforms conforms to socialist corporatism, stressing a key aspect of the institutional structure that the government has set up to control economic interests beyond the past economic planning and distribution of resources. In recent, the declining regulatory authority of the SASAC highlights the relative empowerment of the state planning agency, the NDRC.

The Waning SASAC

The SASAC, as an owner and regulator of China's central SOEs, appears to relatively lose its capacity to monitor the performance of those firms. Despite the growing profits, the declining return on assets and the contested authority over SOE dividends implicitly reflect the SASAC's regulatory incompetence (see Fig. 9.2). According to some estimation, while private companies between 2001 and 2005 managed an average return on assets of more than 9%, Chinese state firms achieved a return on assets of just 0.9% (Holland 2009). As Table 9.1 also shows, regardless of its sheer amount of profit, the rate of net return on assets of the central SOEs has been in decline since 2007, and such poor performance of central state firms reflects the SASAC's regulatory failure to supervise their business management.

Moreover, this story is not much different overall for the SOEs, beyond the central SOEs. As Table 9.2 exhibits, their financial performance has

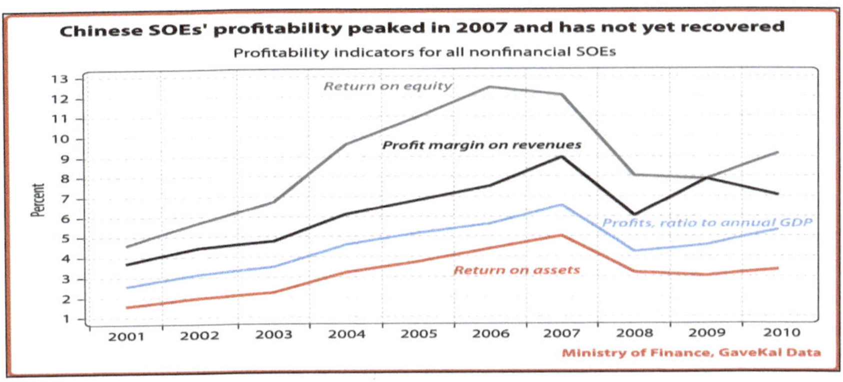

Fig. 9.2 Five hard years (Source: Andrew Batson, "Lazy monopolists or sinister octopi?" *China Economic Quarterly* (December 2012), p. 31)

Table 9.1 Return on assets of central SOEs

	2001	*2002*	*2003*	*2004*	*2005*	*2006*	*2007*	*2008*	*2009*
Rate of net return on assets (%)	−9.12	−7.88	−3.97	−1.95	1.46	4.23	5.33	1.07	−2.44

Source: Unirule Institute of Economics, *Guoyou qiye de xingzhi, biaoxian yu gaige*, p. 52

Table 9.2 SOE financial performance

	Total profits (% of annual GDP)	Return on assets	Return on equity	Profit margin
1998	0.3%	0.2%	0.4%	0.3%
1999	1.3%	0.8%	2.1%	1.7%
2000	2.9%	1.8%	4.9%	3.8%
2001	2.6%	1.6%	4.6%	3.7%
2002	3.1%	2.0%	5.7%	4.4%
2003	3.5%	2.2%	6.7%	4.8%
2004	4.6%	3.2%	9.6%	6.1%
2005	5.2%	3.7%	11.0%	6.8%
2006	5.6%	4.4%	12.4%	7.5%
2007	6.6%	5.0%	12.1%	9.0%
2008	4.2%	3.2%	8.0%	6.0%
2009	4.6%	3.0%	7.9%	7.9%
2010	5.3%	3.3%	9.2%	7.0%
2011	5.2%	3.2%	9.0%	6.6%
2012	4.7%	3.1%	n/a	5.6%

Source: Andrew Batson, "Fixing China's State Sector," *Paulson Institute Policy Memorandum* (January 2014), p. 7

been in a downturn since 2008. "The total return on assets of all SOEs surged from a marginal 0.2% in 1998 and reached a peak of 5% in 2007, but their return on equity rose from 0.4% in 1998 to a high of 12.4% in 2006" (Batson 2014, p. 7). Likewise, the financial performance of Chinese SOEs fell dramatically in 2008 and has yet to significantly recover (Batson 2014, p. 8).

To some extent, the rising profits of SOEs (see figure above) serve as a powerbase for both the firms and their nominal owner, the SASAC. Indeed, SOE profits, as a share of China's GDP, have jumped from 1.7% in 2001 to 3.7% in 2007 (Borst 2012), which later led to a call for the remittance of SOE dividends. Moreover, it is expected that SOE dividends will not only discourage state firms from overinvesting but also will help redistribute their net profits for generating the public funds, which ultimately has the effect of rebalancing the economy by encouraging more consumption as people are relieved from social safety net concerns. Accordingly, the State Council in 2007 announced a decision that requires the central SOEs to pay dividends: "10 percent in highly profitable industries and 5 percent in the industries where SOEs were less profitable" (Ministry of Finance and SASAC 2007). In fact, the SASAC maintained a position against asking SOEs to pay dividends to the national pension fund until the recent anti-corruption campaign topples the top executives of some central SOEs (Yam 2013). Yet, the bureaucratic infightings between the SASAC and the Ministry of Finance impeded the SASAC's rights to manage the dividends. According to the SASAC, an appropriate function of the investor (*chuziren*, 出资人) is the right to collect net profits; therefore, central SOEs should pay dividends to the SASAC first (Wang 2006). Though acknowledging the SASAC's right to own the net profits of the firms, the Ministry of Finance, as the macro-coordinating government body responsible for managing the social economy, emphasizes that, since such profits of the SOEs always lie in the people, they should be transformed into public finance revenues (Wang 2006). In this sense, the dividends should be managed by the Ministry of Finance, not the SASAC. After severe infighting between the SASAC and the Ministry of Finance, the SASAC has lost the authority to collect and manage the dividends (Borst 2012), which led it to suffer from funding the structural adjustments of the firms (e.g., merging). This arguably has weakened its regulatory capacity as both owner and investor.

The Powerful NDRC

The NDRC, which has evolved from the former planning agency, the SPC, over the last three decades, acts as a supra-regulator responsible for guiding macro-level development, not micro-level control like the planning agency (Pearson 2007, 2011). The NDRC designs and enforces policies for economic and social development and proposes "indicative" planning by laying out directions and objectives, such as five-year plans.[11] Although the NDRC-led five-year plan no longer sets a specific target quantity for production or the distribution of resources (Heilmann and Melton 2013),[12] it still makes an aggregate effort to steer the economy. Such moves have been reinforced since the economic crisis. While it is responsible for maintaining macroeconomic stability, the NDRC's more interventionist market regulation can be identified by its enhanced authority to (1) promote technological innovation and structural adjustments through industrial polices, (2) endorse a range of investment projects, and (3) embed the rules in the market. First, as the government is determined to push forward technological innovation and structural adjustments in markets, 12% of all investment schemes from China's stimulus plan were allocated to promoting investment in applied industrial research and industrial restructuring (Naughton 2009, p. 8). For more effective action/execution, the NDRC is asked to "develop a series of 10 sectoral industrial policies, each of them identically labeled a 'long-range plan for adjustment and rejuvenation' (*tiaozheng he zhenxing guihua*)" (Naughton 2009, p. 9). Following up on such proposals, the state-backed development plan, including energy, biotechnology, and information technology, was also announced by Premier Wen Jiabao in the *2010 Report of Government Work* (Hong Kong Economic Daily 2010).[13] Though the details of those industrial policies are beyond the scope of this paper, this plan clearly indicates the changing goals and tools of market regulation by the NDRC. That is, by using ambitious industrial policies, the state's market regulation aims primarily to steer the market rather than to enhance market-oriented rules and mechanisms as was done between the mid-1990s and the early 2000s. Second, the right to approve numerous investments greatly enables the NDRC to adjust the industrial structure by endorsing more energy conservation projects while reining in overcapacity sectors where repeated constructions and blind investments are rampant (*Xinhua News Agency* 2005). In particular, as the 2008 global financial crisis brought the issues of rising inflation and unemployment to the close attention of the center, China rolled out a stimulus program with mounting infrastructure investment plans and industrial restructuring initiatives. Those growing state investments suggest the increased sheer size of government presence in the markets. In this way, the stimulus program, engineered by massive state investments, provides the NDRC with the resources and opportunities to exercise interventionist regulatory control over both the scope and nature of investment by engaging in designing, developing, and approving projects from their outset. For example, the number of investment proposals endorsed by the NDRC increased from 91 in 2005 to 702 by 2010 (see Table 9.3). Although most of this investment has come from government-run corporations and not from the government itself, the government's command of a large share of resources has certainly driven

Table 9.3 NDRC's approval of investment projects, 2005–2013 (Yeo 2012)

	2005	*2007*	*2010*	*2013*
Foreign investments	4	3	6	10
Local-level investment	50	105	584	96
National-level investment	26	19	107	30
Not specified	11	65	5	27
Total	91(5)	192(3)	702(5)	163

Sources: Yukyung Yeo, 'Remaking the Chinese State and the Nature of Economic Governance?' *Journal of Contemporary China*. Vol. 18 (2009), pp. 729–744; NDRC public announcement on project examination and approval, please note that data was available at http://www.ndrc.gov.cn/zwfwzx/xmsphz/ until 3 April, 2015

Notes: The figures in brackets denote projects using multiple sources among the total number; data from the NDRC's official announcement is only available from 2005

the leading state body, the NDRC, to be more assertive and interventionist in governing the Chinese economy than before.

Lastly, the empowered NDRC has become assertive in pushing to embody certain norms of regulation in the market. For example, emphasis on promoting competition, efficiency, and productivity is hardly new throughout the reform. However, what is different from the past is that its tools of regulation are increasingly relying upon bureaucratic instruments, particularly during the post-economic crisis (Naughton 2013, p. 650). In recent, the changing nature of the NDRC is even described as the return of "planning" (Naughton 2013). What is more, when the NDRC overhauls some state firms that are suspected of doing business against the rules, it holds the power to enforce the associated laws without coordinating with other related state agencies in advance. The following presents China's first anti-monopoly case against major state firms and presents how market regulation proceeds when rising state firms meet rising regulatory power, namely, the NDRC.

The Politics of Anti-monopoly Probing Against Telecom Giants

The anti-monopoly investigation of the telecom giants as of 2011 offers a good example of how the empowered NDRC exercises its regulatory control over central SOEs without prior coordination or agreements with other state bodies, such as the telecom regulator MIIT and the SASAC. Furthermore, the case confirms the weakness of large telecom firms as a business enterprise group as well as the limited role of business association (i.e., Chinese Telecoms Enterprises Association) in advancing commercial interests. Accordingly, the power of state planning agency, the NDRC, and weak business associations together present some theoretical benefits of socialist–corporatist institutions, such as the state planning agency in particular, in examining China's state–business relations in the telecom service sector.

In China, the rise of the anti-monopoly regime that has grown out of regulatory reform seems to introduce new rules of the game to the telecom markets. Here, the anti-monopoly regime largely consists of three elements: anti-monopoly law, the norm of disciplining anti-competition behavior, and state agencies in charge. In August 2007, China's anti-monopoly law (*fanlongduanfa*, 反垄断法) (State Council of the People's Republic of China 2007) was finally approved by National People's Congress (NPC) after 13 years of careful considerations. By prohibiting "price-fixing, collusion, excessive market concentration and other monopolistic practices by private and state-owned business alike" (Bradsher 2007), this anti-monopoly law was expected to prevent giant SOEs from abusing their vast privileges, such as the predominant position in the market or political ties to the upper-hand, as well as pursuing market monopoly. China's anti-monopoly law particularly warns giant SOEs against harming fair competition by abusing their monopolistic market status, not the dominant position of large SOEs itself in the market. Although the comments from the pundits are somewhat wide-ranging, the anti-monopoly law is certain to be invoked to manage competition in markets. The NDRC's surprising announcement of anti-monopoly investigation for China Telecom and Unicom in November 2011 did not disappoint such an expectation.

This anti-monopoly investigation began with the report from China Tietong to the NDRC as of June 2011, claiming that China Telecom and China Unicom attempted to monopolize the internet broadband service market by abusing their dominant position in the market (Lang 2011; *Souhu Caijing* 2011). Upon Tietong's report, the NDRC, the leading state agency in the enforcement of anti-monopoly law, made a preliminary conclusion that two telecom giants with two-third of shares in telecom markets abused their predominant position regarding the service charge in the internet broadband service market (Chen et al. 2012, p. 179). According to the government department responsible for the pricing issues of anti-monopoly law, these two operators were attempting to "keep competitors out of the internet access market by demanding prohibitive prices for leasing their networks" (Chen et al. 2012, p. 179). The anti-monopoly law stipulates that "a business operator having market dominance is prohibited from treating equally qualified trade counterparts differently in terms of transaction price or other conditions without legitimate reasons" (Zhang 2011; State Council of the People's Republic of China 2007). China Telecom and China Unicom together accounted for more than two-thirds of the broadband Internet market as of 2011. Such a dominant market position enabled them to demand higher prices than their competitors and to offer more favorable prices to other companies. Soon after, China Telecom and China Unicom submitted a written opinion to make a counter-argument for this initial assessment. For a careful investigation, the NDRC consulted the MIIT, the Legal Affairs Office of the State Council, and the Supreme People's Court about this case in October. Although the opinions from these three institutions were somewhat different, they commonly judged that a decisive evidence to show their monopolistic behavior was absent, asking for making a careful decision (Chen et al. 2012, p. 179). In fact, the NDRC was actually going to make a final decision after hearing from the SASAC and had much discussion with two telecom giants; both parties agreed to resolve the issue amicably (Chen et al. 2012, p. 181). Despite such underlying negotiations and consultations, on November 9th, the NDRC made public its investigation of China Telecom and Unicom without final coordination with the SASAC and the MIIT. Indeed, this was a rare high-profile move against state-owned enterprises. (Hille 2011) After these two telecom giants acknowledged their charges and made efforts to provide a lowered price with a faster network, the NDRC decided to suspend its anti-monopoly probing (Xinhua news Agency 2011).

Above all, the case of anti-monopoly investigation for telecom giants shows how the underlying normative and institutional elements in China led to the predominance of the state planning agency, the NDRC, in shaping state–business relations for the telecom service market. Normatively, this anti-monopoly investigation reflects Chinese state that appears to employ legal measures rather than administrative ones in disciplining the market competition and ultimately controlling the pursuit of business interests and autonomy. Institutionally, the leading position of the NDRC within the fragmented and overlapped institutional structure of China's anti-monopoly governance indicates the resilience and power of state planning agency in making state–business relations as the socialist corporatism highlights. Upon the enactment of the anti-monopoly law in 2008, the State Council set up two administrative bodies: the Anti-Monopoly Commission (*fanlongduan weiyuanhui*) and the Anti-Monopoly Enforcement Structure (*fanlongduan zhixingjiegou*), aiming to supervise the monopolistic behavior of the firms (see Fig. 9.3) (Zhang 2013, p. 45). The Anti-Monopoly Commission is organized with 15 government ministries, including the NDRC, MIIT, SASAC, and the Ministry of Commerce, and mainly responsible for drafting the policies on the anti-monopoly related issues as well as assisting the enforcement of anti-monopoly probing. Yet, the substantial investigation of anti-monopoly is made by the Anti-Monopoly Enforcement Structure organized by the NDRC, the Ministry of Commerce, and the State Administration of Industry and Commerce (SAIC). Particularly, the NDRC is charged of

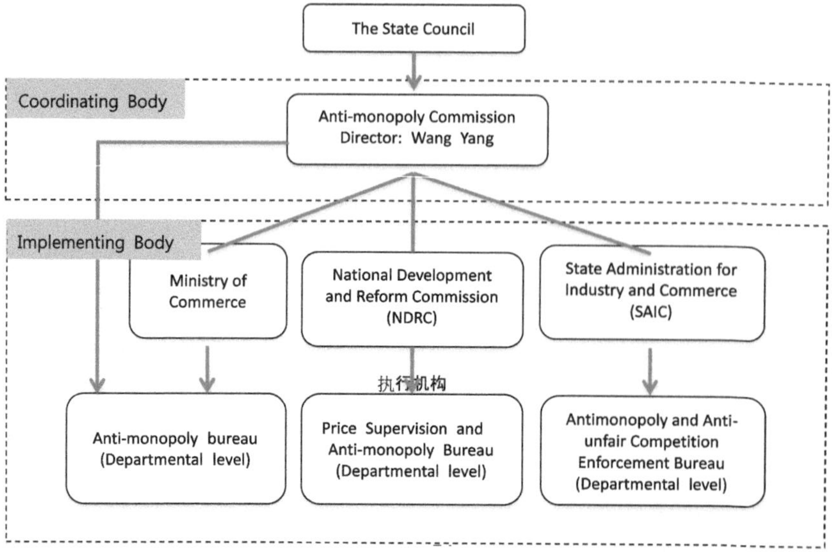

Fig. 9.3 China's anti-monopoly regime (Sources: Zhang Moning, "<Fanlongduan fa>li 'jingji xianfa' youduoyuan—zhuanfang guowuyuan fanlongduan weiyuanhui zhuanjia zixunzu fuzuzhang huangyong [How far away is the "anti-monopoly law" from the "economic constitution"—An interview with Huang Yong, deputy head of the expert advisory group of the State Council's Anti-Monopoly Committee]," *Nanfengchuang* (2013), No. 23, p. 45)

probing the monopolistic pricing, while the MIIT and the SASAC, though members of the anti-monopoly commission, have little influence on the process of anti-monopoly probing. As Fig. 9.3 shows, the institutional structure of the anti-monopoly regime places the state planning agency NDRC at the center as both policy-maker and enforcement body, which incapacitates the regulatory authorities of the SASAC and the MIIT. Indeed, the NDRC focuses on nurturing fair market competition, but the better financial performance of state firms is the key concern for the SASAC. Such conflicting interests led two telecom giants to be squeezed in between the NDRC and the SASAC. According to one Chinese pundit, since telecom firms are under pressure from the SASAC as to business performance, their monopolistic act on internet service pricing could not be avoided (Gu and Zhou 2011). Moreover, the MIIT played a role of the business associations by mediating the accumulated complaints from telecom operators, including China Telecom, Unicom, and Tietong (Lang 2011). To resolve the rising tensions, the MIIT not only asked China Tietong to cancel its report to the NDRC but also requested the NDRC to end the anti-monopoly investigation through a conversation (Lang 2011). Likewise, business association for the telecom sector, such as Chinese Association of Communication Enterprises, was mainly responsible for providing telecom firms with various consultations on technology or related legal rules,[14] not taking collective actions to defend telecom giants against the NDRC's probing. Since the rise of the anti-monopoly regime in 2008, market competition or entry is not primarily supervised by the telecom regulator MIIT (formerly MII), but mainly by the planning agency NDRC, despite the efforts of regulatory reform in China's telecom industry.

Does it tell us that this emphasis on consumers' costs for accessing broadband Internet services signals that China's telecom operators are becoming more accountable to consumers and less concerned about losing state assets? Some argue that the high cost of online services is a sore point for Chinese consumers, but Internet services account for a relatively small piece of the overall business of the telecom giants. This investigation, therefore, would not incur much cost for these companies. Moreover, Chinese telecom pundits also raise doubts about the political goal of the planning bureaucracy, the NDRC, given that there are other market monopolies, such as oil, power, and railway, but only telecom firms are charged with violations (*Souhu caijing* 2011). Perhaps the real intention of the central leadership is to ensure that the public is aware of the monopoly problem, not actually regulating anti-competition activities.

Conclusion

This study examines how, despite increasing material power of giant SOEs in China, the resilient socialist institutions (particularly the empowered indicative planning agency, NDRC) and weak business associations under the guidance and supervision of the government ministry prevent large state firms as business groups from advancing commercial interests. To this end, the chapter points to the rise of statist ideas, the state's ties to business, and the changing balance of power between supra-regulatory commissions, such as the NDRC and SASAC, as the key elements. The recent anti-monopoly investigation against two giant telecom companies serves as a good example of what happens when rising corporate power meets rising state agency. As noted earlier, the nature of market regulation appeared to be already in a shift from market-enhancing to market-steering with state interventionist policies and institutions. The Chinese government had been enthusiastic about enhancing market-oriented system of the economy and creating a level playing field between the early 1990s and the early 2000s. However, the reemergence of "statist ideas" has become apparent, particularly after the super-ministry reform, and even seemed justified/legitimate upon the global financial crisis in 2008, which led the government to publish the stimulus package and industrial policies. These internal and external changes together led to the enhancement of statist policy ideas and the empowerment of state planning agency, the NDRC, in regulating the market and business of large state firms in it. As the empirical findings from the anti-monopoly investigation show, the Chinese central leadership has a clear view on the difference between having a dominant position in the market and monopolizing the market. In other words, it is allowed and even encouraged by the central leadership that key state firms are predominant as its emphasis on creating the national champions; but it is prohibited to monopolize the entire market by abusing such a dominant market share. In order to control such monopolistic behavior of giant SOEs, the Chinese state sets up an institutional structure that gives the NDRC a preferential right to regulate the market as the socialist corporatism highlights. In this way, the political and economic resources have come to be concentrated on the NDRC, while the authorities of the other supra-regulatory commission, the SASAC, have been weakened. Besides the institutional factor, this chapter points to the declining return on state assets and the failure to exercise control over SOE dividends as the sources of the ailing regulator. However, what is equally important to note is that the benefits of socialist corporatism and the leading role of the state planning agency in shaping state–business relations are argued for the top-tier industry that consists of the centrally owned state firms in the most strategic sectors. Since the governing ideas, institutional structure, and business ownership are different across the sectors and tiers, a single theoretical framework may suffer from providing plausible explanations on China's dynamic state–society relations. Indeed, more systematic studies that compare cross sectors and tiers are needed to further articulate the causal mechanism between rising giant SOEs and resilient state commissions in China.

Notes

1. This study distinguishes between corporate power and autonomy. As long as the Chinese state plays a role as "owner" of State-Owned Enterprises (SOEs), politicized corporate governance, exercised through the right to appoint top executives of the firms, and ad hoc interventions or pressures are certainly likely to constrain the decision-making autonomy of the SOEs; yet, it should be noted that such a constrained corporate autonomy does not unilaterally determine/decide their ability to influence the decision-making and implementation.
2. Since Xi Jinping's policy of fight against corruption, without exception, the former leaders of the NOCs were investigated and ousted from the CCP with corruption charge. The major examples include Zhou Yongkang and Jiang Jiemin.
3. Refer to Pearson (2011), China's sheer continental size tends to generate economic tiers: top, middle, and bottom. The strategically most important leading sectors fall under the top-tiered sector.
4. The author appreciates Wu Yongping's very important remark on this point. According to him, any analysis that dismisses the impact of the CCP on government–business relations in China would lose the validity of arguments.
5. Schmitter distinguishes two major variants of corporatism: state and societal.
6. For more information, please refer to Pearson (2005, 2007, 2011), Yukyung Yeo (2009) and Dali Yang (2004).

7. I appreciate one scholar in the Development of Research Centre of the State Council for this insight. Correspondence from Beijing (January 2015).
8. Interviews in the Institute of Enterprise of DRC, Beijing (2011, 2012).
9. Interviews in the Institute of Enterprise of DRC, Beijing (2012, 2013).
10. Author's interview with a Beijing-based official in the Development Research Centre of the State Council by correspondence (January 2015).
11. Its official functions are available at http://en.ndrc.gov.cn/mfndrc/
12. Regarding the evolution of role of the "planning" in Chinese economic reform and the development of NDRC, refer to Sebastian Heilmann and Oliver Melton (2013).
13. Hong Kong Economic Daily (11 March 2010).
14. Zhongguo tongxin qiye xiehui, "Xiehui jianjie (Brief Introduction for Associate)," May 13 (2006), http://www.cace.org.cn/new/content/2006-05/13/content_866410.htm

References

Batson, A. (2012). Lazy monopolists or sinister octopi? *China Economic Quarterly, 16*(4), 29–33.

Batson, A. (2014). Fixing China's state sector. *Paulson Institute Policy Memorandum* [online]. Available from: http://www.paulsoninstitute.org/think-tank/2014/01/09/fixing-chinas-state-sector/. Accessed 10 Oct 2016.

Borst, N. (2012). *SOE dividends and economic rebalancing*. Peterson Institute for International Economics [online]. Available from: https://piie.com/blogs/china-economic-watch/soe-dividends-and-economic-rebalancing. Accessed 10 Oct 2016.

Bradsher, K. (2007). China: Antimonopoly law approved. *New York Times* [online]. Available from: Accessed 10 Oct 2016.

Chen, X. H., Liu, X. C., & Li, H. J. (2012). *Zhongguo weiji gongguan anli yanjiu baogao 2011 juan* [A case study of China crisis public relations]. Huazhong Keji Daxue Chubanshe.

Downs, E. (2008). Business interest groups in Chinese politics: The case of the oil companies. In L. Cheng (Ed.), *China's changing political landscape: Prospects for democracy* (1th ed., pp. 123–124). Washington, DC: The Brookings Institution.

Gu, X. Y., & Zhou, Y. (2011). Dianxin liantong shexian longduan huochi dafadan [Alleged mono polistic conduct by China Telecom and China Unicom or eat a manu of infringement]. *Xinlang Caijing* [online]. Available from: http://finance.sina.com.cn/chanjing/gsnews/20111110/072510787933.shtml. Accessed 20 Aug 2016.

Haggard, S., Maxfield, S., & Schneider, R. B. (1997). Theories of business and business-state relations. In S. Maxfield & R. B. Schneider (Eds.), *Business and the state in developing countries* (1th ed., pp. 36–60). Ithaca/London: Cornell University Press.

Heilmann, S., & Melton, O. (2013). The reinvention of development planning in China, 1993–2012. *Modern China, 39*(6), 580–628.

Hille, K. (2011). Beijing probes claims of telecoms monopolies *Financial Times* [online]. Available from: http://www.ft.com/cms/s/0/e803d3e6-0abc-11e1-b62f-00144feabdc0. html#axzz49MX2JwvA. Accessed 20 Aug 2016.

Holland, T. (2009). State-sector profits nothing but a mirage. *South China Morning Post.* [online] Available from: http://www.scmp.com/article/679083/state-sector-profits-nothing-mirage. Accessed 10 Oct 2016.

Jordana, J., & Levi-Faur, David. (2004). The politics of regulation in the age of governance. In J. Jordana & David Levi-Faur (Eds.), *The politics of regulation: Institutions and regulatory reforms for the age of governance* (1st ed., pp. 1–18). Cheltenham/Northampton: Edward Elgar.

Katzenstein, P. (1985). *Small states in world markets: Industrial policy in Europe.* Ithaca: Cornell University Press.

Kennedy, S. (2005). *The business of lobbying in China.* Cambridge, MA: Harvard University Press.

Lang, L. (2011). Dianxin liantong fanlongduan'an xuannian guangdian huyu checha [China Telecom and China Unicom's anti-trust case is full of suspense, State Administration of Press, Publication, Radio, Film and Television of China asked for an investigation]. *21Shiji Jingji Baodao* [online]. Available from: http://finance.ifeng.com/news/special/fanlongduan/20111122/5110566.shtml. Accessed 9 Nov 2016.

Ministry of Finance and SASAC. (2007). *Zhonggyang qiye guoyou ziben shouyi shouqu guanli zanxing banfa* [The central State-owned capital gains received interim measure]. Command paper. 309. Beijing: MOF and SASAC.

Naughton, B. (2008). SASAC and rising corporate power in China. *China Leadership Monitor, 24*, 1–9.

Naughton, B. (2009). Understanding the Chinese stimulus package. *China Leadership Monitor, 28*, 1–12.

Naughton, B. (2013a). *Wu Jinglian: Voice of reform in China.* Boston: The MIT Press.

Naughton, B. (2013b). The return of planning in China: Comment on Heilmann-Melton and Hu Angan. *Modern China, 39*(6), 640–652.

Pearson, M. M. (1997). *China's new business elite: The political consequences of economic reform.* Berkeley: University of California Press.

Pearson, M. M. (2005). The business of governing business in China. *World Politics, 57*(2), 296–322.

Pearson, M. M. (2007). Governing the Chinese economy: Regulatory reform in the service of the state. *Public Administration Review, 67*(4), 718–730.

Pearson, M. M. (2011). Variety within and without: The political economy of Chinese regulation. In S. Kennedy (Ed.), *Beyond the middle kingdom: Comparative perspectives on China's capitalist transformation* (pp. 25–43). Stanford: Stanford University Press.

Shi, H. C. (2007). Zhongguo tongxin qiye xiehui: jiaoliu, hezuo, ruiyi jinqu, tuidong hangye jiankang fazhan [China association of communication enterprises: To communicate and cooperate, to forge ahead with keen determination and to promote the healthy development of the industry]. *C114 Zhongguo Tongxinwang* [online]. Available from: http://www.c114.net/persona/498/a236005.html. Accessed 9 Nov 2016.

Solomon, G. S. (1983). *Pluralism in the Soviet Union: Essays in Honour of H. Gordon Skilling*. New York: St. Martin's Press.

Souhu Caijing. (2011). Dianxin liantong cunzai longduanma? [Is China Telecom and Unicom facing monopoly?]. *Souhu Caijing* [online]. Available from: http://business.sohu.com/20111114/n325596671.shtml. Accessed 20 Aug 2016.

State Council of the People's Republic of China. (2007). *Zhonghua renmin gongheguo fanlongduanfa [Anti-monopoly law of the People's Republic of China]*. Beijing: The State Council of the People's Republic of China.

State-owned Assets Supervision and Administration Commission. (2016). *Yangqi minglu* [List of central state-owned enterprises]. Beijing: SASAC.

The Central People's of Government of the People's Republic of China. (2008). *Guanyu shenhua xingzheng guanli tizhi gaige de yijian* [*Ideas on deepening the reform of administrative governing system*] [online]. Available from: http://www.gov.cn/jrzg/2008-03/04/content_909225.htm. Accessed 10 Oct 2016.

Wang, H. R. (2006). Guoqi fenhong gai shangjiao caizhengbu haishi guoziwei? [Should SOE dividends be turned over to the ministry of finance or the SASAC?]. *Zhongguowang* [online]. Available from: http://www.china.com.cn/chinese/OP-c/1128726.htm. Accessed 9 Novr 2016.

Weng, S. Y., Yuan Z. H., & Cheng, Z. Y. (2008). China's congress Revitalizes NDRC. *The Economic Observer* [online]. Available from: http://eeo.com.cn/ens/Politics/2008/03/21/94671.html. Accessed 20 Aug 2016.

Wilks, S., & Wright, M. (1987). *Comparative government-industry relations: Western Europe, the United States, and Japan*. Oxford: Clarendon Press.

Xinhua News Agency. (2005, December 22). China posts list of industries facing overcapacities. *Xinhua News Agency* [online]. Available from: http://news.xinhuanet.com/english/2005-12/21/content_3953099.htm. Accessed 10 Oct 2016.

Xinhua News Agency. (2011, December 2). China Telecom, China Unicom pledge to mend errors after anti-monopoly probe. *Xinhua News Agency* [online]. Available from: http://news.xinhuanet.com/english2010/china/2011-12/02/c_131285141.htm. Accessed 9 Nov 2016.

Yam, S. (2013). Reforms for state firms likely to be more talk than real action. *South China Morning Post* [online]. Available from: http://www.scmp.com/business/article/1351291/reforms-state-firms-likely-be-more-talk-real-action. Accessed 10 Oct 2016.

Yang, D. (2004). *Remaking the Chinese leviathan: Market transition and the politics of governance in China*. Stanford: Stanford University Press.

Yeo, Y. K. (2009a). Between owner and regulator: Governing the business of China's telecommunications service industry. *The China Quarterly, 200*, 1013–1032.

Yeo, Y. K. (2009b). Remaking the Chinese state and the nature of economic governance? *Journal of Contemporary China, 18*(62), 729–743.

Yeo, Y. K. (2012). Revisiting China's economic regulatory reform. *The Korean Journal of International Studies, 10*(2), 255–274.

Yep, R. (2000). The limitations of corporatism for understanding reforming China: An empirical analysis in a rural county. *Journal of Contemporary China, 9*(25), 547–566.

Zhang, E. (2011). New rules tackle price-fixing monopolies. *South China Morning Post* [online]. Available from: http://www.scmp.com/article/734812/new-rules-tackle-price-fixing-monopolies. Accessed 9 Nov 2016.

Zhang, M. N. (2013). <Fanlongduan fa>li 'jingji xianfa' youduoyuan – Zhuanfang guowuyuan fanlongduan weiyuanhui zhuanjia zixunzu fuzuzhang huangyong [How far away is the "anti-monopoly law" from the "economic constitution"—An interview with Huang Yong, deputy head of the expert advisory group of the state council's Anti-Monopoly Committee]. *Nanfengchuang, 23*, 45–47.

Zheng, D. H. (2012). Zhongguo tongxin qiye xiehui di wuci huiyuan daibiao dahui zhaokai [The fifth member congress of China association of communications enterprises was held]. *Tongxin chanye wang* [online]. Available from: http://www.ccidcom.com/html/y aowen/201206/05-177377.html. Accessed 20 Aug 2016.

Zhongguo hulianwang xiehui. (2011). Xiehui jianjie. *Zhongguo hulianwang xiehui* [online]. Available from: http://www.isc.org.cn/xhgk/xhjj/. Accessed 20 Aug 2016.

CHAPTER 10

State Structures, Business–State Relations, and Multinational Corporate Behaviours: A Case Study of Chinese Multinational Oil Companies

Jin Zhang

Introduction

This chapter considers the central proposition that the behaviour of Chinese multinational corporations is conditioned by the national characteristics of state structures and state–business relations. The political economy approach (see, e.g., Pauly and Reich 1997; Doremus et al. 1999; Griffiths and Zammuto 2005; Spencer et al. 2005) emphasises the causal importance of macro sociopolitical factors, such as political regimes and ideological orientations, in shaping the organisations, operations, competitive strategies, and innovations of private firms in general and multinational corporations in particular. The state-determinist view of the political economy approach has a problem in explaining the multinational corporate behaviour of large state-owned enterprises (SOEs) in China. If Chinese SOEs are dictated by

J. Zhang (✉)
Cambridge China Development Trust, Cambridge, UK

Judge Business School, University of Cambridge, Cambridge, UK

X. Zhang, T. Zhu (eds.), *Business, Government and Economic Institutions in China*, International Political Economy Series,
DOI 10.1007/978-3-319-64486-8_10

state policy, they are likely to demonstrate the same business behaviour in overseas investment. They would have behaved as state agencies to execute government policy to secure, for example, the supply of natural resources, for national development. However, empirical evidence from the international business literature shows that the motivation of Chinese SOEs is much more complex than the political economy literature would have suggested. One view argues that the pattern of Chinese overseas investment, especially in location and sector distribution, is mainly driven by the goals of enhancing China's political and economic influence and expanding China's international trade relations, rather than the strategic consideration of profit-maximisation of Chinese multinational enterprises (Child and Rodriguez 2005). Another view argues that China has steadily liberalised the regulation of outward foreign direct investment (FDI) and even Chinese SOEs have demonstrated the same commercial motivations as those suggested in the standard FDI theory, that is, resource-seeking, market-seeking, efficiency-seeking, and strategic asset-seeking (Buckley et al. 2007). The identification of the coexistence of commercial and political considerations of Chinese overseas investment suggests a paradoxical situation that the business literature has not yet been able to resolve (Wei 2010).

The apparent paradox demonstrated by Chinese overseas investment suggests the absence of a fundamental question—how Chinese SOEs are governed. Corporate governance deals with the fundamental question of how firms are controlled. If we understand the governance of Chinese SOEs, the extent they are embedded in state structures and their relations with the state, we can confidently begin to explain the apparent paradox of Chinese SOEs being simultaneously political and economic entities in overseas investment. Therefore, this chapter will look into the mechanisms of corporate governance and patterns of overseas investment of Chinese SOEs as the two variables of multinational corporate behaviour (Table 10.1).

The inadequacy of the political economy approach in explaining the motivation of overseas investment by Chinese SOEs can be remedied by the economic sociology perspective (see, e.g., Hollingsworth and Boyer 1997; Casper and van Waarden 2005; Whitley 1999, 2007; Zhang and Whitley 2013) that focuses on relatively micro and meso variables as the major determinants of firms' organisational structures, managerial patterns, and innovation strategies. Variables such as market positions, interfirm relations, and business associations all play an important role in explaining business strategies. These two strands of theoretical approaches—the political economy approach and the economic sociology

Table 10.1 Corporate governance and overseas investment of the Chinese multinational oil companies

Explananda	*Major mechanisms*	*Key features*
Corporate governance	Ownership	100 per cent state-owned at parent group level; 50–90 per cent state ownership in internationally listed major subsidiaries held by the parent group companies
	Board structure	Parallel governance, both legal and political; double hats for executives—CCP committee members and executive positions; independent directors
	Executive appointment	Top executives are appointed by COD
	Executive remuneration	Subject to state wage grade but negotiable with SASAC
	Performance assessment	SASAC devises criteria and executes assessment
Overseas investment	Motivation	Both state policy driven and firm growth driven; a balancing act between executing policy and pursuing economic benefit
	International strategy	Most are equity oil and loan for oil; less mergers and acquisitions
	Access to finance	State-coordinated especially with CDB
	Location	Resource-rich developing countries; mature oil fields

perspective—which are mutually reinforcing rather than mutually exclusive, suggest three key explanatory variables are particularly crucial to the consideration of the central propositions of this chapter: the institutional structures of state economic and political agencies, the organisational configuration of business actors, and the state-firm policy linkages (Table 10.2).

The empirical evidence to support the central proposition will come from the Chinese oil industry. The oil industry is resource-dependent and capital-intensive. Ruigrok and Van Tulder (1995) claim it is the second most capital-intensive industry after the automobile industry. International oil companies seek resources around the globe and develop technology for resource extraction to supply the world that is still heavily dependent on oil. The Chinese oil industry is the first among the country's strategic sectors to have expanded internationally. The three largest Chinese oil firms (oil majors), all of which are central state-owned enterprises,[1] play a critical role in the supply of the country's energy needs.

Table 10.2 State structure and state-business relations

Explanans	*Key attributes*
Institutional structure of the state economic and political agencies	
Role of the CCP	CCP performs three modes of intervention in promoting and regulating big business: institution building and policy entrepreneurship; personnel control; residual mobilisation capacity (Li 2014)
Role of SASAC, NDRC, MOFCOM	SASAC executes government policy to reform SOEs in the aspects of corporate governance, executive remuneration, and performance evaluation; NDRC on project approval; MOFCOM coordinates overseas investment
State-firm policy network	Formal channels mainly through companies; informal channels especially personal networks
Organisational configuration of business actors	
Market position	CNPC, Sinopec, and CNOOC dominate the domestic market in both upstream and downstream businesses; relatively weak competitive position in international market compared with international oil companies in frontier technology and constructing global supply chain
Inter-firm relations	Extensive cooperation with global oil majors and other national oil companies; coordination; cooperation and competition among the three Chinese oil majors both at home and abroad

The chapter will argue that since the 1980s, the reform directives of the Chinese Communist Party (CCP) and the resultant State Council's specific reform measures in China's overall economic reform and especially in the reform of the state-owned sector are decisive in the evolution of the institutional structures of state agencies regulating big businesses, the industry structure of strategic sectors such as the oil industry, and the corporate governance of large Chinese multinational SOEs (Tables 10.3 and 10.4). While the introduction and adoption of Western style of corporate governance structure and mechanisms in SOEs have been administered by the state agency of the State-owned Assets Supervision and Administration Commission (SASAC), the CCP exercises its control through the Central Organisation Department (COD) over the appointment and promotion of the top executives of large Chinese multinational SOEs (Zhang 2017). The changes in the structure of government ministries demonstrate increasing liberalisation of regulation over business activities, and the changes of industry structure show a gradual introduction of market forces into the strategic sectors that directly affect the market positions and inter-firm relations for firms operating in industry. The pattern of overseas

Table 10.3 Co-evolution of state structure, industry structure, and corporate governance in the Chinese oil industry

Year	*CCP decisions*	*Major contents*	*Changes of state ministries*	*Changes in oil industry structure*	*Changes in oil corporate governance*
1978 and 1980s	1978 Communique of the Third Plenary Session of the 11th CCP Central Committee on economic reform 1984 Decision of the CCP Central Committee on Economic System Reform adopted at the Third Plenary Session of the 12th CCP Central Committee A series of State Council directives on enterprise responsibility system in the 1980s	CCP work focuses on economic affairs and technological revolution Increase enterprise vitality Establish planning economy applying the law of value and developing socialist commodity economy Establish reasonable price system and pay close attention to the role of economic leverage Separate government function from enterprise responsibility and develop state function in managing economic work Establish a variety of economic responsibility systems and distribution on the basis of labour Promote economic varieties and further opening to domestic and foreign economic and technological exchanges Build a team of socialist economic management cadres Strengthen CCP leadership to ensure reform carried out smoothly	Some of the 65 economic ministries were merged or corporatised in 1981 Ministry of Petroleum was abolished in 1981	Out of the Ministry of Petroleum, CNOOC (offshore) was created in 1982, Sinopec (downstream) in 1983, and CNPC (onshore upstream) in 1988 FDI in upstream, downstream businesses and service stations	The three corporations had both business and regulatory functions for the entire industry The corporations had the bureaucratic level equivalent to a ministry Heads of the corporations were appointed by COD

(*continued*)

Table 10.3 (continued)

Year	*CCP decisions*	*Major contents*	*Changes of state ministries*	*Changes in oil industry structure*	*Changes in oil corporate governance*
1990s	1993 Decision of the CCP Central Committee on Some Issues Concerning the Establishment of the Socialist Market Economy adopted at the Third Plenary Session of the 14th CCP Central Committee 1999 Decision of the CCP Central Committee on Major Issues Concerning the Reform and Development of State-Owned Enterprises adopted at the Fourth Plenary Session of the 15th CCP Central Committee	Establish socialist market economy system and modern enterprise system SOEs adopt managerial responsibility system in which managers in charge of businesses and CCP organs playing core political role to ensure the execution of the CCP and the state Strengthen SOE assets management Promote SOE strategic restructuring Establish modern enterprise system Improve SOE balance sheet Step up technological progress and industrial upgrading Develop high-quality managers Strengthen CCP leadership on SOE reform and development	1998 government restructuring reduced state ministries from 40 to 29 Ministry Chemical Industry was abolished Seven 'state bureaux' were created including one for the oil and petrochemicals industry and affiliated to the newly created State Economic and Trade Commission (SETC)	1998/1999 CNPC, Sinopec Group, and CNOOC Group each established a majority-controlled joint stock company PetroChina, Sinopec, and CNOOC, grouping together the core businesses Service stations open to private companies	The listed subsidiaries PetroChina, Sinopec, and CNOOC each adopted governance structure of Board of Directors, Executive Committee, and Supervisory Committee PetroChina, Sinopec, and CNOOC each was listed in international stock market Top executive team were appointed by the parent companies as the largest shareholders
2000s	2003 Decision of the CCP Central Committee on Some Issues Concerning the Improvement of the Socialist Market Economy adopted at the Third Plenary Session of the 16th CCP Central Committee	Improve corporate legal person governance structure Speed up and improve reform of monopoly industries	SASAC was established in 2003 National Energy Leading Group led by the Premier was established in 2005 NDRC National Energy Bureau was established in 2008	Oil trading was opened up to private companies Price regulation on oil products was improved towards more timely adjustment to market situation	Establishment of Board of Directors at the level of the parent companies Appointment of independent executive directors

(*continued*)

Table 10.3 (continued)

Year	*CCP decisions*	*Major contents*	*Changes of state ministries*	*Changes in oil industry structure*	*Changes in oil corporate governance*
2010s	2013 Decision of the CCP Central Committee on Major Issues concerning Comprehensively Deepening Reform adopted at the Third Plenary Session of the 18th CCP Central Committee 2015 the CCP Central Committee and the State Council Guidelines on Deepening the Reform of State-Owned Enterprises	Market playing determining role and state improving its functions Categorise SOEs into two types—commercial ones and those for public welfare Improve modern enterprise system including corporate legal person governance structure Improve SOE assets management system Promote mixed ownerships Strengthen regulation to prevent loss of SOE assets Strengthen and improve CCP leadership over SOEs	None yet	Opening up to investment from domestic privately owned enterprises, e.g., Sinopec has been cooperating with Alibaba to develop an ecommerce cloud platform for oil and petrochemical products since 2014	Anti-corruption campaign reveals 'oil clique' CNPC set up Board of Directors in 2014

Sources: CPC (2015)

Table 10.4 Multinational corporate behaviour and state-business relations

	Corporate governance	*Overseas investment*
Institutional structure of state economic and political agencies		
Role of CCP	Strong in enacting principles of corporate governance reform and personnel control	Strong in enacting principles of 'going global'
Role of SASAC, NDRC, and MOFCOM	SASAC strong in implementing specific reform policy NDRC and MOFCOM not relevant	Moderate in approving and coordinating location and access to finance
State-firm policy networks	State generally strong but with moderating influence from firms due to their embeddedness in the state structure	Firms are stronger mainly due to their market position and inter-firm relations
Organisational configuration of business actors		
Market position	Strong in legal governance by adopting international practice	Strong overall
Inter-firm relations	Moderate through executive rotations, JVs with global oil majors	Strong overall

investment by large Chinese multinational SOEs is, to a much larger extent, determined by their market positions and inter-firm relations vis-à-vis foreign multinational enterprises and host country enterprises. The technological knowledge and expertise of large Chinese multinational SOEs means they are better equipped to propose investment projects. In the end, their embeddedness in state-firm policy networks and their technological expertise would help them to get investment approval and access to finance from the government. The CCP's leadership in promoting large Chinese SOEs by simultaneously restructuring their businesses and governance, introducing market force (Nolan 2001, 2012), and regulating them to serve the national goal of economic and social development explains that large Chinese SOEs have been both economic and political entities. The alignment as opposed to the apparent paradox of the economic, social, and political goals in multinational corporate behaviour is not new. This means large Chinese multinational SOEs operate in a fully dialectical relationship with the CCP and state agencies—their roles and positions are simultaneously unified and contradictory, with the CCP having the final say.

The first section of the chapter will set up the explananda of corporate mechanisms and patterns of overseas investment, followed by the identification of the determinants of state structure and organisational configuration of business actors. The third section will present a case study on the Chinese oil industry, which will be followed by the conclusion.

Multinational Corporate Behaviour of Chinese Oil Majors

Corporate Governance

China's reform has transformed the SOEs into entities with attributes such as legal personality, limited liability, board of directors, and shareholding structures based on contribution of capital, which are promulgated in the Company Law of People's Republic of China. Literature on corporate governance and state-owned enterprises in China largely employ the theoretical framework of the shareholder-oriented model featuring the separation of ownership and control (Berle and Means 1932). However, recent studies by legal academics (Lin and Milhaupt 2013; Wang 2014) argue for the need to understand how the corporate governance mechanisms in China's SOEs function and who is in control.

Wang (2014) suggests a duality of corporate governance structure of Chinese SOEs—one legal and the other political. The reform drive to create modern industrial enterprise established the legal governance structure stipulated in the Company Law. It is characterised by a three-level control system—the shareholders' general meeting, the board of directors and the board of supervisors, the CEO and his executive team. In parallel with the legal governance structure, there are the CPC committee and party organs in the company. The secretary of the CPC committee of the central SOEs is either the chairperson of the board of directors or the chief executive officer. The most important members on the board of directors are the CPC committee members. In shaping the corporate governance mechanisms of Chinese large SOEs, the CPC has the ultimate power in control; this control is exercised through the 'nomenklatura system' (Brodsgaard 2012; Downs 2008). The performance of China's oil majors are regulated mainly by the State-owned Asset Supervisory and Administrative Commission (SASAC), a ministry-level department under the State Council. The executive salaries are tied to the overall grade (Naughton 2010: 453).

Overseas Investment

There is a complex relationship of home governments and outward foreign direct investment by multinational enterprises (Stopford and Strange 1991). Chinese outward investment was largely from state-owned enterprises in the decades prior to 2001 (Buckley et al. 2007). In the 1980s and early 1990s, the Chinese FDI was encouraged and directed by government towards investments to support export, secure natural resources, and gain knowledge and learning of international operation. Natural resources-oriented FDI was highly concentrated by value in developing countries. Between 1992 and 2001, Chinese outward FDI is associated with host natural resources endowments (Buckley et al. 2007).

By 2013 China (excluding Hong Kong) had 93 firms in the *Fortune Global 500* ranked by revenue and 43 firms are central SOEs. Among the top 100 Chinese multinational enterprises ranked by foreign assets (CEC/CEDA 2014), 43 are central SOEs and 40 central SOEs are among the top 50 in the list. The three Chinese oil majors are ranked as the top three Chinese MNEs.

State Structure and State–Business Relations

In the Chinese context, the institutional structures of state economic and political agencies refer to the role of the CCP and the policymaking power of relevant departments, such as SASAC and NDRC (National Development and Reform Commission). The organisational configuration of business actors involves the market positions of firms and inter-firm linkages[2] (Table 10.2).

Institutional Structure of State Economic and Political Agencies

The Leadership Role of the CCP

As a political institution, the CCP's leadership position in the country is enshrined in the Chinese Constitution. Its committees, groups, or teams run parallel to the executive system of the government at every level from the CCP Standing Committee of the polit-bureau to the grass-root CCP village committee. The heads of government ministries and central SOEs often hold both CCP and executive positions. Currently there are over 80 million CCP members working in all walks of life, approximately 6 per cent of the whole population. The governance of the Chinese political economy can be characterised as a dual structure with the CCP in the leadership position (Table 10.2). Studies on the role of the CCP in China's political economy show that the CCP is an adaptive political entity (Shambaugh 2009). In the broad context of China's economic reform, the CCP leads the process of gradual yet steady reform towards 'socialist market economy' (Table 10.3). Each step reflected in the CCP directives and State Council reform measures leads to major changes in the bureaucratic structure and the industry structure of strategic industries as well as the firm-level governing mechanisms (Table 10.3).

The CCP promotes enterprise reform by encouraging enterprise autonomy and commercial success of its central SOEs while regulating them through the 'nomenklatura system'—the appointment of the Chairmen and Presidents of the largest central SOEs and the cadre transfer system that enabled the rotation and transfer of these business leaders to senior state and CCP positions (Li 2014; Brodsgaard 2010, 2012). COD is responsible for the appointment, administration, and training of cadres and high-level government officials including those Chairmen and Presidents of the 53 largest central SOEs in which CNPC, Sinopec, and CNOOC are currently ranked number 11th, 12th, and 13th (SASAC

2015). In addition, most of the top executives of the largest 53 central SOEs are CPC members, of which 12 of the leaders of these companies were elected to the 17th CCP Central Committee in 2007. Some of them have been transferred to ministerial and provincial leadership positions. The current 18th CCP Central Committee, 205 full members and 171 alternate members, has 14 members from central SOEs, 4 full members, and 10 alternate members.

The Executive Role of State Agencies

The CCP has become less and less involved in detailed regulatory and industry-specific issues; the government makes most of these decisions (Kennedy 2005). The process of corporatisation and overseas listing of large SOEs was accompanied by the reorganisation of government structures with the objective to create a market-friendly environment and increase the state capabilities in regulating business (Table 10.3). In 1981, the central government had 100 ministries, of which no fewer than 65 were responsible for economic management. During the 1980s, some of the 65 economic ministries were merged or corporatised. For example, out of the Ministry of Petroleum, three Chinese oil majors were created—CNOOC in 1982, Sinopec in 1983, and CNPC in 1988. A major government reform programme was launched in 1998, which reduced the number of government ministries and state commissions to 29 from 40 (Zhang 2004: Figure 5-1). Industrial ministries were restructured and transferred into seven newly created 'state bureaux', which included oil and petrochemicals, affiliated to the ministerial-level State Economic and Trade Commission (SETC). In 2003, SASAC was established to oversee further reform of the SOEs. Under SASAC, the state-owned enterprises are grouped into two categories. The central SOEs are those that are directly supervised by SASAC at the state ministry level, while local SOEs are those that are supervised by SASAC at the provincial and municipal level. Other significant state agencies regulating large SOEs include NDRC for price and investment regulation and the Ministry of Commerce (MOFCOM) for overseas investment (Table 10.2).

State-Firm Policy Linkages

The variable of public–private networks has been modified into state-firm policy networks. The Western policy network approach has its limit in capturing the different political and administrative system in China from those in Western countries (Zheng et al. 2010). It has been suggested that the role of the CCP and the meaning of personal networks need to be considered. For Chinese SOEs, the interaction between the state and the firm takes place within the broad institutional structure of the state economic and political agencies through both formal and informal channels. The variable of the state-firm policy networks, hence, is a better term to capture the institutional reality of the Chinese oil industry. Its incorporation into the institutional structure of the state economic and political agencies demonstrates that the state-owned oil firms are part of the state economic structure, influencing policy through both formal and informal channels.

Organisational Configurations of Business Actors

Market Position

In the domestic market, market positions of the three Chinese oil majors vary across the value chain of the oil industry. Traditionally, CNPC is strong in onshore upstream business, Sinopec in refining and downstream business, and CNOOC in offshore upstream business. The upstream exploration of resources is regulated by the state through a licensing system administered by the Ministry of Land and Resources (Fig. 10.1). Major international oil companies participate in the upstream exploration onshore and offshore through forming partnerships with the Chinese oil majors. In the segment of domestic oil production, the three Chinese oil majors account for 94 per cent of the total volume of production of 210 million tons in 2014 with CNPC at 54 per cent, Sinopec 21 per cent, and CNOOC 19 per cent. Compared with CNPC's market share of around 90 per cent 15 years ago, CNPC's dominant position in oil production has been reduced by 40 per cent. The downstream refining and petrochemical segments were liberalised since the 1980s. China's oil production cannot keep up with the rapid growth of the country's economy. In 2014, 60 per cent of the oil consumption was met by oil imported from foreign countries. The oil import business is now dominated by five SOEs—Chinaoil (joint venture between CNPC and Sinochem), Unipec (joint venture between Sinopec and Sinochem), CNOOC-Sinopec United International Trading, Sinochem, and Zhuhai Zhenrong Company. Together they account for 90 per cent of China's oil imports, and the rest is for the several dozen private enterprises.

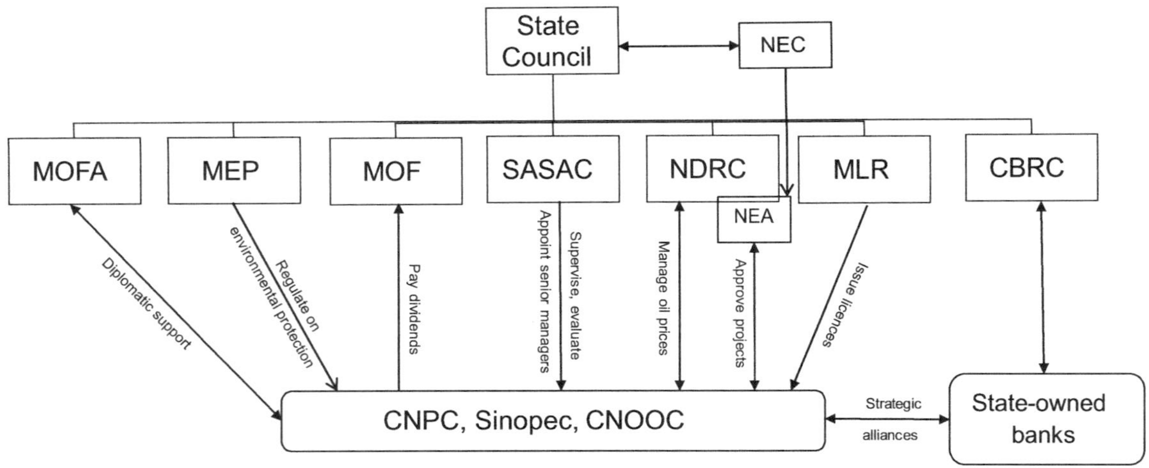

Notes: NEC – National Energy Commission; MOFA – Ministry of Foreign Affairs; MEP – Ministry of Environmental Protection; MOF – Ministry of Finance; SASAC – State Asset Supervision and Administration Commission; NDRC: National Development and Reform Commission; NEA – National Energy Administration; MLR – Ministry of Land Resources; CBRC – China Banking Regulation Commission

Fig. 10.1 Governance structure of the Chinese oil industry (Source: Zhang 2015)

China is poorly endowed with oil and gas reserves (Zhang 2015). With the rapid growth of demand for oil and the declining of production at major oil fields, CNPC has developed technology in developing mature oil fields that are usually deemed to be worthless in the industry. The Chinese oil majors still lag behind global oil majors in state-of-the-art technologies in for example deep-sea exploration and development (Zhang 2015).

Inter-firm Linkages

The global oil majors are deeply interested in developing their business in China from upstream to downstream. The three Chinese oil majors have formed cooperative partnerships and joint ventures with many of these global players across the value chain from upstream to downstream (Zhang 2015). In most areas, global oil majors are technologically ahead of their Chinese counterparts in upstream contracts and downstream joint ventures. From the perspective of the foreign partner in these joint ventures, the Chinese majors form a part of the companies' respective global business systems, typically a single business unit. In recent years, large Chinese SOEs have increasingly entered into cooperative relationships with other national oil companies especially in refining and petrochemicals and with domestic privately owned firms on customer services.

The Case of the Oil Industry

The evolutionary path in business development and governance structure of the three Chinese oil majors provides a useful perspective to examine the influence of the state structure and state-business relations.

Co-evolution of State Structures, Industry Structure, and Corporate Governance

The Determining Role of the CCP

The determining role of the CCP is reflected in three aspects—directing the reform of the oil industry, controlling over the personnel of the three oil majors, and mobilising SOEs to serve national policy goals in emergency circumstances such as disaster relief and coping with financial crisis. First, the transformation of the Chinese oil industry is inseparable from the CCP's directives on broad economic reform strategy and on SOEs reform in particular (Table 10.3). The resultant reform measures by the State Council executed by the state agencies and corporations alike gradually transformed the oil industry from government ministries into an industry today that is dominated by the three vertically integrated Chinese oil majors with other market participants such as international oil companies, other national oil companies, and private companies (Zhang 2004).

Second, all of the top 9 executives of CNPC and the top 11 executives of Sinopec Group hold similar positions in PetroChina and Sinopec Corp. Moreover the same person usually serves as the head of both the parent company and the listed company. For example, Wang Yilin is simultaneously the Chairman of the listed PetroChina and CNPC the parent group company. He is also the Party Secretary of CNPC. Independent directors are typically drawn from other government department and organisations. For example, the independent directors of Sinopec are all party members and worked for the government. The CCP committee at the board level and the party organs throughout the central SOEs indicate the party is at the core of the governance system. The career of the CEOs at central SOEs such as the three oil majors is dependent on both financial performance of their firms and serving the national policies promoted by the CCP. The performance of CNPC, Sinopec, and CNOOC is to a large extent dependent on their respective internationally listed companies PetroChina, Sinopec Corp., and CNOOC Ltd. At the time of the flotation, CNPC controlled around 90 per cent of PetroChina; Sinopec controlled around 56 per cent of Sinopec Corp; CNOOC controlled around 70.6 per cent of CNOOC Ltd. It is in the interest of the group companies that these listed companies perform well in the market.

The corporate governing mechanisms that the CCP uses to promote and regulate oil companies are executive appointment, executive rotation among the big three, and executive promotion to national leadership positions (Downs and Meidan 2011). COD is responsible for the appointment, administration, and training of cadres and high-level government officials including those Chairmen and Presidents of the 53 largest central SOEs. The mechanism of appointment of the business leaders was described as a process of consultations, suggestions, recommendations, and deliberations among company employees as the first step. It is followed by SASAC, approved by COD, selecting the top ten candidates for the top position from which the company employees elect, by vote, their nominees. The list will be ranked by the number of votes. If SASAC and COD disagree with the result, the second round of voting will take place.

Finally, the number of candidates will be reduced to two. Once the incumbent top executive steps down, SASAC, in consultation with the company board, makes their recommendation for which of the two candidates should be the new leader. All are subject to the approval of the COD (Brodsgaard 2012). Some of the top executives of the three oil majors have been promoted to ministerial and provincial leadership positions. The control of the personnel at the oil majors is exercised through not just appointment and promotion, but also rotations among central SOEs. In recent years there has been a reshuffle among the top leaders of the oil majors. In April 2011, it was announced that top executives of the parent companies would swap positions with their rivals. Fu Chengyu, the then Chairman of CNOOC, replaced Su Shulin at Sinopec as the Chairman, and Wang Yilin, Vice President of CNPC, filled Fu's position at CNOOC. The executive rotation aims to share the business and management expertise of the top executives and also prevent them to serve in one company for too long. Furthermore, there is an implicit understanding that successful executives will be rewarded with an appointment to a position in the government. For example, Wei Liucheng, President of CNOOC, was promoted to become the Governor of Hainan Province in 2003 and Wang Yupu was promoted to become the Vice Governor of Heilongjiang Province from his Chairmanship at Daqing, the largest oil field in China. Mr Wang is currently the Chairman of CNPC. Cao et al. (2009) find a strong positive relationship of the likelihood that a CEO is promoted politically with firm performance. They argue that 'political career concerns are consistent with incentives for value-maximisation in Chinese SOEs'.

Third, the oil majors are keeping in line of the CCP's mobilisation in tackling national disasters and coping with financial crisis. The oil majors all participated in the disaster relief efforts during the 2008 Sichuan earthquake. In the wake of the financial crisis, the CCP and the State Council urged SOEs to invest. Oil majors responded by increasing their borrowing from state-owned banks and increasing production capacity that was not necessarily desirable.

The Executive Role of State Agencies

The three Chinese oil majors were created out of the Ministry of Petroleum—CNOOC in 1982, Sinopec in 1983, and CNPC in 1988. As part of the 1998/1999 major reform programme, three vertically integrated oil majors were created through asset swaps among themselves, which fundamentally changed the structure of the oil industry in China (Table 10.3, Zhang 2004, 2015). In 2003, the establishment of SASAC is the most important policy measure to the reform of SOEs including the oil industry. Currently, the state agencies that are most relevant to the oil industry are SASAC, NDRC, and MOFCOM (Fig. 10.1).

SASAC

The function of SASAC is twofold. It acts as the shareholder of the state assets while leading reforms on corporate governance and restructuring the state-owned assets across industrial sectors. SASAC regards corporate governance mechanisms as crucial for SOEs to establish modern enterprise management system. Since 2004, it has been guiding the process of establishing company boards in central SOEs. It stipulates the principles and compositions of boards in these enterprises. The company boards have a 3-year term and should have no less than nine board members, one of which must be elected by the employees as their representative on the board. The Chairmen and Vice Chairmen as well as independent directors are appointed by SASAC approved by COD. The remuneration of board members including independent directors is determined by SASAC. By 2013, the three oil majors except for CNPC have established company boards. In the meantime, SASAC evaluates the performance of the central SOEs on the basis of financial performance and management performance (SASAC 2006) and regulates the overseas investment of the central SOEs. The executive appointment and remuneration are two important managerial rights for company boards. The remuneration of central SOEs employees are significantly higher than those working for other SOEs in China but significantly lower than those from international companies of similar scale in the same industrial sector. These are very sensitive issues for SASAC to tackle. As there is no specific guideline for medium- or long-term incentive compensation such as stock-based compensation, oil majors that wish to use it as part of the compensation package must negotiate the terms with the SASAC on a case-by-case basis (Li 2010). In July 2014, SASAC published a reform plan in line with the spirit of the Third Plenum of the 18th CPC Congress. The plan selected six central SOEs as pilot projects for reform, focusing on bringing in shareholders from the non-state sector and improving SOE corporate governance, for example, giving company boards more power to appoint executives and decide executive remuneration (Wen and Ma 2014).

The State Council delegates to SASAC to represent the state as the shareholder of the central SOEs. However, SASAC's power is limited in supervising the central SOEs including the oil majors. SASAC neither collects dividend nor makes appointment for the heads of the central SOEs. The financial oversight comes from the Ministry of Finance. Legally, SASAC has the legal mandate to appoint or remove senior executives and members of the two boards, as well as propose candidates for directors and supervisors to the shareholders' general meeting. In practice, it is COD that exercises the appointment and removal of senior executives.

NDRC

The disbanding of the Ministry of Energy in 1993 and the reorganisation of the Chinese government in 1998 injected new complexity into energy policymaking (Zhang 2015). By 1999, China no longer had ministerial-level government department with broad policymaking authority to direct energy policy; energy policymaking and regulation became highly fragmented with a lack of policy coordination. The governance structure of the energy industry is fragmented, and the designated energy-specific bureaux often lack bureaucratic clout (Kong 2010). For the Chinese oil majors, this fragmentation in policymaking and coordination actually strengthened their power in driving forward projects and policy within the oil industry.

In recent years, institutions have been developed to address problems in policy coordination and implementation. These include the Energy Leading Group (ELG), set up in 2005, led by then Premier Wen Jiabao. The ELG's members include two vice premiers and nine members from ministries involving in energy policy issues. The main function of the ELG was to study prominent issues regarding energy development policy, formulating specific policies, and overseeing their implementation. In 2008, the National Energy Administration (NEA) was created under the administration of NDRC. In 2010, the National Energy Commission (NEC) was set up. Today the NEC, led by Premier Li Keqiang, has 22 ministers gathered from government ministries and commissions as its members. This shows a further consolidation of the leadership of the energy industry at the highest level of the government (Fig. 10.1). The NEC has the responsibility of determining national energy development strategy, addressing energy security and energy development, and coordinating domestic and international investments. The NEA undertakes the daily work of the NEC and takes responsibility to devise and implement plans and industrial policy for the energy industry. Although none of the leaders of the three oil majors is a member of the NEC, they are likely to remain powerful actors driving projects and policies, making full use of their knowledge in the industry and their role in securing energy supplies both at home and abroad.

From a governance perspective, the three Chinese oil majors are unequivocally part of the Chinese state. However, it would be a mistake to think the state is in absolute control of the central SOEs. The lack of a ministry-level department means the three Chinese oil majors have enormous knowledge and lobbying influence over policy and investment in the industry.

MOFCOM

The regulation on overseas investment by MOFCOM has gradually moved towards allowing more business autonomy. Previous to the latest Measures for the Administration of Investment Abroad issued in 2014, outward direct investment had to be approved based on the value of the investment. The latest Measures stipulate that outward direct investment need be approved by MOFCOM if it is towards countries that have not established diplomatic relations with China and countries under sanctions by the United Nations, investment need also to be approved if it is in sectors that contain products or technology under export control and that potentially affect the interest of over one country or a region. It can be said that MOFCOM acts as the focal point to get approval or recordation for China's outward investment. Furthermore, the latest Measures indicate MOFCOM no longer approves investment projects based on the value of investment. Instead, it coordinates with other ministries to regulate central SOEs' overseas investment to keep them in line legally and diplomatically.

State-Firm Policy Linkages

As discussed in the analytical context, state-firm policy linkages are a suitable term to reflect the ways in which central SOEs interact with the government on policy issues. Kennedy (2005) has explained that while the CCP is very important, when companies or actors try to influence policy, they tend to go to government agencies and address officials in their respective administrative government capacities. The CCP is less and less involved in detailed regulatory and industry-specific issues; the government makes most of these decisions. But this is not to say that the CCP does not have jurisdiction, but rather that it has been focusing on broader, strategic-level questions, such as security, social, and economic issues. But it is important when approaching government officials in their administrative capacity to be aware of the party hat that this official might also wear (and how that affects power dynamics as well). And this is not just true for government officials; in state-owned enterprises, officials who wear these multiple hats can be especially influential because they represent both the party and a commercial interest group. This makes their voices especially important for industrial policy matters.

In the oil industry, the relationship between the Chinese oil majors and the Chinese government is complex and dynamic. The growing financial power combined with their technical knowhow and their political rank allows the oil majors to have considerable power in energy policymaking (Downs and Meidan 2011). Moreover, the oil majors today were born out of the corporatisation of the previous energy ministry. When they were established, they were expected to operate as both a commercial and regulatory entity. For example, they devised industry and environmental protection standards (Zhang 2004; Kong 2010). The first generation of leaders with the oil majors believed that the companies they lead represented the national interests. Although successive rounds of reform emphasised the separation of the regulatory functions for the commercial business, the oil majors tend to amalgamate corporate interests with national interests to suit their own needs and achieve their own agendas. As in many central SOEs, Chairmen and CEOs in the oil industry strive to use their corporate careers as springboards into the national leadership by growing their companies in ways that advance the interests of the party and the state and thus building their own personal political capital (Downs and Meidan 2011).

One key feature of the state-firm policy networks as compared with central SOEs in other sectors is that the energy industry including oil does not have an overarching department to oversee the industry. This means the oil majors have enormous power in energy-related policymaking process. The government often has to rely on the oil majors' technical know-how and market expertise for making policy. However, it is not that the oil majors can always get what they wanted. One exception is the price of oil products. While the government liberalised crude oil price, it still controls oil products prices at a level that is not consistent to the international oil price for fear of the impact of passing-through inflation and the affordability of rural farmers who operate oil-fuelled agricultural equipment.

The oil majors have to balance operational losses and state imperatives. For example, CNPC bears losses from the downstream business through cross-subsidies that are financed through heavy taxation of its upstream business (Jiang and Sinton 2011). Their reluctance to sell oil products at huge losses has frequently contributed to artificial fuel shortages in China (Liou 2009).

However, there have been some moves towards fuel price and tax reforms. In June 2008, the government moved to increase retail gasoline and diesel prices by 17–18 per cent, the first increase in 8 months, following months of spreading fuel rationing as refiners cut production to trim deepening losses incurred by record crude costs. Tan and Wolak's (2009) careful analysis shows that Chinese prices are now reliably approaching Western prices and the era of subsidies seems to be ending.

It is nothing new to attempt to align commercial interests with government foreign and trade policies (Jiang and Sinton 2011). For the Chinese government, the capability of the Chinese oil companies in securing energy supply is of vital importance. Both CNPC and Sinopec are bureaucratically ranked at the ministry level, the same as SASAC, NDRC, and other ministries in the governance structure (Fig. 10.1). The leaders of the oil major are both business executives and senior members of the CCP. It is in the interests of both the CCP and the government that the major Chinese oil companies are commercially successful and that they are able to secure adequate energy supplies.

Market Positions, Inter-firm Relations, and Overseas Investment

The Chinese oil majors are still emphatically oriented towards the domestic market (Zhang 2015). Their competitive capabilities in business and technology have not yet been on a par with that of the global oil majors in the aspects of tackling the most technically demanding areas of exploration and development across the world and in organising an efficient and effective global supply chain. The relatively weak market position of the Chinese oil majors compared with the global oil majors and their experience of cooperating with international oil majors in the domestic market influence the location and the pattern of the international investment of the Chinese oil majors. Most of the overseas investment by Chinese oil majors has been in upstream exploration and development, and much less investment has been in downstream refining and petrochemicals.

Motivation
Scholars and analysts debate on the motivation of the international expansion of the Chinese oil majors. Some analysts claim that energy security is the main driver for China's 'going out' strategy (Downs 2010). Others argue that although Beijing has encouraged overseas investment in the past, it is less enthusiastic now due to the small effect such actions have on gaining energy security for the country (Houser 2008). Only about 10–20 per cent of all the oil that is produced overseas actually makes it back to China (Dirks 2006). The more profitable light, sweet crude tends to be sold in the international market where profits are higher. Furthermore, companies have little incentive to bring crude oil back to the Chinese market due to the low prices set for oil products by NDRC. How much of the different crude types CNPC brings back for the domestic market is a point of tension between the Chinese government and CNPC. The exact proportion that is settled on is a negotiation between the government and the company (Jiang and Sinton 2011).

The economics and politics of the international expansion of the Chinese oil majors have another dimension that is under appreciated in the debate. It is the industrial policy of creating and developing globally competitive integrated Chinese oil firms (Nolan and Zhang 2002; Zhang 2004, 2015). Both the government and the oil majors have a balancing act to play between achieving policy objectives and commercial success. On the one hand, the government would like to see the oil majors play a critical role to secure energy supply, which implies the government would like to secure energy at whatever the costs are; on the other hand, the government supports the oil majors to become competitive and commercially successful companies in the world market, which implies they have to be profitable and viable to carry out long-term investment.

Tension has been observed between the Chinese government and the oil majors on the topic of overseas investment. Any major overseas venture requires approval by the central government. The Chinese oil majors, like other central SOEs, are subject to the governance of the SASAC in terms of foreign assets and investments. They are also subject to the regulation of NDRC and MOFCOM. Any overseas investment in mineral resources valued between USD 30 million to USD 200 million is subject to the approval of NDRC. Overseas investment over USD 200 million must be approved by the State Council. The three central oil SOEs, however, have autonomy to decide overseas investment below USD 30 million. In the meantime, MOFCOM will also approve overseas investment in consultation with Chinese embassies in the host countries.

Analysts from the International Energy Association (Jiang and Sinton 2011) argue that CNPC has strong business interest to expand internationally as overseas operations are more profitable and more autonomous than those within China. The Chinese government provides political and diplomatic support to open markets. For example, China's Export-Import Bank extended loans to Angola and other African nations in 2006 (Faucon 2006). But it is CNPC's business decisions that are now the dominant explanation for the push overseas. Energy security might have started out as a main driver for China's going out policy, but in key places such as Kazakhstan, Venezuela, and Iran, it is certainly not the main reason for why the trend has continued and grown.

However, the combination of the long lineage associated with the government ministries, the large size of the companies in the oil industry, a strategically important 'pillar' industry, and the company leaders' high ranks within the CCP resulted in much large lobbying power of the oil majors relative to the government agencies tasked with overseeing them (Jiang and Ding 2014). China's oil majors have been able to manipulate the government to adopt policies consistent to their interests (Andrew-Speed 2004; Cunningham 2007; Downs 2010).

There is little evidence that Chinese oil majors' expansion abroad is motivated by anything other than a desire to secure diversified resources to support continued economic growth as well as to improve the competitive capabilities of Chinese oil majors in technology and supply chain management, as well as management expertise (Zhang 2004, 2015; Zweig and Bi 2005). While Chinese firms have appeared willing to invest in some countries that Western majors have little presence in, this is largely motivated by securing resources to meet the growing demand for energy and diversifying supplying sources. Furthermore, international investment by Chinese oil companies has actually helped to diversify the global supply base, making it more competitive and ultimately benefiting all oil-consuming economies. A 2010 study examined the 16 largest Chinese natural-resource procurement arrangements and found that Chinese efforts fall predominantly into categories that help expand and diversify the global energy supply system (Moran 2010). The Chinese government wants both enhanced supply security and competitive global companies. This is the mandate by which China's national oil companies operate.

Internationalisation Strategies

The overseas investment by the Chinese oil majors have taken a number of forms, including equity investment, acquisitions, and loans for resources. During the decade between 2002 and 2013, the main path for international expansion of Chinese oil majors has been through minority investments in oil and gas assets, mostly mature oil fields in developing countries, often partnering with other national oil companies and global oil majors. The Chinese oil majors, especially CNPC, have developed technologies to turn around mature oil fields that production has been declining. The three Chinese oil majors now operate in upstream and downstream businesses in over 30 countries in the world, mainly in developing countries. The International Energy Agency (IEA) estimates that by the end of 2013, the combined overseas oil and gas production by Chinese companies totalled 2.5 million barrels of oil equivalent per day, in which the three Chinese oil majors and their listed companies accounted for 85 per cent, with production in Iraq accounting for 26 per cent (Jiang and Ding 2014). In 2013, the Chinese oil majors produced overseas equity shares of 2.1 million barrels of oil per day, a significant increase from 1.1 million barrels per day in 2009 and equivalent to half of China's domestic production in the same year. There is no evidence that this production is required to be exported to the Chinese market. Instead, the marketing for overseas production is largely based on commercial considerations, the production-sharing contracts involving the investments, or both (Jiang and Ding 2014).

The speed of Chinese oil majors' international acquisitions has been accelerating. Between 2002 and 2010, the Chinese oil majors spent USD 65 billion in acquisitions. In comparison, their spending on international acquisition between 2011 and 2013 reached USD 73 billion. This incremental growth is large, but it remains a fraction of the total value of international mergers and acquisitions in the oil and gas sector. For example, China's international oil and gas acquisitions totalled USD 38 billion in 2013, doubling the total value of USD 18 billion it reached in 2009. In 2013, the total value of global oil and gas acquisitions reached USD 237 billion (EY 2014), which means China's share was just 16 per cent.

The IEA reports a total of 90 international oil and gas acquisitions by Chinese companies between 2002 and 2013 (Jiang and Sinton 2011; Jiang and Ding 2014). Of these, 44 were less than USD 1 billion and 41 were between USD 1 and USD 5 billion. Only five deals were above USD 5 billion. Furthermore, most of the international acquisitions by the

Chinese oil majors are asset deals, not corporate deals, and mainly from developing countries. Of the 90 deals between 2002 and 2013, 50 deals are acquisitions of assets from resource-rich developing countries or divestments from international oil companies from their assets in developing countries. Among the 41 upstream deals between 2002 and 2010, 27 are in developing countries from the Middle East, Central Asia, South America, and Africa.

In recent years, global oil majors have increasingly formed partnerships with the Chinese oil majors to access the fast-growing Chinese market while also selling assets to the Chinese oil majors in international projects. This practice is considered an 'asset swap' and is the 'unspoken rule' for successfully working with the Chinese oil majors (Jiang and Ding 2014). CNPC has signed agreements with Iran, Iraq, and Qatar for investment in upstream activities and technical services, committing the company to 20–30 years of investment. These commitments are all done through partnerships with international oil companies such as Shell, BP, and Total as well as national oil companies from developing countries such as Turkish Petroleum and Petronas (Jiang and Sinton 2011). Meanwhile, the Chinese oil majors have used partnerships with resource-rich developing or emerging countries as a commercial strategy. Through the adoption of the 'market for resources' strategy, they have been able to gain preferential treatment for cooperation or to increase their opportunities to buy more oil in resource-rich countries by offering these countries' national oil companies opportunities in the Chinese domestic market. For example, Saudi Arabia, Qatar, Venezuela, and Kuwait are the major suppliers of China's oil imports. Saudi Aramco entered into partnerships with CNPC and Sinopec to develop petrol stations and refineries in the coastal provinces of China. Kuwait National Petroleum and PDVSA have set up joint ventures with Sinopec and CNPC respectively to construct refineries with capacities of more than 10 million tons per year.

The nature of the inter-firm linkages between CNPC and Sinopec are both competitive and cooperative. CNPC and Sinopec compete on oil products, service stations, and chemicals while cooperate in national projects such as West-East Gas Pipeline. They also cooperate, with the coordination from the NDRC, to secure the annual energy supply for economic growth. The most ferocious competition between CNPC and Sinopec takes place in the bidding for international oil assets. Liou (2009) looks into the case of south-east Sudan and concludes that the central government is by no means omnipotent in regulating the oil majors' overseas activities.

Access to Finance

China's oil majors also work closely with the major state-owned banks especially the China Development Bank (CDB) to structure and execute these large-scale domestic and international transactions. CDB's energy-backed loans are better understood as the result of a convergence of divergent interests rather than as the execution of a state master plan (Downs 2011). The two policy banks, CDB and the China Export & Import Bank, are the two most important strategic partners for Chinese oil majors. Since 2009, in their effort to secure long-term supplies of oil and gas, China has concluded 16 deals of 'loan for oil' and 'loan for gas' with Turkmenistan, Kazakhstan, Angola, Ghana, Venezuela, Brazil, Bolivia, and Ecuador, as well as Russia. These various deals total USD 120 billion, with the USD 25 billion loan to Rosneft and Transneft by far the largest (Jiang and Sinton 2011; Jiang and Ding 2014). The Chinese beneficiaries of these loans are the three Chinese oil majors.

Locations

The Middle East remains the largest source of China's crude oil imports, although African countries, particularly Angola, have begun contributing more to China's imports in recent years. As part of China's policy of energy supply security, the Chinese oil majors have been attempting to diversify supply sources in various regions through equity share investments and loan for oil schemes. Saudi Arabia and Angola are China's two largest sources of oil imports; together they account for 33 per cent of the country's total oil imports. The Chinese government has for many decades cultivated relationships with developing countries in Africa and the Middle East. For example, the Chinese government has been providing development aid to Africa since the 1950s. The goodwill created has indirectly beneficial to commercial activities. At the same time, Chinese oil companies have also enlisted diplomatic support from the Chinese government in initiating and closing deals in energy supply and investment.

Conclusions

The multinational corporate behaviour in corporate governance and overseas investment in the Chinese oil industry can be explained by the institutional structure of state economic and political agencies in which they are embedded and by which they are regulated as well as by the organisational configuration of business actors in which they compete and cooperate. First, the CCP's reform directives and the resultant State Council's specific reform measures in China's overall economic reform and especially in the reform of the state-owned sector have determined the evolution of the institutional structures of state agencies regulating big businesses, the industry structure of strategic sectors such as the oil industry, and the corporate governance of large Chinese multinational SOEs (Tables 10.3 and 10.4). Second, the reform of SOE corporate governance has introduced and adopted Western style of corporate governance structure and mechanisms, which has been administered by the state agency of SASAC. Meanwhile, the CCP exercises its control through COD over the appointment and promotion of the top executives of large Chinese multinational SOEs. With further reforms, market-oriented norms and institutions will continue to be learned and the leadership is likely to contextualise them by creating their own rules and organisation (Yeo 2013). Third, the changes in the structure of government ministries demonstrate increasing liberalisation of regulation over business activities, and the changes of industry structure show a gradual introduction of market forces into the strategic sectors that directly affect the market positions and inter-firm relations for firms operating in industry. The pattern of overseas investment by large Chinese multinational SOEs is, to a much larger extent, determined by their market positions and inter-firm relations vis-à-vis foreign multinational enterprises and host country enterprises. The technological knowledge and expertise of large Chinese multinational SOEs means they are better equipped to propose investment projects. In the end, their embeddedness in state-firm policy networks and their technological expertise would help them to get investment approval and access to finance from the government.

The CCP's leadership in promoting large Chinese SOEs by simultaneously restructuring their businesses and governance, introducing market force, and regulating them to serve the national goal of economic and social development explains that Chinese multinational SOEs operate in a fully dialectical relationship with the CPC and state agencies—their roles and positions are simultaneously unified and contradictory, with the CCP playing the determining role.

Notes

1. A group of over 100 large SOEs operating in industrial sectors that are considered to be strategic for the development of the national economy and mostly evolved from various government ministries in the pre-reform era (SASAC 2015).
2. The business associations initially created by the government have also become part of the hierarchical state bureaucracy, and the influence of their advocacy is constrained by the ownership of their members and by the bureaucratic level of the government departments they are associated with. On 8 July 2015, the State Council issued the 'Overall Programme of Disassociation of Business Associations from Administrative Agencies', requesting business associations sever their administrative relations with government ministries and departments. The process of disassociation will be carried out in a staged fashion. The business associations for the oil industry—the China Petroleum and Chemical Industry Federation and the China Chamber of Commerce for Petroleum Industry—are not included in the list of the first batch of 148 business associations to carry out the disassociation.

References

Andrew-Speed, P. (2004). *Energy policy and regulation in the People's Republic of China*. The Hague: Kluwer Law International.

Berle, A. A., & Means, G. C. (1932). *The modern corporation and private property*. New York: Macmillan.

Brodsgaard, K. E. (2010). Governing capacity and institutional change in China in the reform era. *The Copenhagen Journal of Asian Studies, 28*(1), 20–35.

Brodsgaard, K. E. (2012). Politics and business group formation in China: The party in control? *China Quarterly, 211*, 624–648.

Buckley, P. J., Jeremy Clegg, L., Cross, A. R., Liu, X., Voss, H., & Zheng, P. (2007). The determinants of Chinese outward foreign direct investment. *Journal of International Business Studies, 38*, 499–518.

Cao, J., Lemmon, X. P., Qian, M., & Tan, G. (2009). *Political promotion, CEO compensation, and their effect of firm performance*. Research Collection Lee Kong Chian School of Business, Paper 1816.

Casper, S., & Van Waarden, F. (2005). *Innovation and institutions: A multidisciplinary review of the study of innovation systems*. Cheltenham: Edward Elgar.

CEC/CEDA (China Enterprise Confederation and China Enterprise Directors Association). (2014). Top 100 Chinese multinational enterprises 2013. http://www.cec1979.org.cn/c500/chinese/content.php?id=146&t_id=1. Accessed 1 Aug 2014.

Child, J., & Rodriguez, S. B. (2005). The internationalization of Chinese firms: A case for theoretical extension? *Management and Organization Review, 1*(3), 381–410.

CPC (Communist Party of China). Database of CPC National Congresses 1st–18th. http://cpc.people.com.cn/GB/64162/64168/351850/index.html. Accessed 1 May 2015.

Cunningham, E. A. (2007). *China's energy governance: perception and reality.* MIT Centre for International Studies. http://web.mit.edu/cis/pdf/Audit_03_07_Cunningham.pdf. Accessed 15 Jan 2016.

Dirks, G. (2006). *Energy security: China and the world.* Paper presented at the International Symposium on Energy Security: China and the World, Beijing, 24–26 May 2006.

Doremus, P. N., Keller, W. W., Pauly, L. W., & Reich, S. (1999). *The myth of the global corporation.* Princeton: Princeton University Press.

Downs, E. (2008). Business interest groups in Chinese politics: The case of the oil companies. In C. Li (Ed.), *China's changing political landscape.* Washington, DC: Brookings Institute.

Downs, E. (2010). Who's afraid of China's national oil companies? In C. Pascual & J. Elkind (Eds.), *Energy security: Economics, politics, strategies and implications.* Washington, DC: Brookings Institute.

Downs, E. (2011). *Inside China, Inc: China development bank's cross-border energy deals.* Washington, DC: Brookings Institute.

Downs, E., & Meidan, M. (2011). Business and politics in China: The oil executive reshuffle of 2011. *China Security, 19*, 3–21.

Ernst and Young (EY). (2014). Global oil and gas transactions review 2013. http://www.ey.com/GL/en/Industries/Oil---Gas/Global-oil-and-gas-transactions-review-2013---Overview#.U647Wo1dVqs. Accessed 22 June 2014.

Faucon, B. (2006, November 30). China makes headway in Angola with multiple trade ties. *Dow Jones International News.*

Griffiths, A. B., & Zammuto, R. F. (2005). Institutional governance systems and variations in national competitive advantage: An integrative framework. *Academy of Management Review, 30*(4), 823–842.

Hollingsworth, J. R., & Boyer, R. (1997). *Contemporary capitalism: The embeddedness of institutions.* Cambridge: Cambridge University Press.

Houser, T. (2008). The roots of Chinese oil investment abroad. *Asia Policy, 5*, 141–166.

Jiang, J., & Ding, C. (2014). *Update on overseas investments by China's national oil companies: Achievements and challenges since 2011.* Paris: OECD/International Energy Agency.

Jiang, J., & Sinton, J. (2011). *Overseas investments by China's national oil companies: Assessing the drivers and impacts*. Paris: OECD/International Energy Agency.

Kennedy, S. (2005). *Business of lobbying in China*. Cambridge, MA: Harvard University Press.

Kong, B. (2010). *China's international petroleum policy*. Santa Barbara: ABC-Clio LLC.

Li, J. (2010). Contractual arrangements with top executive in state-owned enterprises in the current institutional perspective. *Reformation, 9*, 112–114.

Li, C. (2014). *China's centralised industrial order: Industrial reform and the rise of centrally controlled big business*. London: Routledge.

Lin, L.-W., & Milhaupt, C. J. (2013). We are the (national) champions. *Standard Law Review, 65*(4), 697–759.

Liou, C.-S. (2009). Bureaucratic politics and overseas investment by Chinese state-owned oil companies: Illusory champions. *Asian Survey, XLIX*(4), 670–690.

Moran, T. H. (2010). *China's strategy to secure natural resources: Risks, dangers and opportunities*. Washington, DC: Peterson Institute of International Economics.

Naughton, B. (2010). China's distinctive system: Can it be a model for others? *Journal of Contemporary China, 19*(65), 437–460.

Nolan, P. (2001). *The global business revolution and China*. Basingstoke: Palgrave.

Nolan, P. (2012). *Is China buying the world?* Cambridge: Polity Press.

Nolan, P., & Zhang, J. (2002). The challenge of globalization for large Chinese firms. *World Development, 30*(12), 2089–2107.

Pauly, L. W., & Reich, S. (1997). National structures and multinational corporate behavior: Enduring differences in the age of globalization. *International Organization, 51*, 1–30.

Ruigrok, W., & Van Tulder, R. (1995). *The logic of international restructuring*. London/New York: Routledge.

Shambaugh, D. (2009). *China's Communist Party: Atrophy and adaptation*. Berkeley: University of California Press.

Spencer, J. W., Murtha, T. P., & Lenway, S. A. (2005). How governments matter to new industry creation. *Academy of Management Review, 30*(2), 321–337.

State Asset Supervision and Administration Commission (SASAC). (2006). Detailed criteria of performance evaluation of central SOEs. http://www.sasac.gov.cn/n1180/n1211/n2695/n4592/12349041.html. Accessed 7 Aug 2014.

State Asset Supervision and Administration Commission (SASAC). (2015). List of the Central State-Owned Enterprises. http://www.sasac.gov.cn/n86114/n86137/c1725422/content.html. Accessed 28 Apr 2016.

Stopford, J., & Strange, S. (1991). *Rival states, rival firms: Competition for world market shares*. Cambridge: Cambridge University Press.

Tan, X., & Wolak, F. (2009). *Does China underprice its oil consumption?* Stanford University Working Paper 2009/2/6.

Wang, J. (2014). The political logic of corporate governance in China's state-owned enterprises. *Cornell International Law Journal, 47*, 631–669.

Wei, Z. (2010). The literature on Chinese outward FDI. *Multinational Business Review, 18*(3), 73–112.

Wen, Y, & Ma, C. (2014, July 18). Guoqi gaige yi shijian bojie maodun (SOE reform: solving problems through practice). *Guangming Daily*. http://www.sasac.gov.cn/n1180/n1271/n20515/n2697175/15968596.html. Accessed 1 Aug 2014.

Whitley, R. (1999). *Divergent capitalism*. Oxford: Oxford University Press.

Whitley, R. (2007). *Business systems and organizational capabilities: The institutional structuring of competitive competences*. Oxford: Oxford University Press.

Yeo, Y. (2013). Contextualizing corporate governance: The case of China's central state enterprise groups. *Journal of Contemporary China, 22*(81), 460–475.

Zhang, J. (2004, reissued as paperback in 2016). *Catch-up and competitiveness in China: The case of large firms in the oil industry*. London: Routledge.

Zhang, J. (2015). China's oil industry: Investment in developing countries. In C. P. Freeman (Ed.), *Handbook on China and developing countries* (pp. 287–317). Cheltenham/Northampton: Edward Elgar.

Zhang, J. (2017). Western ideas of corporate governance: China's reform of large state-owned enterprises. In M. Warner (Ed.), *The diffusion of Western economic ideas in East Asia*. New York: Routledge.

Zhang, X., & Whitley, R. (2013). Changing macro-structural varieties of East Asian capitalism. *Socio-Economic Review, 11*(2), 301–336.

Zheng, H., De Jong, M., & Koppenjan, J. (2010). Applying policy network theory to policy-making in China: The case of urban health insurance reform. *Public Administration, 88*(2), 398–417.

Zweig, D., & Bi, J. (2005). China's global hunt for energy. *Foreign Affairs, 84*(5), 25–38.

CHAPTER 11

Business–State Interactions and Technology Development Regimes: A Comparative Analysis of Two Metropolises

Xiaoke Zhang

Introduction

This chapter explores how variations in business–state relations encourage divergent approaches to developing technology development regimes across two metropolises—Shanghai and Shenzhen. Technology development regimes are understood as the combinations of state industrial policies and corporate entrepreneurship strategies to deal with major challenges involved in managing technical change. State policies and corporate strategies are granted analytical primacy here, mainly because technology development patterns and outcomes are empirically shown to have resulted from the ways in which state and business actors interact to pursue product, process, and organizational innovations, particularly in developing and emerging market economies (Fagerberg et al. 2010; Lall and Urata 2002). These policies and strategies are causally connected, this chapter argues, with two critical dimensions of business–state relations—the state organization of industrialization processes and business coordination of

X. Zhang (✉)
Alliance Manchester Business School, University of Manchester, Manchester, UK

X. Zhang, T. Zhu (eds.), *Business, Government and Economic Institutions in China*, International Political Economy Series,
DOI 10.1007/978-3-319-64486-8_11

economic and innovation activities. It posits that regional or subnational political economies with divergent configurations of state organization and business coordination are expected to differ in their respective patterns and outcomes of technology development.

This chapter focuses on Shanghai and Shenzhen in its account of institution–technology connections, primarily because they represent two divergent archetypes of high-tech industrial governance. As will be shown below, they have demonstrated systematic variations in their respective technology development regimes and in the corresponding configuration of state–business interactions. An empirical focus on these two metropolises thus helps leverage the explanatory power of the theoretical argument of this chapter. Furthermore, there are also important methodological reasons for developing the comparative analysis of the chapter in the context of the ICT industry. Confining the empirical locale to a single industry ensures that the key analytical dimensions along which state policies and corporate strategies to deal with major technology development challenges are characterized and contrasted will be of comparable importance. More significantly, the ICT industry has constituted a sectoral focus of government and business efforts to promote high-tech industrial development across the two localities. The data for this study come from more than 150 interviews with senior managers of ICT firms, leaders of business associations, government officials, and academics conducted during numerous research trips to Shanghai and Shenzhen between 2013 and 2017 as well as from various secondary sources.

The chapter starts by suggesting four dimensions for contrasting the sorts of state industrial policies and corporate strategies that interact to tackle major challenges facing the process of technology development, particularly in emerging market economies. It then distinguishes two combinations of these policies and strategies or two technology development regimes that are shown to have become established in Shanghai and Shenzhen. In the following sections, the chapter exposits how state organization and business coordination have combined to yield distinctive institutional structures of industrial governance in the two metropolises and demonstrates how variations in their respective technology development regimes are causally interactive with these different structures. The chapter concludes by discussing the innovation outcomes of the different configurations of business–state interactions in the two regional political economies and by reflecting on the major policy and theoretical implications of the empirical findings.

Technology Development Challenges

In late industrializing economies, the development and accumulation of technological capabilities reflect prevalent ways of dealing with four sets of interrelated challenges. The first of these challenges results from innovations generating technical uncertainty and giving rise to unpredictable market outcomes. In advanced industrial societies, new technologies and industries often evolve through the three stages of emergence, consolidation, and maturity, with the level of technical and market uncertainty inherent in the innovation process being the most acute at the emergence stage (Ergas 1987; Utterback and Abernathy 1975). By contrast, new industries in late industrializing economies generally begin at the mature, standardized end of this evolutionary path, although there may be variations in different technologies and industries; firms in these economies gradually assimilate and improve upon imported technologies through incremental learning. As a result, technical feasibility and market acceptance are relatively well established. However, as latecomer firms work backwards from the mature technology stages to the more design-intensive and complex innovation stages, they are likely to encounter greater technological uncertainties and risks (Bell and Pavitt 1995; Hobday 1995).

How well firms manage market and technical uncertainties is contingent on their ability to acquire new knowledge from foreign and domestic sources, a second technology development challenge. The acquisition of foreign technologies is not a linear and automatic process and may be impeded by various cognitive and organizational constraints affecting the process of identifying appropriate foreign technologies and translating blueprints embodied in imported capital goods into specifications and procedures specific to local products and markets (Lall and Teubal 1998; Perez and Soete 1988). Furthermore, new technologies diffused through imported plants and equipment are only partially articulated in codified information and usually have to be acquired through trial and error. This suggests that latecomer firms can only understand and apply foreign technologies through the accumulation of tacit knowledge in particular organizational and technical contexts.

As new industries expand and as innovation capabilities accumulate in late industrializing economies, firms may draw increasingly on domestic sources for technological inputs. As with the diffusion of foreign technologies, inter-organizational knowledge transfer is not straightforward and effortless. While organizations may have explicit knowledge, such as blueprints and technical procedures, these are useful, applicable, and innovation-creating only when their members possess the requisite tacit knowledge to utilize them (Kim and Nelson 2000; Teece et al. 1997). The fact that an organization's knowledge is tacit and proprietary means that it usually has significant organization-specific dimensions. For knowledge receivers, understanding and learning the specifics of knowledge sources is a time-consuming and costly process. Equally, knowledge that provides information for the development of innovations may derive from a wide variety of scientific and technological fields and come from different departments and groups within organizations and their business partners, public research institutions and universities (PRIUs), and other agencies. This cognitive and organizational complexity of knowledge implies that the success of such transfer processes depends on investment in developing search and assimilating capabilities on the part of recipients.

This last point suggests a third major challenge—the development of firms' 'absorptive capacity' (Cohen and Levinthal 1990: 128). Developing absorptive capacity is essentially a learning process in which firms learn how to combine new with existing knowledge and use and improve organizational competences in new ways through problem-solving experiences. Central to this process is the aggregation of individual knowledge and skills gained from these experiences at the firm level that is necessary for organizational learning to enhance innovation performance. This varies with the extent to which certain organizational structures and practices, such as subordinates' participation in decision-making processes, the rotation of employees across functions and units and manager–worker interdependence, facilitate the sharing of relevant knowledge and the free flow of information among members of the firm, promote problem-solving and creative action, and enable knowledge transformation and exploitation (Jansen et al. 2005; Zahra and George 2002).

A fourth and final major challenge facing latecomer firms in their effort to accumulate technological capabilities concerns their ability to integrate and coordinate their internal and external activities. Such capacity is particularly important at two levels. In the first place, while firms may be able to develop knowledge production and technical problem-solving competences internally, this can limit access to new knowledge and skills that do not easily fit into the firm-specific technological framework and restrict learning from business partners and public researchers (Kim 1999; Lall and Teubal 1998). As a result, firms that focus on developing innovation capabilities internally can be disadvantaged in sectors where technical change is high and dependent on a wide variety of knowledge from different fields. As latecomer firms move from the mature technology stages to the more design-intensive innovation stages, they would have to rely more heavily on external sources of knowledge and, more importantly, integrate these with their internal competences in order to develop robust R&D skills and innovation capabilities.

Furthermore, the ability of latecomer firms to combine internal competences with external knowledge varies with the ways in which they integrate intra- and inter-organizational learning processes. Internal learning can be structured and promoted through various kinds of training in technical know-how, the intra-organizational sharing of ideas, and the participation of individual members in collective problem-solving activities (Malik and Kotabe 2009; Zollo and Winter 2002). Internal learning is likely to be enhanced if it is embedded in the process of inter-organizational learning. This involves not only the joint development and exploitation of knowledge for producing new products and services but also the establishment of collaborative training schemes and R&D facilities and the promotion of competence-creating activities between firms in specific technological fields. Inter-organizational learning is particularly effective in those firms that have long-running collaborative ties with other firms and operate in dense and durable inter-corporate networks (Baum and Ingram 2002; Knight 2002).

Divergent Technology Development Regimes

In Shanghai and Shenzhen, state industrial and technology policies have interacted with corporate entrepreneurship strategies in different ways to deal with these four major challenges in the process of promoting the growth of the ICT industry. They have each adopted a distinctive approach to managing technical and market uncertainties, organizing technology diffusion, developing the absorptive capacity of ICT firms, and integrating knowledge production and learning processes both within firms and between firms, PRIUs, and other third-party entities. These differences in technology development regimes, which are summarized in Table 11.1, will now be discussed in more detail.

Shanghai has adopted a strongly dirigiste approach to tackling major technology development challenges in the process of developing the ICT industry. This is particularly salient in the two-pronged strategy of the municipal government to help firms manage market and technical

Table 11.1 Divergent technology development regimes

	Shanghai	*Shenzhen*
Technology development regimes	Dirigiste	Inter-dependent
Management of technical and market uncertainty	Active state support; weak corporate strategies, particularly among small firms	Active state support; relatively strong corporate effort
Organization of extramural knowledge transfer	Strong state role in helping firms, particularly large ones, acquire new technology; limited corporate effort, except in state-directed projects	Strong state effort to help firms to acquire new knowledge from various sources; corporate strategies facilitated through inter-organizational networks
Development of absorptive capacity	Strong state support, mainly directed to large firms; considerable among large firms but limited among smaller ones	Joint state and corporate efforts
Integration of knowledge production and learning processes	Considerable in state-mediated developmental activities but weak corporate strategies	Relatively strong and balanced efforts on the part of state and business actors

uncertainties. On the one hand, the key industrial and planning agencies have dictated the selection of semiconductors and telecommunications as the strategically important sectors and encouraged and even cajoled firms to operate in these capital-intensive and potentially high-risk sectors through the targeted use of financial, fiscal, and other policy instruments. On the other hand, they have established, nurtured, or utilized large companies of hybrid ownership as the spearheads in the development of new technologies in the selected ICT industries. While the government has never explicitly undertaken to underwrite the investment and technical risks of their operations, many of these companies have clearly believed that their size and strategic importance are an effective guarantee against these risks (interviews SHQY7, SHQY16, SHQY30, SHQY31, SHQY40, and SHQY46). Indeed, the importance of size in this sense cannot be overemphasized, since state actors are likely to be forced into the role of the lender of last resort, if market downturns and technical risks land large ICT companies, be they state-owned or joint ventures, in financial troubles.

State actors have also been actively involved in the process of structuring the transfer of new technologies from foreign and domestic sources in Shanghai. A dozen of research institutes and technology service centres across the ICT industry have been established by various central and local government agencies to aid identification of appropriate foreign technologies and adapt selected technologies for diffusion among local firms. In the meantime, elaborate fiscal and investment policies have been implemented to shape and expedite knowledge transfer from abroad through technology licensing and capital goods imports and, more importantly, by encouraging leading ICT MNCs to operate R&D and training centres in collaboration with local research institutes, universities, and companies (Liefner and Zeng 2008; Sun et al. 2006). While the transfer of foreign technologies has been given priority, state actors have also pushed for extramural knowledge transfer among ICT firms, R&D centres, and PRIUs by shepherding them to develop research partnerships, form product development alliances, or engage in technology-sharing activities, often in state-directed projects and largely through administrative decrees (interviews SHQY6, SHQY11, SHQY22, SHQY25, SHQY32, SHXH1, SHZF1, and SHZF4).

Apart from these macro policy and institutional manifestations, the statist mode of technology promotion has been embodied in the effort of industrial policy-makers to micro-manage the development of absorptive capacity among individual firms in the targeted ICT sectors. Crucial to this has been their ability and willingness to shower large semiconductor and telecommunications companies with enormous financial and organizational support and, more significantly, stimulate them to assimilate and apply new knowledge through the setting of challenging goals for them (interviews SHXH1, SHXH3, SHZF1, and SHZF5). While economic officials have often had difficulty in bringing the behaviour of favoured firms in line with government performance criteria, they have demonstrated a strong and tenacious disposition to coordinate the accumulation of R&D resources and skills at the firm level. Policy support and disciplinary action aside, they have spurred ICT firms to exploit new technologies by creating a competitive industrial environment. Nowhere has this been more manifest than in their arduous attempt to strengthen the presence of MNCs, not only as a conduit of new knowledge but also as an instrument to incentivize local firms to invest in the development of their innovative competences.

Perhaps, this top-down approach has borne most significantly on the integration of research activities and organizational learning efforts across Shanghai's ICT industry at three different yet interrelated levels. First, state actors have orchestrated cross-sector knowledge production and investment activities, mainly through their efforts to establish high-tech industrial parks to link various ICT firms together and develop joint product-developing and technology-sharing forums. Second, the government has exerted shaping influence over the formation of production chains, particularly in the semiconductor and telecommunications sectors, making risky upstream investments, alleviating coordination failures, and inducing firms to proceed with technology development. And third, local industrial officials have invariably depended on large or state-owned companies for leading the agglomeration of research and investment activities in the ICT industry and for crafting a regional technology system, often at the cost of developing inter-organizational learning and innovative capabilities across a wide range of firms through extensive collaborations with business partners and external agencies.

In Shanghai, the municipal government's forceful and dirigiste policies have contrasted sharply with weak and weakly organized corporate efforts to deal with major challenges facing the development of the ICT industry. While large companies have managed market and investment risks through their enhanced access to financial, organizational, and informational resources, small firms have tended to avoid technical uncertainties by operating at the relatively standardized end of product life cycles (interviews SHQY1, SHQY4, SHQY10, SHQY13, SHQY34, SHQY37, SHQY47, SHYD2, and SHYD7). Similarly, some ICT conglomerates and a few entrepreneurial ventures have been able to absorb and apply externally sourced technologies, integrate these with their organizational routines, and generate novel products and processes. But many firms, particularly in the IC design and software sectors, have not developed a strong ability to identify market opportunities arising from changing technologies and to exploit them by enhancing their research skills and designing products that incorporate new knowledge (interviews SHQY3, SHQY5, SHQY8, SHQY17, SHQY25, SHQY41, SHXH2, and SHXH4).

The weak absorptive capacity of many firms has in large measure reflected the lack of a balanced, diversified, and integrated structure of extramural knowledge transfer in the ICT industry. With the state dominating the acquisition of foreign technologies, large firms have not acted actively to extract technology transfer deals with foreign companies that would allow them to enhance their design, engineering and project management skills. Small firms, many of whom operate on the periphery of the industry, have had neither resources nor incentives to source a wide range of new technological inputs. Furthermore, while state-controlled business groups and investment companies often operate across multiple ICT sectors, they have played little role in facilitating technology diffusion and integrating learning and innovative activities both within and between these sectors (interviews SHQY5, SHQY27, SHXH1, SHXH4, and SHXH6). Similarly, not only have linkages among the prominent ICT-oriented industrial parks, such as Zhangjiang, Caohejing, and Zizhu, remained weak, inter-organizational networks between leading firms have also been fragmented within these parks (Breznitz and Murphree 2011; Zhang 2016). These weaknesses have amplified the negative impact of knowledge specificity and complexity on the transfer of knowledge across ICT firms, despite the effort of the municipal government to promote such transfer through the establishment of research institutes, technology development centres and other collaboration schemes.

In Shenzhen, the technology development regime has been increasingly structured around joint business–state efforts to tackle market and organizational challenges facing the development and upgrading of the ICT industry. Since the late 1980s and early 1990s when the city government reoriented its development strategy towards a more innovation-based one, it has identified telecommunications, micro-electronics, and software design as the key strategically important sectors and made consistent and forceful attempts to spur these sectors to upgrade. As crucial measures to hedge ICT firms against real and possible investment risks attendant on more design-intensive and complex innovation activities, industrial policy-makers have provided them with start-up capital, tax breaks, or enhanced access to long-term financing, particularly through the launching of a small and medium enterprise board on the Shenzhen Stock Exchange and the development of the venture capital industry. At the same time, to encourage innovation, firms that have invested in the development of research skills, production technologies and new brands are eligible for grants from municipal authorities.

In its efforts to stimulate industrial upgrading through policy and financial inducements, the Shenzhen government has adopted an inclusive approach and has not discriminated between ICT firms of different ownership types or sizes. Indeed, industrial policy-makers have encouraged small and private companies to experiment with new ways of organizing innovation activities and helped them deal with technical uncertainties, often in collaboration with their interest-representing organizations (interviews SZXH1 and SZXH2). This has created a socio-economic environment that has supported entrepreneurship and emboldened ICT firms to develop an array of organizationally ingenious strategies to manage and minimize market risks associated with technology development. Some, particularly small firms, have engaged in the process of imitative innovation by adapting imported technologies to the domestic market, for instance; others have learnt to innovate from their experiences as OEM or ODM producers for leading foreign ICT companies; still others, such as Huawei and ZTE, have developed research skills and innovative competences through the incremental improvement of designs, products, and technologies (Fu 2015; interviews SZQY3, SZQY4, SZQY5, SZQY12, SZQY19, SZQY20, SZQY21, SZQY25, SZQY36).

State and business actors have also interacted closely to facilitate the transfer of knowledge both between domestic and foreign companies and among domestic academic institutions and enterprises. While the Shanghai government has depended on MNCs for obtaining new technologies for domestic ICT firms, its Shenzhen counterpart has focused on nurturing indigenous high-tech enterprises and actively encouraged them to invest in the development of innovative capabilities. Once they have improved existing product platforms and developed their own core technologies, they have caught the eyes of leading foreign ICT firms and become their contracted manufacturers. The ensuing OEM and ODM collaborations have granted local firms enhanced access to the latest technologies in mobile telephony, software design, or IC manufacturing and aided their efforts to further strengthen their research and development competences (interviews SZQY1, SZQY3, SZQY4, SZQY9, SZQY20, SZQY24, SZQY33, and SZQY36).

Furthermore, the city government has encouraged, since the 1990s, top research institutions and universities, both Chinese and foreign, to establish branch campuses, laboratories, incubators, or postgraduate training programmes in Shenzhen. It has co-located most of these facilities with ICT and other firms in the Shenzhen High-Tech Industrial Park (SHIP), in an attempt to help transfer knowledge from academic entities to the market and incorporate local firms into PRIU-sponsored research activities (Chen and Kenney 2007; Cheng et al. 2013; interviews SZYD2 and SZZF2). Equally important, economic officials and private market players have made arduous efforts to develop dense and cross-cutting production networks across high-tech industries in general and the ICT sectors in particular, starting with the launching of the Saige Electronics Supply Market (SESM) in the late 1980s. While some studies have expressed reservations about the role of such networks in facilitating the diffusion of technologies between firms (see Wang et al. 2010), many others have confirmed that the tight clustering of firms and PRIUs has allowed social capital grow, fostered long-term partnerships, smoothed information exchanges, and encouraged innovation (Breznitz and Murphree 2011; Chen 2014; Fu 2015).

To strengthen the ability of entrepreneurs to absorb new knowledge from various external sources, the Shenzhen government has spurred ICT firms to enhance their technology-assimilating capabilities through thematic funding, encouraged them to cooperate with universities to develop their R&D resources, and joined forces with business associations and academic institutions to nurture a SHIP-centred skill formation system, as noted above. Financial inducements and institutional support have been coupled with official efforts to incentivize firms to invest in the accumulation of absorptive capacity by leveraging environmental drivers for the creative exploitation of new technologies. This has manifested itself in the effort of industrial officials to press less innovative entrepreneurs to search for and acquire new knowledge and force out ICT firms or even sectors that have failed to commit themselves to technological learning or lost competitive advantages by redesigning tax regulations and removing export subsidies (interviews SZQY 3, SZQY6, SZQY16, SZQY27, SZQY37, SZXH2, SZZF1, and SZZF3; Yang 2014). Leading ICT firms appear to have responded to these policy and institutional stimuli relatively strongly, as their R&D expenditures are shown to have been among the highest across the key high-tech regions in China (Breznitz and Murphree 2011; Chen 2014; Zhou et al. 2011).

The inter-dependent mode of technology development has also asserted itself in the development of a regional innovation system that has involved the integration of organizational learning and innovation activities across economic actors and entities. Unlike in Shanghai where industrial planners have orchestrated the establishment of high-tech parks, key parks in Shenzhen have been operated through joint public–private endeavours in which the city government has regularly provided land and preferential policies whereas private firms have contributed funding and managerial expertise (Cheng et al. 2013). Furthermore, economic officials played an important part in initially building the basic regulatory and institutional structures for the SESM. These structures have subsequently been improved through business efforts to broaden and sustain ICT production networks between suppliers, producers and customers in Shenzhen and beyond (interviews SZQY5, SZQY7, SZQY11, SZQY14, SZQY15,

SZQY19, and SZQY27). By the same token, while local state agencies have taken the lead in completing an industrial value chain across the telecommunications and semiconductor sectors, ICT firms have enhanced its innovation-promoting role by organizing inter-corporate exchanges of information and skills and horizontal coordination of investment activities (Fu 2015; interviews SZQY1, SZQY2 SZQY8, SZQY17, SZQY20, SZQY27, SZQY28, SZQY31, SZQY32, and SZQY37). Finally, institutional co-evolutions between business and government have worked their way through the process of state actors co-locating high-tech firms and PRIUs in the SHIP and entrepreneurs co-developing new products with academics by combining their organizational competences with external research skills.

It is clear from the above that Shanghai and Shenzhen have differed significantly in terms of technology development regimes. The combination of state-orchestrated strategies to promote technology development and weakly developed corporate efforts to tackle collective action problems and market failures has yielded a dirigiste pattern of high-tech industrial governance in Shanghai. The inter-dependent technology development regime in Shenzhen has featured joint business–state efforts to organize collective learning, promote knowledge diffusion, and coordinate research and investment activities across ICT firms, academic institutions and intermediary entities.

Business–State Interactions and Technology Development Regimes

In searching for the sources of different technology development regimes, this chapter emphasizes the causal importance of business–state interactions. While market pressures, development patterns and links with global production networks have certainly affected the process of high-tech industrialization in Shanghai and Shenzhen, their impact is significantly mediated through distinctive socio-political structures of economic governance in the two metropolises. More specifically, these structures comprise the state organization of industrialization processes and the business coordination of economic and innovation activity. The chapter argues that it is subnational variations in the configuration of state organization and business coordination that have generated contrasting patterns and trajectories of technology development in Shanghai and Shenzhen.

The state organization of industrialization processes can be defined in terms of four different yet interrelated dimensions: (1) the degree of state controls over financial institutions and resource allocation; (2) the organization of interactions and hierarchies both within and between PRIUs; (3) the nature and structure of policy linkages between industrial policy-makers and private market players; and (4) the organizational and policy-making coherence and centralization of state economic agencies. In considering how subnational states organize and steer high-tech industrial development in tandem with private market players in Shanghai and Shenzhen, the interactive impact of these four dimensions is particularly crucial.

The ability of state officials to formulate and implement technology development strategies is, in the first place, contingent on the extent to which they control the operation of financial markets and allocate resources in support of their policy priorities. In China, the sustained process of market liberalization has not eliminated cross-regional differences in the ways in which local governments direct financial institutions to influence industrial development (Walter and Howie 2011). In those regional political economies where states exert significant influence over the organization and allocation of financial resources, industrial policy-makers are well positioned to manage market uncertainties through state equity participation, hedge targeted sectors and firms against investment risks by providing them thematic funding, or build institutions for acquiring knowledge from various sources.

Furthermore, the role of state actors in organizing public research systems and structuring inter-relationships between various PRIUs has a direct and clear impact on the management of technology development challenges. In a more state-led pubic research system, economic officials pursue more dirigiste science and technology policies through state-orchestrated funding mechanisms and research coordination strategies. These policies are generally buttressed by PRIUs attached to individual ministries or local governments as well as by state-owned or controlled banks and investment companies. In such a public research system, the policy interests of state actors heavily influence the process through which academic institutions obtain funding, formulate research strategies, and develop links with industry. Given the central role of public research systems in the innovation process of both developed and emerging market economies (Albuquerque et al. 2015; Whitley 2003), divergent state approaches to structuring such systems are likely to generate variations, not only in PRIU-industry research links but also in the ability of firms to source external knowledge inputs and absorb new technologies.

The nature and structure of public–private policy linkages also play an important part in shaping the ways in which state and business actors interact to promote the accumulation of technological capabilities. Across China, these policy linkages have long existed at the regional, sectoral, or interpersonal levels and taken such forms as deliberative councils, policy consultation platforms, business associations, or guanxi connections (see Kennedy 2005; Unger 2008). However, they differ along two structural attributes across regional political economies: first, the organizational stability, durability and cohesion of public–private networks, and second, the configuration of power relations between state and business actors. These differences bear significantly on the ability of industrial policy-makers to tackle technology development challenges in interaction with firms. Where public–private networks are stable and durable and develop through equal and inclusive partnerships, state actors are more capable of obtaining timely and accurate information to identify new technologies, orienting corporate behaviours with official performance criteria, and committing firms to strengthening their absorptive capacity and research skills. By contrast, if the economic bureaucracy is connected to the private sector through ad hoc, transitory, or particularized mechanisms, industrial officials may be deprived of necessary informational and organizational resources to introduce appropriately fitting foreign technologies to the private sector, encourage entrepreneurs to invest in the improvement of their R&D skills, or incentivize firms to assimilate and apply new knowledge.

Finally, the effectiveness of industrial policies in helping firms develop innovative capabilities is an important function of state structures. Three points are crucial here. First, the ability of state officials to organize industrial financing, structure public research systems and develop policy networks for the purpose of promoting technological innovations varies with the degree of organizational and decision-making coherence and centralization both within and between state agencies. Formulating high-tech industrial strategies and engaging firms in the management of technical change in particular require not only financial, research, and associational resources but also centralized and cohesive bureaucratic apparatuses that provide an institutional underpinning for the integrated and effective deployment of these resources. Where decision-making powers are fragmented, inter-agency conflicts prevalent, and policy processes erratic within the economic bureaucracy, state actors may be unable to employ resources effectively to reduce market and investment risks for entrepreneurs, encourage PRIUs to develop close links with industry, and sustain innovation-promoting networks with the business community.

Second, the effective management of various challenges associated with high-tech industrial development is predicated on the ability of economic officials to integrate a wide array of managerial expertise and competence and coordinate the implementation of diverse policy instruments among various state economic agencies in a coherent manner. Such ability is likely to be strong, where industrial policy-making authority is concentrated in the hands of a relatively small number of agencies and where there is a considerable degree of inter-bureaucratic acculturation and cohesion between these agencies. Third, the development of a well-coordinated technology development regime not only involves the integration of inter-firm knowledge production and learning processes but also commends concerted official efforts to realign the policy resources and objectives of relevant agencies involved in the making of industrial and technology strategies. The centralization of economic bureaucratic apparatuses that enhances inter-agency communication and coordination is likely to facilitate such efforts. Where the interdependence of research and innovation activities is limited across firms and sectors, this may reflect the fragmentation of decision-making powers and the lack of organizational cohesion within the economic bureaucracy that undercut official efforts to coordinate the development of an integrated technological system.

While these four dimensions of state organization combine to exert shaping influence on technology development regimes, socio-economic groups and hierarchies, particularly firms, are also important mechanisms for governing innovation processes. It is important to emphasize that the state direction of industrial and technology policies is mediated through the action and organization of socio-economic actors. How firms compete, strategize, and coordinate has profound effects on the ways in which they interact with state actors to manage innovation challenges. Particularly important is their ability to reorient the behaviour of individual firms to collective ends, promote inter-corporate collaborations, and nurture technological entrepreneurship. How firms coordinate their actions and decisions in relation to the management of technical change and the organization of innovation activities hinges on: (1) the role of leading firms; (2) the configuration of inter-firm linkage relationships; and (3) the pattern of interactions between socio-economic actors through associational mechanisms.

Large firms play a crucial role in leading and coordinating innovation activities, mainly because they have more financial and organizational resources, a stronger ability to absorb and utilize new technologies, and more extensive linkages with external knowledge holders (Hervas-Oliver and Albors-Garrigos 2008; Munari et al. 2011). However, where national or regional technology systems are locked into the technical profiles, development pathways and strategic expectations of leading firms, this may not only make small firms within these systems vulnerable to external crises affecting leading firms but also block alternative innovation trajectories in response to market and technological changes (Bailey 2003; Hassink 2010). These negative effects can be mitigated if large firms are embedded in dense, cross-cutting and horizontally structured inter-firm networks that enable small firms to exercise a collective voice in the process of industrial governance, interact with a wide range of organizations, and pursue diverse technology development strategies (Sternberg and Tamasy 1999; Sacchetti and Tomlinson 2009).

The configuration of inter-firm relations also impinges directly on the governance of technology development, particularly through its impact on the management of market and technical uncertainty, knowledge diffusion, and learning processes. Inter-corporate linkage relationships differ in both the extent to which firms are committed to long-term collaboration with each other and the scope of activities involved in developing and maintaining intra- or inter-sector networks (Hagedoorn et al. 2000; Whitley 2007). When firms share various resources across a wide range of production and innovation activities, they develop strong and long-term collaborative ties. Such ties provide firms with a variety of informational sources and enable them to incorporate external knowledge into organizational competences. Firms that engage in frequent and intensive inter-corporate alliances are thus more able to pool resources to manage market risks and develop robust absorptive capacity. On the other hand, where firms interact across a narrow range of activities, for limited purposes and over a short period time, inter-firm linkage relationships are more likely to develop on an arm's-length, ad hoc and low commitment basis. This limits the ability of firms to collaborate to deal with technical uncertainty, assimilate new research skills and technologies from diverse sources, and integrate knowledge production across organizational boundaries.

Finally, the business coordination of innovation activities has an organizational correlate in associational mechanisms. Such mechanisms, which may involve firms, financial institutions, or PRIUs, are mainly embodied in business organizations, R&D consortiums, or product-development forums both within and across sectors. They contribute to the diffusion of knowledge, the collective management of investment risks, the organization of technological collaborations, and the upgrading of innovative capabilities (Tomlinson 2011; Wolfe and Nelles 2008). Associational mechanisms play these roles differently across national or regional political economies, reflecting variations in their internal organizational structures and external relationships with state agencies. Their contribution to technology development is strong, where they are cohesively structured and possess rich resources to organize collection action and where they have institutionalized linkages with but operate independently from state agencies. By contrast, the role of associational mechanisms in helping firms manage innovation challenges is likely to be weak, if they operate at the mercy of state actors, are not delegated important policy and regulatory functions, and lack organizational resources to engage entrepreneurs, financiers, and academics in collective and collaborative activities.

Divergent Business–State Relations and Corresponding Technology Development Regimes

Cross-regional variations in the dominant structure of state organization and business coordination between Shanghai and Shenzhen, characterized in terms of the constitutive dimensions discussed in the preceding section, are summarized in Table 11.2. Shanghai represents a state corporatist pattern in which a structurally fragmented business sector operates under the shadow of a centralized and interventionist state. Shenzhen shares many characteristics of a co-governed configuration that features extensive state direction and robust business coordination. Based on the above theoretical propositions, this section outlines the causal pathways through which the different patterns of business–state interactions have generated divergent technology development regimes in the two localities.

In Shanghai, the dominant structure of industrial governance in the ICT and other high-tech sectors has been defined by strong state direction but weak business coordination. This has rested fundamentally with an elaborate and centralized economic bureaucracy. While the making of industrial and innovation policies often involves participation and inputs from several functional bureaus, these policies are centrally deliberated

Table 11.2 Business–state interactions and technology development regimes

	Shanghai	*Shenzhen*
State organization		
State controls over financial and other resources	High	Considerable
Organization of interactions within and between PRIUs	Considerable	Some and more autonomy granted to PRIUs
Nature and structure of public–private policy linkages	Extensive but state-dominated	Extensive, stronger business role and more equal ties
Organizational and policy-making centralization and coherence	High centralization and some coherence	Considerable centralization and some coherence
Business coordination		
Role of large firms	Very strong	Considerable
Inter-firm linkage relations	Limited except in some ties between MNCs and local firms	More extensive and collaborative networks
Interactions through associational mechanisms	Some but state-directed and organized	Better structured and extensive
Corresponding technology development regimes	Dirigiste	Inter-dependent

and finalized by small leading groups that have overarching controls over the direction of technology development strategies. The overall process of industrial policy-making has thus been concentrated, despite there being inter-agency disputes and rivalries (interviews SHZF2, SHZF3, and SHZF4). Associated with the centralized bureaucratic apparatus have been vertically structured public–private policy linkages. While economic officials have frequently interacted with firms of various ownership types and business organizations and often depended on them for crucial inputs in the formulation of industrial policies, it has invariably been the former that have dominated the process of interactions. Similarly, while various channels of consultations and deliberations have existed, these have been used by state agencies not so much to seek firms' cooperation and engage them in the implementation of technology development strategies as to discipline their behaviours and impose state policies on them (interviews SHXH1, SHXH3, SHXH5, and SHZF2).

The heavy dirigisme of high-tech industrial governance has also been reinforced by tight state controls of financial resources and by extensive coordination of PRIU structures and activities through administrative means. Despite market-oriented reforms of the past decades, state agencies have maintained their direct ownership control over key segments of the financial system in Shanghai, including commercial banks, venture capital companies and the stock market (Walter and Howie 2011). Equally significant, while PRIUs and universities in particular have been granted increased autonomy in curriculum development and internal administration, they have had to organize R&D programmes, commercial activities, and industrial linkages within the regulatory and policy parameters of the municipal as well as central governments. Not only have state actors imposed onerous restrictions on the commercial engagements of academics, they have also dictated the establishment of research institutions in key technological areas and structured inter-relationship between various PRIUs in line with their policy priorities (Huang and Qian 2010; interviews SHYD3, SHYD5, and SHYD6). While some PRIUs have developed formal research links with high-tech firms, particularly MNCs and large SOEs, these links have derived not so much from PRIU initiatives as from the municipal government's policy dictates (interviews SHYD1, SHYD3, SHYD5, and SHZF4).

By dint of centralized policy-making apparatuses, vertically structured public–private networks, and direct controls over financial and organizational resources, state actors have been able to establish or incentivize large firms to undertake high-risk investments in the various segments of the ICT market. In order to strengthen their absorptive capacity, industrial officials have provided the targeted ICT firms with enormous financing and coordinated sustained R&D support for their developmental projects, often in state-funded PRIUs. The well-entrenched institution of state dominance has enabled economic policy-makers to pursue the acquisition of foreign technologies through focused trade and investment policies and orchestrate the diffusion of knowledge and skills, particularly among favoured firms, by setting up technology development agencies, research centres and programmes, and other similar mechanisms. Invested with powerful and elaborate policy instruments, they have also pushed for the growth of an integrated innovation system in Shanghai by shepherding ICT firms to join R&D alliances, cajoling MNCs to strengthen their research ties with local partners and mobilizing PRIUs to link up with high-tech industries.

In stark contrast to the forceful state direction of high-tech industrial pathways, the business coordination of economic and innovation activities through collaborative and associational means has been weak in Shanghai. The structure of industrial organization has been hierarchical, with large SOEs and MNCs dominating the ICT and other high-tech sectors. These corporate players that have been co-opted into the growth-oriented coalition of the local state as key development agents have had favourable access to financial, human and research resources of various kinds (Wu 2009; Zhang 2002). Small firms, which have remained on the periphery of the regional high-tech industrial system, are often deprived of these resources. The hierarchical structure has essentially segregated ICT firms of different ownership and organizational types into mutually isolated groupings and fragmented linkage relations between them. This has impeded information flows and spawned distrust between them and dampened the prospects of them developing close inter-corporate networks (interviews SHQY8, SHQY9, SHQY26, SHQY30, and SHXH3).

Furthermore, business associations in the ICT and other high-tech industries are largely state-controlled and have acted more as institutional extensions of the local state than as independent mechanisms of interest representation (interviews SHQY6, SHQY19, SHQY34, SHQY41, SHXH1, SHXH3, and SHYD3). Organizationally incohesive and institutionally subordinate within the socio-political milieu of state corporatism, they have been unable to reorient their member firms towards collective activities and promote inter-firm collaborations. Moreover, the municipal government has initiated or sponsored R&D consortia and joint technology development forums among ICT firms, PRIUs, and finance firms. However, most of these consortia and forums have either fallen apart or failed to achieve their desired goals, mainly because of the weak ability of participants to develop commonly accepted norms of reciprocity and resolve differences in favour of collective interests (interviews SHQY8, SHQY13, SHQY16, SHQY26, SHXH4, and SHXH7). In Shanghai, economic officials and business leaders have often lamented the lack of collaborations among high-tech entrepreneurs, academics, and financiers without fully realizing that the long and strong arm of the state and the attendant weaknesses of associated mechanisms are in large part culpable.

Weak inter-corporate networks and associational mechanisms in the ICT sector suggest that firms have been unable to organize themselves collectively to deal with technology development challenges and coordinate innovation activities independently of state actors. ICT conglomerates that have had their investment risks covered through access to policy largess have tended to develop their technological competences in-house and had little incentive to manage market uncertainty with and diffuse R&D skills to other firms. Similarly, key PRIUs that have been showered with so much funding that they are generally poorly motivated to cultivate research links, particularly with smaller ICT firms (interviews SHYD4 and SHYD 5; Wu 2007). While large ICT companies have maintained strong absorptive and innovative capabilities, small market players have invariably found themselves unable to develop organization-specific routines for assimilating and applying new research skills and technologies. As a result, state strategies to integrate learning processes, knowledge production, and capacity-building across firms, PRIUs and MNCs have often fallen short of their desired objectives.

In Shenzhen, the inter-dependent technology development regime rests on an integrated structure of industrial governance: state-guided initiatives have been tempered and balanced by entrepreneurial forces. As in Shanghai, the municipality of Shenzhen has enjoyed considerable policy-making autonomy, particularly in industrial policy arenas, although it has to operate within the policy purview of the central government. Strategies designed to promote the growth of the ICT and other high-tech industries are often deliberated through various functional agencies before they are formulated and finalized by the planning authority. Economic officials are also well equipped with a range of financial, fiscal, and administrative policy instruments to implement these strategies (Yang 2014; Zhang 2012). However, unlike in Shanghai, state actors have maintained close, inclusive and horizontal policy links with private market players in Shenzhen. As the city was built up virtually from scratch in the early 1980s, the SOE sector was relatively weak to start with and further weakened in the subsequent process of privatization. Moreover, the growth of the ICT and other electronics industries hinged, first, on Hong Kong and Taiwanese firms and then on local, mostly, private companies. State officials in Shenzhen have thus seen creating private entrepreneurship and developing public-private partnerships as a key to the management of innovation challenges in high-tech industries (interviews SZXH1, SZZF1, SZZF3, and SZZF4).

While Shenzhen may have made more significant progress towards marketization and opening of finance than Shanghai, state control over the banking sector and equity markets has, on balance, remained considerable. However, in another departure from its Shanghai counterpart, the Shenzhen government has not only created a policy environment supportive of PRIU–industry collaborations but also granted PRIUs significant operational autonomy. Many of these PRIUs, which are established as the extended facilities or branch campuses of universities and research institutions headquartered in the other parts of China, are far away from their respective supervising authorities and have thus gained greater latitude in developing their commercialization activities. More importantly, fully aware of relatively weak higher education and research infrastructures in Shenzhen, the city government has consciously worked to attract prestigious PRIUs, encourage them to locate in the SHIP, and stimulate them to collaborate with local high-tech firms through a range of policy and institutional inducements (Breznitz and Murphree 2011; Cheng et al. 2013). Top universities in Hong Kong that have been frustrated by the lack of state support for PRIU–industry links have found the grass much greener on the other side of the border and established an array of collaborative innovation programmes with the ICT and other high-tech industries in Shenzhen (Sharif and Tang 2014).

The inter-dependent technology development strategy has also been underpinned by the robust business organization of economic action. Over the past decades, several large ICT companies, such as Huawei, Tencent, and ZTE, have emerged across the high-tech industrial landscape of Shenzhen, playing a leading role in coordinating production and innovation activities, primarily through their efforts to develop and sustain close supplier linkages with smaller firms in the city and beyond. Unlike in Shanghai, large companies have found themselves extensively immersed in dense and deep networks, not only among local ICT firms but also between them, MNCs and PRIUs. These networks have helped to temper the increasingly hierarchical structure of industrial governance with horizontally structured inter-organizational relations and balance the technical specialization of large firms with technological diversity across the regional industrial system. As a result, inter-corporate linkage relationships, both along production chains and across sectors, have been more crosscutting and collaborative in Shenzhen than in Shanghai.

More collaborative ties are attributable, in large part, to the strong intermediating role of business associations, particularly in the ICT and other high-tech industries. While business associations are kept under state control in Shanghai, their Shenzhen counterparts have received support from and have been given operational autonomy by the local government. Economic officials granted key intermediary bodies, such as the Shenzhen Semiconductor Industry Association, the Shenzhen Software Industry Association and the Shenzhen Computer Industry Association, powers to regulate the behaviour of their members and engaged these bodies in the making of technology development strategies, the setting of technical standards and the development of supplier networks (interviews SZXH1, SZXH2, SZXH3, SZZF1, and SZZF2). Reflecting state actors' lack of policy options due to a weaker SOE sector and their eagerness to nurture private entrepreneurs, this approach has enhanced the credentials of business associations with their members and provided them with organizational legitimacy and resources to promote inter-firm collaborations. Both as a cause and a consequence of strong business organizations, R&D consortia and product–development alliances have also become a crucial node in the governance of high-tech development. Unlike in Shanghai, many of these consortia and alliances have been established on the initiative of local ICT firms rather than by administrative decrees. However, once they are up and running, state actors have directed financial institutions to support their operations and mobilized PRIUs to provide them with technological inputs (interviews SZQY2, SZQY6, SZQY7, SZQY10, SZQY15, SZQY20, SZQY29, SZQY38, SZXH2, and SZXH3). The role of state agencies in facilitating rather than directing the development of associational mechanisms has encouraged ICT firms to craft independent strategies to organize collective action and maintain durable collaborative forums.

In Shenzhen, state officials, operating within the centralized bureaucratic apparatus and endowed with elaborate policy instruments, have thus been able to implement forceful strategies to develop key technologies in the ICT industry, target sectors and firms for specific promotion, and foster the growth of a local innovation system. Through an array of structural incentives and institutional inducements, industrial policy-makers have steered and stimulated private firms to assimilate new knowledge and enhance their R&D skills by combining organizational competences with external resources. State efforts to manage technological change have been reinforced by robust corporate strategies to deal with market and investment risks and diffuse production technologies through strong inter-firm ties, PRIU–industry interactions and associational mechanisms. This has created extensive and institutionalized networks on which ICT firms have drawn to exchange information, elicit commitments, and make collective endeavours to improve innovative capabilities and coordinate learning activities. In this process, state actors and market players have found themselves pressed by the same technology development imperatives to co-govern an increasingly inter-dependent innovation system.

Conclusions and Implications

This comparative analysis suggests that socio-political institutions bear strongly on technology development regimes by shaping the ways in which industrial policies and corporate strategies interact to manage innovation challenges. In the more dirigiste regime of Shanghai, while the strong state organization of industrialization processes has underpinned forceful policies to help ICT firms deal with technology development challenges, the efficacy of such policies in improving the R&D skills and competences, particularly among small firms, has been compromised by the inability of business actors to organize innovation activities across firms and sectors. Shenzhen has cultivated an inter-dependent regime in which strong state direction and robust business organization have generated the coordinated efforts of policy-makers and market players to promote technology development in the ICT industry.

The divergent socio-political structures of technology development regimes appear to have generated different innovation outcomes, measured in terms of both inputs and outputs. It is difficult to obtain consistent time series data on innovation inputs and outputs that are systematically and reliably comparable across Shanghai and Shenzhen. However, the local statistical authorities of the two metropolises have published survey data on innovation activities, which are broadly in line with case study and other qualitative evidence. Table 11.3 shows the key dimensions of innovation outcomes at the regional, sectoral, and firm levels across the two localities in 2013, the most recent year for which comparative data are available. It should, though, be noted that there may be some differences in the respective methodologies that the local statistical authorities have employed to collect and compile data; conclusions that are drawn from the table should thus be treated cautiously.

As suggested in Table 11.3, governmental contributions to gross expenditure on R&D (GERD) and R&D expenditures in the ICT industry performed by the government were broadly comparable in Shanghai and Shenzhen, reflecting the equally forceful industrial policies to target ICT firms for promotion and enhance their research skills and absorptive capacity in the two metropolises. In line with strong financial support from the government and the robust role of large firms in leading innovation activities in Shanghai and Shenzhen, in-house R&D expenditures across ICT firms were also largely similar. However, while ICT firms in Shanghai spent more on R&D activities than their Shenzhen counterparts, they appeared less capable of developing new products, as shown in

Table 11.3 Business–state interactions, technology development regimes, and innovation outcomes (2013)

	Shanghai	*Shenzhen*
Governmental contribution to GERD (%)	31.6	28.9
R&D expenditure performed by government in the ICT industry (%)	32.6	31.7
R&D expenditure per sample firm (thousand yuan) in the ICT industry	20,398	18,196
Number of product innovations per sample firm in the ICT industry	3.62	4.11

Sources: SMCST and SMSB (2014) and SMSB (2014)

Table 11.3. This difference is even more striking, given that Shanghai is widely believed to have better industrial infrastructures in the ICT sector than Shenzhen. The stronger innovative capabilities of ICT firms in Shenzhen can be plausibly attributed to more extensive and collaborative inter-firm networks and more robust associational interactions between firms, state agencies and PRIUs.

The major empirical findings of this chapter call into question the central propositions of prominent studies (see Wan et al. 2015; Williamson and Yin 2014) that have taken a grossly aggregated approach to examining innovation processes across regions and industries in China. While more nuanced analyses (Chen 2014; Nahm and Steinfeld 2014) have demonstrated crucial regional or sectoral differences in technology development patterns and trajectories, they have tended to privilege empirical elaboration over causal explanation and failed to explore the fundamental sources of these differences. This chapter has taken as its starting point the central idea that technology development regimes are not cut from the same institutional cloth but vary significantly with regional or sectoral structures of industrial governance. These structures that hinge on the interface between state organization and business coordination shape the process through which technology development challenges are managed. To better understand regional or sectoral variations in technological change and industrial competitiveness, we need to bring to the fore the divergent configurations of business–state interactions. This chapter that emphasizes such interactions as the socio-political underpinning of innovation activities provides a new point of theoretical departure for thinking about the dynamics of technology development across regional political economies in China.

References

Albuquerque, E., Suzigan, W., Kruss, G., & Lee, K. (Eds.). (2015). *Developing national systems of innovation*. Cheltenham: Edward Elgar.

Bailey, D. (2003). Globalisation, regions and cluster policies. *Policy Studies, 24*, 67–85.

Baum, J. A. C., & Ingram, P. (2002). Inter-organizational learning and network organizations. In M. Augier & J. March (Eds.), *The economics of choice, change and organization* (pp. 191–218). Cheltenham: Edward Elgar.

Bell, M., & Pavitt, K. (1995). The development of technological capabilities. In I. u. Hague (Ed.), *Trade, technology and international competitiveness* (pp. 69–101). Washington, DC: World Bank.

Breznitz, D., & Murphree, M. (2011). *Run of the red queen*. New Haven: Yale University Press.

Chen, L. (2014). Varieties of global capital and the paradox of local upgrading in China. *Politics and Society, 42*, 223–252.

Chen, K., & Kenney, M. (2007). Universities/research institutes and regional innovation systems. *World Development, 35*, 1056–1074.

Cheng, F., van Oort, F., Geertman, S., & Hooimeijer, P. (2013). Science parks and the co-location of high-tech small- and medium-sized firms in China's Shenzhen. *Urban Studies, 3*, 1–17.

Cohen, W. M., & Levinthal, D. A. (1990). Absorptive capacity: A new perspective on learning and innovation. *Administrative Science Quarterly, 35*, 128–152.

Ergas, H. (1987). Does technology policy matter? In B. R. Guile & H. Brooks (Eds.), *Technology and global industry* (pp. 191–245). Washington, DC: National Academic Press.

Fagerberg, J., Srholec, M., & Verspagen, B. (2010). Innovation and economic development. In B. H. Hall & N. Rosenberg (Eds.), *Handbook of the economics of innovation* (Vol. 2, pp. 833–872). Amsterdam: Elsevier.

Fu, W. (2015). *Towards a dynamic regional innovation system*. New York: Springer.

Hagedoorn, J., Link, A. N., & Vonortas, N. S. (2000). Research partnerships. *Research Policy, 29*, 567–586.

Hassink, R. (2010). Locked in decline? In R. Boschma & R. Martin (Eds.), *Handbook of evolutionary economic geography* (pp. 450–468). Cheltenham: Edward Elgar.

Hervas-Oliver, J.-L., & Albors-Garrigos, J. (2008). The role of the firm's internal and relational capabilities in cluster. *Journal of Economic Geography, 9*, 263–283.

Hobday, M. (1995). *Innovation in East Asia*. Cheltenham: Edward Elgar.

Huang, Y., & Qian, Y. (2010). Is entrepreneurship missing in Shanghai? In J. Lerner & A. Schoar (Eds.), *International differences in entrepreneurship* (pp. 321–346). Chicago: University of Chicago Press.

Jansen, J. J. P., van den Bosch, F. A. J., & Volberda, H. W. (2005). Managing potential and realized absorptive capacity. *Academy of Management Journal, 48*, 999–1015.

Kennedy, S. (2005). *The business of lobbying in China*. Cambridge, MA: Harvard University Press.

Kim, L. (1999). *Learning and innovation in economic development*. Cheltenham: Edward Elgar.

Kim, L., & Nelson, R. R. (Eds.). (2000). *Technology, learning and innovation*. Cambridge: Cambridge University Press.

Knight, L. (2002). Network learning: Exploring learning by inter-organizational networks. *Human Relations, 55*, 427–454.

Lall, S., & Teubal, M. (1998). Market-stimulating technology policies in developing countries. *World Development, 26*, 1369–1385.

Lall, S., & Urata, S. (2002). *Competitiveness, FDI and technological activity in East Asia*. Cheltenham: Edward Elgar.

Liefner, I., & Zeng, G. (2008). Cooperation patterns of high-tech companies in Shanghai and Beijing. *Erdkunde, 62*, 245–258.

Malik, O. R., & Kotabe, M. (2009). Dynamic capabilities, government policies, and performance in firms from emerging markets. *Journal of Management Studies, 46*, 421–450.

Munari, F., Sobrero, M., & Malipiero, A. (2011). Absorptive capacity and localised spillovers. *Industrial and Corporate Change, 21*, 429–462.

Nahm, J., & Steinfeld, E. S. (2014). Scale-up nation. *World Development, 54*, 288–300.

Perez, C., & Soete, L. (1988). Catching up in technology. In G. Dosi, C. Freeman, R. Nelson, G. Silverberg, & L. Soete (Eds.), *Technical change and economic policy* (pp. 458–479). London: Pinter.

Sacchetti, S., & Tomlinson, P. R. (2009). Economic governance and the evolution of industrial districts under globalisation. *European Planning Studies, 17*, 1837–1859.

Shanghai Municipal Commission of Science and Technology (SMCST) and Shanghai Municipal Statistics Bureau (SMSB). (2014). *Shanghai statistical yearbook on science and technology*. Shanghai: Shanghai KEPU Publishing House.

Sharif, N., & Tang, H.-H. H. (2014). New trends in innovation strategy at Chinese universities in Hong Kong and Shenzhen. *International Journal of Technology Management, 65*, 300–318.

Shenzhen Municipal Statistics Bureau (SMSB). (2014). *Shenzhen statistical yearbook on science and technology*. Beijing: China Statistics Publishing House.

Sternberg, R., & Tamasy, C. (1999). Munich as Germany's No. 1 high technology region. *Regional Studies, 33*, 367–377.

Sun, Y., Du, D., & Huang, L. (2006). Foreign R&D in developing countries. *The China Review, 6*, 67–91.

Teece, D. J., Pisano, G., & Shuen, A. (1997). Dynamic capabilities and strategic management. *Strategic Management Journal, 18*, 509–533.

Tomlinson, P. R. (2011). Strong ties, substantive embeddedness and innovation. *Knowledge and Process Management, 18*, 95–108.

Unger, J. (Ed.). (2008). *Associations and the Chinese state: Contested spaces.* Armonk: M.E. Sharpe.

Utterback, J. M., & Abernathy, W. J. (1975). A dynamic model of process and product innovation. *Omega, 3*, 639–656.

Walter, C. E., & Howie, F. T. (2011). *Red capitalism.* Singapore: John Wiley & Sons.

Wan, F., Williamson, P. J., & Yin, E. (2015). Antecedents and implications of disruptive innovation. *Technovation, 39-40*, 94–104.

Wang, C. C., Lin, G. C. S., & Li, G. (2010). Industrial clustering and technological innovation in China. *Environment and Planning A, 42*, 1987–2010.

Whitley, R. (2003). Competition and pluralism in the public sciences. *Research Policy, 32*, 1015–1029.

Whitley, R. (2007). *Business systems and organizational capabilities.* Oxford: Oxford University Press.

Williamson, P. J., & Yin, E. (2014, Summer). Accelerated innovation. *MIT Sloan Management Review*, pp. 26–34.

Wolfe, D. A., & Nelles, J. (2008). The role of civic capital and civic associations in cluster policy. In C. Karlsson (Ed.), *Handbook of research on innovation and clusters* (pp. 374–392). Cheltenham: Edward Elgar.

Wu, W. (2007). Cultivating research universities and industrial linkages in China. *World Development, 35*, 1075–1093.

Wu, F. (2009). Globalization, the changing state, and local governance in Shanghai. In X. Chen & Z. Zhou (Eds.), *Shanghai rising* (pp. 125–149). Minneapolis: University of Minnesota Press.

Yang, C. (2014). Government policy change and evolution of regional innovation systems in China. *Environment and Planning C, 32*, 99–121.

Zahra, S. A., & George, G. (2002). Absorptive capacity: A review, reconceptualization and extension. *Academy of Management Review, 27*, 185–203.

Zhang, T. (2002). Urban development and a socialist pro-growth coalition in Shanghai. *Urban Affairs Review, 37*, 475–499.

Zhang, J. (2012). From Hong Kong's capitalist fundamentals to Singapore's authoritarian governance. *Urban Studies, 49*, 2853–2871.

Zhang, X.-K. (2016). Socio-political structures and market organization in regional industrial systems. In R. Whitley & X.-K. Zhang (Eds.), *Changing Asian business systems* (pp. 229–256). Oxford: Oxford University Press.

Zhou, Y., Sun, Y., Wei, Y. H. D., & Lin, G. C. S. (2011). De-centring "spatial fix"—Patterns of territorialisation and regional technological dynamism of ICT hubs in China. *Journal of Economic Geography, 11*, 119–150.

Zollo, M., & Winter, S. G. (2002). Deliberate learning and the evolution of dynamic capabilities. *Organization Science, 13*, 339–351.

CHAPTER 12

Conclusions and Reflections

Tianbiao Zhu and Xiaoke Zhang

This book has addressed three key questions. The first one is how state–business relations in China have changed both across regions and industries and over the past decades. It has examined this question by developing a typology of business–government relations based on two key analytical dimensions: the authoritative governance of the economy and the market coordination of socio-economic activities. On the one hand, the state structures its relationship with business actors through industrial targeting and economic intervention, plays a key role in managing and regulating the development of product, labour or financial markets, and shapes inter-linkages between various economic agents and shape associational arrangements among them. On the other hand, business actors coordinate their decisions and actions through inter-firm linkages and also develop collaborative ties with such third-party entities as financial institutions, research organizations, or legal and consultancy services.

T. Zhu (✉)
Institute for Advanced Study in Humanities and Social Sciences, Zhejiang University, Hangzhou, China

X. Zhang
Alliance Manchester Business School, University of Manchester, Manchester, UK

X. Zhang, T. Zhu (eds.), *Business, Government and Economic Institutions in China*, International Political Economy Series,
DOI 10.1007/978-3-319-64486-8_12

The interaction between the authoritative governance of the economy and the market coordination of socio-economic activities reflects the organizational diversity of business–government relations in China. There are interdependent, networked, statist, and atomistic modes of business–government relations across regions and sectors in China. State and business actors are mutually dependent or interdependent (i.e. the interdependent mode) when strong authoritative governance meets robust market coordination; state and business actors are connected in close, cross-cutting, and highly structured ties (i.e. the networked mode) when authoritative governance is relatively modest or limited, but socio-economic producer groups play the key role in coordinating market activities; state and business actors are organized in a top-down and vertically structured manner (i.e. the statist mode) when strong authoritative governance coexists with limited market coordination of socio-economic activities; and state and business actors tend to be connected in atomistic fashions (i.e. the atomistic mode) when both authoritative governance and market coordination are weak and limited.

The second key question that this book has examined focuses on understanding and explaining the causes of changes and variations in business–government relations in China. The major causal variables are drawn from three levels of analysis: global and normative pressures, national socio-political transformations, and regional and sectoral configurations of state institutions and market structures. The key argument developed out of this book is that while global pressures and national transformations are crucial to changes in the general pattern of state-firm interactions, regional or sectoral configurations are the primary sources of variations in the behaviour of similarly situated state and business actors.

Political and economic competitions among nation-states at international level generate the pressure of late development for all developing countries. In particular, the impact of economic globalization on the transformation of business–government relations in China has worked through both market mechanisms and constraints and subjective pressures of transnational norms. The open-door policy invited trade and capital flows, and growing influence of MNCs, and the rise of neo-liberalism in international policy circles coincided with China's integration into the global economy. National socio-political transformations, in particular marketization and decentralization, have not only led to China's fast economic growth but also fundamentally changed its state-society nexuses. Both global pressures and national transformations create a background for regional and sectoral configurations to shape China's business–government relations directly. Those configurations include development ideologies (interventionism versus liberalism) associated with different regions and sectors, the internal organizational structure of local governments, and relations between the centre and regions or industrial sectors, firm size, ownership forms, and transnational linkages.

While China's business–government relations are influenced by various factors, they in turn also shape the development and transformation of economic institutions in China, a third and final key issue discussed in the book. How the structural dimensions of business–government relations—the authoritative governance of the economy and the market coordination of socio-economic action—affect the constitutive features of emergent market institutions is one of the central focuses of the book. The argument is certainly not just limited to the structural constraints of business–government interactions, the role of agency in determining how state actors and business leaders interpret and respond to pressures for institutional reforms is also crucial to a number of authors in the book. Various forms of internationalization and national socio-political transformations continue to interact with regional and sectoral configurations of business–government relations in China, which generate divergent processes and outcomes of institutional change across regions and industrial sectors.

As China has gradually integrated into the global economy, its business–government relations have experienced crucial changes over the past three decades. Today, global economic downturn and the rise of international terrorism as a fundamental challenge to nation-states may temporarily tip the balance power of business and government towards the latter. However, it seems that few people would doubt that the process of China's integration into the global economy will be reversed over the long run. This then will lead to a more balanced relationship between business and government, as civil society in general and the business community in particular are growing stronger. To be sure, even a more balanced power-relation would continue to be uneven across regions and industries in China. Divergent processes of local and sectoral developments would continue to be a key feature of China's business–government relations.

Both the government side and business side are facing major problems in an evolving global economy. The rise of global value chains has been seriously challenging the vertically integrated industrial structure and traditional form of industrial policy. On the other hand, the profit margin of manufactured goods is going down everywhere. Technological innovations are happening in an ever-faster pace, which generate huge stress for business all over the developing world. It looks that the traditional forms of business–government relations have to change. The focus of new relations has to be on the nurturement of business capability to innovate. In that sense, China is an interesting place, where different forms of business–government relations stand side by side, and different experiments continue to play on. It would be difficult to predict how China's business–government relations will evolve in the future, but one can be sure that the evolution process will definitely be a multiple, diversified, and complex one.

Index[1]

[1]Note: Page number followed by 'n' refers to notes.

X. Zhang, T. Zhu (eds.), *Business, Government and Economic Institutions in China*, International Political Economy Series,
DOI 10.1007/978-3-319-64486-8

Q

R

FSC
www.fsc.org
MIX
Papier | Fördert gute Waldnutzung
FSC® C083411

Kolibri 360 GmbH
Ferdinand-Jühlke-Straße 7
99095 Erfurt, Deutschland
produktsicherheit@kolibri360.de